Transnational Perspectives
on Culture, Policy, and Education

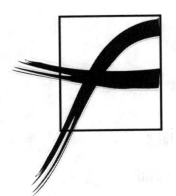

Intersections in Communications and Culture

Global Approaches and Transdisciplinary Perspectives

Cameron McCarthy and Angharad N. Valdivia
General Editors

Vol. 21

PETER LANG
New York • Washington, D.C./Baltimore • Bern
Frankfurt am Main • Berlin • Brussels • Vienna • Oxford

Transnational Perspectives on Culture, Policy, and Education

Redirecting Cultural Studies in Neoliberal Times

Edited by
Cameron McCarthy and Cathryn Teasley

PETER LANG
New York • Washington, D.C./Baltimore • Bern
Frankfurt am Main • Berlin • Brussels • Vienna • Oxford

Library of Congress Cataloging-in-Publication Data

Transnational perspectives on culture, policy, and education: redirecting cultural studies
in neoliberal times / edited by Cameron McCarthy, Cathryn Teasley.
p. cm. — (Intersections in communications and culture:
global approaches and transdisciplinary perspectives; v. 21)
Includes bibliographical references and index.
1. Culture—Study and teaching. 2. Popular culture—Study and teaching.
3. Education. I. McCarthy, Cameron. II. Teasley, Cathryn.
HM623.T737   306.01—dc22   2008009682
ISBN 978-0-8204-9731-0
ISSN 1528-610X

Bibliographic information published by **Die Deutsche Bibliothek**.
Die Deutsche Bibliothek lists this publication in the "Deutsche
Nationalbibliografie"; detailed bibliographic data is available
on the Internet at http://dnb.ddb.de/.

Cover design by Joni Holst
Cover art, *Notes to Basquiat* (*The Coming of the Light*)
by Gordon Bennett (2001)

The paper in this book meets the guidelines for permanence and durability
of the Committee on Production Guidelines for Book Longevity
of the Council of Library Resources.

Table OF Contents

Acknowledgments vii

Introduction: Redirecting and resituating cultural studies
   in a globalizing world. 1
   Cathryn Teasley and Cameron McCarthy

Part 1: Problematizing conceptions and constructions
of culture and identity

Chapter 1. Freedom, community, and Raymond Williams's
   project of a common culture. 17
   Álvaro Pina

Chapter 2. Manning the borders: Blackness, nationalisms,
   and popular culture. 39
   Susan Harewood

Chapter 3. Relativism, racism, and philanthropy 55
   Teresa San Román

Chapter 4. Remaking civic coexistence: Immigration, religion
   and cultural diversity 73
   Eduardo Terrén

Part II: Transnational cultural policy, global neoliberalism,
and racism

Chapter 5. Elite discourse and institutional racism 93
   Teun A. van Dijk

Chapter 6. The popular racial order of "urban" America:
Sport, identity, and the politics of culture. 113
Michael D. Giardina and Cameron McCarthy

Chapter 7. Governing doped bodies: The World Anti-Doping Agency
and the global culture of surveillance 143
Jin-kyung Park

Chapter 8. Pro(fits) of a future not our own: Neoliberal reframings
of public discourse on social justice 159
Emily Noelle Ignacio

Part III: Critical cross-cultural projects in education

Chapter 9. School culture and the fight against exclusion:
An optimistic curriculum 183
Jurjo Torres Santomé

Chapter 10. Educational change, cultural politics,
and social reinvention 219
Mar Rodríguez Romero

Chapter 11. The challenges of migration: Anthropology,
education, and multiculturalism 241
Dolores Juliano

Chapter 12. Ethnic group, class, and gender: Paradoxes
in the education of Moroccans and Roma in Spain 257
Mariano Fernández-Enguita

Chapter 13. New racisms in Spanish society 277
Juan José Bueno Aguilar

Chapter 14. Roma youth at school: Instituting inclusion from
a legacy of exclusion 293
Cathryn Teasley

Chapter 15. Understanding the neoliberal context of race
and schooling in the age of globalization 319
Cameron McCarthy

Coda: Terrorism, globalization, schooling, and humanity........................... 341
James G. Ladwig

Contributors 351

Index 355

Acknowledgments

This volume is the product of ongoing transatlantic exchange and the simultaneous meeting of cross-cultural minds. Translation has played a central role in this endeavor, which would not have been possible without the valuable support of colleagues on both sides of the Atlantic: at the University of Illinois at Urbana-Champaign (U.S.A.) and at the University of A Coruña, in Galiza (Spain).

Our gratitude goes to all of the contributors to this volume; we have learned so much from all of you, and we acknowledge and appreciate the extra work invested by those authors whose chapters were, in addition, translated. We would further like to extend our heartfelt thanks to those who participated in the translation work itself, most especially Viviana Pitton and John Barlow, who both carefully revised several of the chapters. Teresa San Román would like to thank David Owen for his translation work on her chapter, as would Mar Rodríguez Romero for James Fowlie's input on her own piece. And James Ladwig would like to thank Dr. Wendy Amosa for proof reading and commenting on his essay. We are further grateful to Soochul Kim for his technical support, and to Michael Giardina for his careful reading of an early draft of this work.

Cameron McCarthy wishes to acknowledge the generous support of the University of A Coruña in the form of a summer fellowship award in 2006. Cameron also wishes to thank the Center on Democracy in a Multiracial Society at the University of Illinois for fellowship support extended to him in the fall of 2006.

A special thanks goes to Jurjo Torres Santomé for having planted the initial seed of contact, back in 1999, which has since given rise to ongoing exchange and a highly productive relationship, one of the products of which is the present volume. Finally, Cathryn Teasley would like to acknowledge her family's unfailing support throughout this adventure, and most especially that received from Celso Álvarez Cáccamo, without which this project may never have come to fruition.

Introduction: Redirecting AND resituating cultural studies IN A globalizing world

CATHRYN TEASLEY

University of A Coruña

CAMERON MCCARTHY

University of Illinois, Urbana-Champaign

With *Transnational perspectives on culture, policy, and education: Redirecting cultural studies in neoliberal times,* our aim is to offer a kind of "voyage out"—to borrow a notion Virginia Woolf so compellingly pursued from her own particular ethno-national situatedness in the imperial center[1]—out of the as-yet Anglocentric realm of cultural studies and toward a more expansive, cross-cultural, and interdisciplinary plane of inquiry. The world is now witness not only to a surge in the volume of movement across borders: a movement of people, information and material goods that goes hand in hand with the neoliberal pulse of the global marketplace; it is also witness to a transgression of orthodoxies and gatekeeping in conceptual spheres. Within this scenario, understanding how popular culture articulates with formal culture (i.e., public policy, institutions, etc.) is our major concern here, for, in the greater, fluctuating scheme of things, the inhabitants of this limited planet, of societies both young and old, must negotiate their respective identities, histories, and possibilities within growing world dynamics marked by interdependency, domination, and power. In this volume, these cultural processes are explored through scholarly insights emerging primarily from the Iberian Peninsula of Europe, the Caribbean, Latin America, and East Asia, the alternative voices of which bring new perspectives to the kind of cultural inquiry that, regardless of its origins, remains focused on a shared concern for human rights and dignity, social justice, and peaceful coexistence.

As the cumulative effects of worldwide scholarship coalesce into an ever-expanding global knowledge base, the clearly collective nature of research becomes undeniably apparent, this despite the progressive atomization of academic inquiry so characteristic of our late modern times. Ironically, even as novel research inevitably influences the course of development of this growing corpus of knowledge—at times challenging its very foundations—academic tradition continues to tame and mold such epistemological instability into canonical categories of certainty and predictability, imposing boundaries on the various schools of thought and on the extent to which they can be questioned or destabilized. Some scholars have argued that such resistance to change is primarily the result of methodological conservatism or preservationism (a critique most evident in postmodern theorists such as Derrida, Lyotard, or Baudrillard), while others have placed greater emphasis on ideological, cultural, gendered, and economic power plays that seek to secure turf, territory, or place, in our highly stratified and increasingly globalized world—consider the work of Foucault, and that of postcolonial scholars such as Bhabha, Hall, or Said; or feminist researchers Butler, Benhabib, and Fraser; not to mention Birmingham School ideologues Hoggart, Thompson and Williams; or neo-Marxists Bourdieu and Eagleton. Yet despite the respective differences in emphasis among these informed thinkers, all would likely agree that resistance to paradigmatic breakdown, or to deprivileging the traditional objects and centers of study, is due, above all, to an *interaction* between the aforementioned key factors of method and place in the conservation of privilege, as these operate within the overlapping spheres of scholarly activity, material gain, and hegemonic culture.

The very persistence of such avid investment in academic stability makes the degree to which it is challenged so central to cultural studies. In keeping with this critical cultural project, we propose that the present volume be considered an exercise in degree. While the intercultural aspirations within the field have been significant, an overwhelming bias toward its Anglo origins nevertheless remains: the bulk of research in cultural studies is written in English and the majority of its scholars live in English-speaking countries (Spivak and Harasym, 1990; Bhabha, 1994). When they reside elsewhere around the world, they tend to work in English or Communications departments, both of which are dominated, once again, by pan-Anglo cultural perspectives (e.g., on the Iberian Peninsula, the few existing forums on cultural studies have been initiated by scholars of English). Thus, while the contributors to this volume indeed subscribe to the *raison d'être* for the interdisciplinary exploration of culture pursued in cultural studies, they must do so from the periphery, for most live and work in linguistic, national, economic, and academic contexts located beyond the habitual range of exchange of cultural studies scholarship. Herein lies the degree to which this volume moves beyond the dominant realms of cultural inquiry: over half of the authors speak mother tongues other than English (Spanish, Galizan-Portuguese, Portuguese, Catalan, Korean, and Dutch), and reside in countries where English is not an autochthonous language. Finally, six of the chapters have come to this volume by way of third-party translation.

The overall purpose of this book, then, is one of multiple border-crossing, which requires, at a minimum, an investment in both *relationality* (McCarthy and Dimitriadis, 2000) and translation, and at a maximum, transgression. This volume puts into practice the theoretical orientation of critical relationality and radical contextualization by bringing diverse national, epistemological, and linguistic perspectives to the analysis of popular and institutional culture, for the purpose of uncovering points of articulation across cultures that promote social justice in these new times of popular culture and public policy, dominated as they are by neoliberalism and the ever-expanding corporatism and re-feudalization of the public sphere. Where translation is concerned, while many of the chapters have effectively been translated in the literal sense, the act of translating—indeed, the very notion of translation itself—entails so much more. Taking the concept beyond mere linguistic operations, scholars such as Boaventura de Sousa Santos (2005) or Homi Bhabha (in Rutherford, 1990) have pointed out that translation is a profoundly cultural and potentially transformational undertaking. According to Santos, *cultural translation* facilitates reciprocal intelligibility amongst, on the one hand, knowledge bases and cultures, and on the other, social agents and practices. It is therefore the kind of work that is at once intellectual, political, and emotional in nature because it directly confronts issues of access, understanding, and mutual respect, and can pave the way for establishing intercultural links while simultaneously identifying cultural gaps.

More than this, however, this volume constitutes an exercise in transgression to the extent that most of its contributors are "outsiders" to the field of cultural studies, and not merely because their academic specializations vary, but because their access to the English-language forums of cultural studies has been limited, and their experience and professional dialog with cross-cultural realities diverse. For example, the interdisciplinarity reflected in these contributors ranges from fields such as sociology and anthropology, to pedagogy, psychology, linguistics, communications studies, and English philology, while their transnational and ethnocultural affiliations include ties to Barbados, Korea, Japan, the Philippines, Argentina, El Salvador, Portugal, Spain, and the Netherlands, as well as the United Kingdom, Australia, and the United States. Further, all of the authors are committed to removing the cultural obstacles to fair representation and a minimally decent standard of living in the worldwide neoliberal scheme of things today—an ideologically and politically informed stance that more often than not requires opposing and transgressing the established modes of production of both official knowledge and material gain in the academy and beyond.

REDIRECTING CULTURAL STUDIES (THE VOYAGE OUT)

Because *Transnational perspectives on culture, policy, and education: Redirecting cultural studies in neoliberal times* has been forged by way of the aforementioned principles of relationality, translation, and transgression, it brings to the field of cultural studies, the fresh voices of scholars—most of whom are firmly established in their respective national contexts—that have nonetheless seldom had access to globally privileged English-speaking forums. For example, several of the Iberian contributors are concerned with issues related to the relatively recent role of immigration in the young democracy of Spain, and how this novel reality is being met through popular culture and public policy. Moreover, the authors' respective national origins can be mapped along a continuum ranging from the so-called First World to the Third World, with Spain and Portugal still having qualified, in the not-too-distant past, as "Second World" countries—that is, until the legacies of dictatorial rule finally began to fade following the collapse of the Franco and Salazar regimes in the mid-1970s.

These alternative interdisciplinary voices and contexts of inquiry lend a uniqueness to this volume that counters a trend in other recently edited books on popular culture and cultural studies that attempt to incorporate transnational perspectives. For example, if we consider the collective volume *Global ethnography: Forces, connections, imaginations in a postmodern world* (Burawoy et al., 2000) the international contexts addressed in this book are overwhelmingly articulated through their peripheral connections to immigration and corporate capital flows centered in the United States. Likewise, the collection *Media and cultural studies: Keyworks* (Durham and Kellner, 2001) maps a canon for an emergent field of research clearly dominated by West European and North American scholarly traditions, contexts, and points of reference, to which the book's few postcolonial contributors are nonetheless invariably linked. In the present volume, Michael Giardina and Cameron McCarthy point out in Chapter Six that the rapidly expanding, global interconnectivity of popular cultural artifacts, which Kellner (1995) has identified as the *global popular*, is "raising challenges to the problematic place-boundedness of the (British) cultural studies tradition" (Giardina and McCarthy, this volume, p. 115; see also Carrington, 2001).

Transnational perspectives on culture, policy, and education: Redirecting cultural studies in neoliberal times thus "redirects" our attention to *other* (subaltern) centers of critical scholarship on popular and institutional culture. These contributors' diverse cultural experiences, national contexts, and scholarly pursuits—many of which circulate widely, albeit outside the dominant Anglo circuits—stand not only to inform and enrich, but to broaden the cultural scope and to decenter the professional priorities of an interdisciplinary and cross-cultural field of research such as cultural studies. In this sense, the volume embodies a form of cultural translation and transgression: it performs a kind of inclusion, or access, aimed at eventually transforming the world-hegemonic centers of knowledge production that inevitably ride the tide of economic globalization. The ultimate goal, then, with projects such as this one is to transform such established canons into more porous, malleable, equitable, multilingual, multinational, and transcultural spaces of integration and exchange.

NAVIGATING THE PERIPHERIES OF CULTURAL STUDIES

The sixteen international contributors to this volume take on highly current issues of global scale and impact, such as: the role of religious diversity in cosmopolitan societies; forging interdisciplinary arrangements that enrich the collective contribution of research to the advancement of social justice in today's interdependent world; deconstructing the pessimism associated with cultural difference and social transformation; understanding the nuances of power in and between popular and institutionalized cultural expressions; and cultural resistance to the marginalizing effects of neoliberal globalization. These themes articulate with each other to the extent that they widen the cultural lens and the transnational understanding of intercultural phenomena and processes as these play out in a world dominated by privileged centers of knowledge and global mechanisms of economic control.

Part One ("Problematizing conceptions and constructions of culture and identity") addresses convergent and divergent conceptions and constructions of cultural identity as these emerge from popular experience and institutional structures. General concerns are raised around how disparate assumptions about culture are confronted and reconfigured.

For instance, in Chapter One, Álvaro Pina opens this section of the book with a thought-provoking exploration into community, culture, and freedom, and the ways these can be articulated to form the foundation of rigorous cultural studies practice—one that incorporates the principled intellectual analyses of Raymond Williams and Edward P. Thompson, and one that is capable of renewing and developing their solid democratic project. By focusing on community, culture, and freedom as concepts and practices, he analyzes their theoretical status and political potential in today's societies. By constructing a position founded on the articulation of these three key components, he proposes a mode of intellectual inquiry of the contemporary that can offer alternative views of the world we live in, and open independent configurations of the human, the social, and the cultural. Through this form of articulation, Pina takes on recent challenges to cultural studies; he reexamines Williams's common culture project, and he reassesses this project as a basis for a democratic view of common humanity which is further informed from Zygmunt Bauman's recent work.

Firmly committed to understanding the deeper implications of the popular for cultural analysis, Susan Harewood takes us on a journey in Chapter Two into the power of popular art, masquerade, and music in breaking dominant molds for perceiving and conceptualizing blackness, national identity, and difference. Parting from the premise that cultural studies' discussions of blackness follow predictably consistent tropes, and that race relations in academic Anglocentric centers such as Britain and the United States have dominated the discussions and truncated the analysis of blackness, Harewood posits a way of broadening our understanding of both blackness and its relations to nationalism by focusing on Barbadian popular musical performance. Using the examples of Barbadian calypso/soca musicians, she explores their performances of competing nationalist narratives. These narratives illuminate the ways in which artists' imaginative work exceeds the limits set by academic criticism, and thus can challenge cultural critics to rethink some of those concepts that have become settled, such as binary discussions of nationalism and blackness, which tend to focus almost exclusively on blacks either as victims of racist white nationalist movements or as participants in black nationalist movements.

Parting from a shared concern regarding the ways race-related matters are addressed in academia, Teresa San Román explores in Chapter Three the changing role of philanthropy in cosmopolitan societies. She draws our attention to the all-too-familiar arguments proclaiming the incompatibility of cultures that are used as much to reinforce mixophobia as to justify a desire for the public integration of diverse cultural groups. Yet, the problem may only sometimes lie in incompatibility. When incompatibility in a given context is genuine, this must indeed be negotiated, as it may not necessarily apply in a general sense to the cultures in contact, or to their respective peoples. This is so, according to San Román, because a cultural project, considered in overall terms, cannot be objectively measured because we cannot judge or valorize other cultures without relying on preexisting cultural values. However, one thing is to give equal value to all cultures, while it is quite another to assign equal value to all cultural phenomena (our own and those of "others"). Because this latter action constitutes a particularist assessment, it cannot be universally imposed; while it can instead be *universally proposed* without this implying either an overall exaltation of the culture upon which the proposal is based, or a complete disapproval of the same. What San Román argues that we have to find, then, is that comfortable niche that Todorov sought somewhere between dogmatism, which seeks to possess the truth, and skepticism, which denies all truths.

Related to this, in Chapter Four Eduardo Terrén grapples with redefining coexistence in heterogeneous social contexts where religious diversity is intentionally polemicized and artificially polarized. Like Pina, Terrén finds inspiration in Bauman's work inasmuch as the notion of "togetherness" has implications for cosmopolitan coexistence in Mediterranean Europe. He argues that with the transition from the 20th to the 21st century, a series of phenomena tied to economic globalization and population movements are opening new horizons for citizenship, including the identity demands—particularly those related to religion—of very diverse collectives. He highlights the ways in which the growing multiculturalism of resident populations in the same national space clearly oblige us to reflect on the necessity of forging a new concept of citizenship: one capable of providing an alternative project around rights, participation, and belonging to an increasingly complex and heterogeneous civil society. It is within this context that contemporary Europe is facing the challenge of redefining its own identity, a challenge with particular dimensions for South European countries now transformed, according to Terrén, into kinds of semi-reluctant hosts. While immigration is not the only source of cultural diversity in Spain, it obviously places new demands on a country used to five centuries of cultural homogenization; only within the last twenty years has Spain become a viable destination for immigrants. A very old state with a very young democracy (as young as its experience with immigration) is now forced to rethink and reconfigure the way in which "coexistence" has been constructed historically. This chapter starts off by approaching cultural diversity as an opportunity for reinforcing democracy and civil society, and then focuses on the barriers to this project, as rooted in the cultural and historical experience of Mediterranean countries such as Spain.

Part Two of the book ("Transnational cultural policy, global neoliberalism, and racism") problematizes prevailing forms of extra-state neoliberal policies and governance, and the transnational cultural institutions, practices, and discourses attendant to this process of control.

Such policies are manifested through elite (institutional) discourse. Teun van Dijk opens this section, in Chapter Five, with a revealing examination of the racial logics of this kind of discourse in the European context, where the challenges to public policy from popular cultural trends have taken center stage in the European Parliament and other institutional settings. Within the broader framework of a theory of racism as a social system of ethnic domination, van Dijk argues that, contrary to the positive self-image and denial of racism that most symbolic elites project, they play a prominent role in the reproduction of racism in society. This thesis is based, on the one hand, on arguments contending that these elites control (access to) public discourse in political, scholarly, educational, corporate, legal, and communications arenas, and that the acquisition of racist ideologies, which is a condition for the reproduction of racist practices in society, takes place especially through the influence of such elite discourse and institutions. The impact of elite discourse in the perpetuation of racism is further illuminated, van Dijk argues, through international empirical research, which has shown that, rather than providing solutions, more often than not the elite embody a major source of racism. More specifically, this chapter summarizes the findings of various projects on discourse and elite racism in Europe.

In Chapter Six, Michael Giardina and Cameron McCarthy critically interrogate the prevailing contemporary figurations of so-called "urban" popular culture, as suggested within and against filmic narratives of sport and the racial logics of late capitalism. Attempting to forge a contextual understanding of the conflicting representations of (urban) subjectivity, the authors locate "urban" America within broader conjunctural developments that have given rise to its mainstream appellation. They then focus on how urban popular culture is currently represented within broader "pop" culture formations—especially Hollywood cinema—before concluding with a close read of the Spike Lee film *He Got Game*, which, they argue, is both an example and a symptom of popular racial representation that is compatible with the politics of a conservative (black) middle class.

Where nongovernmental regulating institutions are concerned, Jin-kyung Park examines, in Chapter Seven, the impact of one such institution on Third World athletes: that of the World Anti-Doping Association (WADA). Her chapter examines the governing practices of the this agency as a global organization established in 1999 to cope with the crisis of illicit performance-enhancing drug use in international sports. She analyzes the background, structure, and policies of WADA while reflecting upon recent debates on governmentality and cultural policy. In so doing, Park illustrates how WADA policies fundamentally work to police athletic bodies, while impacting in particular ways on the Third World. In this sense, she suggests that WADA embodies a First World, technologically driven governance of doping.

On the related issue of transnational instruments of corporate control, Emily Noelle Ignacio takes up, in Chapter Eight, the cultural effects of international accords such as the Central American Free Trade Agreement (CAFTA). She reveals the links such policies have to the selective, discursive reframing of popular demands for social justice in El Salvador, the United States, and beyond. Because many scholars have argued that racial discourses are simultaneously formed within and across nations in relation to specific political and economic contexts, Ignacio establishes the imperative that we study racial formations in relation to changing cultural, political, and economic contexts. She argues that we must also examine how the emphasis on the success of civil rights and other social movements, peace accords (such as in El Salvador), and multiculturalism policies have been used to exacerbate racism and hide the negative impact of globalization and free market agreements on racially subordinated groups and/or widening social class inequalities in the Americas and around the world. This emphasis on our successes, coupled with inadequate discussions about the impact of border-crossing neoliberal economic policies, make it difficult, in turn, to talk about pervasive and global structural racism. Using Michael Omi and Howard Winant's theory of racial formation, George Lakoff's theories about values and framing, Stuart Hall's theory of representation and articulation, and, more generally, Antonio Gramsci's theory of hegemony, Ignacio focuses on the reconstruction of the writings and speeches of Martin Luther King, Jr. in the United States, and of Monseñor Oscar Arnulfo Romero in El Salvador.

Finally, Part Three ("Critical cross-cultural projects in education") explores the complexities and implications of education as a modern institution, and its role in the reproduction or transformation of diverse cultural dynamics.

For instance, in Chapter Nine, Jurjo Torres Santomé confronts neoliberal and hegemonic forms of cultural exclusion through what he refers to as "an optimistic curriculum." He argues that there is an urgent need to revise both the selection of cultural contents taken up in classrooms, as well as the methodological strategies employed therein, for it is at the compulsory level of education that mental habits are formed, which then characterize citizens' modes of thinking about reality. For most of us who have passed through classrooms, the contents of schooling remain too abstract, ahistorical, and vague. According to Torres Santomé, there is also a tendency to protect students from considering social inequalities and injustices, to shelter them within a kind of artificial paradise—which explains the childish and affected format of most textbooks. This "Walt Disneyfication" of life in general, and of school culture in particular, works in turn to stimulate the consumption of cultural products from multinationals, and to enclose children's lived experience in artificial paradises, while giving rise to excessive silences around reality. Preventing children from engaging more realistically with the world around them perpetuates a negative image of the potential for positive human intervention and transformation of the world. One of the essential tasks for teachers, then, is to awaken a reflective and critical spirit in their students. Torres Santomé thus finds it of paramount importance that we offer images of human achievements. This can be accomplished through institutionalized education, despite its reproductive capacity. It can and should also be a space for educating people in the commitment to opposing injustice, and in their capacity to intervene in, and improve reality.

Mar Rodríguez Romero takes educational change further by addressing, in Chapter Ten, the potential of situated educational reform for contending with the oppressions of today's globally reconfigured social landscape. She asserts that the field of educational change has been colonized by managerial discourses, and that the most recent reforms in education insist upon increasing social exclusion and symbolic control. In order to challenge this situation and stimulate the construction of alternative visions for education, this chapter reconfigures educational change as a cultural politics. Rodríguez Romero analyzes reform as a versatile social practice, constructed and defined by a multitude of conflicting social interests. Special attention is dedicated to the discourses and practices of those social groups that attempt to expand the spaces of dissidence through recognizing difference and achieving equality. Reform is explored as a strategy that can challenge both forms of injustice, creating uneasy and contingent alliances among the various social actors. Specifically, situated reform strives to contend with the diverse faces of oppression, using the power of local commitment and democratic deliberation to create heterogeneous public spaces in schools that are more responsive to the rights of traditionally disenfranchised student groups and individuals.

Focusing on higher education, in Chapter Eleven Dolores Juliano questions the lack of dialog across academic fields, such as educational studies and anthropology, and explores the benefits for multicultural school populations if these camps were to mutually inform each other to a greater degree. She argues that some of the social demand for anthropological support in solving problems related to multicultural coexistence in schooling and society is based on a functionalistic conception of culture and the assumption that cultural diversity in schools has significantly increased. Juliano notes, however, that a multiple world must not be regarded as a mere patchwork of different cultures, but as a complex field of interrelations and mutations, one that produces ever-evolving identities and spatial movement, and one that values these developments: a world in which we feel that we learn from life as the landscape around us changes. Nonetheless, scholars of anthropology in the Spanish State context, Juliano contends, have failed to develop sufficient interest in the ways these events are playing out in formal learning contexts, for students of anthropology are not systematically engaged with educational issues; nor have anthropologists made enough effort to remain current on the theoretical and practical proposals arising from the educational sector. Forums for dialog with educators have thus failed to emerge to the extent that might be considered desirable. But while anthropology offers no clear answers to the problems, it does offer the opportunity to see them in a different light. Likewise, the change from strong to weak paradigms that goes hand in hand with postmodernism does not provide stand-alone answers, but opens the door to trial and error as well as to individual thought. This is one way, according to Juliano, in which the most productive form of cross-cultural coexistence can be sought.

In Chapter Twelve, Mariano Fernández Enguita articulates the institutions of school, work, and family to reveal the fractures and links between subaltern groups and the dominant culture of Spain, and within each minoritized collective. He explores, for instance, the functions of universal schooling, with its successive expansions in terms of time and scope, and its role in postponing young people's entrance into the labor market while preparing them for integration into a model of economic activity centered on the marketplace as a mechanism of exchange, and on formal, bureaucratic organization as a mechanism of cooperation and discipline—both of which are predicated on the displacement of any other form of socialization around attitudes toward, and qualifications for, work. Within the dominant culture, the educational institution, and the teaching profession itself, this process of preparation is assumed to be unproblematic, even as it faces a manifest, yet unplanned challenge: the (non)meeting of, on the one hand, an accelerated expansion of the educational system, with, on the other hand, the alternative economy of the Roma/Gypsies, or with the distinct patterns of transition to adult and economic life that characterize significant sectors of the immigrant population of Spain, especially among Arabic North Africans. Enguita goes on to point out another such encounter at the intersection between educational policy and gender relations: in a school institution initially designed to meet the demands of ethnically dominant males, uniformity and bureaucratic equity policy have together translated into noteworthy gains for the integration of ethnically dominant women, as well as significant gains for women from minority groups, relative to the male members of those groups. But the same educational policies have done little for ethnic minorities in general. Finally, these institutional effects, taken together, configure a complex and charged panorama, replete with (mis)encounters between the teaching profession and the new publics at school, and with unpredictable consequences for action.

In Chapter Thirteen, Juan José Bueno Aguilar maps the ways in which emergent forms of racism in Spanish society are projected through the mass media and education. He analyzes, for example, the dynamics of racism in relation to the diverse cultures now coexisting in Spain and the construction of a multicultural society, which is increasingly influenced by the relatively recent phenomenon of immigration. Bueno Aguilar shows how these new racisms diverge from older forms by means of translation: earlier biological and differential racisms are transformed into new constructs, attitudes, and behaviors that may, in the long run, prove even more pernicious to humankind, especially to those groups who have most suffered from racism. Even so, the immigration factor is complex and dynamic, for it affects Spanish society as a whole and, more clearly than ever, education in particular. Bueno Aguilar offers analytical proposals drawn from critical multicultural perspectives in education that are aimed at contesting these new racisms as they inundate the various cultural spheres of our media-driven reality today.

Cathryn Teasley addresses racism in Spanish society and schooling as well, but prefers to focus, in Chapter Fourteen, on deeply rooted forms of racism and the ways that these inform the biased institutional dynamics through which "diversity" is instituted at school. Specifically, critical ethnographic inquiry guides her examination of the ways in which a group of experienced teachers at an urban secondary school in Spain have responded to a series of new regulations of their practice in the context of markedly increased student diversity at the school. Teasley's analysis centers on the ideological stances represented and produced through the educators' discourses and actions, and on the implications for the education of the school's Roma/Gypsy students, as members of what is generally considered to be the most disenfranchised ethnic group of Spain. This chapter concludes with the exploration of some alternative means, especially through action research, for producing professional commitments that are more conducive to socially just and culturally responsive educational interventions.

To close this section of the book, in Chapter Fifteen Cameron McCarthy explores scholarly writing on the topic of globalization processes, which are too often cast in terms of simplistic binary oppositions: "homogenization" versus "heterogeneity," "uniformity" versus "diversity," "cosmopolitanism" versus "localism," "centralization" versus "decentralization," etc., and how these views influence educational contexts. Because globalization is often seen as a set of processes happening "way out there" in the world, far from what educators, teachers and students actually do, it is therefore depicted as embodying movement and dynamism. On the other hand, schooling, particularly in the urban setting, is frequently represented within the discourse of "stasis" and tradition. McCarthy confronts this unreflexive dualism, showing how globalization, when articulated to neoliberal policies—such as, for example, the Bush government's "No Child Left Behind Act" of 2002 in the United States—is effectively restructuring the organization of knowledge in educational institutions and undermining their vital function as institutions dedicated to the public good. McCarthy argues that "movement" and "stasis" are therefore intimately related in the reorganization and restructuring of education, and in the larger processes of the re-feudalization of the public sphere.

IN CONCLUSION

In the Coda to the volume, James Ladwig gets at the heart of what drives the various authors to engage as they do with the intersections between popular culture, race, public policy, and the neoliberal times in which we live. To quote Ladwig (this volume), "Race in this analysis is about the culturally created social groups stratified by some bizarre moral universes that have littered the pathways of human history" (p. 343). This history, as well as the future of such "bizarre moral universes," are confronted on multiple fronts in this volume, for, as the respective chapters can attest to, certain dominant forms of (bizarre) "normalcy" across the globe have, ironically, encouraged the emergence of social injustices where popular culture, institutional culture, and the political economy intersect, at both local and global levels. The particulars of the situated, transnational experiences and practices around identity, cross-cultural coexistence, racism, sexism, and other forms discrimination brought together in this book, are, moreover, addressed through theoretical levels of analysis that provide one of the keys to transforming the epistemology of an academic field in formation, such as cultural studies. It is our hope that this volume contribute, through these subaltern perspectives, to the opening up of a rapidly forming canon, and that, in the process, a more inclusive and informed approach to sociocultural justice be forged.

NOTE

1. In her distinctive first novel, *The voyage out*, Virginia Woolf (1915) explored an empowering process of self-discovery in a young English woman who embarked on a touristic journey to South America.

REFERENCES

Bhabha, H. (1994). *The location of culture*. London: Routledge.

Burawoy, M., Blum, J. A., George S., Gille, Z., Thayer, M., Gowan T., Haney, L., Klawiter, M., Lopez, S. H., and Riain, S. (2000). *Global ethnography: Forces, connections, imaginations in a postmodern world*. Berkeley, CA: University of California Press.

Carrington, B. (2001). Decentering the centre: Cultural studies in Britain and its legacy. In T. Miller (Ed.), *A companion to cultural studies* (pp. 275–297). Oxford: Blackwell.

Durham, M. G. and Kellner, D. M. (Eds.) (2001). *Media and cultural studies: Keyworks*. Malden, MA: Blackwell Publishing.

Giardina, M. and McCarthy, C. (2008). The popular racial order of "urban" America: Sport, identity and the politics of culture. In C. Teasley and C. McCarthy (Eds.) *Transnational perspectives on culture, policy, and education: Redirecting cultural studies in neoliberal times* (pp. 113–141). New York: Peter Lang.

Kellner, D. (1995). *Media culture: Cultural studies, identity, and politics between the modern and the postmodern*. New York: Routledge.

Ladwig, J. (2008). Terrorism, globalization, schooling and humanity. In C. Teasley and C. McCarthy (Eds.) *Transnational perspectives on culture, policy, and education: Redirecting cultural studies in neoliberal times* (pp. 113–141). New York: Peter Lang.

McCarthy, C. and Dimitriadis, G. (2000). Globalizing pedagogies: Power, resentment, and the renarration of difference. In R. Mahalingham and C. McCarthy (Eds.), *Multicultural curriculum: New directions for social theory, practice, and policy* (pp. 70–83). New York: Routledge.

Rutherford, J. (1990). The third space (interview with Homi Bhabha). In J. Rutherford (Ed.), *Identity, community, culture, difference* (pp. 207–221). London: Lawrence and Wishart.

Santos, B. de S. (2005). *El milenio huérfano: Ensayos para un nueva cultura política.* Madrid / Bogotá: Trotta/ILSA.

Spivak, G. C. and Harasym, S. E. (1990). *The post-colonial critic: Interviews, strategies, dialogues.* New York: Routledge.

Woolf, V. (1915/1991). *The voyage out.* New York: Bantam Books.

Part I. Problematizing conceptions and constructions of culture and identity

CHAPTER ONE

Freedom, community, AND Raymond Williams's project OF A common culture[1]

ÁLVARO PINA

University of Lisbon

Over the last four years I have been working with graduate students at the University of Lisbon on a cultural studies project exploring articulations of culture and freedom, community, and freedom; and community, culture and freedom. More recently, within that project's theoretical framework, I have organized sessions and/or presented papers at several international conferences—in Lisbon, at the 5th Culture Conference, in 2001; in Tampere, at the 4th "Crossroads in Cultural Studies" Conference; in Tarragona, at the 8th "Culture and Power" Conference; and in Évora, at the "Language, Communication, Culture" Conference, in 2002. My articulation of community, culture, and freedom, both as concepts and practices, is an attempt to construct a position to analyze the developments and changes in North Atlantic societies over the second half of the 20th and the beginning of the 21st centuries, and to recover for cultural studies a principled practice of political engagement with the social, in the radical tradition of Raymond Williams and Edward P. Thompson.

A PROJECT OF POLITICAL ENGAGEMENT WITH SOCIAL LIFE

There is much in cultural studies today that takes too many aspects of society and culture for granted. I want to remind cultural studies workers and scholars that cultural studies emerged as a project from the refusal to take for granted, and leave unchallenged, not only the structures and relations of power but also the knowledges and theories that naturalized, and were naturalized by, those relations and structures, and that inscribed them in a "natural" order of things.

To make my position clear, I shall begin by taking into account a number of voices that have challenged cultural studies of late. Tom Steele (1997) is a good voice to start with.

> Because mainstream cultural studies regards any attempt to map cultural phenomena onto accounts of capitalist development as economic reductionism, (ironically, exactly the demon Thompson was trying to exorcise), they have lost the possibility of political engagement with social life. Instead, they comment upon social life from a distanced and increasingly ironic standpoint. In some of their more recent manifestations, mainstream cultural studies adopt an aristocratic nihilism which utterly refuses to distinguish between the social life and its simulations—with ludicrous results, such as in Baudrillard's analysis of the Gulf War. (pp. 206–207)

In a remarkable book, Russell Jacoby (1999) asked, "What happens to cultural studies when its original object, working-class culture, vaporizes?" (p. 79). His answer strikes two notes. On the one hand,

> [i]f nature does not abhor a vacuum, intellectuals do. Knock-off French theories and Instant Gramsci fill up the spaces. The orientation of cultural studies changes from criticizing to interpreting, reading, deconstructing and, increasingly, championing mass culture. (p. 79)

On the other, "The ailment is not the banality of the subject matter, but the banality of the analysis":

> This is the heart of the matter. The self-satisfied break with old elitism can be tolerated, perhaps even applauded; the incessant repetition of the new academic commonplaces, however, betrays the project. These are not gutsy scholars plowing new ground, but cautious souls trimming their front lawns. (Jacoby, 1999, p. 81)

Francis Mulhern (2000) observed that "Kulturkritik reasoned politics out of moral existence, as a false pretender to authority" (p. 151), and added:

> Cultural Studies, inverting the social commitments of that tradition but retaining its discursive form, has been tempted to follow suit. And to the extent that it has yielded, it has disclosed its character as a strictly limited mode of opposition to Kulturkritik, with which it continues to share the discursive space of metaculture. (p. 151)

Terry Eagleton (2000) wrote that cultural studies today "fails to see not only that not all political issues are cultural, but that not all cultural differences are political" (p. 43):

> And in thus subordinating issues of state, class, political organization and the rest to cultural questions, it ends up rehearsing the prejudices of the very traditional *Kulturkritik* it rejects, which had little enough time itself for such mundane political matters. … What *Kulturkritik* and modern-day culturalism also share is a lack of interest in what lies, politically speaking, beyond culture: the state apparatus of violence and coercion. Yet it is this, not culture, which is most likely in the end to defeat radical change. (p. 43)

Zygmunt Bauman (2001) has issued in recent years many challenges to cultural studies which cannot be overlooked. In one, he has pointed out that "claims to recognition tend nowadays to be voiced with no reference to distributive justice" (p. 88):

> What is assumed … is that having legally guaranteed freedom of choice means being free to choose—which, blatantly, is not the case. On the way to the "culturalist" version of the human right to recognition, the unfulfilled task of the human right to well-being and a life lived in dignity falls by the board. (p. 88)

Selecting these five voices enables me to make them present in my article to briefly state that my practice of cultural studies involves political engagement with social life, as Steele rightly stressed, which refuses the change from criticizing to interpreting, and the banality of lawn-trimming analysis that Jacoby highlighted. It does not reason politics out of existence, this concurring with Mulhern; and, in agreement with Eagleton, it does not subordinate issues of state, class, and political organization to cultural questions, but is, above all, focused on the unfulfilled task of the human right to well-being and a life lived in dignity, in Bauman's principled remark.

Such emphases also enable me to outline the theoretical framework of the project I am working on with my students. By articulating community, culture, and freedom together, as both concepts and practices, not only can I examine the direction of change in North Atlantic social relations over the second half of the 20th and the beginning of the 21st centuries, but I can also ground my cultural studies work in the democratic intellectual project and practice of Raymond Williams and Edward P. Thompson. In Williams's definition of that practice, it was an intellectual analysis that wanted to change the actual developments of society (Williams, 1989a, p. 158).

A TRUNCATED DEMOCRACY

Over the second half of the 20th century, social changes in North Atlantic modernity have been swift and far-reaching. There are at least a few key vectors in these changes that the intellectual practice of cultural studies cannot ignore, and must indeed be fully aware of. Because these changes and their vectors have been best perceived and analyzed in recent sociological studies, I shall quote from the important work carried out by Zygmunt Bauman and also by Ulrich Beck. Bauman (2000) has rightly underscored that "the job in which sociologists are the experts, the job of restoring to view the lost link between objective affliction and subjective experience, has become more vital and indispensable than ever" (p. 211), and unlikely to be performed by practitioners of other fields of expertise. Cultural studies can—indeed must—learn with sociologists to make that "lost link" visible, if it is to contribute again to human and social dignity, and to human and social freedom, by means of a better, more productive understanding of human and social conditions—that is, an understanding which makes clear the possibility and the reality of the changes needed by humankind.

In one of Bauman's analyses (1998), producer societies have passed over into consumer societies, and this passage has entailed many profound changes; arguably the most decisive among them is, however, the fashion in which people are groomed and trained to meet the demands of their social identities (i.e., the fashion in which men and women are "integrated" into the social order and given a place in it). Panoptical institutions, once crucial in that respect, have fallen progressively out of use (p. 24).

Cultural studies must examine these many profound changes. The passage from producer to consumer societies has disrupted the social order and its processes of social identification to such an extent that the very concept and practice of society have been made ineffective, this having dramatic consequences for citizenship, work, and education. Studies of consumption that not seldom turn out to be celebrations of consumption, tend to overlook, or turn a blind eye to, that disruption and its dramatic consequences.

Another of Bauman's studies (2000) makes the contemporary strategy and configurations of power visible. The changes produced fluid, liquid modernity, "the epoch of disengagement, elusiveness, facile escape and hopeless chase," in which "it is the most elusive, those free to move without notice, who rule" (Bauman, 2000, p. 120):

> Domination consists in one's own capacity to escape, to disengage, to "be elsewhere," and the right to decide the speed with which all that is done—while simultaneously stripping the people on the dominated side of their ability to arrest or constrain their moves or slow them down. (p. 120)

Disengagement plays here a decisive role: "Labour has been let out of the Panopticon, but, most importantly, capital has shed the vexing burden and exorbitant costs of running it," Bauman wrote (2000, p. 121). What is more significant, however, in my argument, is the politics of shedding all moral, social, and cultural responsibilities by capital, the state servicing it, and most critically the institutions of knowledge. Capital demands and gets from national governments flexible conditions for its flows and increased profits. The state resorts to disengagement as the leading vector of its own policies, thus making society a void: an un-society. The institutions of knowledge disengage from culture understood as the making of a better, solidary, and just world—a praxis of human-making. In conversation with Keith Tester, Bauman stressed that it

> is not the *knowledge* of good and evil that we are missing; it is the skill and zeal to *act* on that knowledge which is conspicuously absent in this world of ours, in which dependencies, political responsibilities and cultural values part ways and no longer hold each other in check. (Bauman and Tester, 2001, p. 131)

In Ulrich Beck's analysis (1999), we have moved from the first to the second modernity, from "modernity based on nation-state societies, where social relations, networks and communities are essentially understood in a territorial sense" (pp. 1–2), to "a phase of development of modern society in which the social, political, ecological and individual risks created by the momentum of innovation increasingly elude the control and protective institutions of industrial society" (p. 72). The second modernity is that of manufactured uncertainties and insecurity created by technological innovation developed and carried out with no knowledge of its consequences, as in the fields of atomic energy, genetic engineering, and chemical industry. But Beck (1992) makes us aware of the human consequences of advanced modernity: "individualization takes place under the general conditions of a societalizing process that makes individual autonomizations increasingly impossible" (p. 131):

> The individual is indeed removed from traditional commitments and support relationships, but exchanges them for the constraints of existence in the labor market and as a consumer, with the standardizations and controls they contain. The place of *traditional* ties and social forms (social class, nuclear family) is taken by *secondary* agencies and institutions, which stamp the biography of the individual and make that person dependent upon fashions, social policy, economic cycles and markets, contrary to the image of individual control which establishes itself in the consciousness. (p. 131)

In Beck's (1992) famous definition, "how one lives becomes the *biographical solution of systemic contradictions*" (p. 137), only a small minority can hope to find, or boast of finding, such biographical solutions (Bauman, 2001, p. 101); while the majority of human beings are caught and trapped in the systemic contradictions that endanger, and put at risk, their human freedom and dignity.

What lies behind the move from solid to liquid modernity, from the first to the second modernity? Bauman's emphasis on disengagement, elusiveness, facile escape, and hopeless chase—as characteristic of liquid modernity—coupled with Beck's account of innovation—as developed and carried out without knowledge of its consequences—help us understand, and deal with, the driving force behind the changes in North Atlantic modernity and in the societies it influences, subordinates, and exploits. Richard Sennett (1998) has noted that the "new capitalism is an often illegible regime of power" (p. 10), and that "knock-off French theories and instant Gramsci" (p. 10), to borrow Jacoby's phrase, are not particularly suited to read that regime—at least not in cultural studies, where Althusser and Foucault have been made particularly influential in leading teachers and students to look back, and the other way, to find excuses for not attempting to read flexible capitalism and its regime of power.

Jürgen Habermas (1996) examined modernity as the project of Enlightenment, that is, as consisting in the relentless development of the objectivating sciences, of the universalistic foundations of morality and law, and of autonomous art—all in accord with their own immanent logic, but also as releasing cognitive potentials and attempting to apply them in the sphere of praxis, and to encourage the rational organization of social relations (p. 45). In his examination, Habermas also noted that in the process of social modernization, the autonomous, systemic dynamics of the economic and administrative systems inhibit the reconnection of modern culture with everyday praxis; such reconnection will only prove successful if the process of social modernization can also be turned in other noncapitalist directions (Habermas, 1996, pp. 52–53).

Habermas (1987) looked further into modernization and perceived that it dissociates modernity from its modern European origins and stylizes it into a spatiotemporally neutral model for processes of social development in general, while at the same time breaking the internal connections between modernity and the historical context of Western rationalism. He writes, "so that processes of modernization can no longer be conceived of as rationalization, as the historical objectification of rational structures" (Habermas, 1987, p. 2). And he adds that

> it is precisely modernization research that has contributed to the currency of the expression "postmodern" even among social scientists. For in view of an evolutionary autonomous, self-promoting modernization, social-scientific observers can all the more easily take leave of the conceptual horizon of Western rationalism in which modernity arose. (Habermas, 1987, p. 3)

I am bringing together Habermas's (1987) look at modernization and Beck's (1992, 1999) view of innovation as a way of explaining why I agree with Tom Steele (1997) that cultural studies must persist in its attempt to map cultural phenomena onto accounts of capitalist development as a condition of its political engagement with social life. As capitalism turns flexible, modernity turns liquid. Those who rule, as Bauman points out, are those most elusive and free to move without notice. Capitalism, in its different stages and strategic modes, has been effective in moving without notice and in eluding the democratic structures and institutions which were the result of long democratic struggles. As Beck emphasizes,

> industrial society has produced a "truncated democracy," in which questions of the technological change of society remain beyond the reach of political-parliamentary decision-making. As things stand, one can say "no" to techno-economic progress, but that will not change its course in any way. (1999, p. 70)

Against the truncated democracy capitalism has produced in the North Atlantic modern societies and all over the world, precisely because "we lack the agencies that could push human affairs the way we would wish them to go" (Bauman and Tester, 2001, p. 131), I want to recover Raymond Williams's (1989b) argument for a common culture, which he defined as an *educated and participating democracy* (p. 37). As Terry Eagleton (2000) recently remarked, "Williams's position would no doubt seem to [contemporary culturalism] quaintly residual, not to say positively archaic; the problem in fact is that we have yet to catch up with it" (p. 122).

A COMMON CULTURE

Williams's (1963) argument for a common culture was first developed in the "Conclusion" to *Culture and Society 1780–1950*, the chapter in which he moved beyond the English "culture and society tradition," which the book so innovatively reviewed and analyzed while making both his review, and his moving beyond it, the condition of possibility of "a new general theory of culture." As he himself put it, he had sought to clarify the tradition, but it might be possible "to go from this to a full restatement of principles, taking the theory of culture as a theory of relations between elements in a whole way of life" (Williams, 1963, pp. 11–12). The review was only possible, however, by going beyond: as Francis Mulhern (2000) noted, there was "much still to rethink and to discover, but by the turn of the 1960s Williams had established the irreducible distance between Kulturkritik in all its variants—reactionary or reforming—and an integrally socialist politics of culture" (p. 72).

The "Conclusion" opens with the well-known remark that the "history of the idea of culture is a record of our reactions, in thought and feeling, to the changed conditions of our common life" (Williams, 1963, p. 285), followed a few lines below with the perception that

> [t]he idea of culture describes our common inquiry, but our conclusions are diverse, as our starting points were diverse. The word, culture, cannot automatically be pressed into service as any kind of social or personal directive. Its emergence, in its modern meanings, marks the effort at total qualitative assessment, but what it indicates is a process, not a conclusion. (Williams, 1963, p. 285)

Williams's (1963) proposal of a new general theory of culture as a theory of relations—later the study of relations between elements in a social order—is still of great importance for cultural studies today because it treats culture as a process, both common and differentiated, shared and conflicted, which cannot be used, "pressed into service," as a "directive" and a "conclusion." As an inquiry, culture is open to, and aware of, diverse starting points, and develops in dialogue and conflict; as an effort at total qualitative assessment. Culture is open to, and aware of, relations between elements in the social order and the social order itself—what is to be assessed is the social order and its relations. It is this Williamsian understanding of culture, both as a concept and as a practice, that makes its articulation with community and freedom more significant and effective for today's inquiry and assessment.

To go back, however, to the "Conclusion" (Williams, 1963), the *common* in "our common life" and "our common inquiry" is likely to sound vague and ambiguous today, but the note it strikes at the opening of the "Conclusion" must not be lost sight of, must indeed be recovered, as it runs through, and shapes, Williams's entire argument. Here I shall explore only three lines of its development.

First, "there are in fact no masses; there are only ways of seeing people as masses" (Williams, 1963, p. 289). It is not only that "to other people, we also are masses" and "masses are other people"; it is also, and more significantly, that "a way of seeing other people which has become characteristic of our kind of society, has been capitalized for the purposes of political or cultural exploitation" (Williams, 1963, p. 289).

What is at stake here, Williams (1963) notes, is democracy—democracy as historically produced and advanced in social changes by the struggle of working people:

> If a majority can be achieved in favour of these changes, the democratic criterion is satisfied. But if you disapprove of the changes you can, it seems, avoid open opposition to democracy as such by inventing a new category, mass-democracy. (p. 288)

The consequence, then, is that the "submerged opposite is class-democracy, where democracy will merely describe the processes by which the ruling class conducts its business of ruling" (Williams, 1963, p. 289).

Beck's (1992) comment on the "truncated democracy" quoted above is directly relevant to our understanding of Williams's (1963) analysis, in light of which not only questions of technological change lie beyond the reach of political-parliamentary decision-making; but so does the entire business of ruling. The whole process of social change over the last three or four decades has been conducted with no regard for the majority of the populations in North Atlantic societies and all over the world. Indeed, this process has been strategically conducted with no regard for, and in contempt of, democratic decision-making. It is not only the case that nation-states have been made instrumental, and are proving decisively effective, in subordinating national populations to global capitalism and the regime of power active in its flows; it is above all the case—more central to the concerns of this article—that this dismantling of the nation, and its social protection systems and structures, is a dismantling of the very relations and structures of democratic community-making which over the last two centuries have been effective as instruments of freedom for working people, protecting their human right to well-being and a life lived in dignity. Those relations and structures of democratic community-making were what Williams called "the collective democratic institution" created by working-class culture (1963, p. 314).

Second, "communication is not only transmission; it is also reception and response" (Williams, 1963, p. 301). Williams's (1963) argument in making this point is worth looking into. He writes:

> Any governing body will seek to implant the "right" ideas in the minds of those whom it governs, but there is no government in exile. The minds of men are shaped by their whole experience, and the most skilful transmission of material which this experience does not confirm will fail to communicate. (Williams, 1963, p. 301)

He then observes that

> mass-communication has had its evident successes, in a social and economic system to which its methods correspond. But it has failed, and will continue to fail, when its transmissions encounter, not a confused uncertainty, but a considered and formulated experience. (Williams, 1963, p. 301)

As with class democracy, the "submerged element" Williams's (1963) analysis brought to the surface, is so now with communication reduced to transmission: Williams offers the clear recognition that this "long dominative effort" (1963, p. 303) corresponds to, and is part of, the social and economic system that requires that its business be conducted without reception of, and response to, its transmissions.

Williams's new theory of culture, as a theory of relations between elements in a whole way of life, is a socialist politics of culture, and must be recognized as such.

In another context, clearly pedagogical but no less clearly socially committed, Paulo Freire (1998) explored the opposition between what he called "banking" and liberating education in terms worth remembering here: "Instead of communicating, the teacher issues communiqués and makes deposits which the students patiently receive, memorize, and repeat" (p. 67), he wrote of the banking concept of education; of the liberating, he wrote that in response to the essence of consciousness it "rejects communiqués and embodies communication" (p. 74). Freire's thesis that "solidarity requires true communication" because "only through communication can human life hold meaning" (p. 72) is underpinned by his perception that "the presence of the oppressed in the struggle for their liberation will be what it should be: not pseudo-participation, but committed involvement" (p. 67)—as E. P. Thompson (1968) famously put it, the working class was present at its own making (p. 9).

Third, "we have to unlearn, as the price of survival, the inherent dominative mode" (Williams, 1963, p. 322):

> This is a real barrier in the mind, [...] a refusal to accept the creative capacities of life; a determination to limit and restrict the channels of growth; a habit of thinking, indeed, that the future has now to be determined by some ordinance in our own minds. We project our old images into the future, and take hold of ourselves and others to force energy towards that substantiation. We do this as conservatives, trying to prolong old forms: we do this as socialists, trying to prescribe the new man. (Williams, 1963, p. 322)

Williams's (1963) cultural studies project emerged and developed in his effort to unlearn that dominative mode. "Project" is an adequate definition of Williams's work: it was "always purposive, embodying a sense of work *to be done*" (Wallace, Jones, and Nield, 1997, p. 1), and at the same time it provided "a guarantee against the reduction of the necessary and the possible to the actual" (Wallace et al., 1997, p. 15). But also because how "we 'place' the work is essentially the question of where we go with it from here" (Prendergast, 1995, p. 3)—which means that Williams's work is a project open to the future and looking forward to being taken up as an "uncancelled challenge" (Tredell, 1990). In Edward Said's words, his own work since *Orientalism* "has depended very much on Raymond [Williams]'s work, or one sentence [...] I always struggle to realize, [...] the need to unlearn the inherent dominative mode" (Williams and Said, 1989, p. 181). Freire (1998) warned that in the task of liberation the leadership cannot merely "implant" in the oppressed a belief in freedom: "the conviction of the oppressed that they must fight for their liberation is not a gift bestowed by the revolutionary leadership, but the result of their own *conscientização*" (p. 64).

Democracy—full democracy with equal participation of all human beings in all their individual difference—and communication—full communication with transmission, active reception, and intelligent response—are key elements in Williams's (1963) argument for a common culture, and a common culture is a key element in the unlearning of the old dominative mode. In terms of communication, Williams argues for "a different attitude to transmission, one which will ensure that its origins are genuinely multiple, that all the sources have access to the common channels" (1963, p. 304); in terms of democracy, Williams argues for "an effective community of experience" and "recognition of practical equality," "a context of material community," and "the full democratic process" (1963, p. 304).

It is Williams's (1963) argument for full democracy and effective, material community that makes common culture, common experience, common life, common business, or common inquiry, integral to his new theory of culture and his socialist politics of culture—a theory of culture which is a socialist politics of culture. As "The Idea of a Common Culture" a decade later would emphasize, "the culture of a people can only be what all its members are engaged in creating in the act of living" (Williams, 1989b, p. 36):

> A common culture is [...] the creation of a condition in which the people as a whole participate in the articulation of meanings and values, and in the consequent decisions between this meaning and that, this value and that. This would involve, in any real world, the removal of all the material obstacles to just this form of participation. (Williams, 1989b, p. 36)

The need for a common culture, Williams wrote, was asserted both as a recognition of the community of culture and as a critique of capitalist society: "one was using the idea of the *common* element of the culture—its community—as a way of criticizing that divided and fragmented culture we actually have" (Williams, 1989b, p. 35). The critique begun as cultural had to be extended to the social and the political. "The argument about culture can never pass in a simple way to an argument about politics; but when a political case is made, in these terms, it tries always to base itself on the originating values" (Williams, 1989b, p. 37).

Williams (1989b) concluded his common culture article with the comment, "In speaking of a common culture, one is asking, precisely, for that free, contributive and common *process* of participation in the creation of meanings and values" (p. 38).

COMMUNITY

To illustrate what can be achieved by articulating community, culture and freedom, as concepts and practices, to a position, at once critical and politically engaged, from which to study the latest developments and shifts in North Atlantic capitalism, I shall look again at some of these developments and shifts. Examining the crisis-decades of the 20th century, Eric Hobsbawm (1995) wrote that as the "transnational economy established its grip over the world" (p. 424).

> [O]rganizations whose field of action were effectively bounded by the frontiers of their territory, like trade unions, parliaments and national public broadcasting systems, therefore lost, as organizations not so bounded like transnational firms, the international currency market and the globalized media and communications of the satellite era, gained. (p. 424)

Hobsbawm analyzes three elements of the crisis: the new separatist nationalism, the collective egoism of wealth, and, as more relevant to my pursuit in this context, "the 'cultural revolution' of the second half of the [20th] century, that extraordinary dissolution of traditional social norms, textures and values, which left so many of the inhabitants of the developed world orphaned and bereft" (p. 428). He notes, "Never was the word 'community' used more indiscriminately and emptily than in the decades when communities in the sociological sense became hard to find in real life" (Hobsbawm, 1995, p. 428).

The indiscriminate emptiness in the use of community criticized by Hobsbawm (1995) is indeed a problem, but not the main problem in our times. It is part of capitalism's flexible strategies against the common cause of those it inflexibly exploits and subordinates. The main problem, as I see it—indeed, the tragedy—is that the subordinated and exploited pursue and celebrate "exclusionary identity politics" (Hobsbawm, 1995, p. 429); they accept and celebrate the fragmentation of society, and in this way abet the making of an un-society. Bauman (2001) cogently points out that

> the pulverization of public space and its saturation with intercommunal strife is precisely the kind of political "superstructure" (or should we now call it "understructure"?) that the new power hierarchy serviced by the strategy of disengagement needs and would openly or surreptitiously cultivate if allowed to do so. Global order needs a lot of global disorder. (p. 105)

The pulverization of public space signifies that subordinated and exploited groups have also disengaged from society as the space of engagement for common causes, and spells out their rejection of the community-making needed to oppose and defeat the unmaking of society. This is the serious problem multiculturalism and multicommunitarianism either overlook or appear committed to silence and dismiss. As Bauman (1999) argues,

> [t]he multi-cultural and multi-communitarian programmes are two different strategies meant to deal with a similarly diagnosed situation: the co-presence of *many*

cultures within the same society. It seems, however, that the diagnosis is false to start with. The most prominent feature of contemporary life is cultural variety of societies, rather than *variety of cultures* in society. (p. xliii)

Where society not so long ago was, a void now yawns (Bauman, 2001, p. 112), the result of hegemonic strategy as well as unprincipled surrender by subordinated groups to the pressures of domination. Taking up from this angle the question put forth recently by Glenn Jordan and Chris Weedon (2000), "When the subalterns speak, what do they say?" my answer in this context must be that subalterns acting out the discourses of multicommunitarianism and multiculturalism remain trapped within the politics of disengagement of the hegemonic elites. This is one side of the problem.

The other is, as Bauman (2000) observes, that

> the "citizen" is a person inclined to seek her or his own welfare through the wellbeing of the city—while the individual tends to be lukewarm, sceptical or wary about "common cause," "common good," "good society" or "just society." What is the sense of "common interests" except letting each individual satisfy her or his own? (p. 36)

The unmaking of society is the unmaking of solidarity and common cause, the unmaking of class and citizenship, and the celebration of socially and morally unaccountable individualization. In the absence of the citizen, "cloakroom" and "carnival" communities have replaced the "common cause" of the "heavy/solid/hardware modernity" (Bauman, 2000, p. 200).

The common culture Raymond Williams argued for at the turn of, and in, the 1960s, belonged to the solid modernity of the nation-state as rectifying social injustices, and the welfare state as promoting the well-being of its citizens—the modernity in the meantime liquefied by the transnational economy and the flexible shifts of capitalism. What is the point, then, of recovering Williams's principled argument for our times and our societies?

UNIVERSAL COMMUNITY, UNIVERSAL CITIZENSHIP

One answer could be based on E. P. Thompson's (1993) observation that we

> shall not ever return to pre-capitalist human nature, yet a reminder of its alternative needs, expectations and codes may renew our sense of our nature's range of possibilities. Could it even prepare us for a time when [...] human nature may be made over in a new form? (p. 15)

We shall not return to the solid modernity of industrial society and the nation-state; yet, a reminder of its needs, expectations, and codes may renew our sense of the range of possibilities of our practice and our theory as human nature is being made over in a new form.

Another answer, which is no less committed to "the great causes of the Enlightenment: reason, progress, and the betterment of the conditions of all human beings" (Hobsbawm, 2000, p. 162), can take into account Terry Eagleton's (2000) endorsement of Francis Mulhern's (1998) argument about communities— namely, that communities are "not *places* but *practices* of collective identification whose variable order largely defines the culture of any social formation" (Mulhern, 1998, p. 111).

> They can be as much universal as local, and to limit the notion to the latter is to fetishize it. One can speak of "abstract communities," or see the nation as a "community of known strangers." The relations between culture and politics are similarly variable, depending on the context. There should be no Enlightenment assumption that politics always has the edge over culture, or—with so much culturalist thought—that it is enough simply to invert this order of priorities. (Eagleton, 2000, p. 80)

Because communities can be as much universal as local, and because "citizenship is not an optional extra, a mere add on, to what it is to be human" (Clarke, 1994, p. 29), what must be affirmed in today's world is the human community of universal citizenship. As Bauman (2001) argues, "universality of citizenship is the preliminary condition of all meaningful 'politics of recognition'. And, let me add, universality of humanity is the horizon by which all politics of recognition, to be meaningful, needs to orient itself" (p. 140).

Williams's common culture is, then, to be recovered, I suggest, at two levels: at the level of national citizenship, in defense of, and in struggle for, that "free, contributive and common *process* of participation in the creation of meanings and values" that Williams (1989b, p. 38) stressed; and at the level of our common humanity, which is "a political task still to be undertaken," in Eagleton's words (1993, p. 6)—that is, the level at which a cultural studies practice standing in the radical line of Williams and Thompson can best analyze and criticize the transnational economy, and move beyond the horizons that capitalism—although appearing to be flexible—inflexibly sets as limits to the possibility of full democracies: educated and participatory democracies.

At the level of the struggle for full national citizenship,

> Williams's theory of a common culture [...] involves political transformations whose full implications are revolutionary; [...] the conditions for this complex cultural development can be laid only by politically securing [...] socialist institutions. And this certainly involves common belief, commitment and practice. (Eagleton, 2000, pp. 121–122)

The political terrain of the nation remains a decisive site of both opposition to capitalism and the struggle for alternative developments through the sharing and making of a community of belief, commitment, and practice, which will lead to "the process of sharing in political life" as "a vital means by which one exercises free self-determination" (Eagleton, 1996, pp. 84–85).

The political terrain of the North Atlantic modern nation is, however, also the site of power over other nations. The industrial development of the North Atlantic modern producer societies demanded colonial empires, formal and informal colonies, colonized and exploited peoples (Hobsbawm, 1999), and such limited improvement in the living conditions and well-being of their working people as was achieved by the latter's struggles that was always made possible by, and contingent upon, the inhuman conditions of the colonial working peoples. The change from producer to consumer societies in North Atlantic liquid modernity did not alter that structure of unequal relations. Not only was poverty not eradicated in these societies, but the very supply of consumer goods within them is only possible because other societies all over the world have been condemned to dire poverty, hunger, disease, and war. As Bauman (1988) has noted, consumer societies are

> a privileged minority in relation to the rest of the world. They have all transcended that threshold of commodity supply beyond which consumer attractions become effective factors of social integration and systemic management—but they attained this privilege through a disproportionately huge share of world resources and the subordination of the economies of less fortunate nations. (p. 94)

COMMON CULTURE, COMMON HUMANITY

It is for these reasons that recovering the democratic political potential of Williams's common culture argument must be articulated to the democratic political goal of a common humanity—to undertaking the political task of common humanity. Jeffrey Weeks (1993) argued for the common humanity to be constructed as the community of free human beings, the "wider human community" of "universal solidarities" in his "radical humanist project" (p. 194ff). As he wrote:

> "Humanity," in the sense of the unity of the species, may be seen as yet another community, though one that the social struggles and upheavals of the last two and a half centuries (the period of "modernity") [have] given a special meaning. The challenge is to construct that unity in a way which achieves ("invents" or "imagines") a sense of "universal human values" while respecting human variety and difference. (Weeks, 1993, p. 199)

The full significance of Weeks's argument appears, however, with his definition of humanity:

> The task of the radical humanist project, then, is to tease out of the multiple forms of difference, rooted in contingency and a radical historicity, those common strands which can make the human bond. [...] Humanity is not an essence to be realised, but a pragmatic construction, a perspective, to be developed through the articulation of the variety of individual projects, of differences, which constitute our humanity in the broadest sense. (1993, pp. 199–200)

Bauman (2001) has recently also argued for a common humanity, and it is worth noting that he does so in terms which remind us of Williams's defense of the full democratic process to be achieved through the project of a common culture. Bauman (2001) imagines the search for common humanity as carried out by explorers united by solidarity:

> While we all, singly or collectively, are embarked on the search for the best form of humanity, since we would all wish eventually to avail ourselves of it, each of us explores a different avenue and brings from the expedition somewhat different findings. (2001, pp. 135–136)

He adds:

> None of the findings can *a priori* be declared worthless, and no earnest effort to find the best shape for common humanity can be discarded in advance as misguided and undeserving of sympathetic attention. On the contrary: the variety of findings increases the chance that fewer of the many human possibilities will be overlooked and remain untried. (Bauman, 2001, p. 136)

This argument is indeed very close to Williams's defense of his common culture project, but the similarity is most striking as Bauman (2001) goes on:

> Each finding may benefit all explorers, whichever road they have themselves chosen. It does not mean that all findings are of equal value; but their true value may only be established through a long dialogue, in which all voices are allowed to be heard and bona fide, well-intentioned comparisons can be conducted. In other words, recognition of cultural variety is the beginning, not the end, of the matter; it is but a starting point for a long and perhaps tortuous, but in the end beneficial, *political process*. (p. 136)

FREEDOM

Cultural studies have not paid much theoretical attention to freedom. It is fair to say, as Bauman (1988) said of sociology, that the attention of cultural studies practitioners turned to *unfreedom* rather than freedom (p. 4). But this needs some contextualizing:

> If orthodox sociology, born and developed under the aegis of solid modernity, was pre-occupied with the conditions of human obedience and conformity, the prime concern of sociology made to the measure of liquid modernity needs to be the promotion of autonomy and freedom; such sociology must therefore put individual self-awareness, understanding and *responsibility* at its focus. For the denizens of modern society in its solid and managed phase, the major opposition was one between conformity and deviance; the major opposition in modern society in its present-day liquified and decentred phase, the opposition which needs to be faced up to in order to pave the way to a truly autonomous society, is one between taking up responsibility and seeking a shelter where responsibility for one's own action need not be taken by the actors. (Bauman, 2000, p. 213)

In the intellectual practice of Williams and Thompson, freedom was articulated to democratic participation, community-making, and social change. Not directly or explicitly theorized in their work, freedom was implicit in their theorizing of class-making culture and common culture, and in their theorizing of culture and social change. Emerging from adult education as a democratic and socialist politics of culture, the intellectual practice of cultural studies was predicated on the democratic processes of social change resulting from the victory over German Fascism in the Second World War, and from the Labour victory in Great Britain in the 1945 elections. In that context, the focus of the emergent cultural studies was on the educated participation of the working people in the making of a democratic society.

With its institutionalization, and after the encounter with French structuralism, the focus of cultural studies was shifted to unfreedom, to the opposition between conformity and deviance, dominance, and resistance. Social change as the collective human praxis of freedom-making was pushed to the margins of the cultural studies project, the consequence of which was that theorizing freedom went unrecognized and unacknowledged. It is now time to recognize that need, which will necessarily mean to recover, and to update, the intellectual practice of Williams and Thompson.

Bauman (1988) has given us a serious, historically contextualized study of freedom. Freedom is a social relation of difference and power, and you are free only insofar as others are not free, and you have power over them. One important point Bauman makes is that the

> [l]ack of prohibition or punitive sanctions is indeed a necessary condition for acting according to one's wishes, but not a sufficient one. You may be free to leave the country

at will, but have no money for the ticket. You may be free to seek skills in the field of your choice, but find that there is no place for you where you want to study. You may wish to work in a job that interests you, but find no such job available. [...] Thus freedom has more to it than lack of restrictions. To do things, one needs *resources*. Our expression ["This is a free country"] does not promise you such resources, but pretends—wrongly—that this does not matter. (1988, p. 2)

Freedom, I argue, must be considered as both a concept and a practice. On the one hand, the concept of freedom gains new content and scope, and new meanings in history as new practices and social relations open new horizons and expectations in the everyday; this is part of its power of attraction. On the other hand, the practice of freedom in history reveals that the strategic action of some classes and social groups open up horizons and expectations for the members of those classes and groups as individuals, while for the members of other classes and social groups, who are also placed in society as individuals in that strategic process, such expectations and horizons remain unattainable.

There is a contradiction between the concept and the practice of freedom in the history of Western societies that has been rendered most significant in North Atlantic modern societies. The practice of freedom, which involves both overcoming constraints and the appropriation of resources required for successful social action, has always distinguished and promoted the power or empowerment of certain individuals of those groups, classes, or fractions of classes best positioned in social relations to subordinate all other classes and groups. At the same time, that practice has successfully represented itself in culture as a concept which is offered to all individuals for social guidance and through which the resources and power of certain individuals of certain classes are disembedded from class relations and made examples of human—mostly manly—achievement.

In North Atlantic modern societies this contradiction has been rendered especially significant. Modernity was theorized and practiced as freedom, as human and social freedom grounded in European rationalism, and claiming universal human and social value. In the historical conditions obtaining in modern Europe, freedom was appropriated by capitalism and contained within its instrumental logics, once again practiced by ruling elites with power and resources, and once again, represented in culture for the benefit of subaltern groups as an abstract human value unrelated to power and resources. What was new in modern Europe, however, because modern Europe was produced in social collective action, was that the theory and practice of modernity as freedom could be appropriated also by individuals and subcultures in subaltern groups who theorized and practiced freedom in opposition to the logics of capitalism and to capitalism itself. The making of the working class in European nations was part of the practice and theory of freedom in modernity aimed at a noncapitalist alternative modernity.

We have, then, two leading vectors to consider in the analysis of freedom in modern societies: the individualizing vector, as a strategy of power based on relations of inequality and subordination that uses freedom to ensure consent to the exercise of power; and the community-making vector, predicated on solidarity and common interests and defining complex temporal and spatial trajectories of negotiation, opposition, and independent cultural creation to achieve as much human dignity and well-being as possible in the present and the future. It is to this community-making vector that hope as an intellectual practice and as a space of freedom owes its resources even today, when the individualizing vector appears to claim the whole field of the social.

Freedom, in my argument, must be articulated to community, common culture, and common humanity—to the practice of community-making in the process of democratic participation, and in the political task of common humanity. I again quote from Bauman (1999):

> The idea of creativity, of active assimilation of the universe, of imposing on the chaotic world the ordering structure of the human intelligent action—the idea built irremovably into the notion of praxis—is indeed comprehensible only if viewed as an attribute of community, capable of transcending the natural or "naturalized" order and creating new and different orders. (p. 95)

The notion of praxis as active assimilation of the universe cannot be dissociated from the practice of community as world-making and world-changing. But it is the new articulation of freedom and community that interests me here:

> Furthermore, the idea of freedom, associated in turn with the notion of creativity, acquires an utterly different meaning when considered as a quality of a community, from when it is discussed in terms of a solitary human individual. In the first case it is the freedom to change the human condition; in the second, freedom from communal coercion and limitation. The first is a real, genuine modality of the human existence; the second often happens to emanate from a misplaced nostalgia for a new, more suitable human-ordering-of-the-world, cast into the illusory realm of individualism by the obfuscating impact of an alienated, ossified, immobile society. The community [...] is therefore the medium and the bearer of praxis. (Bauman, 1999, p. 95)

The community, it must be recognized, as the medium and bearer of praxis, is also the medium and bearer of culture. It is to the community of the common culture and the common humanity that freedom must be articulated—not to individualism, not to the market, not to consumption—if freedom is to become integral to changing our human condition through changing the actual developments in our societies. And this is a recognition cultural studies cannot afford to ignore.

NOTE

1. This chapter is based on an article of the same title and authorship published in *Cultural Studies* ↔ *Critical Methodologies*, 5(2), May 2005, pp. 23–249.

REFERENCES

Bauman, Z. (1988). *Freedom*. Milton Keynes: Open University Press.

Bauman, Z. (1998). *Work, consumerism and the new poor*. Buckingham: Open University Press.

Bauman, Z. (1999). *Culture as praxis*. New edition. London: Sage Publications.

Bauman, Z. (2000). *Liquid modernity*. Cambridge: Polity Press.

Bauman, Z. (2001). *Community: Seeking safety in an insecure world*. Cambridge: Polity Press.

Bauman, Z. and Tester, K. (2001). *Conversations with Zygmunt Bauman*. Cambridge: Polity Press.

Beck, U. (1992). *Risk society: Towards a new modernity*. Translated by Mark Ritter. London: Sage Publications (Original work published 1986).

Beck, U. (1999). *World risk society*. Cambridge: Polity Press.

Clarke, P. B. (1994). *Citizenship*. London: Pluto Press.

Eagleton, T. (1993). *The crisis of contemporary culture*. Oxford: Clarendon Press.

Eagleton, T. (1996). *The illusions of postmodernism*. Oxford: Blackwell.

Eagleton, T. (2000). *The idea of culture*. Oxford: Blackwell.

Freire, P. (1998). *The Paulo Freire reader* (A. M. Araújo Freire and D. Macedo, Eds.). New York: Continuum.

Habermas, J. (1987). *The philosophical discourse of modernity*. Translated by Frederick Lawrence. Cambridge: Polity Press (Original work published 1985).

Habermas, J. (1996). Modernity: An unfinished project. Translated by Nicholas Walker. In M. Passerin d'Éntrèves and S. Benhabib (Eds.), *Habermas and the unfinished project of modernity* (pp. 38–55). Cambridge: Polity Press.

Hobsbawm, E. (1995). *Age of extremes: The short twentieth century 1914–1991*. London: Abacus.

Hobsbawm, E. (1999). *Industry and Empire: From 1750 to the present day*. Revised edition (Revised edition, with C. Wrigley). London: Penguin Books.

Hobsbawm, E. (2000). *The new century: In conversation with Antonio Polito*. Translated from the Italian by Allan Cameron. London: Abacus (Original work published 1999).

Jacoby, R. (1999). *The end of utopia: Politics and culture in an age of apathy*. New York: Basic Books.

Jordan, G. and Weedon, C. (2000). When the subalterns speak, what do they say? Radical cultural politics in Cardiff Docklands. In P. Gilroy, L. Grossberg and A. McRobbie (Eds.), *Without guarantees: In honour of Stuart Hall* (pp. 165–180). London/New York: Verso.

Mulhern, F. (1998). *The present lasts a long time: Essays in cultural politics*. Cork: Cork University Press, in association with Field Day.

Mulhern, F. (2000). *Culture/metaculture*. London/New York: Routledge.

Prendergast, C. (Ed.) (1995). *Cultural materialism: On Raymond Williams*. Minneapolis, MN/London: University of Minnesota Press.

Sennett, R. (1998). *The corrosion of character: The personal consequences of work in the new capitalism*. New York: W. W. Norton & Company.

Steele, T. (1997). *The emergence of cultural studies: Adult education, cultural politics and the "English" question*. London: Lawrence and Wishart.

Thompson, E. P. (1968). *The making of the English working class*. Harmondsworth: Penguin Books.

Thompson, E. P. (1993). *Customs in common*. London: Penguin Books.

Tredell, N. (1990). *Uncancelled challenge: The work of Raymond Williams*. Nottingham: Paupers' Press.

Wallace, J., Jones, R., and Nield, S. (Eds.) (1997). *Raymond Williams now: Knowledge, limits and the future*. Houndmills/London: Macmillan.

Weeks, J. (1993). Rediscovering Values. In J. Squires (Ed.), *Principled positions: Postmodernism and the rediscovery of values* (pp. 189–211). London: Lawrence and Wishart.

Williams, R. (1963). *Culture and society 1780–1950*. Harmondsworth, UK: Penguin Books.

Williams, R. (1989a). The future of cultural studies. In T. Pinkney (Ed.), *The politics of modernism: Against the new conformists* (pp. 151–162). London: Verso.

Williams, R. (1989b). The idea of a common culture. In R. Gable (Ed.), *Resources of hope: Culture, democracy, socialism* (pp. 32–38). With an Introduction by Robin Blackburn. London: Verso.

Williams, R. and Said, E. (1989). Media, margins and modernity. In T. Pinkney (Ed.), *The politics of modernism: Against the new conformists* (pp. 177–197). London: Verso.

CHAPTER TWO

Manning THE borders: Blackness, nationalisms, AND popular culture

SUSAN HAREWOOD

University of the West Indies

Perhaps "manning" is not a word that sits as easily today as it used to. It carries a number of meanings—supplying troops or workers, reinforcing defenses, acting in a manly fashion—all of which, because they derive from the verb "to man" seem to ascribe legitimate control and work to masculinity. It is precisely for this reason that I have selected this word for the title of this chapter in which I seek to rethink some questions of nationalism, masculinity, race and popular culture. Cynthia Enloe points out that nationalism is often a particularly masculine endeavor: "nationalism has typically sprung from masculinized memory, masculinized humiliation and masculinized hope" (Enloe, 1990, p. 45). Manning seems an appropriate word, therefore, which draws together simultaneous constructions of masculinity and borders that are fundamental to nationalism. In this chapter I want to look at the ways in which nationalist borders have been reinforced, manned if you will, by cultural studies scholarship. This might not necessarily seem to be a new contention. Two of the key moments in the genealogy of cultural studies have been when feminist scholars challenged the iterative scholarly telling of the stories of British lads with no reference to British women and girls; and when black scholars questioned foundational scholarship that equated whiteness with Britishness. In both cases those cut out from the story pointed out that the scholarship effectively erected a border that defined who could and who could not be British. In this chapter I contend that the time is overdue to challenge borders again because, even as these black scholars transgressed the borders of Englishness and Americanness they actually reinforced the borders of what blackness can mean in relation to nationalism. By considering nationalism and blackness exclusively through the prism of European-American race relations, they often reinscribed the sense that blackness is necessarily always and already at the margins of the nation. In this chapter I consider what happens to our understandings of blackness, nationalism, and the political projects of cultural studies when we seriously consider nationalism(s) in the Caribbean.

I begin by examining the difficulties that cultural studies has had, up to this point, with defining text beyond the set of circumstances found in Europe and America. This has the impact of reinforcing the borders of race because, despite a commitment to transnational scholarship, the experiences in Europe and America are the only ones that inform the theorizing on race and nationalism. I then turn my attention to examine the importance of "the nation" in the Caribbean context. The chapter focuses on the contributions that calypso criticism has had in mapping out the nation and the ways that this has informed cultural policy. Competing nationalist narratives are also highlighted. The objective in all of this is not to posit black investment in nationalism as emancipatory. Rather, the objective is to shake up the standard narratives about race and nationalism as these have failed to consider the political projects and the ethical duties that are confronted when academia's "go to" minority are no longer the minority.

BORDERS OF BLACKNESS

Over twenty years ago Stuart Hall drew our attention to "Blackness without Guarantees" (1996). However there are ways in which blackness, by being articulated through national and urban racial politics of British cultural studies and American cultural studies, remains fixed. Blackness frequently operates in analysis as a homogenous minority underclass that is subject to, and does not have agency in, state power. Blacks' relation to nationalism is only understood as either the source of essentialist black nationalism or as the cause of white fear/desire that results in racist nationalism. I will briefly turn to Paul Gilroy's major works to clarify the above point. I specifically have chosen Gilroy because of the rigor of his scholarship and its particular importance for examining the theoretical significance of the transnational performance of black popular music. However, Gilroy's work is particularly helpful here also because it displays both the major strengths and some of the weaknesses of British/American cultural studies. Gilroy demands that cultural studies take race seriously and successfully challenges the notion that one cannot be both black and British. He advances a well-conceived examination of the theoretical sophistication of black popular music; it is an understanding of black popular music from which I draw in my own work. He attempts to move beyond the national in his conceptualization of the transnational *Black Atlantic* and, in very compelling fashion, he challenges racial absolutism. However, in many ways Gilroy's work travels the groove that moves from England to the United States in which cultural studies frequently locates itself, even in spite of its protestations of being international (Miller, 2001). Thus Gilroy's work begins with the task of defining Britain and British concerns. This is a task in which Caribbean popular culture has, in fact, played a significant part. As I have pointed out elsewhere (see Harewood, 2007), foundational cultural studies texts have all looked at reggae and its role in British style. Reggae allowed these scholars to explore the complex meaning-making strategies in which British youth were engaged, and it also allowed the scholars an opportunity to challenge monolithic, racist understandings of what it meant/means to be British. However, it was a Britishness, that within the conventions of subcultural studies, fixed (or to use Hall again, guaranteed) blackness as always subcultural, resistant, counter-hegemonic, and progressive in very specific ways. For example, reggae is only lauded where it "chants down Babylon." Little space is made for other styles of reggae and dancehall, such as the smooth pop style of John Holt or the slackness of Yellowman. Reggae is required, then, to fit a preselected set of political moves. In other words, Caribbean popular culture is emptied of much of its complexity and ambivalence.

With the rise (and publishing dominance) of American cultural studies, Gilroy, like other British cultural scholars, turned to look "across the pond" with some consternation. Stuart Hall admitted to being dumbfounded by American cultural studies (Hall, 1992) yet in some ways he seems transfixed by it. In a similar way, though *The Black Atlantic* (1993) expressly attempts to explore transnational blackness, it is an exploration whose primary focus is its effort to challenge (black) American claims to cultural and theoretical particularism. *The Black Atlantic* remains an argument between England and the United States predicated upon definitions of black life drawn from reading the similarities of experiences under British/American racism(s). I would argue that this accounts for Gilroy's inability to recognize the variety of ways in which blackness is lived and defined, and, specifically, the limited examination of nationalism. Gilroy assumes that blackness always stands outside of "the nation." He limits his examination of nationalism and blackness to black nationalism failing to recognize that black life can take multiple positions in relation to the nation as it is imagined. As Laura Chrisman points out, Gilroy presumes, "that nationalism can only be ethnically purist and exclusivist, and is incapable of pluralisation" (Chrisman, 2003, p. 78). I am not attempting to claim here that nationalism is emancipatory within the Caribbean context. Gilroy's charge that nationalism is often tinged with Fascism holds true, and the ways in which nationalists seek to impose unities will be born out in the examples I draw below. Nevertheless, an examination of the multiple positions that blacks can take and have taken in relation to nationalism, to my mind, invites our scholarship, in the strongest way possible to tear its gaze away from the metropolitan centers just long enough to consider blackness outside of the lines that are drawn, redrawn, and drawn again in academic research.

CALYPSO AND THE MAKING OF NATIONS

Making national histories

Considering calypso and its relationship to various projects of nationalism in the Caribbean should make it clear that criticism, policy, and performance are all deeply and inextricably enmeshed. Despite the way in which calypso, and a great deal of popular music, is depicted, calypso performance does not stand at a discrete distance from governmental strategies so that it might take on the tasks of "progressive politics" that we academics, critics, and fans hope for. It is deeply enmeshed in the complex relations of power and, as such, has been part of both radical and conservative politics and, I would say, continues to carry vestiges of both at all times.

Calypso is usually said to have emerged at the end of slavery, although it should not be assumed that it marks a complete break with the forms of slave music and performance. Thus calypso carries with it the counter-hegemonic theoretical and activist strategies of slave and ex-slave arts. This counter-hegemonic work in calypso can lead us back to Paul Gilroy's work and his cogent exploration of the philosophical/political work of black music to which I have already made mention. Linking Gilroy with the rich historiographies of calypso by Trevor Marshall (1986), Gordon Rohlehr (1990), Hollis Liverpool (1998), and Louis Regis (1999), demonstrates the ways in which calypso has been actively engaged in the assertion of, first, black humanity, and, later, the pursuit of black citizenship. Given my focus on blacks and nationalism, it is not necessary to go into more detail on 19th century and very early 20th century calypso. The histories mentioned do this very successfully. My focus is much more on the achievement and shape of the modern Caribbean nation-state and calypso's multidimensional role in those processes. Nevertheless, it is important to recognize that these artistic labors toward theorizing and achieving justice remain clearly audible and strongly felt parts of calypso, and, as I go on to write about some of the more conservative projects which have sought to recruit calypso, it should also be recognized that calypso, like all music forms, is a complex form in which contradictions constantly crisscross.

The historiographies just mentioned are invaluable resources for understanding the history of this musical form. However, they are more than this. They are extremely important in constructing what we perceive the "nature" of calypso to be, and the commonsense understandings of the role of calypso in the construction of the Caribbean nation-state. In other words, this criticism forms an important part of the discourse that makes the nation, and it articulates the role of calypso in the task of nation-making. The historiographies have formed an important part[1] of the nationalist narratives for Trinidad and Tobago[2] as well as many of the territories in the Eastern and Southern Caribbean. In these narratives, the leadership of the black male, and particularly the middle-class black male intellectual, is affirmed as the legitimate leadership for the Caribbean nation-state. These narratives and the policies and performance practices that emerge from them—which I will be looking at later in this chapter—demonstrate how critically important the making of the nation is to the black middle-class male. And, as I will show later, a different, although related conceptualization of the nation is also important to the black lower income male.

Much of the research on calypso has paid particular attention to drawing a link between calypso and the fortunes of the liberal democratic nation-state in the Anglo-Caribbean. This emphasis on calypso and liberal democratic politics has resulted in the tendency to emphasize a unified audience expressed as a mirror image of a homogenized body politic. Researchers have focused their attention on the calypso as an integral part of the anticolonial struggles and the movement toward universal adult suffrage. Generally writers have paid the most attention to the relationship between the politicians, the calypsonians, and the audience viewed as the electorate. The literature has suggested that both the Caribbean politicians and the calypsonians formed alliances that allowed them to effectively represent the interests of the electorate. By and large, the work on calypso equates aesthetic representation and political representation and defines "representation" as meaning standing in for. Thus, time and again, researchers suggest that the calypso art faithfully reflects, and thus stands in for, the reality facing Caribbean citizens. This leads to a position which suggests that the calypsonian can stand in for these same citizens, representing their interests to the political directorate. This argument also has the effect of legitimizing the parliamentary system used in Trinidad and Tobago and other Anglo-Caribbean states, as it is through these different tiers of representation that the politician is said to be an effective representative of the citizenry.

Two consistent tropes are used in calypso research that present calypso as an accurate archive of historical events and the calypsonian as both recorder of those events and faithful representative of his audience. These are the descriptions of the calypso as the "poor man's newspaper" and the calypsonian as the "voice of the people." The "voice" trope appears time and again. For example C. L. R. James, making reference to The Mighty Sparrow, describes him as *vox populi* and suggests that Sparrow "faithfully reports public sentiment" (James, 1973, p. 376). Writers like James, therefore, suggest that the experiences of the underprivileged and the artistic expression of the calypsonians are the same. What is important to recognize here is that neither the idea of "the people" nor "the poor man" is problematized in the literature. There is an undifferentiated lumping together of Caribbean citizens under the leadership of the black middle-class male. In a region as demographically diverse as the Caribbean this is clearly problematic. As Shalini Puri asks, "What does it mean to the place of Indo-Trinidadians in the national imagination that calypso has been seen as simultaneously *Afro*-Trinidadian and *national*?" (Puri, 1997, p. 121). But my task is not to prove that the pursuit of nationalism is necessarily emancipatory. Rather my hope is that in pointing to the ways in which nationalism has been important we might begin to do three things. First, we might be pushed to think about politics in much more nuanced ways when the guaranteed "safety"[3] of moral authority of *knowing* what is progressive politics is stripped away. Second, we might be pushed to seriously think "what is our next step" when we recognize that nationalism can be ambivalent. In other words, how do we approach, in a politically mature fashion, the fact that the national project challenged imperialism and meant a better life for many Caribbean citizens (the majority in most territories) whilst it *simultaneously* robbed other Caribbean citizens (the majority in some territories) of their right to full political participation. Third, and this is a question for cultural studies in general, how might answering these questions push us to move beyond the taken-for-granted political stances that continue to appear in cultural studies.

The dominant nationalist narrative that has been a major part of calypso criticism has also shaped cultural policy. In order to demonstrate the ways in which this has occurred I am going to focus my attention on music policy in Barbados and the ways in which the bourgeois nationalist project has been become part of that policy.

Making the bourgeois nation

Barbados gained constitutional independence in 1966, and the development of a national cultural policy really got underway in the 1970s. This move was not unique to Barbados. At the international level, it was felt that the cultural policies emerging from UNESCO, which had been transformed by the many former colonies joining its ranks, might be vital in assisting "Third World" countries in "triggering" their economic development.

In 1978 Barbados set up its Ministry of Culture, and in 1979 the government published a document entitled *A Report on Cultural Formation in Barbados with Proposals for a Plan for National Cultural Development*, which was compiled by Barbadian historian and poet Edward Kamau Brathwaite. It was the first of a number of similar cultural policy documents. These documents had an expressed objective of producing the "ideal Barbadian citizen."

The cultural report and those that have followed it contain many of the key elements that have shaped the dominant nationalist project in Barbados. The reports view the cultural energy of the nation to come from the "folk," which we understand from Brathwaite's other writings to comprise the black lower classes. However, this creative energy has gone underground due to the brutality of imperialism. It is up to the black professional/bureaucratic classes, therefore, to reclaim and refine the folk culture in the interests of national integration and national advancement. Thus, for example, in the 1979 report it is stated that the imperial bourgeois culture mandated the eradication of "folk expressions of foreign national culture, especially in those overseas plantation/colonies where the 'folk' were non-European, non-bourgeois" (Brathwaite, 1979, p. 74). The report calls for a rediscovery of Barbados's "true culture" which, it is argued, had hidden itself in the face of imperial aggression. In this, then, the *Report* participates in what Stuart Hall (1994) has recognized as an important, although often limiting, "act of imaginative rediscovery" of an essential identity which has frequently accompanied decolonization efforts. Even though the "folk" are identified as the source for this rediscovery, it is the bourgeois state managers, particularly Ministry of Education and Culture officials, who are charged with the task of strengthening Barbadian culture. He asserts that their task will be to define what it means to be a Bajan[4] and to educate Bajans how to be Bajans. This emphasis on training Bajans to be Bajans has continued to be the theme drawing together policy documents and the activities of state cultural institutions, at least up to the new millennium.

The first policy document emerged at the same time that the institutional framework to implement cultural policy was also being established. The main institution that emerged to facilitate the cultural policy was the National Cultural Foundation (NCF), which was established in 1984. The NCF Act outlines four functions for the organization:

a. to stimulate and facilitate the development of culture generally;
b. to develop, maintain and manage theatres and other cultural facilities and equipment provided by the government;
c. to organize cultural festivals; and
d. to do anything necessary or desirable to assist persons interested in developing cultural expression. (NCF Act, 1984, p. 4)

These functions emphasize government's managerial role and its responsibility to provide venues, both physical and temporal, for artistic activity. The NCF has played a key part in the implementation of Barbados's music policy. Cultural

Officers were appointed for the different artistic disciplines, including music. However, it is perhaps the huge popularity of calypso that has made it so important to the NCF mission. The popularity of Barbadian calypso can be linked to the reestablishment of the plantation harvest celebration, the Crop Over Festival (COF), in the 1970s. A Pan African organization, the Yoruba Foundation initially attempted to revive the festival in 1972, but, probably due to their focus on black empowerment, they received little support from the new and cautious government. However, in 1974 the Barbados Board of Tourism adopted the festival as a means to boost summer tourist arrivals to Barbados. Initially, as conceived by the Board which was dominated by members of Barbados' social elite, calypso was not part of the COF. However, calypsonians led by The Mighty Dragon fought to get calypso included on the festival agenda. Clearly, these calypsonians believed that calypso should be part of any national and nationalist agenda. By the 1980s, the calypso competition had become one of the most important aspects of the festival, if not the very engine of the celebration (see Marshall, 1986). The popularity of local calypso seemed almost to guarantee that calypso would come under careful scrutiny. State managers set about the task of shaping and refining calypso music performance practices *and* calypso audiences in the service of the idealized nation-state.

A number of decisions were taken with a view to "improving" and regulating performers, performances, and audiences. The major decisions were made within the contexts of the national calypso competition, the "Pic O De Crop." This competition, although it mirrors calypso competitions throughout the region, reasserts the importance of the nation-state through its regulations. Traditionally, calypsonians who have wished to compete have been required to be members of state-sponsored calypso tents.[5] Only citizens and those who have been residents for over five years are allowed to participate in the competition. Lyrics must be vetted before performance in order that they conform to defamation and libel laws of Barbados as well as the more vaguely defined dictates of "good taste." Jocelyn Guilbault (2002) has called the calypso competition an important part of the regulatory processes of the State. Part of these regulatory processes involves defining the aesthetics as well as what the State determines to be the authentic limits of the national culture. Certainly, in the Barbadian case, competitions have had disciplinary effects. Besides having such effects, they draw our attention not only to the coercive power but also to the negotiations over "commonsense" ideas of the nation, citizenship, and musical value.

This can be seen in the efforts to determine the "authentic" sound of calypso by professionalizing the Festival Band (Mottley, 2003). The Festival Band is the backing band for all the calypsonians who make it to the Finals night. The efforts to produce the "authentic" sound can also be recognized in the style of calypsos that seem to have been favored by the judges. An examination of both the competition winners over the years and the common discourses about what constitutes a "crown song" or a winning song in Barbados, suggests that the judges favor a song that through its tempo and content indicates a seriousness of purpose. "Crown songs,"[6] it would seem, tended to have a slower tempo, with a narrative lyrical style and content that dealt with ways of improving the young nation, and/or ways of defining the national identity.

Both the calypso style and the competition structure have had a role to play in the mapping out of the cultural landscape of Barbados. The competition structure results in the assignment of value based on the judges' positions as a special class of experts qualified to make assessments. It therefore reinforces the central importance of the educated and professional classes in guiding the young nation. Similarly, the privileged calypso style can be linked to middle-class efforts to assert their right to lead by asserting their ability to master a Victorian ideal of intellectual labor (Edmondson, 1999). This ideal privileged the literary over the embodied. This is clearly apparent in the role that the West Indian novel has had in contesting and challenging colonial power. But it has also had an impact on the way in which calypso is conceived. Academic and lay criticisms have tended to emphasize calypso almost as a *literary* rather than a musical form. Calypso research has concentrated on the lyrical content of calypso at the expense of all other aspects of performance. In part, this literary focus can be seen as a type of writing back to the racist tropes in colonial research on the Caribbean that had reduced blacks to bodies alone. For example, early anthropological research on the Caribbean and traveler accounts had fetishized the black bodily movements that accompanied black musics.[7] For black leaders in the Caribbean to imagine themselves worthy inheritors of the Enlightenment project and legitimate leaders of the Caribbean societies, they had to eschew the dark cavorting bodies and hot rhythms that had been used by the colonial powers to mark black difference and inferiority. They needed to be able to claim their space, alongside the colonial leaders, as men of letters.

The ways in which the dominant national project was encoded in cultural policy should be quite clear by now. Cultural policy has been part of the process of mapping national space and ordering social life. At its core, the policy was conceived as way of constructing a national identity based on black cultural forms. Nevertheless, there was a clear class dimension to this. The lower income citizens were seen as the source for the creative energy, and the process was guided by bureaucrats, the professional classes, and educated elites. Nevertheless, it would be a mistake to view this exclusively in terms of domination, as if "The State," conceived as a homogenous unstoppable force, imposed its exclusive vision of the nation on the rest of the population. There has always been much more negotiation than would be suggested by such a characterization of the state. In addition, it must be recognized that at that point in the history of the young, newly independent nation, the very real possibility of alliances between state managers and citizens existed around the hope of the independence project. I am not suggesting that everyone in the Caribbean leapt into constitutional independence with the same positive vision for an independent future. Such a significant change was bound to involve controversy at the time. Nevertheless, independence afforded the citizens an opportunity to conceive of having a nation and building a nation as opposed to standing at a distance from the metropolitan colonial center.

Challenging the bourgeois nation

Although the paragraphs above discuss the deployment of the dominant bourgeois ideal of the nation-state in criticism and policy, it should not be assumed that this was the single narrative of the nation. Nationalist elites often seek to give the impression that their version of the nation is the only version, and, by focusing almost exclusively on the dominant nationalist narratives, nationalism research often inadvertently reifies the dominant narratives. However, it has always been my contention that nationalist narratives are heteroglossic (see Harewood, 2006). Thus, there are always competing stories of the nation, and calypso performance has been a space to experience these as well as many other cultural forms. Nevertheless, in the new millennium, the competing visions came to occupy, quite literally, center stage.

Beginning in the 1980s, the revolution in digital music technology began to transform music production in Barbados. Not only did the new technology mean that there were new ways of creating sound, but also new producers stepped forward and changed the structure of the local music industry. The possibility for more people to get involved in music production and the ability to draw from a larger palette of musical sounds—hip hop and dancehall especially—led to the development of what Curwen Best (2004) has called "hard core soca." Part of the hardness might have come from the new musical sources and the edginess of digital production. However part of the hardness might also have come from difficult socioeconomic conditions that the musicians, like the rest of the population, were experiencing.

In 1990 Barbados' GDP declined for the first time in seven years. There were decreasing revenues from tourism, sugar, and manufacturing, as well as rising interest on the large foreign debt incurred in the 1980s. That debt had fueled the social welfare programs of the 1980s that provided Barbadians with a better standard of living, although not necessarily a sustainable one, as it was linked more to patterns of consumption than to production. In 1991 the government instituted an International Monetary Fund (IMF) sponsored austerity program. The unemployment rate rose to between 27 and 30%.

The faltering economy made it difficult for many, particularly the youth who were hardest hit by unemployment, to have confidence in the promises of independence and the dominant national project. Fissures in the independence promise therefore started to appear. Within the arena of calypso performance, this seemed to lead to the development of the hard core style which rejected many of the terms of Victorian gentlemanly behavior. Whereas the bourgeois nationalist project emphasized the literary over the embodied, the new soca style emphasized the body—faster rhythms that encouraged dancing; repetitive lyrics that created a bricolage of lyrical images rather than a linear, lyrical narrative; an emphasis on a confrontational chanting style of vocal delivery rather than the more melodic style traditionally favored in calypso; and the use of the cut-and-paste sampling technologies of the digital music revolution rather than the use of brass instruments or even traditional calypso's idea of one man, one guitar.

This new style posits a different way of constructing the nation. It offered a competing aesthetic that challenged the dominant bourgeois nationalist project, especially the position of the middle-class/professional class as the arbiters of taste. It has been met with some resistance and some efforts at accommodation by those who have invested heavily in creating the dominant nationalist narrative. The hard core styles are often dismissed as trivial by academic and media critics. For instance, each year during the Crop Over Festival, calypso purists lament the ways in which "the youth" have debased the art form. There are repeated calls to get back to the true principles of calypso, not only on the radio call-in programs and in the newspaper commentaries, but also on the calypso stage. As Gordon Rohlehr (1998) has pointed out, one of the repeated themes in calypso competitions is showing how other calypsonians have drifted away from the art form. In addition to these admonishments, there have also been efforts by state managers to accommodate, discipline, and make a profit from the new style. Party and soca monarch competitions have been added to the traditional calypso competition in many Caribbean territories and communities. Thus, even though the hard core styles are dismissed as "mere party music," efforts have still been made to discipline the performances through the competitions and reaffirm the position of the judges as arbiters of taste.

Although the new hard core styles are a challenge to the dominant bourgeois nationalist narrative, I would not argue that they are necessarily emancipatory. Rather, they are efforts by differently situated citizens to jockey for political, cultural and economic visibility within the nation. They are national projects in themselves in which efforts are made to contribute to the heteroglossic narrative of the nation. Elsewhere (Harewood, 2006) I have written of the ways in which Caribbean women have used the new hard core styles to challenge their invisibility within the national project. However, hard core styles are also used by some male performers to *reaffirm* masculinity as the key qualification for leading the nation. These performances, in many ways, seek to marginalize the performances of women, nonblack citizens, LGBT citizens, and so on, and challenge their claims for legitimacy in public life. The calypso/soca arena is therefore a contestatory terrain in which the limits and ideals of the nation are negotiated in a variety of ways. I have only managed to give the broadest outline of the type of contestations that take place around the idea of "the nation" in the Caribbean.

CONCLUSION: NATIONALISM MATTERS

As scholars, we have grown accustomed to the idea that the nation is an imaginative project, yet there are times when we seem to think that it is an immaterial one. By "immaterial" I do not mean that it has no physical substance, rather, I mean that it does not matter, or maybe, that it *should not* matter. The brutal suppression of difference that has so often accompanied nationalism makes many of us want to have nothing to do with nationalism. This desire to reject the violent excesses of nationalism is a laudable one. However, there seems to be, perhaps, a lack of self-awareness if we do not acknowledge the place that academic scholarship has had in various nationalist projects.

Certainly cultural studies has played its part in nationalist projects, particularly in manning the borders of Britain. As I pointed out in this chapter, early British cultural studies was heavily criticized for the ways in which it reinscribed the idea of White British Maleness as the legitimate subject of research and the "authentic" British citizen. Black British cultural studies launched an extremely important critical assessment of that research and has provided us with fundamentally important work that has given us the tools to challenge racial absolutism and think of our research in transnational terms. Nevertheless, in spite of this, black British cultural studies has inadvertently protected its own borders too.

By limiting the consideration of blackness to the experiences of blacks in the metropolitan countries, the scholarship has not really been successful at imagining what different experiences of blackness mean to the terms of our analysis. It is for this reason that nationalism matters. It matters not because nationalism will bring about social justice. It matters because it is a deeply contestatory terrain that has been flattened thus far in the literature. The dominant literature assumes that blacks stand at a distance from the state and therefore should display no interest in nationalism. In the Caribbean this could not be farther from the truth. In the Caribbean, the nation is constructed through both discourse and material institutional practice.

In this chapter I have highlighted the important place that calypso criticism has played in the telling of the dominant nationalist narrative. This narrative has informed musical policy and the disciplinary projects encoded in that policy. The policy and the criticism reveal the ways in which the black intellectual and bureaucratic classes have positioned themselves as the brokers of symbolic capital in the region. This is not a position that goes unchallenged. In this chapter I have also made mention of the challenge from young lower-income men. Elsewhere I have mentioned the challenges from women. The key points to notice are that, first, many different groups are invested in challenging their position in the nation and using the idea of the nation to jockey for political and economic visibility. The nation matters to them. It has deep materiality in their lives. The second thing to recognize is that if we examine something so fraught with tensions as "the nation" and consider deeply the number of different positions blacks take in relation to the nation, then we actually move a step closer to research that does not fix blacks into the counter-hegemonic position of the eternal outsider. Contestations over nationalist narratives in the Caribbean reveal a range of differences of class, gender, sexuality, age, faith, and race, which interrogate the ideas of margin and center. In the same way that calypso research as an area of study and a practice must begin to interrogate what it means by "the people," cultural studies must be equally critical of the ways in which it has used blackness to guarantee its moral authority and its, at times, uninterrogated assumption that we already know what a progressive politics looks like and it is whatever we say it is.

NOTES

1. I would argue that the calypso criticism is actually part of a triumvirate through which the national narratives of the independent Caribbean nation-state is told. Thus the historiographies of calypso can be related to, and similarities can be seen in, the ways in which cricket and the West Indian novel are drafted into the processes of national integration.
2. By far the vast majority of research on the calypso focuses on Trinidad.
3. Safety is a difficult word to use here. Certainly the position of being outside the national imaginary is one of the most dangerous places to be for blacks who live in the North. Moreover, citizens of the Caribbean are often painfully aware of the dangers of living outside the overdeveloped centers and what it can mean if a microstate is deemed "a threat" by these centers in their perpetual wars on terrorism, drugs, and anything that might challenge their accumulation of wealth. I am actually thinking more about the safety of the outside position in academia—a type of easy, although seemingly disengaged, type of guaranteed politics.
4. People from Barbados are either referred to as Barbadians or Bajans.
5. A calypso tent is often defined as the venue for calypso performance. In the early years of calypso the venues were likely to be open spaces covered with some makeshift material—quite literally a tent. However, today tents are often modern auditoria and halls. However "a tent" is also the mode of organization. In Barbados registered tents of a specified size hosting a specified number

of performances per week receive a subvention from the NCF. The details for this are negotiated each year along with the rules for the competition, the composition of the judging panel, and competition performance fees with the Barbados Association of Tent Managers (BATMAN). It should be noted that this is a union of tent managers and not calypsonians (even though a tent manager could very well be a calypsonian too).

6. The winner of the *Pic O De Crop* is declared the Monarch—hence the idea of a "crown song."
7. For example, in Edward Brathwaite's (1971) analysis of life in Jamaica from 1770 to 1820 he points out that European observers dismissed black music and dance as noise and debauchery. Similarly, Jerome Handler and Charlotte Frisbie (1972) highlight the difficulty of attempting to glean an understanding of the slave music practices from the ethnocentric accounts of European travelers.

REFERENCES

Best, C. (2004). *Culture at the cutting edge: Tracking Caribbean popular music.* Jamaica/Barbados/Trinidad: University of the West Indies Press.

Brathwaite, E. (1971). *The development of Creole society in Jamaica 1770–1820.* Oxford: Clarendon Press.

Brathwaite, E. (1979). *A report on cultural formation in Barbados with proposals for a plan for national cultural development.* St. Michael, Barbados: Ministry of Education and Culture.

Chrisman, L. (2003). Journeying to death: Paul Gilroy's Black Atlantic. In L. Chrisman (Ed.), *Postcolonial contraventions: Cultural readings of race, imperialism and transnationalism* (pp. 73–106). Manchester/New York: Manchester University Press.

Edmondson, B. (1999). *Making men: Gender, literary, authority, and women's writing in Caribbean narrative.* Durham/London: Duke University Press.

Enloe, C. (1990). *Bananas, beaches and bases: Making feminist sense of international politics.* Berkeley, CA: University of California Press.

Gilroy, P. (1993). *The Black Atlantic: Modernity and double consciousness.* Cambridge, MA: Harvard University Press.

Guilbault, J. (2002). The politics of calypso in a world of music industries. In D. Hesmondhalgh and K. Negus (Eds.), *Popular Music Studies* (pp. 191–204). London: Arnold Publishers.

Hall, S. (1992). cultural studies and its theoretical legacies. In L. Grossberg, C. Nelson and P. A. Treichler (Eds.), *cultural studies* (pp. 277–294). New York/London: Routledge.

Hall, S. (1994). Cultural identity and diaspora. In P. Williams and L. Chrisman (Eds.), *Colonial discourse and post-colonial theory: A reader* (pp. 392–401). London: Harvester Wheatsheaf.

Hall, S. (1996). New ethnicities. In D. Morley and K. Chen (Eds.), *Stuart Hall: Critical dialogues in cultural studies* (pp. 465–475). New York: Routledge.

Handler, J. S. and Frisbie, C. J. (1972). Aspects of slave life in Barbados: Music and its cultural context. *Caribbean Studies*, Vol. 11, No. 4, pp. 5–46.

Harewood, S. (2006). Transnational soca performances and gendered re-narrations of Caribbean nationalisms. *Social and Economic Studies*, Vol. 55, Nos. 1 & 2, pp. 25–48.

Harewood, S. (2007). Masquerade as methodology … or, why cultural studies should return to the Caribbean. In C. McCarthy, A. Durham, L. Engel, A. A. Filmer, M. D. Giardina, J. Logue and M. Malagreca (Eds.), *Globalizing cultural studies: Ethnographic interventions in theory, method, & policy* (pp. 61–78). New York: Peter Lang Publishing Group.

James, C. L. R. (1973). The mighty sparrow. In D. Lowenthal and L Comitas (Eds.), *The Aftermath of Sovereignty: West Indian Perspectives* (pp. 373–381). Garden City, NY: Doubleday Anchor.

Liverpool, H. (1998). Origins of rituals and customs in the Trinidad carnival: African or European. *The Drama Review,* Vol. 42, No. 3 (Fall), pp. 24–37.

Marshall, T. (1986). *History and evolution of calypso in Barbados.* Cave Hill: University of the West Indies.

Miller, T (2001). *A companion to cultural studies.* Oxford, UK: Blackwell Publishers.

Mottley, E. (2003). *Identities Volume 1.* Barbados/Jamaica: Fat Pork Productions.

Puri, S. (1997). Race, rape, and representation: Indo-Caribbean women and cultural nationalism. *Cultural Critique* No. 36 (Spring), pp. 119–163.

Regis, L. (1999). *The political calypso: True opposition in Trinidad and Tobago 1962–1987.* Jamaica and Florida (FL): University of the West Indies Press and University Press of Florida.

Rohlehr, G. (1990). *Calypso and society in pre-independence Trinidad.* Trinidad: Self-published.

Rohlehr, G. (1998). "We getting the kaiso we deserve": Calypso and the world music market. *Drama Review,* Vol. 42, No. 3 (Fall), pp. 82–93.

CHAPTER THREE

Relativism, racism, AND philanthropy[1]

TERESA SAN ROMÁN

Autonomous University of Barcelona

UNALTERABLE CULTURE, IDENTITY, AND INTEGRATION

We constantly hear arguments proclaiming the incompatibility of cultures. Such assertions are used not only to reinforce mixophobia but to justify a desire for the public integration—not necessarily the assimilation—of diverse cultural-minority or subaltern groups. Yet the problem may only sometimes lie in incompatibility. When incompatibility in a given context is genuine, it must indeed be negotiated, as it may not always apply in a general sense to the respective cultures in contact, nor to their peoples. This is so because a cultural project, broadly considered, cannot be measured in objective terms, as people cannot judge or valorize other cultures without relying on their own, preexisting cultural values. However, one thing is to give equal value to all cultures, while quite another is to assign equal value to all cultural phenomena ("our own" and those of "others"). Because this latter action constitutes a particularist assessment, it cannot be universally imposed; however it can instead be *universally proposed* without this implying either a complete exaltation of the culture in question, or a total disapproval of the same. What we must find is that comfortable niche that Todorov (1989, pp. 70–71) sought somewhere between dogmatism that seeks to possess the truth, and skepticism that denies all truths. We should stop talking about differences between cultures in holistic terms and start talking instead about degrees of compatibility between cultural phenomena. To an even lesser extent than an ethnic identity, a culture does not vanish simply because a cultural phenomenon itself changes or disappears. This is also true for what we deem to be "ours." Negotiation does not imply "ceasing to be;" rather, it involves concrete changes in specific cultural phenomena or in the relationship between these phenomena. A negotiation toward the compatibility of Catholicism with modern, democratic principles, for example, does not involve discrediting or abandoning the Catholic faith, but might involve modifying its most fundamentalist versions, such as those encompassing intransigence, exclusion, and inquisitorial imposition. Indeed, seen from the outside, such a movement toward making Catholicism compatible with a modern democratic world may have been present in the incipient negotiation of Pope John XXIII's Catholic ecumenicalism, which was to a large extent frustrated, incidentally.

Both the dialectic and "real" problems in this area are extremely obvious. There are two arguments used by cultural fundamentalists (and by certain misguided antiracists) to argue that there is no alternative to incompatibility. One is that culture is understood as an all-encompassing irreducible entity, and the process of enculturation as a determinant, a finished product; the other is the danger of *anomization* when presenting different cultural models that generate asymmetrical identities, this leading to the socializing or acculturating individual becoming destructured in terms of his or her identity. It seems rash to discuss this latter process without the expertise of psychologists and psychoanalysts, and for this reason it will not fall within the remit of the current discussion. Nevertheless, some cultural theorists have ventured to refute this claim regarding the supposed *anomie*-producing quality of unstable, hybrid identities. For instance, Bhabha (1994), Hall (1996), or Bauman (2005) argue that identity is fluid, variegated, and in constant flux, and that this pervasive reality has not been generally acknowledged because of the ideological interests of other cultural analysts set on tailoring and packaging identity to their own epistemological conventions and criteria.

Barth (1969) made a distinction, which I believe is still useful, between "cultural stuff"—the range of a culture's patterns, values, beliefs, tools, and techniques—and "ethnic identity." The latter term relates only to certain features of the "cultural stuff" that become symbols of those who share such an identity, but they do not necessarily serve as symbols of the entire culture.[2] This means that a people, identifying themselves by means of their opposition to other peoples, can change many aspects of their own collective culture throughout a history of contacts, mixtures, alliances, and wars, without losing their identity. Guillaumin (1972), however, argues that this "opposition" is not in fact a matter of classification but instead involves a surreptitiously concealed *hierarchization*, and as such constitutes a form of confrontation. This, I believe, is a judgment of intentions, which may be accurate in some but by no means in all cases. Opposition, when referring to concepts such as identity, identification, classification, and categorization, can never mean anything other than A is A insofar as it contrasts with B; in this sense an "I" exists because there is a "you," and an "us" exists because there is a "them." Opposition, hence, does not necessarily (or even probably) involve rejection, isolation, or aggression. On the contrary, it can involve cooperation, interdependence, complementariness, and even love, which we note requires an "other"—someone similar but in other ways different—to find its true expression. Thus, differentiated identities in no way presuppose rejection or isolation.

This *ethnic identity*, or identity as a people, therefore allows a culture to change from within, a process that is as obvious as it is natural for any people, including the cultural (as opposed to strictly individual) adoption and selection of features that can symbolize its lack of continuity with groups that are set off as different or even in opposition. An enlightening example—one of many other cases involving strong forms of identity—is the Catalan language, which is spoken in northeastern Spain and is used in public institutions committed to the expression of Catalan identity. Indeed, for as long as the Phoenician-Latin alphabet has been in use in Catalonia, it has been used to write Catalan. However, because the written forms of all other languages of the Iberian Peninsula found expression through the same Latin alphabet, this writing system never became a distinguishing feature of Catalonian identity as did the Catalan language itself—as opposed to Spanish, Galician, or Basque. In this way, it is the *selection* of the signs and symbols of identity that distinguishes one sense of identity from others against which it has been historically constructed.[3]

What *ethnic militancy* actually defends is the interests of a people (or of whoever speaks in its name, which is not necessarily the same thing) through the symbolic vehicle of ethnic markers, in the language of the ethnicity. And it is the protection of, and regard for, these ethnic symbols, which are selected from the culture as a whole, that is taken to be the protection of, and regard for, identity itself, although reference to actual *cultural content* is minimal in many cases. The cultural symbols themselves sometimes vary with the passing of time and are often interpreted in different ways by different social segments of the *same* society. For example, Romanes, the most widespread language among Europe's Gypsies, is usually identified as a symbol of Gypsy identity by Gypsies themselves. However, what Romanes actually means for each group varies, as does each group's understanding of what the common characteristics of Gypsy identity are. This understanding often has very little relation to what all Gypsies actually think and do, but tends to be subethnocentric in nature. In the case of Romanes, the extent of its strictly cultural use—as opposed to its mere use for *identifying culture*—ranges from everyday communication to a total lack of knowledge of this language. Romanes is thus an ethnic symbol in Saussure's (1915/1971) strictest sense of the word—that is, precisely what it is not.

Identity is therefore not subject to any and all types of cultural change. If that were the case, there would be no identity because culture undergoes constant change throughout history even while ethnic identity may remain constant. However, the question remains that when more than one identity affects an individual or group, might this not allow anomie to set in? In principle, the confluence or coexistence of various forms of identity is necessary if differentiation is to take place; likewise, differentiation would be a precondition for such coexisting identities. Nevertheless, doubt remains as to whether the presence of more than one identity could prove anomic if this occurs during the enculturation period of childhood. I make no claim to being an authority on all aspects of this issue, and so will refer only to some of the many studies of Francophone and Anglo-Saxon Canadian identities, as well as to studies of nationalist movements and identities that appeared for the first time during the period of colonial domination.[4] These movements and identities took some time to develop a common cultural substratum that allowed shared symbols of identity and, above all, permitted common codes for a potential common government. Such identities evolve through emigration and contact with others; they are new identities emerging from various pre-existing ones (Lieberson and Waters, 1989; Bhabha, 1994; Appadurai, 1996) and from the empirically verified presence of healthy yet multireferential identification.[5]

Todorov (1989) also criticizes the assertion that there is a necessary progression from intercultural communication to homogenization, and from homogenization to the disappearance of separate cultures and identities. Because many empirical observations can be used to refute this position, to accept it unquestioningly would be a mistake. Although Todorov wholly accepts that there is more homogeneity in an expanding industrial society, and that the democratic ideal and the role of science are taking this process to extremes, he seriously questions whether *indifferentiation* takes place, and points to the important role played by differentiation today. To assume that the aforementioned expansions imply *indifferentiation*, however, is akin to assuming that the sole causes of difference lie in a failure to communicate and mutual ignorance, and reveals how the differences involved in this process may be displaced or transformed, but nonetheless remain (Todorov, 1989). More strikingly, uprooting and destructuring appear to be more extensive when the move is from rural areas to large urban centers within single modern societies than when, for example, it takes place among political exiles living together or with people from other cultures in the host society (Todorov, 1989, p. 93). I take issue with contemporary antiracist ideas that reduce the issue to one of a dialogue among cultures. They appear to assume that if dialogue takes place, and mutual comprehension and knowledge is achieved, then coexistence (and—in certain cases—more naive notions, including equality) can be assured. On the contrary, any proposal for coexistence and equality of civic status based on the same common rights for all involves communication and knowledge. However, to the extent that both this coexistence as well as the establishment of a society's legal statutes themselves depend on overcoming disparate interests, and triumphing over inequality and differences regarding asymmetrical content and relationships, dialogue is as necessary as it is insufficient. What is needed is a process of negotiation, and, to that end, parity is required so that negotiation might take place, indeed, so that it might even begin. The problem therefore resides in how to include parity in such a relational context—a context that nonetheless offers no clear site for establishing such parity, if philanthropy itself does not by its very nature provide a rational justification for renouncing the advantages conferred by power. I will deal with this issue later.

A problematic aspect of ethnic identity is that it can be applied by its "users" to establish links of internal solidarity, and the ethnicity of a minority can be seen by certain sectors as a potential danger, a threat to power relationships and to the distribution of power for those holding it (and not only for the more obviously dominant sectors). We might, perhaps, look at this issue from quite a different a point of view from the usual: in 17th and 18th century Spain, for example, there were a number of legislative and administrative provisions made with regard to Gypsies, in order to bring about their assimilation. Gypsies were ordered to renounce the use of their language, to give up wearing their traditional clothes, and many of their customs were prohibited. But there were also two further prohibitions: mentioning the word "Gypsy," and the meeting, assembly, cohabitation, and residence as neighbors of Gypsies, including intermarriage. These were provisions aimed at the destruction of their ethnic solidarity, which was strongly maintained by Gypsies for purposes and reasons not entirely relevant to the current discussion. What concerns me here is not so much difference in and of itself, but rather its potential power—that is, the acquisition of the potential power of that difference: having the opportunity to gain the kind of power that such difference can offer people who identify with each other and make their identity a unifying criterion of solidarity (San Román, 1994). There are at least some fears of difference that cannot be understood without this type of consideration.

There is another problem: the dialectical tactic (or the erroneous claim to this) of arguing for an irreducibility, invariability, and impenetrability of culture that would also justify the affirmation of its incompatibility. However, one characteristic common to all human beings is their ability to adapt, change, and accept cultural elements from others and to transfer their own, regardless of whether these elements are pure ideas or practical tools, or anything in between. It is precisely this malleability that is thought to be the basis of their adaptive success and, I would modestly suggest, the key to the worldwide dissemination of the human species. This species has developed an enormous ability for *general* adaptation. By not adapting *perfectly* to anything, it seems that we humans are able to unobtrusively adapt to everything. (This is unobtrusive from the point of view of our adaptation to the planet, though clearly it is not so when we consider the planet's adaptation to us—a contradiction in evolutionary terms for which we will pay dearly.) We are therefore a species with no frontiers, but which places more frontiers internally than any other species. However, this malleability and this general ability to adapt are what enable contact, exchange, and understanding *without really knowing exactly how this takes place*, as well as the ability to culturally translate, absorb, select, and change. Human beings can change their country, place, relationships, and lifestyle and yet continue to exist. It may well be the incredible capacity for change, identification, adaptation, acceptance as well as emission of diffusion, acculturation, enculturation, and permanent, ongoing socialization that makes human beings different to that "being" who has already been determined, and who is only—and exclusively—historical: the dead. This malleability makes humankind flexible above and beyond its assignments, which are always potentially contingent.

What roles do assignment and belonging have, then, if they seem transitory from this perspective? Human beings can change, and do change constantly, but they are what they are at each point in time and in each context. Assignment and belonging are as human as change itself. The irreducibility and immutability of culture are refuted by the sheer weight of fact. Cultures are obviously penetrable and changing. They all are; we all are, although we change in directions that do not always coincide.

In any event, as far as the immeasurable nature and incompatibility of cultures as compared to their implacable nature is concerned, the hope is to find a point between the dogmatic and the skeptical, a relativist relativism, a well-founded hope. It would seem considerably more difficult for a French member of *SOS Racisme* (an antiracist organization) to understand, communicate, and negotiate with Le Pen on critical social issues than it would be with an Algerian taking part in an *SOS Racisme* demonstration. And for this reason, the problem of the *capacity in principle* for comprehension among peoples appears to be saved from becoming a problem by the most unexpected solution and to be redeemed as a hope, in the most unexpected manner.

The difference between *social integration* and *ethnic assimilation* is essential in a proposal for negotiation, and goes far beyond words. Assimilation implies leaving behind ethnically significant differences and their corresponding ethnic identities in order to adopt the identity and culture that are deemed significant for identity as an "other." Instead, however, integration (or insertion, if preferred) refers to the *position* of individuals and/or groups, in the sense that an integrated position is one that enables people to make use of their civic rights as political beings or as political entities in a *polis*. Islam thus has little to do with the civics of a lay state, but it certainly is implicated in lawful, contract-regulated employment or in full legal access to benefits conferred by the social welfare system. In the civic sense of integration, nothing prevents a North African dressed in a *chilaba*, or a Senegalese with two wives, from visiting a pediatrician; nor does anything prevent the captivating voices of Gypsy girls from the Pentecostal choir from intermingling with the melodic peals of the parish church bells. And all of these people have a right to state unemployment benefits. *A distinction thus has to be made between assimilation and integration.* To do so, I refer to another question: the emphasis placed by Abdelmalek Sayad[6] on the political aspects of the migratory process, which I extend to a discussion of the assimilation-integration distinction, as well as the obsolete nature of the concept of citizenship in the nation-state, outlined by Habermas (1991), which I will address below.

Social integration concerns the full participation (or inclusion) of those who have otherwise been removed or marginalized from politics and civil rights so that such people can provide the responses to their own needs and have access to their rights, according to the norms of the society in question. Whether or not an attempt can even be made to change conceptions and structures existing within the "simple"(!) limitations of internal social inequality is also a consequence of their integration. If so, it is at this point that these people can meet and choose their fellow travelers from among the members of their own ethnic group, or from other groups.

In light of this process, however, assimilation implies the substitution of ethnic identity and critical acculturation, as well as the acceptance of the worldview offered by the host society, and the means for its social embodiment. Nevertheless—and this should not be overlooked—acculturation of one type or another is always occurring to a greater or lesser extent, and it is usually *selective*, taking the initial culture as a benchmark as it is shaped by the dynamics of social, economic, and political integration. As a result, nothing prevents an African immigrant or a marginalized Spanish Gypsy from being able to obtain an official identification document; seek employment; possess a Social Security benefit card; reside in a normal home; find a school for their children; or push a cart around a supermarket with his wives—in the case of the African man—or with, say, his latest wife—in the case of the Gypsy man. The former remains faithful to Islam, the latter baptizes his children but does not always get married in church; one prefers to cook semolina and the other hates purées; one is sexist, so too is the other (and, indeed, so are the *hosts*). And of course all other members of society will potentially interact and perhaps argue with all three of these, from time to time. But in the meantime, the school and the church and the council will incorporate respect for Islam while concurrently striving to improve their own knowledge and understanding of it. The nursery schools attended by Gypsy children will not always serve purées; the state might recognize Gypsy weddings by activating civil procedures, and possibly also by recognizing polygamy for polygamous ethnic communities.

Coexistence is possible. Ethnic and national identity—whether or not these are based on a state—can flourish regardless of the transformations, rejections, and acceptances within the dialectics of a relationship based on direct negotiation that is open to all cultures. It is no greater a Utopia than any other respectable Utopian orientation (in the Christian or Marxist paradises, for example). It is what Don Juan, the wise Indian of Castaneda, called "*un camino con corazón*": a path with a heart, one with an uncertain destination, certainly, but one that is well worth following.

THE DIMENSIONS OF RACISM AND THE DEFINITION OF THE ADVERSARY

In the social sciences, analyses of racist discourse are seldom considered in conjunction with inquiries into antiracist discourse, just as interrogations of social relationships based on heterophobia are rarely explicitly linked to the examination of heterophilia, in terms of both the direct social and institutional relationships between these objects and forms of inquiry. Although such issues are usually considered together, the discourses associated with racism, antiracism, heterophobia, or heterophilia are often understood in the reductive sense as legitimizing certain actions or social dynamics, which themselves appear only at very global and abstract levels ("exploitation," "differences in culture," or "the economic world"). Even when more specific relationships and phenomena are emphasized, and the analysis is focused on delimited and precise empirical benchmarks, the arguments put forth tend merely to scratch the surface, for they take such dynamics at face value. A deeper analysis of the discourse, one that considers its consistencies, and critiques its suppositions and postulations, must be accompanied by references to the need for an empirical basis for this process of inquiry, and by the need for its verification; yet such needs remain unfulfilled. This is a challenge we face, and one about which I would like to make some brief comments.

In 1967, Banton distinguished between what could be called the *three dimensions of racism*. The first was its *ideological dimension*, which includes racist doctrine not only in the strictest sense but also its contextualization within an interpretation of history and a view of the world and the relationships among the peoples for whom it makes sense. The second dimension was *racial prejudice*, that is, orientations prior to action, and willingness to be guided by ethnic and racial stereotypes. Finally, the third dimension deals with social, economic, political, and cultural relationships in their broadest sense, between individuals and between groups, which could also be described as racism, and which Banton calls *racial discrimination*. He considers this to be observable collective behavior, which is often a measurable part of social relationships, and linked to intra- and intersocietal functioning (Banton, 1967).

Taguieff (1987) explicitly used this proposal to distinguish between what he called a *racism-attitude* or prejudice, a *racism-conduct* or discriminatory behavior, and a *racism-ideology* that covers various doctrines ranging from racial theory to the differential nationalism of "national preference."

In Taguieff's view, the phenomena that we currently term "racism" take a variety of forms (racism, anti-Semitism, xenophobia, etc.), and it was of course possible to identify such phenomena even before the term "racist" appeared at the beginning of the 20th century.[7]

If, in addition to these dimensions, we consider their *functions* and the cultural and political *conditions* to which they are linked, we can establish relationships that—although often overlapping in many ways—might be expressed as seen in Table 3.1.

The great value of Taguieff's work, notwithstanding the criticisms that certainly can be made—the brevity of his final proposals, the absence of both a fuller ascertaining of facts, and reference to works on specific situations—is that it provides a criticism of the ideas that situate defined racisms in opposition to the fallacy of a single kind of racism, and shows that antiracism follows in the slipstream of discursive innovations made by racism. Thus, antiracist criticism of a

Table 3.1. Interrelated Considerations on Racism

Cognitive Operations of Racism	Dimensions of Racism or Alterophobia	What Racism is	Categorizations of Racism		Social Consequences of Racism
			Components	Functions	
-Perceive -Classify -Create a hierarchical structure (and put it into practice)	1. Racism as: attitude or "racialism"	-Attitudes -Dispositions -Feelings	-Opinions -Verbalizations	-Passionate orientation of action	-Latent hostility
	2. Racism as: behavior or "discrimination"	-Behavior -Social relationships	-Acts of exclusion or exploitation	-Satisfaction of interests	-Oppression -Aggression
-Justify	3. Racism as: ideology or "racism"	-Ideas	-Representations -Explanations -Evaluations	-Legitimization of acts and their consequences	-Maintenance of discrimination and exploitation of peoples

given type of racism is actually assumed by racists and enables them to thereby create a new racism; antiracism meanwhile remains anchored to arguments that make no sense in light of these updated versions of racism. Instead of gaining a true awareness about racists, this antiracism simply recalls or reinvents them. Taguieff (1987) talks of a "twisting" (*retorsion*) strategy that consists of taking the argument made by your opponent, reducing it to its ultimate extreme, then turning it back on your opponent as a means of countering his arguments. This is an important point and I would like to develop this further here. If, for example, a racist says that there is a biogenetic and hierarchical difference between races, the antiracist's reaction is that the nonexistence of such differences has been empirically confirmed. Furthermore, the discourse of antiracism denies the inequality upon which differentiation in culture is based and rejects the notion of a hierarchical structure here, since cultures fall within perceptions of the world that cannot be measured, and thus cannot be compared. In the case of Europe, the continent's response to great cultural diversity has been an ethnocentric and imperialistic attempt to impose its dominant culture; the antiracist position, on the other hand, is to stress that each culture has value in itself and is valuable in itself. Thus, racists then effectuate a "twisting" movement on this position, taking it to its logical extreme. Hence, they argue, there is no biological differentiation, no superiority, no possible commensurability; each culture is valuable in itself and is a unique product; respect is therefore a matter of separating and isolating cultures, and of defending one's own. Faced with this, antiracists routinely counter-argue with the heavy-handed language of empirical science—with a depth charge, as it were—insisting on the nonexistence of races and the right to be different. Racism and antiracism thus provide a curious sort of mutual fulfillment, mixing together against their will. I will return to this.

What is interesting here is that if such a binary approach is taken, then other approaches may open up as a result. It is possible to rearrange the relationship between racism and antiracism and shed light on different dimensions of each of these by taking this clarification beyond an analysis of the discourse that (with good reason) interests Taguieff. The "theories of the other," and of their correlates—the other dimensions of racism—can be set out in another way.

EQUALITY VERSUS DIFFERENCE—ABSTRACT EQUALITY AND THE EDGES OF EQUALITY

As expected, we reach one of the darkest points of our attempt at clarification—namely, equality and difference. Indeed, the problematic antinomy of these terms has been widely discussed in recent studies on racism and antiracism. It seems we cannot ask people to be both the same and different at the same time.[8] This is perhaps the greatest source of frustration (and even depression) for those working in this area. However, I must confess that (maybe simply because of my own resistance to depression) I fail to see here a very clear antinomy.

Is it not the case that difference and equality, in abstract terms, are antinomous in that they are assumed to constitute part of the same whole, and to be related to the same thing? Difference and equality *in what?* Both terms imply a comparison, and all comparisons suppose the existence of a common point of comparison, something that enables differences, and indeed similarities, to be expressed. But I do not believe that cultural or ethnic differences and equality regarding specific rights point toward common criteria for comparison. In this regard, "equal" is not in opposition to "different" but to "hierarchical." "Different" is not in opposition to "equal" but to "identical" or to "similar." We are not using the same criteria when we affirm the equality of all human beings and the existence of differences among them. In each case the criteria for comparison varies. The assumption of equality refers to the rights of human beings. One might say that it refers to the "dignity of human beings," but this is too vague and abstract, excessively manipulated, full of connotations, and subject to the constant corruption of its use. We might rather talk about the equality both of human rights (and demand the negotiation of their principles) and, following Taguieff (1987) once more, of human beings (he says "men") rather than talking about humanity. It is therefore these specific rights that establish a joint and binding level among all human beings, and that can be demanded by all, above and beyond their differences. Today, these rights are those specified in the Universal Declaration of Human Rights. They are the rights we have, and at least we *do* have them. They are in many ways ethnocentric and are constantly being subverted, manipulated, and distorted. But again, at least we *do* have them. Perhaps one day there will be a universal declaration of rights for human beings, proposed by and agreed upon by all. What we have today was an unthinkable Utopia in the 16th century. "Equal" is therefore not an abstraction in this context. It is the result of comparing the rights that human beings actually have to the rights declared to be universal.

The assumption of difference refers to the empirical attributes of human beings, and is often a matter of the prejudicial conferring of attributes on "other" human beings. Equality, on the other hand, is a convention of universal rights, based not on a verifiable theory (it is not a scientific statement) but rather on a belief, on a very strong conviction. This is true to the same extent that the need for hierarchy is also a belief. Not so with difference; notwithstanding any reservations as to what may be considered metaphysical and theoretical, differences can be listed theoretically, and their existence can be put to the test. Hence, we cannot compare equality and difference even in this respect.

Differences refer to human beings' attributes in various senses: the physical (skin color, stature, agility, strength); the mental (intellectual coefficient, affective characteristics, psychomotor characteristics); and the cultural (beliefs, religious rites and organization, language, family organization, means of production). In short, if difference was irreconcilable with equality, fat and thin people, the bald and the hairy, the affectionate and surly, as well as Catholics and Anglicans, would logically be considered unequal. However, in the same way that similarity does not necessarily imply equality (just look out of your window onto the street), not all differences create inequalities. They may do so (differences in property, for example), but they may also be wholly neutral or may even counteract each other. Let us again examine the European context, so as to minimize the complicating issues of ethnocentric interpretation: there are notable linguistic differences among the European languages of power: English, French, and German. In international terms, these have a hierarchical structure, with English ranking the highest, but this hierarchical structure is not always automatic, and can sometimes be altered. For example, German is relatively underused compared to French, this based on the size and power of the two countries. Other differences in Europe, in fact millions of them, are utterly unproblematic. It is indeed somewhat curious to consider that in asking whether equal rights are possible for those whose skin color or forms of marriage differ from the dominant norm we are doing so within a European context in which members of opposing political parties or even opposing football teams can detest each other passionately, without this passionate hatred leading (as far as I know) to one such group seeking to reduce the "other" to slavery or casting them into the Mediterranean. Our (mean-spirited) sense of minimal panhuman equality is infinitely more tolerant of other "insurmountable differences" than of ethnic ones.

As far as these differences are concerned, if we abandon the radical holistic vision of a rampant "decaffeinated" functionalism, the impossibility of reconciling cultural differences and equality seems even more inadmissible. This is the case for several reasons. The first is because the difference that is incompatible with another coexisting cultural attribute never affects the entire culture, nor indeed ever reaches all relationships among those participating within it. Second, there will always be similarities—whether these are universal or not—upon which agreements can be based in practice. This is well known to many who have experienced an "intercultural" social life. Third, no culture is internally homogenous and internally consistent; in any one society it may be that some people believe a characteristic of a foreign group to be incompatible with their own culture, while others consider it to be perfectly compatible, even desirable. As a result, it is difficult to reach firm agreement on cultural contents or details and their interpretation. There are always factions and disagreements, and it is not unlikely that even when we think we have erred on some point of interpretation here, many will tell us that in fact we were right. We may receive applause from one sector but condemnation from another. Dialogue does not necessarily take place *en bloc*, nor does it occur without surprises within a group (a common, everyday occurrence). Finally, as I mentioned above, no human group and no culture is impermeable; on the contrary, they are receptive (to a greater or lesser extent) and diffusive (depending on their power to impose themselves, among other things).

However, let us pause for a moment to think about exactly *what* we mean when we defend "equality." In principle, it seems that we are referring to the universalist and abstract formulation of panhuman equality that is the basis for various egalitarian ideologies in today's world. Nevertheless, this abstraction weakens in its practical versions, which come up against differing realities, interests, and factions (especially those of power), all of which allow for interpretations to be made in terms of time, space, and the various social segments that form part of egalitarianism. The abstraction itself is all-or-nothing in nature, and may hence give rise to various types of restrictive interpretations that can, ironically, foster inequality. "Equality" includes lightweight notions such as "all men are equal in dignity," which is an elegant way of saying nothing. However, there are also multiple restrictive formulae. As Sayad (1983) observes,

> [...] the possibility of delimiting political territory allows for the reconciliation both of law (that is, the "democratic passion" of equality) and of fact (that is, discrimination and segregation, which are thereby regulated and made legitimate) [...] This enables the democratic order of nation-states to be considered as "transparent." In other words, as arbitrarily unified, homogenous, by means of, or thanks to, the identification thereby conferred onto it. (p. 303)[9]

This is reminiscent of the Racial Democratic Party of Andalusia of southern Spain, in the 1970s, which proposed the expulsion of all nonwhites and nonnationals as well as Gypsies and Jews in order to attain the *universalist* ideal of equality among those remaining. Democratic equality seems therefore to be strictly limited by criteria of inclusion and exclusion from its body politic and its civic rights, and by prerequisite criteria restricting internal inequality. Equality, thus understood, rests on a premise of asymmetry among those who are supposedly equal, as regards their political inclusion.

Thinking, then, about equality in pure and simple terms would lead us to live without frontiers, and would thus prove harmful to our own interests in the same way that it would compromise the equal distribution of wealth throughout the world. Our unjustified privilege (that of the vast majority of "us" in the developed world) becomes truly clear only when this latter image of equality is projected onto ourselves. It is the panic that this image may cause in us that is the most dramatically grotesque reflection of our status as restrictive egalitarians: egalitarians, but within our own borders.

EMPIRICAL SPECIMENS AND IRRATIONAL PHILANTHROPY

> Pure love for humanity has a radically different basis to the individual perception of the empirical examples of the human race.
>
> —P.A. TAGUIEFF (1987, P. 418)

Perhaps the common objective, the purpose of dialogue for any negotiated universal declaration concerned with human rights, can find a basic benchmark in the Rousseauesque compassion that Aranzadi (1991) has rearticulated into a guiding undercurrent for the actions and attitudes of *some* toward *others*. The commitment is, hence, to philanthropy. But this is not an "either-or" dilemma between philanthropist and alterophobe. If we ignore rational assessments—which are always ethnocentric—the *empirical specimens* or concrete individuals of "ourselves" and of "the others" neither lead us toward love nor would I say push us irretrievably toward hate. Taguieff notes that "the condition of pure philanthropy is the conviction that the other's self has the same reality as that of my own self" (1987, p. 431).

Philanthropy is an ethical commitment made through empathy and in the absence of scientific rationality. Why should we be philanthropists? There is no reason to tolerate or to reach agreements that we ourselves do not need to reach, and which are neither imperatives, nor revelations—religious or lay—nor endowed with faith and conviction. Indeed, on this argument philanthropy lacks any firm rational basis. We are philanthropists, rather, because we want to be, because of a conviction or a faith without revelation; we submit to consciously assumed principles, an option to which science is absolutely silent, since it has nothing to say. Max Horkheimer (1978) allows grounds for optimism that might be understood as a philanthropic basis: "It consists of what we must try and do, despite everything […]."[10] There is no reason why. We are antiracists because we are philanthropists. We could have been something else. But this is what we want to be.

Philanthropy needs a purpose that replaces the aims of ethnocentricity. I believe that Aranzadi—with whom I disagree on other issues—is right to suggest that compassion is the guiding feature of philanthropy. As a general rule, save perhaps a few exceptions, human beings prefer to suffer as little as possible; compassion, then, is the recognition of the "other's" suffering and the emergence of intersubjective interest as a result. Compassion may just be—and in many ways become—the political driving force behind philanthropy. If there is no compassion, there is no basis for guiding criticism or philanthropic action. Criticism alone cannot be entrusted to confront cruelty; criticism merely limits cruelty, and compassion itself is not obtained through criticism, which is powerless in this respect. Nonetheless, criticism and compassion are considered similar entities by many people, across many (perhaps all) cultures, and thus serve to promote philanthropy. Yet I agree with the need to rethink antiracism. This is necessary because it helps us to clarify our position and uncover the reasons for our anxiety and confusion. And perhaps it is also useful because it brings into clearer focus the criteria of those who live off the ideology of racism.

In the end I believe I have two things more or less clear in my mind. The first has to do with an irrational philanthropy and a compassion that guides the direction of philanthropy for its own sake. If communication is evident, but not enough value is attributed to it, and if similarity is also evident, but again insufficient value is attributed to it, then neither racists nor antiracists will have scientific arguments for their positions; nor will they if differences are evident but not enough value is attributed to them, or if equality is obviously nonuniversal but is valued either as an asset to humanity or as something harmful to the nation. If we do not already have an argument to use as a basis, I would be willing to state that we are antiracists without logic or empirical basis, and we are so because we share other people's pain, regardless of the progress of the nation. Without any logical or empirical basis: exactly like racists themselves.

NOTES

1. This chapter has been adapted from San Román (1996 and 1998).
2. This distinction has formed the basis of my research. I have developed it further in other works.
3. These identifying features include, for instance, nomadism among Gypsies, as set off against the Spaniards' strong attachment to the land—this even though most Gypsies of Spain have in fact been sedentary for centuries. The Islamic population distinguished between the Mudejars and the (then) Moriscos, despite their many cultural differences from the Castilian population, or their forced conversion to Christianity. Other examples include the identity features that segregate the Bambuti from the Bantu Pygmies, or in Panama, the fact that the Cuna Indians' light coffee-colored skin distinguished them from whites of European (Spanish, English, or French) origins, or from blacks of African origins, who were freed from slavery at the beginning of the 20th century. Height, skin color, the consumption of "clean food" (milk), and a sense of self-control rigorously instilled during childhood are said to distinguish the Tutsi from the Bahutu and Batwa, and the condition of being God's chosen people distinguishes practicing Jews from everyone else. In these ways, culture alone does not make an identity; it is the people with historically acquired identities who select those aspects of their culture that best represent their difference and uniqueness (see Barth, 1969, pp. 9–38).
4. See, for example, Williams (1990) on British Guyana, in Fox (1990), as well as postcolonial scholars such as Fanon (1967), Said (1993), or Appadurai (1996).

5. When the colonial system is removed, it is common for new national identities to appear that are constructed to "make" the substrata of the newly independent states (Williams, 1991; Said, 1993; Appadurai, 1996). This is true of Rwanda, which brought together its original ethnic groups, and which are now once again separating, engaging in bloody conflict with each other. In the case of Somalia, the Somalis' resistance to colonial rule, along with their high self-esteem, their genealogically-mythically based sense of solidarity, and their enormous contempt for their neighbors, has led them to develop, when conditions have been favorable, a strong nationalism aimed against Western powers and based on their Islamic faith. This subsequently led them to oppose strongly "what the Somalis see as the imperialist policies of the Ethiopian government" (Lewis, 1961). In other cases, such as the Azande people, as well as many earlier African and American empires, the identities of politically silenced peoples conquered by their neighbors emerged after Western colonization, being reinforced to an even greater extent after decolonization. The Aleluya social-religious Pentecostal movements of European Gypsies and the Romany Union Gypsy movement are also examples of emerging identities that have promoted unification of very loosely identified segments or groups in recent years (Williams, 1991).

   Ethnic identity is usually multireferential and segmentary, at the level of local or even continental identification. Evans-Prichard (1940) highlighted the segmentary nature of the Nuer identity by using a system of relationships in which they identified themselves, ranging from the basic lineage to the Nuer being. The Iroquoi, as described by L. H. Morgan (1851) in his research carried out between 1844 and 1858, were grouped into five federated nations, each of which was divided into eight tribes, each tribe in turn being divided in such a way that all of its divisions belonged to one of the nations and not to the others. For example "[...] the wolf tribe was divided into five, and each of these five parts was in one of the five Nations. The other tribes were subject to the same division and distribution [and] [...] there was a link of brotherhood between the separate parts of each tribe, which united the nations with indissoluble links [...]" (Morgan, 1851, p. 77). The Iroquoi thus had multiple identities, ranging from the global League identity to the tribal (wolf or bear, for example) and to their respective nations (Seneca or Mohawk). The community of identities was linked in these ways to bonds of solidarity that led to global solidarity within the League.

   A segmentary identity can be seen in many places and peoples. The Ashanti of West Africa, for example, have a strong sense of patriotism centered around their local community. All group members are considered Ashanti and they emphatically identify themselves at a higher level as an Agogo or Askore people, of which the Ashanti are merely one tribe, or part (Fortes, 1947, 1948, 1950). See also Fox (1990).

6. Several works by Sayad are relevant here. See Sayad (1983), (1984), (1987), and (1991).
7. See Le Bras-Chopard (1986), as quoted in Taguieff (1987, p. 250).
8. See for example the works quoted above by Taguieff (1987), Gosselin (1992), and Delannoi (1993).
9. All quotations from non-English source-publications have been translated into English.
10. As quoted in Taguieff (1987, p. 422).

REFERENCES

Appadurai, A. (1996). *Modernity at large: Cultural dimensions of globalization*. Minneapolis, MN: University of Minnesota Press.

Aranzadi, J. (1991). Racismo y piedad: Reflexiones sobre un judío y un chimpancé. *Claves de razón práctica*, No. 13, pp. 2–12.

Banton, M. (1967). *Race relations.* Tavistock: Basic Books.

Barth, F. (1969). *Ethnic groups and boundaries.* London: Allen and Unwin.

Bauman, Z. (2005). *Identity.* Cambridge: Polity Press.

Bhabha, H. (1994). *The location of culture.* London: Routledge.

Delannoi, G. (1993). La teoría de la nación y sus ambivalencias. In G. Delannoi and P. A. Taguieff (Eds.), *Teorías del nacionalismo* (pp. 9–17). Barcelona: Paidós.

Evans-Prichard, E. E. (1940/1969). *The Nuer: A description of the modes of livelihood and political institutions of a Nilotic people.* Oxford: Oxford University Press.

Fanon, F. (1967). *The wretched of the earth.* Harmondworth: Penguin.

Fortes, M. (1947). The Ashanti. *The Geographical Journal,* Vol. 110, No. 4/6, pp. 149–179.

Fortes, M. (1948). The Ashanti social survey. *Rhodes-Livingstone Journal,* No. 6, pp. 1–36.

Fortes, M. (1950). Kinship and marriage among the Ashanti. In A. R. Radcliffe-Brown and D. Forde (Eds.), *African systems of kinship and marriage* (pp. 252–284). Oxford: Oxford University Press.

Fox, R. G. (Ed.) (1990). *Nationalist ideologies and the production of national cultures.* Washington D.C.: American Anthropological Association.

Gosselin, G. (1992). L'Anthropologie et les antinomies de l'égalité des cultures. *Ethnologie Française,* No. 4, pp. 402–408.

Guillaumin, C. (1972.) *L'ideologie raciste.* Paris: Mouton.

Habermas, J. (1991). Citidinanza e identità nazionale. *Micromega,* 5 (December–January), pp. 123–146.

Hall, S. (1996). Gramsci's relevance for the study of race and ethnicity. In D. Morley and K.-H. Chen (Eds.), *Stuart Hall: Critical dialogues in cultural studies* (pp. 411–440). New York: Routledge.

Horkheimer, M. (1978). La Theorie Critique hier et aujourd'hui. In L. Ferry (Ed.), *Theorie Critique* (pp. 353–369). Paris: Payot.

Le Bras-Chopard, A. (1986). *De l'égalité dans la difference: Le socialisme de Pierre Leroux.* Paris: Presses de la Fondation Nationale des Sciences Politiques.

Lewis, I. M. (1961). *A pastoral democracy.* Oxford: Oxford University Press.

Lieberson, S. and Waters, M. C. (1989). The rise of a new ethnic group—the "unhyphenated American": A selection from the New Census Monograph on ethnicity. *Social Sciences Research Council Items,* Volume 43, No. 1, pp. 7–10.

Morgan, L. H. (1851). *League of the Ho-De-No-Sau-Nee, or Iroquois* (Vol. 1). New York: Herbert M. Lloyd Publishers.

Said, E. (1993). *Culture and imperialism.* New York: Alfred Knopf.

San Román, T. (1994). *La diferència inquietant* (Part 1). Barcelona: Serveis de Cultura Popular/Altafulla. [Translation into Spanish and expansion of the work: *La diferencia inquietante. Nuevas y viejas estrategias culturales de los gitanos* (1997), Madrid: Siglo XXI].

San Román, T. (1996). Los muros de la separación: ensayo sobre alterofobia y filantropía. Barcelona: Tecnos/Universitat Autónoma de Barcelona.

San Román, T. (1998): Las bases del racismo y de la filantropía. In Departament de Didactiques Específiques de l'Universitat de Lleida (Eds.), *Los valores y la didáctica de las Ciencias Sociales: Actas del IX Simposio Internacional de Didáctica de las Ciencias Sociales* (pp. 75–90). Lleida: Edicións de l'Universitat de Lleida.

Saussure, F. de (1915/1971): *Curso de Lingüística General* [Translated by Amado Alonso]. Buenos Aires: Losada.

Sayad, A. (1983). Maghrebins en France: Emigrés ou immigrés? In L. Talha (Ed.), *Annuaire de l'Afrique du Nord.* Paris: CRESM-CNRS/L'Harmattan.

Sayad, A. (1984). Tendances et courants dans les publications en sciences socials sur l'immigration en France Depuis 1960. *Current Sociology, ISA,* Vol. 32, No. 3, pp. 219–304.

Sayad, A. (1987). Les immigrés algériens et la nationalité française. In S. Laacher (Ed.), *Questions de nationalité: Histoire et enjeux d'un code* (pp. 127–197). Paris: L'Harmattan.

Sayad, A. (1991). *L'immigration ou les paradoxes de l'alterité.* Brussels: De Boecck-Weismal.

Taguieff, P. A. (1987). *La force du prejugé: Essai sur le racisme et ses doubles.* Paris: La Découverte.

Todorov, T. (1989). *Nous et les autres.* Paris: Editions du Seuil.

Williams, B. (1990). Nationalism, traditionalism and the problem of cultural inauthenticity. In R. G. Fox (Ed.), *Nationalist ideologies and the production of national cultures* (pp. 112–129). Washington: American Anthropological Association.

Williams, P. (1991). Le miracle et la necessité: A propos du développement du pentecôtisme chez les tsiganes. *Archives des Sciences Sociales des religions*, No. 73, pp. 79–98.

CHAPTER FOUR

Remaking civic coexistence: Immigration, religion AND cultural diversity

EDUARDO TERRÉN

University of Salamanca

WHY DOES CIVIC COEXISTENCE MATTER NOW?—CULTURE AND POWER FROM A SOCIOLOGICAL STANDPOINT

Ever since Durkheim's classic (1915) analysis of the role of religion in society, cultural sociologists have regarded religion as a source of values, social ties, and solidarity—a focus that clearly diverges from the large body of research on the role of religion in conflict. I seek to understand how the pursuit of cultural integration might be reconciled with the confluence of diverse religious faiths, new hybridities, and other complexities arising from the wave of globalization that characterizes the current conjuncture in social history. In so doing, my aim is to rearticulate the relevance of civic coexistence. As immigration steadily grows and displaces cultural and physical homogeneity in local communities throughout the world, such communities—particularly those with Christian roots—face the paradoxical challenge of preserving their national identities and traditional values, whilst incorporating the cultural diversity brought about by immigration.

What follows, then, is an exploration of the role of immigration as a source of cultural diversity, and as a major impetus behind cultural change. This involves inquiring into the intersections between immigration, religious diversity, and dominant discourse about these cultural developments. By focusing on discourses such as references to the Judeo-Christian heritage in the draft Constitution for Europe, debates on the teaching of religion at schools, interpretations of the *banlieue* riots that took place in France in November of 2005, and on the Muhammad cartoon controversy of 2006; I highlight the resilience of old-age notions and stereotypes relating to cultural and religious diversity, in different contexts of interpretation. To explain this resilience, I also interrogate the ways in which hierarchical perceptions of Otherness (mainly of Muslims) are flourishing within a dichotomized system of representing the foreigner, the outsider, or those who are simply considered "different." A key argument will be that religion is being mobilized, in this recent context of flux, by new forces of cultural conservatism as a marker of racialization, and that the impact on public opinion of this polarized representation of cultural diversity serves as a cornerstone to the current hegemony of conservative fundamentalism.

The complex dynamics of these cultural developments constitute an important challenge that, as I will argue, can only be met through the remaking of civic coexistence, based on the notion of cosmopolitan civic culture. "Civic coexistence" is the very process through which society evolves, in the course of daily life and face-to-face interactions. As a concept, it pertains much more to the various attitudes, representations, and feelings that underlie social relations, than it does to institutional arrangements. Metaphorically speaking, civic coexistence might thus be conceived of as a kind of construction site where the emotional cement of citizenship is churned out. The term "togetherness," as developed through moral philosophy, may serve to clarify the meaning of "civic coexistence." Bauman (1993), for example, identifies two forms of togetherness, or ways of perceiving and interacting with the Other: being *with* the Other, and being *for* the Other. In the first of these, our relationship *with* the Other is guided by ethical norms and conventions. That is, social norms and institutional conventions form the foundation of our actions. We turn from the personal to the general—to the universal rule—in order to understand how we might best manage this coexistence with the Other. Being *for* the Other, on the other hand, is not based on universal principles but on trust and personal communication. The key element in this form of togetherness, then, is our attitude toward Others. What is central here is an emotional commitment that is closely associated to the feelings of respect for, and recognition of, the Other, as illustrated by Richard Sennett (2003): such engagement moves the interaction with the Other away from a world of (stereotyped) certainty and toward a universe of questioning and openness. However, this form of togetherness, which is essential to the process of remaking civic coexistence in the context of cultural pluralism, is hindered by hegemonic discourses on religious diversity that propagate exclusionary and racialized forms of emotional engagement with the Other.

For mainstream social theory, the modern framework for understanding togetherness, or cultural integration, has long rested on a premise of cultural homogeneity given that theorizing integration has generally occurred within the hitherto unquestioned social model of national culture and national religion (no matter how extra-officially a religion attains this status) (Tambini, 2001; Al Sayyad and Castells, 2002). Nonetheless, the contemporary migrations that are so much a part of the current process of globalization are challenging this basic assumption as they lead to more culturally diverse societies; thus the need to rethink civic coexistence. In the meantime, however, dominant representations of cultural diversity through religion may hinder progress toward this goal. For example, in the post 9/11 and 3/11 world, Samuel Huntington's (1993) pessimistic analysis of cultural conflict has influenced the representation of religious diversity, now increasingly perceived as a potential menace to social integration, rather than as an opportunity for redefining the classic model of coexistence and cultural integration. Yet, Huntington's so-called "clash of civilizations" is in fact an essentializing interpretation of conflicts arising between Western societies founded on Christianity, and predominantly Islamic societies, the dominant religious faiths of which are totalized by Huntington to the point that they come to represent the essences of two supposedly separate "civilizations." Notwithstanding the rhetorical fundamentalism of Huntington's analysis, the effects of his discourse are indeed very real to the extent that "the age of Islamic Wars," and the global emergence of Islamic grievances and hostility toward the West have determined, to a significant degree, the contours of academic and political debates. This means that the prospect of cultural exchange through internal criticism and dialogue is being replaced by a ruthlessly undiscriminating adherence in the West to the notion of the incommensurability and incommunicability of cultures. The fault line, in others words, is one of incomprehension (Turner, 2005). This being so, how can we possibly face the primary challenge to coexistence posed by increasingly multicultural and multireligious populations? Clearly, at least part of the answer lies in resisting the fundamentalist logics that inform binary analyses such as Huntington's. Even then, the question remains as to how we might, as an alternative, offer new life and inspiration to the experience of civic coexistence.

This might be accomplished, first, by reconstructing civic experience in the context of cultural pluralism—a process that involves rethinking "Otherness." In fact, some central terms in the vocabulary of togetherness, such as "Other" or "alterity," have only recently gained currency in sociology and cultural studies (Riggins, 1997). Nevertheless, the Other is still a kind of mysterious being. This figure is strange because s/he is hard to define. The image of the Other is constructed from myths and thematic clusters (such as ancient traditions, political and economic "underdevelopment," exoticism, violence, barbarism, etc.), all of which are difficult to reduce to a single and reliable image. Instead, a complex picture emerges, one that evokes an array of often contradictory feelings, including fear, distrust, and even prurient indulgence, but always from a distance (Shaheen, 1984). Since Jean Paul Sartre's study of "the Jewish Question" (see, for example, Judaken, 2007) and, more recently, following Todorov (1985), research on culture has shown how the framing of cultural identities is typically expressed in terms of externalized Others. The dichotomized structure of this discursive practice is still alive, and can be seen, for example, in the ways evil characters in cartoons and films are marked with non-Western cultural or racial traits. The logic of this racial marking, of course, is far from new. The association, for instance, between evil and Muslim otherness is part of the ethnocentric tradition of European and North American literature: the depiction of the "Saracen" or the "black Moor" as dangerous and strange is rooted in many classic texts of the Western canon, as is the case with the violent character in Shakespeare's *Othello*, or Dante's Muhammad, who is cast into the Inferno (Karim, 1997).

Clearly, the persistence of this polarized and racialized representation of religious diversity hinders the extent to which we can meet the challenge of rethinking the ties that bind people of European origins with those of non-European origins who have made Europe their home. Discursive practices that perpetuate racial marking, as does the tacit association of race with religious faith, constitute a major barrier to deepening democracy and strengthening civil society, that is, to transforming civic coexistence. We will see, moreover, how other powerful hegemonic representations of non-Christian religions further serve to racialize diverse peoples who resist modernization.[1]

The theoretical approach to this discussion arises from a concern with the relationship between culture and power, a relationship which tends to remain invisible in the mainstream sociology of culture. As noted earlier, cultural integration has been one of the main objects of the Durkheimian sociology of culture. From this classic point of view, cultural processes are seen as relatively autonomous from structural dynamics, and function according to basic symbolic classification systems, such as those underlying the religious representation of the world through, for example, the symbolic division between "the sacred" and "the profane" (Alexander, 1988).[2] The narrative structure underlying elite discourse on racial conflict associated with immigrants, for instance, is heavily informed by this kind of binarism in that its lexicon is relentlessly polarizing in terms of the sacred and the profane: civilization/barbarism, friend/foe, us/them, from here/from elsewhere, and so on. These dichotomies are implicit, moreover, in many popular metaphors used to stress the "threat" of border-crossing people ("flood," "avalanche," "plague," and "invasion"), and to further associate these people with "pollution" or "infection." Accordingly, any representation of "we-ness" (Alexander, 1988) as sacred or pure involves an implicit reference to its opposite, perceived as pollut-ing, profane, and as such, threatening. Such representations provide a deep gram-mar of polarized categories that permeate hegemonic discourse and shape popular (nonhegemonic) beliefs and discourse on racial conflict. This is why hegemonic renditions of "the sacred" might be seen as pivotal signifiers of difference, and as a source of symbolisms, feelings, and dispositions that are central to the making of civic coexistence in culturally diverse contexts.

But while the Durkheimian perspective provides interesting insights on the inner organization of cultural systems for representing Otherness, it neglects to consider the political uses of culture underlying hegemonic discourse on cultural diversity. It overlooks the link between culture and power and fails to address how a dichotomized grammar of identity is performed in discursive practices within a framework of power relations. To overcome this analytical weakness, it may be worth developing a critical sociology of cultural power, taking as a (combined) starting point Antonio Gramsci's theory of hegemony, Stuart Hall's theory of representation, and Edward Said's theory of Orientalism. These three concep-tual tools are particularly relevant to the exploration of religion as a cultural field, due to their foci on elite discourse, popular culture, cultural domination, and the control of meaning.

Controlling the meaning of cultural (including religious) diversity in every-day and media discourse has become crucial in a society increasingly shaped by the speed of information and by people's mobility. The exercise of power is there-fore increasingly based on the control of the codes, representations, and symbols that frame the flow of information and images about those who arrive to "our" shores. Because this production and rhetorical manipulation of the meaning of Otherness lies at the core of contemporary conflicts, analyzing how such cul-tural power operates (and is operated) requires a theoretical framework capable of revealing and deconstructing the ways in which both hegemonic and popular representations of race relations and cultural diversity—which often characterize immigration as essentially problematic and threatening—influence our disposi-tion to interact with the Other.

It was Gramsci (1971) who first claimed that, in order to identify mecha-nisms of domination, particular attention should be paid to everyday structures and commonsense values. Gramsci's notion of hegemony refers to the ideologi-cal supremacy of a system of values that supports the interests of the dominant classes or groups and expands and is self-reinforced through popular culture, media discourse, and populist politics. This notion is useful for identifying how not only pervasive racist stereotypes, but also subtly destructive representations of, and emergent sentiments toward, racial minorities are (re)produced in soci-ety (Winant, 1994). Indeed, many of the hegemonic representations of cultural diversity emerging from the current period of mass immigration have origins that can easily be traced back to colonialism, as one of the primary forms of cultural domination and ideological representation in the modern era. In this regard, Said's (1978) critical consideration of the relationship between culture and power offers a theoretical foundation for deconstructing hegemonic discourses on religious diversity, for it helps to unveil the Orientalism that permeates dominant Western discourse on diversity. For Said, "Orientalism" is

> the corporate institution for dealing with the Orient—dealing with it by making statements about it, authoring views of it, describing it, by teaching it, settling it, ruling over it: in short, Orientalism as a Western style for dominating, restructuring and having authority over the Orient. (Said, 1978, p. 3)

In addition, Hall's (1997) constructionist approach to representation facilitates understanding how religion can be used to racialize when particular racial groups are made to represent, or are routinely associated with, certain religions. This process can be conceptualized as part of a cultural politics of representation that is currently turning the debate on religious diversity into a cultural/racial battle rather than an arena where a deeper and more democratic understanding of civic coexistence can take place, and so lead to social transformation.

FORGING CULTURAL INTEGRATION:
CULTURAL DIVERSITY AS AN OPPORTUNITY
FOR REINFORCING DEMOCRACY

Since the turn of the century, the confluence of social changes arising from economic globalization, people's mobility, and the identity demands of very diverse groups, is opening up new horizons for cultural integration in the European context. But as immigration gives rise to new debate on cultural diversity, this discursive context is impacted by hegemonic racial discourse focused on religion. It should be noted, moreover, that contemporary Europe is facing the challenges of cultural diversity whilst concurrently dealing with the redefinition of its own historic sense of European identity, and with the demands of new nationalist movements and native cultural minorities. So while contact with immigrants obliges Europeans to redefine the basis of their civic coexistence (i.e., the playground of feelings and attitudes underlying citizenship and a sense of belonging), this is taking place within a preexisting context of "confused identity," that is, "re-negotiated collective identity in Europe." As Al Sayyad and Castells (2002) have pointed out, the more one's own sense of identity becomes blurred, the more difficult it is to accept the identity of Others and to establish a rational dialogue to negotiate and redefine a new common identity.

These complex dynamics provide the context in which contemporary Europeans are now facing the challenge, on various levels, of what Bauman has referred to as "liquid identity" (Bauman and Vecchi, 2004). In the meantime, however, the impact of immigration alone on the growing multiculturalism of populations residing in the same national space is sufficiently powerful to oblige European nations to reflect on the necessity of forging a new concept of citizenship, one capable of providing an alternative project that encompasses recognition, participation, and feelings of belonging to an increasingly complex and heterogeneous civil society. This challenge is particularly significant in South European countries, as they now see themselves becoming hosts—often reluctantly so—to large immigrant populations.[3] However, this challenge is not only felt in Mediterranean countries, which have effectively taken on the role of border-guard or "gatekeeper" between Europe and the developing world further south; it also constitutes one of the greatest challenges to today's highly interdependent postmodern world. As Moroccan sociologist Mernissi (2003) has asserted, one of the explanations as to why globalization makes us so anxious is that, regardless of origins, getting to know unfamiliar people is never an easy task. This task, however, is essential to the postmodern reconstruction of cosmopolitan civic culture.[4]

In what sense, then, can immigration contribute to a deeper and more inclusive civic coexistence, one which leads to more active, egalitarian, and cosmopolitan interactions and social participation? A new model of cultural integration may help us respond to these important questions. Citizenship in increasingly complex and heterogeneous civil societies implies rethinking legal rights, but also the attitudes and representations that condition the experience of intercultural contact in daily life. Citizenship is thus deeply implicated in the cultural dimension of civic coexistence, as it always implies some kind of collective identity and a certain sense of belonging. The question is whether the cultural frames that have traditionally served as uniting links, such as classical patriotism or national ethnicism (which is very frequently tied to national religions), are still adequate frames from which this new feeling of togetherness and belonging can be forged.

In previous decades, multiculturalist critiques have questioned the assumption that cultural homogeneity (often tied to cultural imperialism) is a necessary moral basis for social integration. This assumption was derived from an idealized model of the polis, understood as a union of ancestors, language, territory and, in most cases, religion (one needs only to consider the etymology of the term "communion"),[5] a model which has not proven sufficiently sophisticated or adequate where recognizing the true multicultural character of most political communities is concerned (Morley and Robin, 1995; Appadurai, 1996; Tambini, 2001; Al Sayyad and Castells, 2002; Held, 2003). This traditionally modern way of building civic identity on the basis of national cultures seems at odds with the new phenomenon of "postnationality" (Tambini, 2001), that is, with the novel or alternative feelings of belonging emerging from current migratory fluxes and the accelerated transnational movement of information. The same could be said of essentialist conceptions of cultural identity in light of the complex identities now claimed by those who are involved in, or influenced by, these movements.[6]

Nevertheless, the persistence of national forms of identity accounts for the fact that cultural diversity is too often perceived as a threat or a danger, since such diversity is assumed to undermine the grounds of a shared national identity (Appadurai, 1996). This is why—in a context of increasing cultural and religious pluralism that is bombarded by media representations and populist discourses associating immigration with menace, decadence, and disorder—many Europeans feel disoriented, anxious, or troubled.

What is more, and as noted earlier, most nations can be characterized by a dominant religious faith. One of the main tasks faced by an increasingly multicultural Europe, then, is the redefinition of the civic relationship with religion. It is worth bearing in mind here Alain Touraine's (1997) "weak principle of integration" as a key for searching for a new model of cultural integration. Touraine suggests that the time has come to accept that sharing a common culture does not necessarily mean sharing the same values, or even the same individual identity (which should not be confused with a common identity). But how can this be accomplished? How can we achieve a multilaterally acceptable common context of existence without sharing values or similar ways of thinking? What indeed do we need to share, and what are we entitled not to share? These are the main questions that cultural diversity poses to the renewal of the experience of civic coexistence.

Assuming that one of the main research questions for cultural sociology is how the discursive representation of cultural diversity in civil society affects the production of the emotional cement of citizenship, it may be worth avoiding easy formulas, such as those stemming from the idea of the supposed incompatibility of cultures, or from the not less simplistic idea that difference in itself is always good and enriching. While recalcitrant xenophobia is bad company, forced xenophilia is not an alternative. Beyond any metaphysics of difference, multiculturalism must be considered from a realistic perspective, one that is independent from any previous assessments, and considered as a simple fact. This is indeed a troubling issue, because, given the monocultural and Eurocentric framework that has characterized the institutional development of modernity (Hall, 1992; Appadurai, 1996), the coexistence of individuals with different visions of the world makes recognition and treatment of Others difficult. Since cultural diversity accounts for different conceptions of good and evil, the ways in which we define who we are, and the cement that binds us together, need to be reformulated.

This task, if properly handled, can provide an important source of renovation for the process of civic learning. Contrary to the exclusionary hegemonic representations of religious pluralism erected in response to immigration, the consideration of cultural diversity as problematic does not imply seeing it as a threat or as civic "gangrene." Rather, it is a challenge—a situation that offers us the possibility of rethinking the ties that unite us, and seeing them as a form of intercultural solidarity. Reassessing our feelings of belonging and the attitudes we develop toward culturally diverse people is a process that, when based on the common denominator of intercultural coexistence, can lead to a stronger democracy, because interculturalism and cosmopolitanism deepen our interactions and commitments with those whose cultural identities differ significantly from our own.

In order to make progress toward this end efficient and meaningful, a realistic perspective must first be established. For if, as already noted, an initial step here is the avoidance of simplistic and idealistic formulas for building solidarity and inclusion, a second step might involve considering the barriers that hinder the development of this project for cultural change. The populism of hegemonic representations of religious diversity that prove divisive to social cohesion—though not the only barrier—is the main element considered here.

THE "WAR OF POSITIONS" AROUND RELIGIOUS DIVERSITY

Power, in Gramsci's view, is exercised by privileged groups or classes in two ways: through force or coercion, and through hegemony. In his efforts to delegitimize unjust dominant belief systems, Gramsci (1971) believed that it was necessary to create a "counter-hegemony" of resistance. In terms of the present discussion, the dichotomized discourse on religious pluralism produced by the Catholic Church and other elites that rhetorically manipulate the meaning of diversity has achieved a certain degree of hegemony, especially in South European countries. The populist ambitions that pervade their discourse of fear and complaint deploy religion as a racializing marker of cultural difference. This is why *laïcité*[7] constitutes a potentially powerful alternative basis for the consideration of civic cohesion in the midst of cultural diversity, as it may allow for working toward a cosmopolitan remaking of civic coexistence. Given that hegemonic values permeate many spheres of civil society—schools, churches, the media, voluntary associations—civil society itself represents the battleground in the struggle for hegemony between laic and confessional stances; hence, the "war of positions."

This in mind, it is not difficult to understand why redefining civic engagements with religion is such an urgent task in modern, multicultural Europe, and why *laïcité* might be seen as a legitimate counterhegemonic project. Indeed, throughout history, secularization has always centered on the place and role of religion in the relationship between state and civil society. This concern is still relevant to the challenge of accommodating the cultural diversity brought about by immigration. Because religion and cultural homogeneity are historically related—as evidenced by the fact that traditional ties between European nation-states and Christian churches remain strong (Al Sayyad and Castells, 2002)—the role of religion as a source of cultural domination needs to be properly situated in its historical dimension. This contextualization leads us to a brief consideration of some legal and policy issues, so that we might better understand the real configuration of power in which religious organizations control a system of symbols, and thus contribute to the hegemonic production of the meaning of diversity.

The current debate on religious diversity can, to a certain extent, be traced back to the hegemonic position enjoyed by the Roman Catholic Church in the late Middle Ages. Nowadays, however, the relationship between church and state in Europe is extraordinarily complex, and it varies according to each country's history of secularization.[8] Nevertheless, almost half of the European countries have established state churches or concordats that have long endowed the Catholic Church with extensive powers for negotiating and institutionalizing numerous privileges. Conservative elites, who maintain strong ties with the church's interests, and who retain the power to exert political pressure, have managed to substitute the debate over identity and religion with a debate on the nature of the relationship between church and state. Even when their strategy has not proved successful enough to achieve the *constitutional* recognition of the Christian legacy of Europe, it has succeeded in achieving the recognition of churches as representative bodies of civil society, whose views must be taken into account by the state. In this scheme of things, however, is every faith treated equally?[9] Following lengthy debate, all attempts to include Europe's Christian legacy in the drafts of the proposed European Constitution have, in fact, failed (perhaps to prevent reaction from Muslim sectors that now represent the second religion of Europe). This should not be understood, however, as a rejection of religious beliefs and identities in favor of a laic cultural identity, even though some media commentators now speak of a "moral panic" caused by the so-called laic revolution—an idea that can lead, paradoxically, to a sense that the church itself is a victim of state-sanctioned exclusion.[10]

The question about the place of religion in schools is equally troubling. In Italy, the controversy over crucifixes, which still hang on the walls of classrooms in state-funded schools, has served to expose the power of the Catholic Church, which, as is the case in Spain, has a decisive institutional role in civil life. In France, where the Muslim population represents between five and six million people, the matter of the *hijab* (or veil) has for more than a decade put the country's tradition of state neutrality—which arose from its republican *laïcité*—to the test. Fourteen years ago, the fact that women used the *hijab* was declared as incompatible with France's official secularism. At that time, though, the matter was left to be dealt with at the local level (a similar legal arrangement was established in the United Kingdom during the same period). Today, however, the same issue is seen as inciting national conflict because wearing the *hijab* is now considered to be a violation of a recent national law that prohibits the display of any religious symbols in public institutions. In Holland, the *Submission* affair, and the murder of film-maker Theo van Gogh (due to his critique of Islam), sent shock waves through the country.[11] Anxiety over jihadists is increasing throughout the continent in the aftermath of terrorist attacks in London and Madrid, due to the association of Islam with terrorism. By merely scanning the press over the last year, one finds that many of these countries are currently working on plans to control and monitor the socialization practices developed in mosques and Islamic schools.

Considering that socialization embodies both the way in which a society envisions itself, and the ways in which it re-creates the basis of its civic culture, the role of education here seems especially relevant. The educational systems of various European countries are currently engaged in discussions about how best to achieve the formal and curricular accommodation of religious diversity in schools. It is worth noting, nonetheless, that the issue has specific implications in those countries that still have limited experience with receiving immigrant families—countries whose traditional model for cultural "integration" is based on Catholicism. Spain, for example, lacks *laïcité* in its public life, even though it has no mainstream neo-Fascist or extreme-right political parties (unlike France, Austria, and Italy). This absence of secularism is to a great extent a legacy of Franco's dictatorship (1939–1975), which was confessional in nature and gained much of its legitimacy and hegemonic power from the Catholic Church. Thus, the concept of *laïcité* in Spain is still frowned upon, and indeed remains unfamiliar to many. Some movements, though, are trying to raise awareness about the principles of tolerance and peaceful coexistence among people from different cultures, some of whose traditions and religions vary from the norm. But even when such principles are promoted as entirely necessary for 21st-century Europe, Catholic discourse on state affairs sinks to the level of complaint and victimization.

Similar developments are taking place in the United States where, despite religious pluralism, confessional schools abound, and fundamentalist Christians are also lobbying. In this case, they are demanding the exclusion of evolutionary theory from the school curriculum, thereby extending the reactionary shadow that had already begun with Ronald Reagan and the New Right's attempts to introduce mandatory daily prayer in schools. Thus, even if our concern is focused on European countries such as Spain, where immigration is a relatively new phenomenon, the issue should be seen from a global perspective. In the global arena, the kind of spiritual leadership that advocates cultural closure as a response to the uncertainties of social change is spearheaded by neoconservative Anglo-Americans, whose arguments revolve around threatened Western values. In Europe, we have seen how this type of cultural fundamentalism can be found in those who seek to include Christianity as a symbol of identity in the European Constitution. They argue that "the European identity" was historically created in opposition to third parties ("barbarians" or "infidels"). The influence of this neo-conservatism can also be found in mainstream politics, where politicians some-times scarcely conceal their belief that the presence of non-Europeans in Europe is an uncomfortable necessity that can best be dealt with in terms of its beneficial effects on the labor market, or indeed as an act of charity. This belief is evident in Oriana Fallaci's recent work (Fallaci, 2002), in which she employs the exclusionary and alarmist language of those who regard themselves as members of a higher civilization, who count on "the power of reason" (as sacred), and complain that immigration has become an "invasion" (a source of pollution). More recently, the controversy that erupted in 2006 over a series of illustrations of Muhammad in the European press has also revealed how religious imagery is deployed as a racializing marker.[12] Another example is the Bush Administration's use of the "crusade" metaphor, and depiction of Saddam Hussein as the latest "Great Satan," as a means of legitimizing the second Gulf War. This deployment of religious imagery turns institutionalized faith into an arena of cultural conflict, and generates dialog within a framework of fear and distrust. The spiritual leadership of Western conservatism, then, informs the dominant discourses that frame most public discussions on cultural diversity in civil society. These discussions are thus conditioned by a defensive and polarized discourse that promotes a simplified, undesirable and threatening image of the Other rather than addressing the need to redefine identity itself. This discursive operation of racializing and denigrating Others through references to religion illustrates an ideological maneuver that Norbert Elias (1997) identifies as typical of the discourse of "the established": through their identification of superiority, merit, and an established self-image.[13]

In this sense, religion not only serves as part of the classificatory, asymmetrical, and patronizing character of the West's sacred self-image, but it is deployed as a cultural weapon in the "war of positions" now waged against cultural diversity. As we have seen, some of the clearest examples can be found in the portrayal of Islam implicitly present in these representations. As Hentsch (1992, p. 1) notes, "The Muslim is Europe's Other *par excellence.*" In the context of the United States,

Huntington (1993) argued with similar urgency that after the demise of the communist threat, Muslims were remerging as the West's chief enemy. Portraying Islam as the principal threat to the West's sacred self-image, however, is in fact little more than a vague and ill-defined imaginary intended to neatly sum-up the collective fear of terrorism. Clearly, it is a representation that fails to account for the tremendous diversity of Islam.[14] This type of asymmetrical representation is equivalent to identifying the whole of Christianity with the massacre of 200 civilians in Uganda by God's Liberation Army, or with North American Christian fundamentalists' defense of Creationism as a pedagogical model for biology classes.

The riots taking place in France in November of 2005 further demonstrate how the mainstream media depiction and popular interpretations of this civil unrest turned Islam into a scapegoat, this constituting a prime example of the hegemonic, populist use of religion as a racializing marker of identity serving to both praise the "we," or the sacred, and stigmatize the (darker-skinned) Other (of North African or Arab origins), as outsider or profane. Indeed, the riots were set off by a series of violent clashes between, on the one hand, thousands of youth from poor suburbs (predominantly from second or even third generation immigrant families), and on the other, the French police. According to various press reports, the social context from which the riots erupted was ripe for civil unrest.[15] The inhabitants of these large city suburbs (*banlieues*) suffer from unemployment at far higher levels than does the rest of France, and unemployment amongst those of foreign origin is even higher than the average rate in the *banlieue*. But frustration from this disproportionately high unemployment rate can only account for part of cause of the riots, for racist discrimination in the *banlieue* has also found expression through police harassment of those with dark skin or Muslim-sounding names, and has been cited in the press as a major cause of discontent in the affected districts. Yet, from the first outbreak of protest, many commentators associated the riots with Islam. Despite the fact that interviews and reports from the riot scenes often made it quite clear that religious issues were not directly involved in these events, the media debated fervently over the alleged association between this civil unrest and the Intifada, or the belief that immigrant families that practice polygamy live by an inappropriate model of socialization.

In sum, these examples show that difference continues to be more feared than appreciated. European debates over the accommodation of religion at schools, the cultural contents of a future European Constitution, or the causes of the French riots, have served as the real-life arenas from which old stereotypes concerning Islam are deployed within a framework of binary and asymmetrical representation, and thus operate as ideological artifacts that produce a polarized, resentful, and even belligerent reception of the immigrants' cultural diversity.

CONCLUSIONS

Europeans today are not only facing the challenge of *being* multicultural, but of *considering themselves as such* (Al Sayyad and Castells, 2002). Globalization and the ongoing diversification of multicultural and multireligious societies have given rise to a new objective: that of interculturalism. The heightened pluralism of postmodern societies requires greater mutual understanding and awareness among individuals and groups. This need and demand puts traditional democratic values and patterns of civic coexistence to the test. What is at stake in the postmodern reconstruction of civic culture is, as Alexis de Tocqueville observed, "knowing how to combine" (Tocqueville, 1969/1848), or "the capacity to mediate" (Held, 2003), which must be deepened if we are to remake civic coexistence.

The aim of the present discussion has been to show to what extent hegemonic discourse on the "war of religions" has brought into circulation representations of religious diversity that hinder efforts toward a deeper democracy. The debates on the place of religion in schools and in the European Constitution, or the hegemonic, populist interpretations of the 2005 riots in France, seem to confirm that the belligerent use of religion in racially marking cultural diversity is connected to the persistence of a dichotomized system of representation that comports important exclusionary effects. The ongoing circulation of these binary stereotypes, which are preserved in the collective memory of European countries such as Spain, with important historical ties to the Arab world (Connerton, 1989), reproduces the cognitive practice of Othering embodied in what Edward Said called "Orientalism." Said's notion of Orientalism reveals how Western discourse constructs cultural Others by representing East-West differences in ways that best suit the West's ideological interests. This seems to echo the "us-them" dichotomy, insofar as "we-ness," or the West, is to be thought of as the primary defining force. A connection between both perspectives can be established through Hall's theory of identity and representation, which suggests that the building of self-identity always generates discourses of difference and similarity (Hall, 1992, 1997).

The critical sociology of culture that I have attempted to develop in this chapter by further building upon neo-Gramscian arguments is intended to reveal that, far from being neutral, the binary grammar inherent in the dominant representation of identity in Europe is developed within hegemonic discourse reflecting a predominantly conservative political leaning. "Religious diversity" is a cultural representation, and cultural representations are cultural politics. Negative images of non-Western religions, such as Islam, contribute to the manipulation of Otherness that depicts the rise of Islam as the new post-Cold War Other. The latent Orientalism of this trend is clearly linked to the dialectic of cultural power relations in the globalized postmodern world.

Although contact with minorities and immigrants provides Europeans with an important opportunity to redefine their collective identity and forge a new sense of belonging, the persistence of the dichotomized organization of European representations of Otherness imposes significant limits on their potential to rethink the ties that bind them to newly arrived immigrants. As long as the dominant discourse on religious diversity continues to reproduce old cultural stereotypes in the framework of the friend/foe dichotomy, the kind of intercultural communication necessary for establishing a new kind of civic coexistence will be thwarted, and interactions around religious and cultural diversity will most likely fail to pave the way for a stronger democracy. Feelings of apprehension, distrust, and outright fear of foreigners are very common feelings that are easily exploited by dominant (mis)representations of cultural diversity and racialized discourse practices that use religion as a marker of difference. Through these practices, which heavily condition popular sentiments through the mainstream media, cultural conservatives and religious elites arouse strong emotions that are in turn expressed through incomprehension and exclusion; and by so doing, they hinder the remaking of a civic coexistence that requires inclusion, cosmopolitanism, and intercultural communication.

NOTES

1. Inasmuch as dominant representations constitute elite discourse, they exert powerful influence over popular beliefs. As van Dijk (1993) has pointed out, the preferential access that elite discourse has to the mass media is key to the reproduction of racism, for such discourse can simultaneously pre-formulate, and give easy formulas to, the beliefs and values of whole populations.

2. Mary Douglas's sociological anthropology, for instance, is clearly Durkheimian in that it focuses on the classifying function of symbolic systems. In fact, her theory on pollution as a form of social control that is used to mark deviant or dangerous activities can be seen as an expansion of the notion of profanation Durkheim developed in his later work.

3. In Spain, for example, immigration is placing new demands on the dominant social mold in a country used to five centuries of cultural homogenization, and which just twenty years ago became a viable destination for immigrants. Hence, a very old nation with a very young democracy (nearly as young as its immigration experience) is now forced to rethink and reconfigure the way in which coexistence has hitherto been constructed.

4. A civic culture can be called cosmopolitan when it expands moral and social inclusion to promote the coexistence of people with multiple belongings, complex identities, and divided loyalties (Thomas, 2004). See also Vertovec and Cohen (2003) for a depiction of cosmopolitanism as a mode of managing cultural diversity, as well as Held (2003) and Beck (2002) for a defense of the inclusive sense of cultural identities embraced by cosmopolitism and by a global civil society that encourages interculturalism.

5. Although the term can simply refer to the sharing of thoughts and feelings, in ecclesiastical discourse it refers to participation in the sacrament. In keeping with Augustine's usage, the Latin

communis (common) is derived from *com-* + *unus*, meaning "oneness, union." See "communion" in Harper (n.d.).

6. As Thomas (2004), Held (2003), Bauman (1993), Bauman and Vecchi (2004), Beck (2002), Hall (1992) and many others point out, the intensification of globalization is altering the nature of identities, making them appear not as static and fixed but as fluid and changing.

7. The French term *laïcité* has no exact equivalent in English. Some authors refuse to translate it due to its resonances with European republicanism and egalitarianism (Judge, 2004). The closest equivalent, however, would be the English concept of laity.

8. While the present discussion does not attempt to address the legal treatment of religious diversity, it is concerned with the ideological treatment of this diversity in hegemonic discursive practices.

9. For a quick look at the influence that Vatican and Catholic lobby groups, such as the Opus Dei, exert in demanding recognition of Europe's "religious inheritance" in the project for a European Constitution, see the article by Terras (2004). Also, Judge (2002) provides a comparative study of the public funding of religiously affiliated schools in France, the United States, and England.

10. Reporting about recent educational and legal reforms in Spain, the *Sunday Catholic Weekly* (November 30, 2005, p. 1) stated that "The socialist radicals have spent a year carriyng out a laic revolution that threatens to change the face of this once deeply Catholic country."

11. The assassination of Theo van Gogh was also clearly a sign of the use of religion as a racial marker, but from the side of the racialized. Van Gogh actually died from a gun wound, but the fact that he also suffered a knife wound to the chest warranted, in one case, a five-page report replete with religious references to fidelity and infidelity, and couched in the language of victimization. Van Gogh, a controversial film maker, directed "Submission" a 12-minute movie for the Dutch television. Some of its images were meant to shock. For example, one depicted the opening lines of the Koran written across the naked body of a Muslim woman. Another showed Koranic verses about female obedience scrawled on the back of a woman beaten by her husband, while a female voice accused Allah of condoning the violence. The film and its screenplay were conceived of and written by a 35-year-old Muslim woman, Ayaan Hirsi Ali.

12. For a brief overview of this controversy, see *Guardian* (2006).

13. Nevertheless, it should be noted that this association of race with religion is also to be found in very diverse legal actions concerning blasphemy. In 2005, for example, an organization curiously named the "General Alliance against Racism & for the Respect of French & Christian Identity"—which had been unsuccessful in a previous legal action against the publication *Liberation*, over a cartoon of a naked Jesus wearing nothing but a condom—began legal action against a critic of John Paul II because of his alleged "racial defamation of the Christian community." In 2006, The French Council of the Muslim Cult, having fallen victim to these "racial and religious outrages," took legal action against all French newspapers that published the cartoons of Muhammad.

14. Different types of ethnic or cultural belonging give rise to no less diverse religious experiences with Islam. This includes at least 30% of those who claim not to practice their religion, or who, without turning their back on Islam, consider themselves to be members of lay society. With regard to this diversity in Islam, notably liberal versions of the faith can be found which are struggling to remold the religion into a belief system that can incorporate the concept of citizenship prevailing in Europe. See Al Sayyad and Castells (2002). Also see the website for the international movement of Muslim gay men and lesbians at the US-based site Al Fatiha (2007), as well as references to the Muslim women's movement at the Spain-based site WebIslam (2007).

15. The riots broke out on October 27, 2005, and were originally triggered by the deaths of two teenagers of North African origins in a poor *banlieue* of Paris. They peaked on the night of November 7, 2005. On November 17, 2005, the French police declared a return to normality

throughout France, stating that the 98 vehicles that had been torched the previous night were nothing out of the ordinary. According to the official count, however, more than 8,000 vehicles were set ablaze in the course of the 20 nights of rioting, with 2,888 arrests and 126 police injured. It should be noted, too, that France has the largest concentration of Muslims living anywhere in Western Europe. The vast majority live in the poor suburbs of Paris, Lille, Lyon, Marseille, and other large cities, and in overcrowded housing projects. Aside from *de facto* residential segregation, another factor helps to explain the situation: unemployment among the foreign-born is *1.5 times higher* than it is among those of French origin, this after adjusting for educational qualifications. The bare statistics are even more arresting: for example, an unemployment rate of 5% for French university graduates can be compared to the unemployment rate of 26.5% for university graduates of North African origin (see *BBC News* [2005] and Sidiqui [2005]).

REFERENCES

Alexander, J. (1988). Durkheimian sociology and cultural studies today. In J. Alexander (Ed.), *Durkheimian sociology: Cultural studies* (pp. 1–22). Cambridge: University of Cambridge Press.

Al Fatiha (2007). The website for the international movement of Muslim gay men and lesbians, at http://www.al-fatiha.org (last retrieved September 18, 2007).

Al Sayyad, N. and Castells, M. (2002). *Muslim Europe or Euro-Islam: Culture and citizenship in the age of globalization.* Lanham, MD: United Press of America.

Appadurai, A. (1996). *Modernity at large: Cultural dimensions of globalization.* Minneapolis, MN: University of Minnesota Press.

Bauman, Z. (1993). *Postmodern ethics.* London: Blackwell.

Bauman, Z. and Vecchi, B. (2004). *Identity: Conversations with Benedetto Vecchi* Cambridge: Polity Press.

BBC News (2005) French Muslims face job discrimination. *BBC News,* November 2, 2005, at http://news.bbc.co.uk/2/hi/europe/4399748.stm (last retrieved September 18, 2007).

Beck, U. (2002). The cosmopolitan society and its enemies. *Theory, Culture and Society,* Vol. 19, No. (1–2), pp. 17–44.

Connerton, P. (1989). *How societies remember.* Cambridge: Cambridge University Press.

Durkheim, E (1995/1915). *The elementary forms of religious life* (translated by K. Fields). New York: Free Press.

Elias, N. (1997). *Logiques de exclusion.* Paris: Fayard.

Fallaci, O. (2002). *The rage and the pride.* New York: Rizzoli.

Gramsci, A. (1971). *Selections from the prison notebooks.* New York: International Publishers.

Guardian, The (2006). European elite scrambles to defuse furore over caricatures of Muhammad. In edition dated February 3 at http://www.guardian.co.uk/religion/Story/0,,1701282,00.html (last retrieved September 18, 2007).

Hall, S. (1992). The West and the rest. In S. Hall and B. Giegen (Eds.), *Formations of modernity* (pp. 276–280). Cambridge: Polity Press/The Open University.

Hall, S. (Ed.) (1994). *Representation: Cultural representations and signifying practices.* London: Sage/The Open University.

Harper, D. (n.d.). Communion. *Online Etymology Dictionary* at Dictionary.com Web site: http://dictionary.reference.com/browse/communion (last retrieved September 21, 2007).

Held. D. (2003). Cosmopolitanism: Globalization tamed? *Review of International Studies,* Vol. 29, No. 4, pp. 465–480.

Hentsch, T. (1992). *Imaging the Middle East*. Montreal: Black Rose Books.

Huntington, S. (1993). The clash of civilizations? *Foreign Affairs*, Vol. 72, No. 3, pp. 22–49.

Judaken, J. (2007). *Jean-Paul Sartre and the Jewish question: Anti-antiSemitism and the politics of the French intellectual*. Omaha, NE: University of Nebraska Press.

Judge, H. (2002). *Faith-based schools and the state*. Oxford: Symposium.

Judge, H. (2004). The Muslim headscarf and French schools. *American Journal of Education*, Vol. 111, No. 1, pp. 1–24.

Karim, K. H. (1997). The historical resilience of primary stereotypes: Core images of the Muslim order. In S. H. Riggins (Ed.), *The Language and politics of exclusion* (pp. 153–182). London: Sage.

Mernissi, F. (2003). The cowboy or Sindbad: Who will be the globalization winner? (Speech given on the occasion of the ceremony of the Prince of Asturias Award for Letters, October).

Morley, D. and Robin, K. (1995). *Spaces of identity: Global media, electronic landscapes and cultural boundaries*. London: Routledge.

Riggins, S. H. (1997). The rhetoric of othering. In S. H. Riggins (Ed.), *The language and politics of exclusion* (pp. 1–30). London: Sage.

Said, E. (1978). *Orientalism*. New York: Vintage.

Sennett, R. (2003). *Respect in a world of inequality*. New York: Norton.

Shaheen, J. (1984). *The TV Arab*. Bowling Green, OH: Bowling Green State University.

Siddiqui, A. (2005) Reflections on the riots in France. In *Media Monitors*, November 17, 2005, at http://usa.mediamonitors.net/content/view/full/22767 (last retrieved September 18, 2007).

Tambini, D. (2001). Postnational citizenship. *Ethnic and Racial Studies*, Vol. 24, No. 2, pp. 195–217.

Terras, C. (2004, January). Bajo la presión de las iglesias [Under church pressure]. In *Le monde diplomatique*, (Spanish version), No. 99. Also available online at: http://www.monde-diplomatique.es/isum/Main?ISUM_ID=Center&ISUM_SCR=externalServiceScr&ISUM_CIPH=np8dF7LPzYHamFF-1unkMvyhznWd7V7YuIPL-La2s-mks3BDIAkJm5XvnVuTvbG MqsLY!2qu-dua5KMKlcbyVFQyq!i8w!28JctZtClFN!JmThFUw10FaTNSgfdtVYd1xPa15JOf ehK1!D-3Fd!Vo4oC-MVn-!d4W-N36OhFtXB9cdhjUGgvz3A44WNGomx0ElpsW27OIPIJ2 sNJO7LeeMMBokpub266HQRhUPvaOEvwr59-EsxBZ3VUtYcZutahrh26OZOqAWUAoK! gjR4vEOFmEA8VsRYENJyJmKcPUi8cDIZUyOAlJQ___ (last retrieved March 6, 2008).

Thomas, H. (2004). *Cosmopolitanism and cultural diversity*. Paper presented at the 2nd Global Conference: Interculturalism: Exploring Critical Issues. Vienna.

Tocqueville, A. de (1969/1848). *Democracy in America* (Vols. 1 and 2). 1969 edition J. P. Mayer (Ed.) (translated by G. Lawrence). Garden City, NY: Anchor Books.

Todorov, T. (1985). *The conquest of America: The question of the other*. New York: Harper and Row.

Touraine, A. (1997). *Pourrons-nous vivre ensemble? Égaux et différents*. Paris: Fayard.

Turner, B. S. (2005). Religion and globalisation: Explaining religio-ethnic conflict. In *ISA Bulletin*, 20, at http://www.isa-sociology.org/publ/e_bulletin.htm (last retrieved March 6, 2008)

van Dijk, T. A. (1993). *Elite discourse and racism*. Newbury Park, CA: Sage Publications.

Vertovec, S. and Cohen, R. (Eds.) (2002). *Conceiving cosmopolitanism: Theory, context and practice*. Oxford: Oxford University Press.

WebIslam (2007). References to the Muslim women's movement at http://www.webislam.com (last retrieved September 18, 2007).

Winant, H. (1994). Racial formation and hegemony: Global and local developments. In A. Rattansi and S. Westwood (Eds.), *Racism, modernity and identity* (pp. 266–289). Cambridge: Polity Press.

Part II. Transnational cultural policy, global neoliberalism, and racism

CHAPTER FIVE

Elite discourse
AND institutional racism

TEUN A. VAN DIJK

Pompeu Fabra University

INTRODUCTION

In this chapter I examine some discursive aspects of the role of the elite and the institutions that produce and reproduce racism in European societies.

There are several reasons for focusing on elite racism, rather than on "popular" racism (for details, see van Dijk, 1993). First, many elites often claim that they certainly have nothing to do with racism. Rather, respectable politicians from democratic parties, mainstream newspaper journalists, or reputed scholars blame racism on others, typically on those at the extreme right, or on "the uneducated" who inhabit popular neighborhoods where immigrants also happen to reside.

Second, prejudice and discrimination are not innate but learned, primarily, from public discourse. Such discourse, which includes political debates, news and opinion articles, TV programs, textbooks, and scholarly works, is largely controlled by elites. If such discourse were systematically and predominantly non-racist or antiracist, racism would not be as widespread as it is, assuming that in many respects the elite are the moral guardians of society and thus tend to serve as good or bad examples of social practices.

Third, the history of racism shows that elites have always played a prominent role in ethnic and racial domination. The very notion of "race" and racial superiority were "invented" by scholars, as we know from the most pervasive scientific literature of the 19th and most of the 20th centuries (Chase, 1975; UNESCO, 1983; Haghighat, 1988; Barkan, 1992). Colonialism, eugenetics, segregation, the Holocaust, Apartheid and "ethnic cleansing" were racist practices engaged by (then) "respectable" politicians, and legitimated by journalists, scholars, and scientists.

Their discourses found their way into novels, movies, textbooks, and the "commonsense" discourses of everyday life. Wherever we find forms of "popular" racism, it is largely preformulated by the elites, their political leaders and the mass media. Even when the elites did not explicitly engage in the production of prejudices and stereotypes, and the exclusion of "Others" from their own realm (politics, media, science, etc.), they can at least be blamed for insufficiently combating popular racism where they had the means and the opportunity to do so.

In sum, several reasons support the thesis that elites always have been and still are part of the problem of racism, and much less a part of the antiracist, multicultural solution. However, since elite racism is often quite subtle, indirect, and thus, distinct from the overt and blatant racism of the extreme right, one still needs to investigate which forms such racism assumes today. We are so much accustomed to this kind of racism that we do not notice it anymore, as has been the case with many forms of sexism, so often denied by men.

The racism of the elite is primarily discursive. Through writing and talking, politicians, journalists, scholars, judges, and managers express and reproduce their beliefs, ideologies, plans, and policies. A prominent politician's speech, a star reporter's opinion article, or a renowned scholar's book may have more negative effects than thousands of conversations in the street, on the bus, or in a bar. In this chapter, I examine some of the properties of this discursive racism of elites, which has been coined as "institutional racism." There are different examples of "institutional racism"—the organized discursive practices of the elites—such as parliamentary debates, press news, municipal or national bureaucratic legislation and speeches, and school and university textbooks. Sociological accounts of institutional racism usually overlook individual social practices and focus on the actions or policies of organizations and institutions. However, one should keep in mind that the discourses of these institutions are the products, either individual or collective, of their members, and are legitimated by their elite leadership. An institution is as racist as are its members, especially its leaders. This does not mean that I reduce racism to personal prejudice. Rather, I want to stress that socially shared prejudices are jointly and collaboratively produced and reproduced by (collectives of) social members through the institutional discourses of the political arena, the media, and the education, scholarship, and business domains.

RACISM

The notions of "elite racism" and "institutional racism" presuppose the concept of racism, which I briefly need to define in order to understand the role of discourse and the elites in the reproduction of racism. Racism is primarily a system of domination and social inequality. In Europe, the Americas, and Australia, this means that a "white" majority (and sometimes a minority) dominates non-European minorities. Domination is defined as the abuse of power by one group over another, and is enacted by two interrelated systems of everyday social and cognitive practices, that is, by various forms of discrimination, marginalization, exclusion, or problematization, on the one hand, and by prejudiced and stereotypical beliefs, attitudes, and ideologies, on the other. Indeed, in many ways the latter can be seen as the "reasons" or "motives" that explain and legitimate the former: people discriminate others because they believe that others are somehow inferior, have fewer rights, and so on.

Discourse is the social practice that relates these two realms of racism. It is itself a prominent social practice among others, and almost exclusive to the social practices of symbolic elites and institutions: what these "do" they do by text or talk. At the same time, discourse is virtually the only way racist prejudices are expressed and reproduced in society: these social cognitions are generally acquired through the mass media, textbooks, and everyday conversations with family members, peers, friends, or colleagues—conversations which again may be inspired by what people see on TV or read in the newspaper. Nearly everything most people know about non-European countries, about immigrants and minorities, they learn from the mass media. The same is true for their opinions and attitudes which, in turn, are the basis of the social practices of discrimination and exclusion.

The processes of the public production and reproduction of knowledge, opinions, and ideologies should thus be primarily defined in terms of the discursive practices of the dominant institutions and their elites. This also holds for the reproduction of racist practices and ideologies, and, by the same logic, of antiracism. Due to minority resistance or outside pressure, some change agents among the political, media, and scholarly elites may begin to formulate alternative discourses that question, criticize, and oppose dominant discourses and other practices. When these voices of dissent gain access to the means of public discourse, they are able to stimulate the formation of opposition movements, NGOs, parties, or pressure groups such as antiracist movements in Europe and the Americas.

Nevertheless, serious and systematic change is, once again, only possible when the majority of the elite leadership in politics, the mass media, and scholarship endorse the antiracist ideologies of dissenting groups, as has been the case in postsegregationist United States, post-Apartheid South Africa, or post-Holocaust Europe where the most extreme forms of racism and anti-Semitism are concerned. Nowadays, though, antiracist resistance to the forms of "modern" racism currently prevalent in the countries where Europeans are dominant has so far played only a minor role in politics, the media, or scholarship. Indeed, some forms of racism, especially in politics, are even on the rise as much in the United

States as in Europe, sometimes as a backlash against earlier civil rights movements and antiracist actions, and generally, as a consequence of real or perceived increases of immigration.[1]

DISCOURSE

Most research on racism focuses on forms of discrimination and exclusion, or on prejudices and ideologies, but ignores the fundamental role of language, discourse, and communication in the reproduction of racism in modern societies. Politics and policies are expressed, engaged in, or practiced as many forms of text and talk, from laws and legislation and parliamentary debates, to government deliberations, decrees, and decisions or party programs and propaganda. The media are broadly discursive, as are images, film, and multimedia messages. The same is true for legal process and the courts, as well as for education and scholarship. That is, the symbolic elites are primarily discursive elites. They wield power by text and talk. Racism without text and talk would probably be impossible. Indeed, how else would people acquire prejudices and stereotypes about other people, especially since these are seldom based on everyday observation and interaction with Others? How else could groups share the beliefs that give rise to discrimination and exclusion?

It is therefore crucial that we study racism, and especially elite racism (as well as antiracism) through a detailed analysis of elites' institutional discursive practices in its diverse forms (i.e., parliamentary debates, political propaganda, news reports, editorials, opinion articles, advertising, textbooks, scholarly books, and articles as well as business policies, negotiations, and deals). Such analysis is especially relevant because, as suggested, many forms of elite racism today are indirect and subtle, as is also the case for sexism. We need sophisticated discourse analysis to show how such institutional practices are informed by underlying racist beliefs, or how elite discourses may have deleterious effects on public opinion.

Fortunately, in the last decades a broad development of discourse analysis has emerged from the humanities and social sciences, not only as a "method" of more explicit analysis of discourse data, but also as an independent cross-discipline of discourse studies (see van Dijk, 1997; Schiffrin et al., 2001). This means that in linguistics we now know much more about language use than the analysis of words and sentences in grammar, for our focus has broadened to include a large number of other structures and strategies of text and talk, such as their coherence, overall topics, schematic forms, narrative or argumentative structure, style, rhetoric, speech acts, and conversational strategies, besides many other aspects. In psychology we now know much more about the cognitive processes of the production and comprehension of discourse, how discourse is memorized, and how people learn from discourse (van Dijk and Kintsch, 1983). In the social sciences, the interest in natural forms of discourse and communicative events has led to a broad movement of detailed ethnographic analyses of the forms and conditions of text and talk in interaction and communities. Although there are still vast unexplored areas, we now know much more about the structures, the processes, and the social and cultural contexts of discourse. Parliamentary debates, news reports, courtroom and classroom interaction, textbooks, scientific publications, everyday conversations, and a host of other discursive practices have been studied in great detail.

These developments in discourse studies also allow for a more sophisticated approach to the study of racist practices, especially those of symbolic elites. We are now aware, for instance, that studying subtle modifications in intonation or volume in speech, syntax, lexical choice, topic selection, storytelling, argumentation, or conversational strategies, besides many other elements, can help us to detect the underlying prejudices operating in language users and institutions. Beyond such discursive studies, we are now also better prepared to gauge the effects of discourse in the public sphere, because we know how discourses are understood, and how people form mental models and socially shared representations about other people, including prejudices and ideologies. In sum, a detailed discourse analysis of racism is a powerful tool for understanding the reproduction of ethnic and racial inequality in society.[2]

EUROPE

For many reasons, the racism I am interested in here is "European" racism. Not because white people are inherently racist, but because European racism has historically represented the most pervasive and destructive form worldwide (Lauren, 1988). More specifically, I am interested in the specific racisms practiced in contemporary Europe. As it would be beyond the scope of this chapter to describe in detail the different political and social forms that such racism can take in various countries, I will instead sketch out a general tendency illustrated by examples of discourse-racism in several countries.[3]

It is customary to address and even to excuse current racism in Europe in relation to the massive increases in non-European immigrant populations. This form of justification might be characterized, however, as just another way of "blaming the victim," for there are arguments showing that today's levels of immigration merely trigger or exacerbate racist dispositions that have long existed in Europe. First, there are the many forms of racism that are not triggered by increased immigration because they are directed at existing European minorities, as is the case with widespread anti-Semitism (Wodak et al., 1990; Reisigl and Wodak, 2001) and the discrimination of the Roma people ("Gypsies"), especially in Eastern Europe and Spain (San Román, 1986; Garrido, 1999). Second, during colonialism many Europeans engaged in various forms of racial discrimination and violence in the colonies. Such racism, however, can hardly be attributed to immigrant Others: the Europeans were the ones who "immigrated," that is, stole the land and dominated Other peoples. Third, throughout European history, elites have written racist texts about non-Europeans, even when these Others were not immigrants in Europe. Finally, by examining patterns of contemporary racism in Europe, one finds that it is precisely the elites, whose racism is examined here, that have the least everyday contact with immigrants. This is also true for popular racism, which is not most blatant in poor neighborhoods with many immigrants, but precisely in the (popular or elite) neighborhoods where people fear the likelihood of immigrant settlements.

In other words, contemporary racism in Europe is not a new invention—rather, it continues a long tradition—and is not caused by immigration, but by the consistently negative social representations of Others throughout its history (Barker, 1978; Delacampagne, 1983; Fredrickson, 2002). One has merely to read the everyday discourse of politics, the media, scholarship, the arts, literature, travel, and so on—texts dating prior to the Second World War and even later—to notice how widespread and blatant racist prejudices about Africans, Asians, or American indigenous people always have been. Racist practices and ideologies against non-Europeans were the official norm, not the exception. It is only due to the Anti-Slavery movement in the 19th century, and later, to the postwar reactions to the Holocaust, decolonization, the Civil Rights movement in the United States, the struggle against Apartheid, and the shame associated with the ethnic slaughter carried out in Rwanda and Bosnia, along with the political activities of UNO and UNESCO, that a more generalized but incipient norm against (blatant) racism developed in the world, and hence, also in North America and Europe (Lauren, 1988; Barkan, 1992).

There are two general European social and political currents that address ethnic relations. One is the contemporary variant of an old form of indigenous European racism and anti-Semitism that has a very long history and is directed against non-European peoples in general, and more specifically, when combined with Islamophobia, against "close" and hence "threatening" Turks and Arabs in particular, above and beyond what is already directed against Jewish people and the Roma. Whereas, under colonialism, European racism took a more "racialized" form, especially where Africans, Asians, and indigenous peoples of the Americas, Australia, and the Pacific were concerned, contemporary European racism is expressed more in terms of culture and cultural difference. This is most clearly the case with the rejection of Islamism, especially Islamic fundamentalism—a reality that was exacerbated by the terrorist attacks of September 11 in the United States and March 11 in Spain (Halliday, 2002; Goody, 2004). It should be noted here as well that the cultural grounds of contemporary racism are generally perceived as a more "acceptable" form of discriminating and excluding those who are also seen to be "racially" different—as often is the case with Turks, Arabs, and Jews.

Hence, we are now witness to developments that are concomitant to the daily manifestations of "old" European racism. On the one hand, there are the more subtle and indirect forms of discrimination and exclusion based on cultural, demographic, or other "reasonable" grounds. Setting limits on immigration or applications for refugee status are the most obvious public manifestations of the legal exclusion of Others, which (not coincidentally) affects mostly people from Africa, Asia, and Latin America, that is, those who can be seen as "racial" Others, and much less immigrants from Eastern Europe. Indeed, this kind of exclusion has become the norm in Europe, and not only on the right. On the other hand, we are also witness to the incorporation of official and "international" norms against blatant prejudice and discrimination—norms which have been enshrined in laws and constitutions.

In the current European context, then, these two currents combine in complex ways. One may observe that countries such as the United Kingdom, Germany, and France legislate against anti-Semitism and racism, but at the same time restrict immigration, tolerate explicitly racist parties, and make practically no effort to counter the many forms of everyday racism circulating within the public sphere and its institutions. For instance, in Italy, Austria, Denmark, and Holland more or less explicitly racist parties capture 30% of the votes and even become partners in government coalitions.

Yet even as such developments are at first officially condemned and decried on the basis of a generalized social norm that rejects racism, as occurred with Haider in Austria, liberal principles or *Realpolitik* usually get the upper hand, and racist parties thus come to be tolerated as part of the "democratic" consensus—as simply one more point of view among others, as is the case in Denmark, France, and Italy. And worse still, the ideas and policies that originally emerged from the racist parties of one or two decades ago are now increasingly incorporated into the arguments shared by current mainstream parties in order to limit immigration and restrict the civil rights of refugees, immigrants, and other minorities. Traditionally "tolerant" countries such as the Netherlands and the Scandinavian countries have thus become hotbeds of increasing xenophobia, Islamophobia, and racism. In contrast, however, the promotion of multiculturalism is present in schools, neighborhoods, NGOs, and many other domains of civil society, as is opposition to dominant government politics.

Over the last decade European politics have veered to the right, increasingly integrating anti-immigration policies. The media have supported these measures, especially after the deadly terrorist attacks by Islamist radicals, this allowing for an ever more present process of legitimization and exacerbation of anti-immigration or anti-Islam sentiments across the continent. Indeed, with some exceptions, the dominant mass media in Europe have failed to energetically oppose the growing expressions of racism and xenophobia in European politics and public opinion. On the contrary, as was the case in the Netherlands with the political phenomenon of Fortuyn,[4] the press and many other elites also went to great lengths to emphasize that their anti-Islam and anti-immigration stances should not be seen as forms of racism. Indeed, as soon as xenophobia becomes the generalized commonsense, as something "we all" agree with, it should no longer be called "racism."

Finally, even the social norm that condemns racism (antiracism) seems to be waning in force. For instance, recent Eurobarometer polls indicate that an increasing percentage of Europeans openly acknowledge that they are "racist"—if that means opposing both immigration and the supposed "spoiling" of immigrants. It is therefore not surprising that many voters, including those who do not interact on a daily basis with immigrants, vote for parties that explicitly oppose or seek to limit immigration. That is, people have not only learned the lessons of the elite through discourses circulating in politics and the media, but they also support the politicians who serve as bad examples in the first place. Elite racism thus becomes legitimated through popular racism, a process that also allows openly populist policies to flourish in order to reproduce political power, and not only on the right.

ELITE DISCOURSE AND RACISM

It is against this theoretical, methodological, and political backdrop that some of the properties of elite discourse and racism in the major institutions of Europe must be dealt with. I shall do so by giving a brief summary of the results of various major projects carried out over the last twenty years that address the ways in which immigrants, minorities, refugees, and non-European peoples in general are portrayed, especially in political discourse, news reports, textbooks, and everyday communication (for details, see van Dijk, 1984, 1987a, 1987b, 1991, 1993, 2005, 2007).

The aims of these projects were threefold: (i) to examine the structures of talk and text about Others; (ii) to inquire about the sociocognitive foundations (prejudice, ideology) of such discourse; and (iii) to study its social and political functions. Although each of these discourse genres and contexts retains its own unique characteristics, there are also notable similarities among them due to the generally shared nature of the underlying social representations concerning Others, as reproduced especially through the mass media:

a. Racist discourse follows the general pattern of any ideological discourse and is characterized by an *overall strategy of positive self-presentation and negative Other-presentation* at all levels of text and talk. This polarization between Us and Them and the various ways positive or negative opinions are discursively enhanced may be witnessed in the choice of topics, lexical items, metaphors, hyperboles, euphemisms, disclaimers ("I am not a racist, but …"), storytelling, argumentation, pictures, lay-out, and many other properties of discourse.

b. Parliamentary debates, news, textbooks, and everyday storytelling about Others tend to be limited to a small number of stereotypical topics: illegal immigration; problems of reception and cultural integration; and crime, drugs, and deviance. Overall, the portrayal of the Others emphasizes their Difference, Deviance, and Threat.

c. Part of the overall strategy of positive self-presentation is the routine denial or mitigation of racism, especially among elites.

d. Ethnic minorities have virtually no access to, or control over the discourses generally spoken and written about them by "white" elites.

e. Similarly, discourses *about* Others, or about ethnic issues in general, are not explicitly directed *at* Others, for these tend to be ignored as potential recipients of public text and talk.

These general characteristics of racist discourse will be further explored in relation to the respective genres of institutional public discourse in the next sections.

Parliament and politics

In *parliamentary debates*, discourses practically always focus on problems of "illegal" immigration, and on furthering restrictions on immigration. Typical of such debates is, again, the combination of positive self-presentation, this time in terms of nationalist glorification (about the "long tradition of hospitality for refugees," etc.), and the systematic, but subtle ways in which newcomers are negatively represented as a problem, a financial burden, if not as a threat for "Our" welfare state, the job market, or Western culture, norms, and values in general. Arguments and fallacies are formulated as if keeping Them out is in fact better for Them, alleging that in this way They can contribute to the construction of their own country; can be received closer to home "in their own culture"; and—the most cynical of all fallacies—can be spared the rampant racism in the popular neighborhoods of Our country. Whatever the increasing restrictions on immigration and civil and legal rights, these are always presented as "firm, but fair." And for those countries where immigration occurred later than it did in northwestern Europe, countries such as Italy and Spain, the pervasive if not persuasive argument is that immigration must be restricted because that is what the European Union requires. In the United Kingdom, the focus is on what the right and the tabloids call "bogus refugees," whereas most other countries are engaged in an ongoing debate on the dilemmas of cultural integration. In sum, the main issue in the institutions revolves around the problems allegedly caused by immigrants, but rarely ever around the innumerable problems *experienced by* immigrants and caused by *Us*, ranging from the many forms of discrimination to the hassles of obtaining papers and permits, and facing the related red tape and bureaucracy. Indeed, seldom do parliamentary debates deal with racism, and unlike terrorism, racism is *never* declared to be one of the major problems of the country or of Europe—despite the long devastating history and killing fields of colonialism, the Holocaust, and the "ethnic wars" in Bosnia, Kosovo, and so on. And although for all countries of the EU immigration (in both its legal and irregular forms) has always brought with it a significant economic bonus, instead of bogus refugees, but rarely are such contributions recognized and emphasized in parliamentary debates or in politicians' propagandistic speeches. On the contrary, they know that being "soft" on immigration costs votes among a population that has for decades been brainwashed by political and media discourse to believe that immigration and immigrants are basically bad news. Political programs, policies, and all other political talk and text expressed throughout Europe today are replete with alarming warnings and tough plans to keep *Them* outside of the European Fortress, or to discipline *Them* once they are already inside, for example, by teaching *Them* that they not only have *rights* but also duties.

This general trend in political discourse has reached frantic dimensions after the terrorist attacks of September 11. Whatever the occasional European distance taken with respect to Bush & Co. in the United States, especially with regards to the war in Iraq, terrorism became the number one topic everywhere, as it was closely related to Islamic fundamentalism, and soon to Islam and immigration in general. So much so, that in some countries, such as the Netherlands, Denmark, Austria, and Italy, racist politicians and political parties were able to gain massive followings and enter into government coalitions, even if only for some time—until the mainstream parties realized the propaganda potential of such scare tactics and essentially propagated the same.[5]

The press

The press—its usual symbiosis with national and party politics filling much of its pages—essentially followed suit, with only minor variations as reflected between center-left and the extreme right in politics—the real left being virtually eliminated in Europe (except in poor countries such as Portugal). That is, the topics preoccupying the politicians in parliamentary debates are very similar to those making headlines in the news, and vice versa. Analysis of parliamentary debates has shown that politicians obviously not only read the papers, but also use them as "evidence" in their debates about immigration and minorities. In countries where the right-wing tabloid popular press is powerful, such as the United Kingdom, Germany, Denmark, Austria, and the Netherlands, this means that national politics also is premised on the panic reports of the press.

Yet, despite its dependence on politicians, the press is not their lapdog. It plays its own powerful role in the reproduction of racism, as is shown by numerous analyses in many countries.[6] Even before the news is printed, we find that newsgathering is systematically geared towards the access, or omnipresent voice, of "white" elites when it comes to defining and representing "the ethnic situation." Whatever the ethnic event, it is the (white) politician, mayor, police officer, professor, or other "expert" who is sought out, interviewed, and hence cited. Minority groups, organizations, and spokespersons, which often lack fancy press or public relations departments and specialists, generally have less access. And even when they do, they are much less (and much less credibly) cited, this "weeding" process resulting in one-sided stories that are biased toward "white" commentary. Moreover, I have observed in fieldwork that press releases from minority organizations are, by definition, suspected to be biased and often end up in the wastepaper basket, whereas releases from white people are seen as more "objective."

This is hardly surprising considering that further data show that newsrooms, especially at the top, are generally white. Among elites, ethnic diversity is hardly a prominent value in hiring, especially among those who usually claim to be most cosmopolitan: journalists, scholars, and so on. This means that for a variety of often fallacious reasons, minority journalists seldom get a job at a prominent newspaper, let alone as editors. That is, discrimination already begins at the stage where not even newsgathering and newswriting has begun: in the hiring process. And the fact that the selected white (often male) journalists have less sympathetic understandings of ethnic events, as well as less access to ethnic communities and spokespersons, further explains why the ethnic perspectives of Others are significantly minoritized in the news.

The news on ethnic affairs in the press is conditioned by this context of discrimination and exclusion. It is not surprising to discover that various studies from many different countries have found that topic selection and other news features are, in the best of cases, stereotypical, and in the worst, more or less subtly racist, depending on the newspaper—probably the most blatantly racist being the tabloids, especially in the United Kingdom, Germany, Denmark, and Austria.

First of all, news about the Others is limited to a handful of topics in which various groups may be covered under a large range of topics. As we have seen for political discourse, media discourse in most EU countries focuses primarily on new arrivals and illegal entry; on the problems associated with the reception and integration of immigrants; and on crime and deviance; whereas the problems experienced *by* immigrants receive little attention if any. If racism is dealt with at all, this tends only to occur when the "official" racism of the extreme right is involved (such as that of Le Pen in France or Haider in Austria), but seldom the racisms of the mainstream. There is *never* news on racism in the press, as may be expected, because journalism is not known to be the most self-critical profession—not surprisingly, as journalists seldom read anything negative about themselves in the newspaper. News about the daily lives, work, and leisure of minorities is rare. Their contributions to the economy—hardly a secret—rarely make the headlines. In sum, minorities are portrayed in few, stereotypical and often negative roles.

Beyond these general themes, other aspects of the news are also stacked against immigrants. As may be inferred from the context of news gathering, they are seldom cited, and when they are, they are never cited alone. Rather, news *about* them is gathered from dominant group sources, sometimes even exclusively. In other words, the EU press in general does not define the ethnic situation in terms of the ethnic participants themselves.

Textbooks

In addition to the political and media institutions, educational institutions play a primary role in reproducing social representations in general, and stereotypes and prejudices in particular. Textbooks are defined by their "official knowledge" (Apple, 1993), including the dominant ideologies of the time. This has always been true with the ways in which the world and its people have been represented, for instance, in geography, history, and the (other) social sciences. Textbooks are also known for their national or even nationalist biases, in which the glory days and deeds of the country are magnified and its crimes and misdeeds mitigated or even totally "forgotten." Thus, few are the textbooks in Europe that detail, for example, the horrors and the exploitation of slavery and colonialism.

Textbook analysis shows that similar conclusions should be drawn for the portrayal of non-European minorities and extra-European countries and peoples in general, which more or less subtly feature the usual stereotypes, prejudices, and omissions from a Eurocentric perspective (see Preiswerk, 1980; Klein, 1985; van Dijk, 1987b; Blondin, 1990).

Thus, half of Dutch social science textbooks of the mid-1980s did not even acknowledge the presence of hundreds of thousands of minorities in the country and, even more relevantly, in the classroom. The other half tended to mimic each other in emphasizing cultural differences instead of the similarities between *Us* (Dutch) and *Them* (Turks, Moroccans), while largely ignoring the Surinamese-Dutch population, to whom no different "culture" could be ascribed. Sometimes a few lines would suffice for an entire ethnic community, such as the Moluccans, and such lines in that case would not fail to recall that some younger members once engaged in terrorist acts. Of course, within such a general strategy of positive self-presentation and negative Other-presentation, not much space is dedicated, if at all, to the many forms of everyday Dutch racism against minorities (van Dijk, 1987b).

Further, many other studies of textbooks in Europe and the European-dominated former colonies (the Americas, Australia, and New Zealand) have shown that such representation of minorities in the metropolis is quite similar to the portrayal of non-European peoples and countries internationally. Besides the simplistic stereotypes about a rich North and a poor South (ignoring poverty in the North and riches in many parts of the South, as well as huge differences among the countries of the South), we thus may conclude from topics, lexicon, examples, assignments, maps, photographs, and other discourse features, that whereas *We* are democratic, *They* are dictatorships; that *We* are peaceful and *They* are violent; that *We* are developed and *They* are underdeveloped; that *We* are modern and *They* are backward; that *We* live in houses, and *They* in huts; and so on. At the same time, *We* of course are generous for "helping" *Them*. But the omissions here are sometimes more significant than the stereotypes, for we may read about *Their* poverty, but seldom get even a superficial account of the *causes* of *Their* poverty and *Our* riches.

In the last decade, textbooks have shown some improvement. There are now usually a few pages on immigrants and minorities, and a few (still limited) references to colonialism, discrimination or even racism—but *never* in terms of overall systems of ethnic domination that pervade all domains and at all levels of society, and least of all, among the elites. In this sense, the dominant ideologies of society are faithfully represented and reproduced in the textbooks, even the ethnic ones.

Despite this general situation, education and research are the few domains in society in which alternative views, policies, and principles still have some space. Also, under the pressure of the presence of a growing number of "foreign" students in the classrooms of many European cities, a modest multiculturalism has increasingly been embraced, although usually only in theory, in educational laws, curricula, and textbooks.

Textbooks not only reproduce dominant ideologies; they also represent watered-down versions of earlier science curriculum. Given the racist (and sexist) nature of much science curriculum until at least the Second World War, it is not surprising that contemporary school textbooks are hardly less prejudiced in their depictions of, say, Africans or Asians—or women, for that matter. An analysis of sociology textbooks in the United States and the United Kingdom in the early 1990s, which were written by prominent contemporary scholars such as Anthony Giddens, shows that even the academic study of ethnic relations is not free of biases, stereotypes, and serious omissions, most seriously when (not) dealing with racism (for details, see van Dijk, 1993).

CONCLUSIONS

From this brief survey of some forms of elite discourse and institutional racism in Europe, I would like to emphasize first the prominent role of elites in the reproduction of institutional racism. When confronted with critical analyses of racist structures and strategies in their dominant texts and talk, in all symbolic domains of society (politics, media, education, science, law, etc.), the general tendency among elites has been one of denial and rejection.

True, the blatant and explicit racism of another, prewar era has become exceptional and relegated to the extreme right, even when such groups no longer constitute a mere fringe, or negligible percentage, today. In other words, and as argued earlier, in the perception of many citizens as well, racism is becoming *salonfähig*, and even a "commonsense" reaction to the "invasion" of non-European Others. More seriously, these extremist ideas—for which Others could once again be blamed—are increasingly, and hardly in more attenuated terms, also adopted by mainstream parties in many European countries, and not only on the right.

I have also emphasized that European racism is *not* caused by the massive immigration and presence of Others, but continues a long tradition of racist ideas and practices against Asian, African, or American Others, and against Jewish and Romani Europeans. This historical dimension of the continuity of racist discourse combines with a contemporary sociopolitical dimension in which racism is exercised in terms of ethnic domination, and implemented and reproduced via daily forms of discrimination based on racist ideologies.

We have seen that in all symbolic domains of society, particularly in those "at the top," discourse plays a prominent role in the enactment of discrimination and the reproduction of racist stereotypes, biases, prejudices, and ideologies. Thus, analysis of parliamentary debates and other political discourses shows that whereas racism is officially rejected, elite discourses increasingly represent immigrants, minorities, and refugees as a threat to the welfare state, Western culture, and of course *Our* economic, political, and social domination. This process has been exacerbated by the terrorist attacks perpetrated by some Islamist fanatics, both in the United States and elsewhere. Rightwing parties, with increasingly explicit xenophobic programs and policies, are thus able to garner popular support that may involve more than 20% of the population.

Research shows that the media generally follow suit, or even initiate and emphasize such tendencies, especially in the tabloids and in the rightwing popular press. The rest of the press, although almost never explicitly racist, rarely contributes either to multicultural society through its policies and reporting: hiring of minority journalists is blatantly discriminatory; news gathering is dominated by white males and ignores or problematizes ethnic sources and leaders while favoring elite white definitions of ethnic realities; and reporting on multicultural society itself is usually limited to the coverage of a small number of "problem" topics, such as illegal immigration, the difficulties associated with integration, or crime. As with elites elsewhere, critical analysis of practices, and especially conclusions about the racism in the press, are vehemently rejected. More generally, the media pay much more attention to the problems attributed to minorities than to minorities' experiences and perspectives. And racism, when it is at all reported on, is generally attributed to the extreme right, seldom to mainstream elites, and *never* to the press itself.

With the arrival of growing numbers of minority students, educational institutions have played a prominent role in exploring some of the tenets of multicultural society in areas such as language teaching and some aspects of the curriculum. Yet here we also find many traces of a long history of racist and sexist curricula, often preformulated by the social and natural scientists of an earlier generation. Although improvements have been made during the last decade, textbook analyses show that teaching for multicultural society is at best fragmentary, and that what minimal textual information is offered regarding ethnic minorities and their countries and continents of origin, is replete with stereotypes and prejudices. Overall, Eurocentric bias remains dominant, one in which *We* Europeans (Dutch, English, French, etc.) appear as superior in all relevant domains, while the Others are depicted as inferior. University textbooks may now be more detailed and sophisticated, but they hardly serve as a much better example, for they, too, largely ignore the critical analysis of racism in European society.

In sum, elites and institutions in Europe appear to combine official antiracist doctrine and policies with the popular practices of widespread discrimination and the perpetuation of ethnicist or racist ideologies. When expressed and reproduced in dominant elite discourses, from politics and the media to education and research, these many types of elite racism seriously affect the well-being and civil rights of immigrants, minorities, and refugees. By focusing on illegal immigration, integration problems, crime, violence, terrorism, backwardness, and on the negative characteristics attributed to Others in general, elite discourses are thus able to produce, disseminate, and confirm the widespread prejudices and ideologies that, in turn, give rise to and legitimate everyday discrimination in the domains of immigration, the labor market, housing, politics, education, security, culture, and so on.

Discursive elite racism, thus, is not just "words" or "ideas," but a pervasive and influential social practice that gives rise to concrete forms of ethnic inequality and domination in the daily lives of minorities. This elite racism can be significantly opposed, however, through the production of consistent and critical antiracist discourses of dissent (supported) by both majority and ethnic minority groups and scholars. The future of a peaceful multicultural Europe in the centuries to come depends on such alternative elite discourses, and the ways in which these are able to influence social institutions. Without such dissent, the horrors of ethnic and racial conflict, strife, and even extermination that defined the 20th century are bound to recur. In the contemporary world, both in Europe and elsewhere, there is no alternative for a multicultural and multiethnic society without racism. Antiracist elite discourses and ideologies that support such a society may be able to make it work.

NOTES

1. For details about contemporary racism in general, and "white" European racism in particular, see Back and Solomos, 2000; Boxill, 2001; Bulmer and Solomos, 1999, 2004; Cashmore, 2003; Doane and Bonilla-Silva, 2003; Essed, 1991a and 1991b; Essed and Goldberg, 2002; Feagin, 2000; Feagin et al., 2001; Goldberg, 2002; Goldberg and Solomos, 2002; Marable, 2002; Sears et al., 2000; Solomos and Back, 1996; Wrench and Solomos, 1993; Wieviorka, 1994, 1998.
2. For studies on racism and discourse, see Blommaert and Verschueren, 1998; Jäger, 1992, 1998; Reisigl and Wodak, 2000, 2001; van Dijk, 1984, 1987a, 1987b, 1991, 1993, 2007; Wetherell and Potter, 1992; Wodak and van Dijk, 2000.
3. For further details, see Bataille and Wieviorka, 1994; Bjørgo, 1994; Butterwegge and Jäger, 1993; Evens Foundation, 2001; Hargreaves and Leaman, 1995; Kalpaka and Räthzel, 1992; Mudde, 2004; Poliakov, 1974a and 1974b; Wrench and Solomos, 1993.
4. Pim Fortuyn was a Dutch politician who, after the September 11 attacks on the World Trade Center, gained a massive following in the Netherlands with his anti-Islam politics. He was assassinated in 2002 and that sent a shockwave through the Netherlands where political assassinations had not occurred for many decades. Following his death, his once successful political party slowly disintegrated due to internal conflict.
5. For other studies on racism in politics and political discourse, see Ebel and Fiala, 1983, Goldberg, 2002; Reeves, 1983; Solomos and Back, 1995; van Dijk, 1993; Wodak and van Dijk, 2000.
6. See Chávez, 2001; Cottle, 2000; Hartmann and Husband, 1974; Jäger and Link, 1993; Ruhrmann, 1995; Smitherman-Donaldson and van Dijk, 1987; Ter Wal, 2002; van Dijk, 1991.

REFERENCES

Apple, M. W. (1993). *Official knowledge: Democratic education in a conservative age*. New York: Routledge.

Back, L. and Solomos, J. (Eds.) (2000). *Theories of race and racism: A reader*. London: Routledge.

Barkan, E. (1992). *Retreat of scientific racism: Changing concepts of race in Britain and the United States between the world wars*. Cambridge/New York: Cambridge University Press.

Barker, A. J. (1978). *The African link: British attitudes to the Negro in the era of the Atlantic slave trade, 1550–1807*. London: Frank Cass.

Bataille, P. and Wieviorka, M. (1994). *Racisme et xénophobie en Europe: Une comparaison internationale*. Paris: Éditions La Découverte.

Bjørgo, T. (Ed.) (1994). *Racist violence in Europe*. New York: St. Martin's Press.

Blommaert, J. and Verschueren, J. (1998). *Debating diversity: Analysing the discourse of tolerance*. New York: Routledge.

Blondin, D. (1990). *L'apprentissage du racisme dans les manuels scolaires*. Montréal, Québec: Editions Agence d'Arc.

Boxill, B. R. (Ed.) (2001). *Race and racism*. Oxford/New York: Oxford University Press.

Bulmer, M. and Solomos, J. (Eds.) (1999). *Racism*. Oxford/New York: Oxford University Press.

Bulmer, M. and Solomos, J. (2004). *Researching race and racism*. London/New York: Routledge.

Butterwegge, C. and Jäger, S. (1993). *Rassismus in Europa*. Köln: Bund-Verlag.

Cashmore, E. (2003). *Encyclopedia of race and ethnic studies*. London/New York: Routledge.

Chase, A. (1975). *The legacy of Malthus: The social costs of the new scientific racism*. Urbana, IL: University of Illinois Press.

Chávez, L. R. (2001). *Covering immigration: Popular images and the politics of the nation*. Berkeley, CA: California University Press.

Cottle, S. (Ed.) (2000). *Ethnic minorities and the media*. Buckingham, UK: Open University Press.

Delacampagne, C. (1983). *L'invention de racisme: Antiquité et Moyen Age*. Paris: Fayard.

Doane, A. W. and Bonilla-Silva, E. (Eds.) (2003). *White out: The continuing significance of racism*. New York: Routledge.

Ebel, M. and Fiala, P. (1983). *Sous le consensus, la xénophobie paroles, arguments, contextes (1961–1981)*. Lausanne: Institut de science politique.

Essed, P. (1991a). Knowledge and resistance: Black-women talk about racism in the Netherlands and the USA. *Feminism & Psychology*, Vol. 1, No. 2, pp. 201–219.

Essed, P. (1991b). *Understanding everyday racism: An interdisciplinary theory*. Newbury Park, CA: Sage Publications.

Essed, P. and Goldberg, D. T. (Ed.) (2002). *Race critical theories: Text and context*. Malden, MA: Blackwell Publishers.

Evens Foundation (Ed.) (2001). *Europe's new racism: Causes, manifestations, and solutions*. New York: Berghahn Books.

Feagin, J. R. (2000). *Racist America: Roots, current realities, and future reparations*. New York: Routledge.

Feagin, J. R., Vera, H., and Batur, P. (2001). *White racism: The basics*. New York: Routledge.

Fredrickson, G. M. (2002). *Racism a short history*. Princeton, NJ: Princeton University Press.

Garrido, A. (1999). *Entre gitanos y payos: Relación de prejuicios y desacuerdos*. Barcelona: Flor del Viento.

Goldberg, D. T. (2002). *The racial state*. Oxford: Blackwell.

Goldberg, D. T. and Solomos, J. (Ed.) (2002). *A companion to racial and ethnic studies*. Malden, MA: Blackwell.

Goody, J. (2004). *Islam in Europe*. Cambridge, UK/Malden, MA: Polity Press distributed in the United States by Blackwell Pub.

Haghighat, C. (1988). *Le racisme "scientifique": Offensive contre l'égalité sociale*. Paris: L'Harmattan.

Halliday, F. (2002). *Two hours that shook the world. September 11, 2001: Causes and consequences*. London: Saqi.

Hargreaves, A. G. and Leaman, J. (Eds.) (1995). *Racism, ethnicity, and politics in contemporary Europe*. Aldershot: Elgar.

Hartmann, P. and Husband, C. (1974). *Racism and the mass media*. London: Davis-Poynter.

Jäger, S. (1992). *BrandSätze. Rassismus im alltag*. ('Brandsätze'—Inflammatory sentences/firebombs. Racism in everyday life). DISS-Studien. Duisburg: DISS.

Jäger, S. (1998). *Der Spuk ist nicht vorbei völkisch-nationalistische ideologeme im öffentlichen diskurs der gegenwart*. Duisburg: DISS.

Jäger, S. and Link, J. (1993). *Die vierte gewalt: Rassismus und die medien* (The fourth power: Racism and the media). Duisburg: DISS.

Kalpaka, A. and Räthzel, N. (Eds.) (1992). *Rassismus und migration in Europa*. Hamburg: Argument.

Klein, G. (1985). *Reading into racism: Bias in children's literature and learning materials*. London/Boston, MA: Routledge and Kegan Paul.

Lauren, P. G. (1988). *Power and prejudice: The politics and diplomacy of racial discrimination*. Boulder, CO: Westview Press.

Marable, M. (2002). *The great wells of democracy: The meaning of race in American life*. New York: Basic Books.

Mudde, C. (Ed.) (2004). *Racist extremism in Central and Eastern Europe*. London/New York: Routledge.

Poliakov, L. (1974a). *The Aryan myth: A history of racist and nationalist ideas in Europe*. London: Heinemann.

Poliakov, L. (1974b). *The history of anti-Semitism*. London: Routledge and Kegan Paul.

Preiswerk, R. (1980). *The Slant of the pen: Racism in children's books*. Geneva: Programme to Combat Racism, World Council of Churches.

Reeves, F. (1983). *British racial discourse: A study of British political discourse about race and race-related matters*. Cambridge: Cambridge University Press.

Reisigl, M. and Wodak, R. (Eds.) (2000). *The semiotics of racism: Approaches in critical discourse analysis*. Wien: Passagen.

Reisigl, M. and Wodak, R. (2001). *Discourse and discrimination rhetorics of racism and antisemitism*. London/New York: Routledge.

Ruhrmann, G. (Ed.) (1995). *Das bild der ausländer in der Öffentlichkeit: Eine theoretische und empirische analyse zur fremdenfeindlichkeit* (The image of foreigners in the public sphere: A theoretical and empirical analysis of xenophobia). Opladen: Leske.

San Román, T. (Ed.) (1986). *Entre la marginación y el racismo: Reflexiones sobre la vida de los gitanos*. Madrid: Alianza.

Schiffrin, D., Tannen, D., and Hamilton, H. E. (Eds.) (2001). *The handbook of discourse analysis*. Oxford/Malden, MA: Blackwell Publishers.

Sears, D. O., Sidanius, J., and Bobo, L. (Eds.) (2000). *Racialized politics: The debate about racism in America*. Chicago, IL: University of Chicago Press.

Smitherman-Donaldson, G. and van Dijk, T. A. (Eds.) (1987). *Discourse and discrimination*. Detroit, MI: Wayne State University Press.

Solomos, J. and Back, L. (1995). *Race, politics, and social change*. London: Routledge.

Solomos, J. and Back, L. (1996). *Racism and society*. New York: St. Martins Press.

Ter Wal, J. (Ed.) (2002). *Racism and cultural diversity in the mass media: An overview of research and examples of good practice in the EU Member States, 1995–2000.* Vienna: European Monitoring Center on Racism and Xenophobia.

UNESCO (Ed.) (1983). *Racism, science and pseudo-science.* Paris: Author.

van Dijk, T. A. (1984). *Prejudice in discourse: An analysis of ethnic prejudice in cognition and conversation.* Amsterdam/Philadelphia, PA: J. Benjamins Co.

van Dijk, T. A. (1987a). *Communicating racism: Ethnic prejudice in thought and talk.* Newbury Park, CA: Sage Publications, Inc.

van Dijk, T. A. (1987b). *Schoolvoorbeelden van racisme: De reproduktie van racisme in maatschappijleerboeken* (Textbook examples of racism: The reproduction of racism in social science textbooks). Amsterdam: Socialistische Uitgeverij Amsterdam.

van Dijk, T. (1991). *Racism and the press.* London: Routledge.

van Dijk, T. A. (1993). *Elite discourse and racism.* Newbury Park, CA: Sage Publications.

van Dijk, T. A. (Ed.) (1997). *Discourse studies: A multidisciplinary introduction* (2 Vols.). London: Sage.

van Dijk, T. A. (2005). *Discourse and racism in Spain and Latin America.* Amsterdam: Benjamins.

van Dijk, T. A. (2007). *Racismo y discurso en América Latina.* Barcelona: Gedisa.

van Dijk, T. A. and Kintsch, W. (1983). *Strategies of discourse comprehension.* New York: Academic Press.

Wetherell, M. and Potter, J. (1992). *Mapping the language of racism: Discourse and the legitimation of exploitation.* New York: Columbia University Press.

Wieviorka, M. (Ed.) (1994). *Racisme et xénophobie en Europe: Une comparaison internationale.* Paris: la Découverte.

Wieviorka, M. (1998). *Le racisme: Une introduction.* Paris: La Découverte.

Wodak, R., Nowak, P., Pelikan, J., Gruber, H., de Cillia, R., and Mitten, R. (1990). *Wir sind alle unschuldige täter.* Diskurshistorische studien zum nachkriegsantisemitismus ("We are all innocent perpetrators": Discourse historic studies in postwar anti-Semitism). Frankfurt/Main: Suhrkamp.

Wodak, R. and van Dijk, T. A. (Eds.) (2000). *Racism at the top: Parliamentary discourses on ethnic issues in six European states.* Klagenfurt, Austria: Drava Verlag.

Wrench, J. and Solomos, J. (Eds.) (1993). *Racism and migration in Western Europe.* Oxford: Berg.

CHAPTER SIX

The popular racial order OF "urban" America: Sport, identity, AND THE politics OF culture[1]

MICHAEL D. GIARDINA

CAMERON MCCARTHY

University of Illinois, Urbana-Champaign

Obviously, the political task is not to refuse representational politics—as if we could. The juridical structures of language and politics constitute the contemporary field of power; hence, there is no position outside this field, but only a critical genealogy of its own legitimating practices ... [T]he task is to formulate within this constituted frame a critique of the categories of identity that contemporary juridical structures engender, naturalize, and immobilize.

—JUDITH BUTLER (1990, P. 8)

INTRODUCTION

New times and new trends must always be met with new approaches and ways of thinking aimed at better understanding one's conjunctural moment. Overlooked in the course of America's current global agenda of preemptive war, neoliberal "democracy," and the unremitting assaults on civil liberties in our post-9/11 moment is that "culture and the critical methodologies used for producing truth" (Denzin, 2004, p. 137) have become two of its greatest casualties. From the creation of the Patriot Act, and congressional approval for unilateral intervention in Iraq, to the passage of the "Clear Skies Initiative" (read: increase pollution) and the

"No Child Left Behind" bill (the second-largest unfunded mandate in US history, often referred to by 2004 Presidential hopeful Howard Dean, 2003 as the "No School Board Left Standing" bill), the current state of American democracy as enumerated in its raced, gendered, and class-based struggles stands at the precipice of serious crisis. However, and as we have become all too well aware, the Bush administration's sociopolitical war of position, to borrow a phrase from Gramsci, is not limited solely to geopolitical domination. Increasingly, we see a revitalized neo-conservative agenda gain momentum with respect to popular forms of culture—especially sport—as the current regime carries out mind-numbing assaults on Title IX[2] and uses the master trope of baseball as a myopic rallying cry to foster nation-alist sentiments that ring hollow the patronage of "freedom" and "democracy." Not to be outdone, popular sporting institutions continue to remain beholden to a poli-tics of racial representation that reverberated throughout much of the 1980s and 1990s inasmuch as perpetuating a status quo premised on sport as part and parcel of the (fictional) meritocratic American dream. However, when we look closer at the competing and, often, contradictory, messages being disseminated through popular forms of sporting culture (movies, television, literature, video games, etc.), the co-articulations of race, gender, nation, and democracy within sport writ large can ultimately be read as "pedagogical and policy-making enterprise[s] actively engaged in the cultural landscaping of national identity and the 'schooling' of the minds of young children" and adults alike (Giroux, 1995, p. 65).

In the broader (post-)Clinton/Bush II moment (of which 9/11 is but one aspect), it is important for us to confront such disquieting developments head-on by doing everything we can to unmask the unequal power relations at play that are concerned with the regulation, management, and manipulation of populations in general via technologies of containment, surveillance, and subjectification. While some might ask "Why sport?" at a time when such things as public education, the environment, or civil liberties are under assault, we agree with David L. Andrews and Michael Silk's (2001) assertion that sport carries with it the most legible form of cultural shorthand for understanding the operation of power in a given con-text. Moreover, as David Rowe (1999) reminds us, "sport and the sports media, as cultural goods *par excellence*, are clearly a central element in a larger process (or set of processes) that is reshaping society and culture" (p. 19). In particular, the popular negotiation and representation of race and racialized identity has long been a favored instrument within popular sporting figurations for perpetuating a white capitalist patriarchal hegemony. This is revealed most notably in relation to a slew of recent cinematic endeavors such as *He Got Game* (Lee, 1998), *Hoop Dreams* (James and Marx, 1994), and *Love and Basketball* (Prince-Bythewood, 2000); the rising prominence of a new class of black entrepreneurs as signified by former National Basketball Association (NBA) star Earvin "Magic" Johnson and

Black Entertainment Television (BET) founder and current Charlotte Bobcats (NBA expansion team) owner Robert Johnson (see Giardina and Cole, 2003); and the public-private investment in the future of (white, middle-class) American girlhood as located within the alleged pro-family, pro-empowerment, pro-girl rhetoric of both the Women's National Basketball Association and the Women's United Soccer Association (Giardina and Metz, 2005).

But, as it is increasingly important to point out, "sport," in its multiple incarnations, is, of course, representative of, and influenced by, more than just a US-based context (irrespective of a pre- or post-9/11 demarcation). The shifting conditions and multiple figurations of what Douglas Kellner (1995) calls the "global popular" have yielded a fertile terrain for the rapid interconnectivity of popular cultural artifacts to be experienced the world-over, raising challenges to the problematic place-boundedness of the (British) cultural studies tradition (see Carrington, 2001a), and forcing us to (re-)evaluate our theoretical approach to "doing" sport-related Cultural Studies research (see especially Andrews and Giardina, 2005). For example, recent popular-culture interventions such as the 2002 British film *Bend it like Beckham*, which privileges the voices of British Asians in a narrative of women's empowerment, sporting participation, and multicultural inclusivity, are caught up in a rubric of cultural representation akin to the exploitative and assimilationist rhetoric of the 1980s under Reagan/Thatcher governments, and yet, at the same time, are cast as progressive cultural artifacts in light of complex questions over race, culture, and identity that underpin their political agendas and become manifest in the popular arena of contemporary Britain (Giardina, 2003). Similarly, at the 2000 Olympic Games in Sydney, Australia both reveled in, and revealed, the dynamic tensions of (stylish) hybridity as located in the celebrity-hood of Australian-Aboriginal track star Cathy Freeman *vis-à-vis* fostering a national discussion on race that was, from the start, couched within monological thinking on multiculturalism (Bruce and Hallinan, 2001), but which was correlatively credited for bringing critical tensions over ethnicity to a mainstream (global) audience in a country embroiled in its own struggle to come to terms with its less-than-stellar treatment of native Aboriginals. Likewise, the eminent malleability of professional tennis player Martina Hingis's mediated subjectivity—in terms of its ability to appeal to highly localized cultural meanings and desires—renders such a flexible citizen (see Ong, 1999; Giardina, 2001) as "a highly productive and prophetic instrument of the ascendant global capitalist order" (Andrews and Jackson, 2001, p. 15).

In part, we are experiencing a fresh take on Paul Gilroy's (1995) conceptualization of the "Black Atlantic." Whereas Gilroy speaks specifically to the impact of the trans-Atlantic movement of black people between Africa and Europe and the New World, arguing in the process that the diasporic movement of peoples has had a profound impact on black identity formation in particular, we want to situate our discussion within and against such a configuration on a broader level germane to the contemporary racial order in the United States. Given the intensification of diasporic flows of cultural and economic capital—aided most significantly by deepening patterns of aestheticization in popular culture as foregrounded in transnational advertising and new forms of electronic mediation—the new millennial nation-state now comprises an increasingly hybridized population where practices of identity construction are no longer bounded by physical borders (Silk, 2001; Giardina, 2003). Rather, practices favoring "flexibility, mobility, and repositioning in relation to markets, governments, and cultural regimes" (Ong, 1999, p. 6) are becoming more and more common. Such heightened transnational migration and increasing processes of electronic mediation have now seemingly separated culture altogether from place; difference has become an abstract value that can be dirempted from specific groups and settings and combined and recombined in ways that allow, for example, clothing designer magnates like Tommy Hilfiger to appropriate elements of hip hop culture and sell these elements back into the inner city itself, while these "ghettoized" elements of urban cultural signification are simultaneously marketed, with overwhelming success, to a white consumer audience.

Culture quite obviously plays a pivotal role within this context by actively translating new economic, political, and moral imperatives into popular commonsense ideas of voluntarism, community responsibility, security, and individual entrepreneurship and self-help. In this new world of cultural fluidity, it is the affectively charged realm of the popular that drives, and is driven by, formative encounters with national (and national-*istic*) identities and cultural signification. Most significantly, multicultural narratives have become deeply intertwined with, and understood to manifest themselves as part of, this larger reiterative frame of reference, which reinforces and gives tacit approval to the exploitative images, representations, and practices dominating late-capitalist commodity-sign culture. However, we believe that, as a formation, "culture" has been, and remains, significantly under-theorized within both scholarly writing and popular public policy discourses such as multiculturalism (see also McCarthy et al., 2003). By and large, *it* is often treated as a preexistent, unchanging deposit, consisting of a rigidly bounded set of elite or folkloric knowledge, values, experiences and linguistic practices specific to particular groups (see Hirsch et al., 1993; Bennett, 1998). Moreover, the current approach to culture, as the production and circulation of meaning in stratified contexts—even within more critical discourses and research paradigms such as cultural studies—remains incomplete. Instead, we need to think about culture along the lines suggested by Tony Bennett (1995, 1996), whereby culture is understood not so much as the distinctive forms of "a whole way of life" (Williams, 1961), but, rather as (or also as) a set of dynamic, productive, and generative material (and immaterial) practices that regulate social conduct and behavior, and that emphasize personal self-management (i.e., the modification of habits, tastes, and styles), political affiliation, and transnational identity. Given the power of transnational (cultural) sporting agents, intermediaries, and institutions to actively work as pedagogical sites hegemonically reinscribing and representing neoliberal discourses on sport, culture, nation, and democracy, it is imperative for us as cultural critics to excavate and theorize the "contingent relations, structures, and effects that link sport forms with prevailing determinate forces" (Andrews, 2001, p. 116). In this chapter, we therefore offer a critical, cultural pedagogy of sport that can "help critical researchers make sense of the world of domination and oppression as they work to bring about a more just, democratic, and egalitarian society" (Kincheloe and McLaren, 2000, p. 285) while at the same time inquiring into the "conditions of emergence" (Butler, 1999, p. 15) that constitute "urban" popular culture in general, and urban sporting representation(s) in specific.

To this end, we critically interrogate the prevailing contemporary figurations of urban popular culture as suggested within and against filmic narratives of sport, attempting, in the process, to forge a contextual understanding of the conflictual representations of (urban) subjectivity within American popular culture. We begin by locating urban America within broader conjunctural developments that have given rise to its mainstream appellation. We then move on to focus on how urban popular culture is currently represented within broader "pop" culture formations, especially Hollywood cinema. We conclude by interrogating the Spike Lee (1998) film *He Got Game*, which we think is both an example and a symptom of popular racial representation that is compatible with the politics of a conservative (black) middle class. In doing so, we answer Norman K. Denzin's (2002) call[3] to challenge the popular racial order by advocating for a radical, progressive democracy that adheres to a (post-)performative moral ethic of interpretation, care, and social change.

"REPRESENTING" IN THE 1990S

> How and why have other relations of power and sociality—those, for example, traversing local, national, and global economic institutions—become less central to adjudicating ethical citizenship in the United States?
>
> —LAUREN BERLANT (1996, P. 398)

In 1992, Stuart Hall's essay "What is this 'black' in black popular culture?" offered a preliminary response to the conjunctural specificities out of which the overarching narrative of "black popular culture" was being shaped and defined. Some ten years later—with the legacy of the Clinton years still to be imagined and the phantasmagoric *mediacracy* of postmodern America at center stage—it is perhaps appropriate to begin by rephrasing the question, asking instead, "What is this 'popular' in urban popular culture?" However, to spin Hall's original question is more of a rhetorical observation about such a polysemous formation as "urban popular culture" than a specific theoretical strategy. To attempt to theoretically ground this particular formation—and those various groups that identify with it—would wrongly suggest that it could ever be unproblematically subsumed under one umbrella term. Rather, for our purposes here, neither the "urban" nor the "popular" need necessarily be divorced from its whole: the (re-)iterative discursivity of the formation itself.

That said, the location of such contestation will, invariably, reside in the realm of the popular—the affectively charged landscape that, as Andrews (1998) argues, "advanced the discriminatory logics of Reaganism [... and] reasserted a vision of an America dominated by a white, heterosexual, and patriarchal, middle-upper class" (p. 198). The Trinidadian cultural Marxist, C. L. R. James, similarly maintains that understanding popular culture is crucial to unraveling the interplay of power in modern life. As James critically insists in books such as *American Civilization* (1993), one can get a better insight into the tensions and contradictions of contemporary society by observing and interpreting popular culture than by analyzing canonical texts. His chapter on "The Popular Arts and Modern Society," makes this point abundantly clear:

> It is in the serious study of, above all, Charles Chaplin, Dick Tracy, Gasoline Alley, James Cagney, Edward G. Robinson, Rita Hayworth, Humphrey Bogart, genuinely popular novels like those of Frank Yerby (*Foxes of Arrow, The Golden Hawk, The Vixen, Pride's Castle*) ... that you find the clearest ideological expression of the sentiments and deepest feelings of the American people and a great window into the future of America and the modern world. This insight is not to be found in the works of T. S. Eliot, of Hemingway, of Joyce, of famous directors like John Ford or Rene Clair. (1993, p. 119)

What James is pointing toward through this revisionary—in fact, radical—strategy is the fact that our popular arena is perhaps the clearest window into the contextual specificities of American life; a context deeply informed by the underlying crises and tensions of cultural integration and reproduction in our time (McCarthy and Dimitriadis, 2000).

As witnessed throughout the decade of the 1990s, discourses centering on race and diversity became increasingly prevalent in mainstream popular discussions. In the case of what has routinely been referred to as the overarching sphere of "urban popular culture," a seemingly progressive but transparently conservative shift has occurred over the last decade whereby the faux color-blind "all-Americaness" of such 1980s luminaries as Michael Jordan and Bill Cosby has been replaced by a multiplicity of representations depicting so-called "authentic" urban cultural emissaries. Located within the sociopolitical milieu of the Clinton administration (see below), the (multi-)cultural landscape has coalesced into a *melange* of images and representations that *appear* to shift toward a more diverse and oppositional version of urban cultural signification. But, in the process of (re-)defining acceptable boundaries of diversified social relations (just as we had nefariously seen in the Reagan Era), tropes such as "multiculturalism," "hybridity," and "diaspora" became renarrated "through a proliferation of images and practices into a normalized, non-politically charged discourse that assumed that ethnic minority communities were homogenous and somehow representative of an authentic and unified culture" (Giardina and Metz, 2001, p. 210).

For example, we witnessed the emergence of hip hop culture in the mid-to-late 1970s originally staking out a position as a progressive social movement that cut across racial and ethnic geographies in the face of eroding urban infrastructures (Watkins, 1998). However, as S. Craig Watkins reminds us, it was not until hip hop became intensely commodified—for better or worse—that it began to receive any widespread attention and become an economically viable outlet for the expression of black culture. But this commodified expression of the self became screened through the lens of profitability, not one's culture; narratives of resistance, revolution, and militancy were diluted and/or tailored to meet an ever-growing (white) audience. Farai Chideya (1997) cogently explicates this phenomenon:

> Who's pushing the rawest rhymes to No. 1 on the charts? For years now, the largest volume of hip hop albums has been sold to white kids who've deposed heavy metal and elevated hip hop to the crown of Music Most Likely to Infuriate My Parents. The suburban rebellion—its record buying tastes, its voyeurism of what too often it views as "authentic black culture"—has contributed to the primacy of the gangsta-rap genre. (p. 47)

Given the hearty consumption of hip hop by white youth, it is no surprise that other facets of urban or "street" culture—from the militant to the mundane—have been similarly appropriated and repositioned to meet with the demands of a specific target audience.

Chief among these other facets of stylized cultural signification, the popular resonance generated by and through the NBA and its players during the 1990s stands as a practical exemplar of the renarration of blackness as articulated through the urban center during the Clinton Era. Previously, the "War on Drugs" narrative of the Reagan Era (circa 1986) privileged basketball as a solution to inner-city problems defined by gangs, violence, and out-of-control consumption

(Cole, 1996). As C. L. Cole argues, "Sport and gangs [became] represented not only as channels for what [was] understood to be corporeal predispositions of African-American youth but as the available substitutes for the 'failed black family'" (Cole, 2001, p. 69). In the parlance of modern identities, gang members, whose deviance was coded through notions of laziness, unemployment, and violence thus "produce[d] what/who are normal and acceptable: the urban African-American athlete" (ibid., p. 70). Over time, as witnessed in the early- to mid-1990s, the dialogues surrounding the so-called "Crime Bill" debates of 1994 and the Gingrich Revolution of 1996 moved to articulate basketball with criminality (Cole and Giardina, 2003), criticizing endeavors such as "Midnight Basketball" (see Hartmann, 2001) as a waste of public resources.[4] But now, it seems, there has been yet another shift in the popular acceptance—one might say, celebration—of the urban style. Aside from NBA players and their mediatized representations of the "streetball" lifestyle, we similarly witness: video games such as *NBA Street, Vol. 2* becoming hugely profitable commercial successes on high-end video game consoles like *PlayStation2* and *Xbox*; ESPN, the premier cable sports channel, recently featuring an ongoing documentary about a traveling "streetball" barnstorming group that regularly sells-out local arenas, playing a sort of Harlem Globetrotters meets Rucker Park style of basketball; MTV hosting a "Big Brother"-like reality show called "Who Got Game?" in which street-ball players are voted off the show on a weekly basis; and basketball-themed movies organized around African-American basketball players reeling in rave reviews. Obviously, this shifting view of and intersection with the popular terrain did not happen overnight.

The racial politics of Clintonian neoliberalism

The inauguration of William Jefferson Clinton as the 42nd President of the United States is often marked as a symbolic shift in the representational politics of American cultural identity (Moallem and Boal, 1999). From the outset of his tenure as President, Clinton displayed a flair for acknowledging diversity, trying hard to distance himself (at least, in the court of popular opinion) from the assaultive and exploitative assimilationist rhetoric of his predecessors. Indeed, as Clinton would often proclaim, multicultural racial equality was a keystone concept to fully realizing the promise of the New Democratic (centrist) country he was envisioning (Klein, 2002a). At his inauguration, Maya Angelou further amplified "the significant discursive shift from 'melting pot' to 'mosaic'" (Moallem and Boal, 1999, pp. 246–247) by reciting her poem "On the Pulse of the Morning," which imagined the realization of a multicultural separatist nation. That is to say, where before the effacement and acceptance of difference and diversity had been couched within the prospect of assimilating to white, middle-class value institutions (e.g., as seen in *The Cosby Show*), Clintonian racial politics publicly endeavored to cast the country as being a mosaic, a pastiche of ethnic and racial groupings (i.e., contra "melting pot" allegories), all coming together and working toward a real and imagined strengthening of the nation. However, where issues of race were unavoidable in policy-making decisions, the Clinton administration "sought to portray critical decisions [...] as race-neutral" (Horne, 1994, p. 185). Difference and diversity would be hailed as strengthening the material and symbolic value of the nation, but only when such overt difference could be celebrated within a framework of conservative racial representation.

Woven into and through this focus on diversity was Clinton's promise to energize the American economy and pull it out from under the Bush (George Herbert) recession. From his quest of "building a bridge to the 21st century" (both in terms of accessible technology for all and improved race relations) to balancing the budget, the Clinton administration generally maintained a fiscal conservative approach to the global marketplace. At the same time, however, it held steadfast to its left-of-center appearance by marketing (strands of) neoliberalism as a socially progressive tripartite focus on opportunity, responsibility, and community: what Clinton (and others have) called "Third Way" governance. The President coyly spelled out the social dimension of his Third Way thinking—without ever mentioning it by name—in his 1996 monograph *Between hope and history: Meeting America's challenges for the 21st Century*:

> It was clear to me that if my vision of twenty-first century America was to become reality, we had to break out of yesterday's thinking and embark on a new and bold course for the future, with a strategy rooted in three fundamental American values: ensuring that all citizens have the *opportunity* to make the most of their own lives; expecting every citizen to shoulder the *responsibility* to seize that opportunity; and working together as a *community* to live up to all we can be as a nation. (pp. 7–8, emphasis in original)

This catchy tripartite slogan of opportunity, responsibility, and community was to be repeated *ad nauseum* during the course of his reelection campaign, which stressed at every turn that citizenship was inherently based on one's public(-private) investment in the well-being of his or her fellow citizen.[5]

Specific to the case of the multicultural popular, the administration's abovementioned talking points were all couched within a (neoconservative) cultural context of family values, crime, and imagined community. Policies aimed at fiscal discipline, health care reform, investment in education and training, welfare-to-work legislation, urban renewal projects (i.e., Empowerment Zones), and taking a "hard line" (read: conservative) on crime and punishment all became part of Clinton's (sociocultural) war of position (Giddens, 1998, 2001).[6] Within this framework, as Mary K. Coffey (2003) explains, community was "paradoxically asserted as a natural, pre-political zone yet also as a key terrain for the successful actualization of the goals and aspirations of government" (p. 225). These "aspirations of government," at least in the Clintonian deployment of the Third Way, lean heavily on notions of neoliberalism that seek a middle-ground between state welfare ("socialism") and laissez-faire capitalism. As a result, such a configuration "relies upon mechanisms for governing 'through society,' through programs that shape, guide, channel, and upon responsible, self-disciplining social subjects" (Hay, 2003, p. 166). From the start, however, these subjects are conceived of as having unfettered access to the (fictional) American Dream, and are correlatively imbricated in the formative mechanisms of such a discursive iteration. But the center does not hold. As Lauren Berlant (1997) articulates, the "promise" of this Dream is continually "voiced in the language of unconflicted personhood: to be American [...] would be to inhabit a secure space of liberated identities and structures that seem to constrain what a person can do in history" (p. 4).

In truth, such a dressed-up neoliberal fantasy hails the prospect of racial difference without (making a) difference, projecting a utopian vision of racial and ethnic diversity that allows for—in fact, vigorously encourages—cultural difference, but only when constrained (and, some may argue, contained) within nonthreatening, nonpoliticized formations ready for easy and profitable consumption by mainstream America. Denzin (2002) rightly dismisses the pseudoprogressiveness of such a (right-)centrist perspective, arguing that "only a conservative racial ideology masquerading as white liberalism would contend that racial difference can be so easily transcended" (p. 53). Thus, while signifying a rhetorical break with the previous Reagan/Bush administration's callous vision of an assimilatory racial dynamic on the part of minority populations as the paramount goal for achieving the so-called "American Dream," Clinton was able to be nearly as racially-conservative as his predecessor(s) by trading on his progressive currency within America's popular arena and presenting himself as someone connected to, and understanding of the plight of, marginalized American citizens.[7]

But what the Clinton administration—and, in fact, most conservative essayists—failed to grasp is that race is always and only contextually performative, that is, linguistically and discursively constructed "within specific historical and institutional sites within specific discursive formations and practices, and by specific enunciative strategies" (Hall, 1996, p. 4; see also Butler, 1990; Mirón and Inda, 1999). In recent history, the auratic status of race—the notion of race as residing in "origins," "ancestry," "linguistic" or "cultural" unity—has been shattered, overwhelmed by the immense processes of hybridity unleashed in contemporary life. This is no more so true than in the realm of the popular. A great exemplar of this play of hybridity and rearticulation of race in popular life exists in the form of Hollywood filmic fantasies about the urban experience. These fantasies foreground particularly hard-edged hyperreal narratives about the lived and commodified existence of the inner-city poor and their production of popular cultural forms linked both to the valorization and abuse of the body. We discuss this in greater detail in the next section.

Cinematic revelations

Throughout the late 1980s and into the early 1990s, Hollywood cinema saw an influx of, and was then dominated by, a series of *hood/barrio* films that adhered to the realist code of filmmaking (Denzin, 2002). That is to say, these films presume a near-perfect relationship between a thing and its representation as can exist and, because of this, the images and narratives depicted should be taken as if they were factual. In the process, these films reinscribe a racial order that privileges "White" over "Other"—the assimilation of black/brown culture to white, middle-class, narratives of nation, family, and law. However, if these images are taken as the "facts of life" (a constructed and negotiated term bearing little resemblance to lived textuality) that they proclaim to be, the unproblematic representations of, for instance, the surveillance narrative in hood films, sets in motion a schema whereby to question such a representation would be to question the larger state apparatus that supports the status quo. Contextually speaking, movies in this vein, such as *Menace II Society* (Hughes et al., 1993) and *Boyz n the Hood* (Singleton, 1991), fuel conservative discourses about race and family relations by allegedly professing to present their narrative representations as true-to-life glimpses into the lives of African-American and Latino/a youth—which, at the time of their release, was not a glimpse most middle-class white Americans had been familiar with. In doing so, cinematic representations of graphic gun-and-drug violence in the black hood and the sexual violence within the Latino/a prison system serves to further demonize each group (Denzin, 2002).

Up until 1995 or so, this genre remained relatively unreflexive, leaving larger sociopolitical and socioeconomic factors untouched, and explicitly grounding the source of such violence and moral decadence in the rhetorically tendacious claims of the dysfunctional urban family structure, absent male role models, and instances of personal failure. By representing a community seemingly out of control, on the verge of implosion (be it through *hood*/gang or prison/gang representations), and on the brink of spilling over into white America, the hood/barrio films acted in accordance not with a political, interventionist agenda but, rather, a neo-conservative agenda to inscribe on, and mark, the body—in typical Reaganite fashion—as the root cause of national problems. However, as the Clintonite project began to fully take shape, such filmic narratives slowly began to react and change. Whereas the late 1980s/early 1990s were overrun with cinematic racial allegories of the black and brown hood that "celebrate[d] a violent, mysoginis-tic masculinity" and "turn[ed] women into crack addicts, ho's, bitches, and lazy welfare mothers" (Denzin, 2002, p. 113), the latter half of the 1990s saw filmmakers—especially African-American filmmakers—purporting to reverse such a trend (Denzin, 2003). No longer was the assimilation model explicitly promoted in films addressing issues of urban American culture; rather, it was subtly written into the underlying fabric of the narrative. Films ranging from *What's Cooking?* (Berges and Chadha, 2000) and *How Stella Got Her Groove Back* (McMillan and Sullivan, 1998) to *Soul Food* (Tillman, 1997) and *Bamboozled* (Lee, 2000) marked a new paradigm for representing minority groups and charac-ters in a positive, multicultural light. That is to say, movies such as these publicly endeavored to create a new space for what Manthia Diawara has referred to as a "New Black Planet," by putting forth examples of a progressive, feminist, neo-black aesthetic that screened race not through a white lens but, rather, through a critically informed, race-conscious, female-centric point of view. And yet, whilst moving away from blatant violence and rampant sexism in favor of opportunity, community, and responsibility, the narrative arcs remained locked in a liminal space between progressive and conservative insights. This follows an argument set out by bell hooks (1990, 1995) who—while envisioning a politics of radical black subjectivity as a liberatory site of transformation from the margins of society where counterhegemonic narratives and constructions of the self can be fully real-ized—contends that much of what passes today for counterhegemonic discursive practices are anything but that. Rather, as hooks writes, they are a reinscription of the very same hegemonic structures that such practices allege to disrupt or challenge. Put another way, despite progressive *moments* of liberation found in films in the mid-to-late-1990s (e.g., the explicit and proud ownership of their own sexuality by the two lead female characters in *How Stella Got Her Groove Back* (McMillan and Sullivan, 1998), the positive representation of a lesbian relation-ship in *What's Cooking?* (Berges and Chadha, 2000), or the strong, family-cen-tered narrative of *Soul Food* (Tillman, 1997), a majority of these films ultimately fall back on rather conservative positioning, locating their leading characters in a deeper ideological narrative that sees them as almost within reach of breaking free from the bonds of social entrapment, but ultimately unable to fully overcome the powerful constraints generated by such conservative representations.

So, how does sport fit into this highly contestatory and contradictory dis-cursive space? What is the role of sport in this historical moment of the rising popular saliency of urban cultural forms? Related to the place of sport within 1990s Hollywood cinema, for instance, wildly-successful (pseudo-)documentary films such as *Hoop Dreams* (James and Marx, 1994) were to bring (white) middle-class America face-to-face with urban American sporting narratives, as framed through the "realist" lens of its independent filmmakers (see Cole and King, 1998). "Shocking" white audiences around the country with its "real life" depiction of daily life in urban America—specifically, the Cabrini Green Housing Project in Chicago, Illinois—and receiving near-unanimous praise within the mainstream press (Ebert, 1998), the film was stitched into the ideologically represented fabric of the *hood* as constructed in early-1990s films such as *Boyz n the Hood* (Singleton, 1999) and *Menace II Society* (Hughes et al., 1993). That is, viewers were presented with a narrative reinforcing the idea that "the postindustrial ghetto suffocates the lives and opportunities of poor African-American youths" (Watkins, 1998, p. 222), and that those who live(d) in such a place are there of their own lifestyle choice, not larger systemic problems. Poverty, welfare dependency, and a struggling economy were thus articulated to individual shortcomings and the breakdown of the (mythic) family among minority segments of the population (Jeffords, 1994; Cole, 1998). Correlatively, as Cole and King (1998) write with regard to the representation of the film's two main characters, African-American high school basketball players William Gates and Arthur Agee:

> The figure of the basketball player, defined over and against the criminal (gang member that governs America's representation of African-American men in the mid-1980s to the mid-1990s) [...] functions as a means of displacement that reconciles middle-class America's sense of itself as compassionate as it calls for, and endorses, increasingly vengeful punitive programs. (p. 78)

Success among young black youth had thus been coded with "escaping" from the "inner-city jungle" through the most (allegedly) viable of avenues: (the prospect of playing) professional sport (specifically basketball).

While indicative of the politics of representation governing the first half of the 1990s, *Hoop Dreams* does not resonate quite so well with the latter half of the decade. Or does it? Enter Spike Lee. Already highly regarded as one of America's most important filmmakers—and a self-avowed avid sports fan (of the New York Knicks and New York Yankees)—Lee took his turn in narrating the urban condition through sport with his 1998 release *He Got Game* a coming-of-age drama about a top-ranked high school basketball star from Coney Island, New York, and his turbulent relationship with his (incarcerated) father. In the next section, we take up this film and argue that its narrative structure succinctly captures the (urban) cultural milieu of the Clinton Era as represented in popular culture; that is, a milieu that embodies a "black postnationalist essentialism" (Wallace, 1992, p. 125) which is "compatible with the politics of a conservative black middle class" (Denzin, 2002, p. 154). Further, and while not to (over)-generalize about contemporary

Hollywood cinema, we believe the film to be indicative of the larger racist infrastructure governing the current conjunctural moment in American history.

"SCREENING" RACE IN AMERICA

> The contemporary history of race relations in America is, in large part, a history of the representation of violent, youthful minority group members in mainstream Hollywood cinema and in commercial television.
>
> —NORMAN K. DENZIN (2002, P. 1)

Spike Lee's (1998) urban basketball drama *He Got Game* is sutured into the prevailing sociopolitical landscape of (urban) America in the mid- to late-1990s. Generally speaking, both public and popular dispositions toward US urban centers have over the years followed a contradictory hypermoral impulse. At various times emphasizing cold disinterest, at other times seen as the object of almost laboratory-like social experimentation and intervention, urban America hangs in a liminal state between all-out decay and the possibility of social and economic renewal. This pendulum of neglect and intervention swings, sometimes frenetically, one way or the other, as the urban context continues to be viewed by bureaucratic and cultural elites through a paradigm of cultural deficit and moral underdevelopment. Since the high point of the Civil Rights era and its culminating fruition in the ameliorative programs of the Great Society/War on Poverty initiated under the Lyndon B. Johnson administration in the late 1960s (e.g., Head Start), the urban centers of the United States have been the target of revisionary strategies of both policy makers and policy intellectuals. This revisionary disposition was, to give but one example, operationalized in the policies of benign neglect found during the Nixon/Carter years and the aggressive disinvestment of the Reagan/Bush era. At the same time, the urban centers—despite their profound marginalization in terms of the uneven allocation of public and private resources—have attained a surplus status in popular media and public policy discourses as the site of the most profound problems affecting the country, and as, in fact, the tragic ballast weighing down the ship of state.

It could be said that up until the 1990s the dominant framework around which both public policy and the surplus popular social meanings were generated was the Keynesian formula of (more or less) social welfarism. In the early 1990s, this overwhelming paradigm of Keynesianism was both rhetorically and practically overturned as the newly ordained Clinton administration sought to connect urban centers to its broad-scale, global, neoliberal initiatives *vis-à-vis* universalizing entrepreneurship. As the administration sought to spread the gospel of unfettered capital around the world through the North American Free Trade Agreement

(NAFTA), General Agreements on Tariffs and Trades (GATT), and the World Trade Organization (WTO), it simultaneously turned its brassy new corporatist gaze on the inner city by speaking the language of enterprise zones, self-help, and community voluntarism. The urban center was/is thus a piece of a much larger puzzle of the proliferation of new social meanings that translate the capitalist enterprise form of modern conduct to the conduct of organizations (e.g., charter schools, corporate partnerships, and voucher programs in education) and the conduct of individuals; the "problems" of inner-city life have become the new targets of self-management, regulation, the restraint of individual appetites, and the moral purposive voluntaristic investment of the inner-city dweller him- or herself.

But, as we have also seen, these so-called "problems" have also become highly marketable images for which mainstream American youth culture has become heavily invested in consuming. As we have increasingly witnessed, the marketing armatures of corporate America have aided in turning the urban condition into one of exploding profitability as they rewrite the historical conventions associated with urban culture primarily in terms of the "stylized elements of cool" (Carrington, 2001b; Klein, 2002b), which it has come to signify to a primarily white youth market. As part of this containment and redirection of racial antagonism—seen within an historical context of the rapid changes taking place in the material reality and fortunes of people, their environments, and the institutional apparatuses that govern and affect their lives—Clinton would prove himself a master craftsman, a silver fox speaking in forked tongues to both the African-American poor and the white professional middle classes. What appeared to be smoke and mirrors were actually highly calculated tactics in which representational politics assumed a pivotal role. The State, corporate interest, and private individuals/groups now operate in tandem in a vigorous effort aimed at reorienting the urban centers in the United States from a Keynesian, welfarist ethos toward a post-Civil Rights, post-Keynesian, postwelfarist future. This trend is seen most concretely in the creation of Empowerment Zone initiatives[8] that have heightened public-private investment in historically low-income urban centers. But, as C. L. Cole (2001) is keen to point out, such investment amounts to little more than rewriting the urban communal landscape—organized around the systematic displacement of the "aesthetically disenchanting"—and embedding in the "rebuilt" urban center "highly marketable, sanitized styles and signs of subversion, antiauthoritarianism, and experimentation that designate it as an 'alternative space'" (p. 117).

While *He Got Game* (Lee, 1998) is a direct response to these changing material conditions reflective in and of the urban center—and although it acts in concert with popular representations of race and racialized identity as deployed throughout various forms of popular culture—it is also a response to three specific sporting tropes surrounding African-American athletes that acquired significant media attention as Lee was producing his film. The first is that of high school basketball players foregoing college to enter the NBA draft. In 1995, Kevin Garnett, a high school player from Chicago who was generally considered the top "prep" prospect in the country, declared that he would enter the NBA draft instead of playing at the collegiate level. He was subsequently drafted 5th over-all (by the Minnesota Timberwolves), and signed a (then-)record contract for rookies in the NBA. While the story itself received a fair amount of attention—nominally framed in terms of "getting out of the projects" in favor of financial security—it was not until the 1996 draft that the trend became an issue. In this draft, two more high school players were drafted in the first round—Kobe Bryant (13th overall) and Jermaine O'Neal (17th overall). Coupled with Georgetown University's Allen Iverson leaving school early to enter the draft (selected 1st overall)—the first time a player under head coach John Thompson had left the school early for the NBA—the mainstream press took up the issue as one of crisis, as yet another example of African-American youth choosing the fast-money track (i.e., NBA contract, endorsement deals) over education. This became tied to the second trope, that of minority athletes as criminals. In particular during this time, the NBA saw a rash of players arrested for marijuana possession (e.g., Isaiah Rider, Allen Iverson, Marcus Camby), and other African-American athletes such as Leon Lett (football), and Dwight Gooden and Darryl Strawberry (both base-ball) also made headlines for their brushes with the law *vis-à-vis* drug use.

The third trope Lee picked up on was that of the absent (black) male father as articulated to sport. At roughly the same time as the film was released, an issue of *Sports Illustrated* featured a cover shot with the headline "Where's Daddy?" and included an article titled "Paternity Ward" (Whal et al., 1998). Capitalizing on the general conservative discourse on absentee fatherhood popular at the time, the article went on to discuss absent athlete-fathers, reserving its harshest rhetoric for condemning African-American fathers within the NBA. While acknowledg-ing that paternity suits were prevalent in all sports, the article went out of its way to single out NBA players. Although offering several reasons for the high pro-pensity of paternity suits against NBA players—including road trips, money, and visibility—the article problematically settled on one's race as the most likely answer, stating that "the NBA has a higher proportion of black players (80%) than football (67%) or baseball (17%) [...] and that out of wedlock births are a persis-tent problem in the African-American community" (p. 68).

Spike Lee's urban ghetto

And so, entrenched within this discursive space, we get Lee's ode to basketball, fatherhood, and urban America. *He Got Game* opens with a series of stereotypical images that speak to, and are readily identifiable to, most people in the United States—fair-haired white youth a la *Hoosiers* (Pizzo and Anspaugh, 1986) shooting baskets amidst pastoral scenes of Middle America, juxtaposed with images of young black youth engaged in raucous games of "playground ball" within the projects of inner-city America. Open-spaced farmlands versus fenced-in urbanscapes. Freedom versus restraint. Suburbia versus the Cabrini Green Housing Project. As the opening montage fades—complete with the obligatory gesture to Michael Jordan by way of his statue outside the United Center in Chicago—we are left with Jesus Shuttlesworth (played by photogenic NBA star Ray Allen) and his cousin Booger, shooting jump-shots on a fenced-in basketball court, as they are dramatically shadowed by their towering project development. Whereas we have just been inundated with rolling countrysides, clean outdoor parks, and stunning visuals of Middle America, the only thing visually appealing to the camera in the Coney Island project is the chained-in courts—newly resurfaced—with an expensive professional-style plexiglass backboard. As Jesus takes his shots, the camera switches back and forth to his father (played by *uber*-celebrity Denzel Washington)—an inmate at Attica prison—who shoots jump-shots from the top of the key in the prison recreation yard under the watchful eye of a machine-gun carrying, white prison security guard. In these initial minutes of the film, we are presented with a spin on what Cole (1996) has called the sport-gang dyad; that is, the idea that "Sport and gangs are represented not only as channels for what are understood to be corporeal predispositions of African American youth but as the available substitutes for the 'failed black family' [...] splitting black youth into forces of good and evil" (Cole, 1996, pp. 370–371).

The storyline of *He Got Game* is straightforward, if not overly melodramatic. Jesus is the top-ranked prep player in the country, drawing scholarship offers from leading collegiate powerhouses such as Duke and Arizona, as well as the prospect of jumping straight into the NBA. Concurrently, his father, Jake, is serving a 15-year prison sentence for the manslaughter of Jesus' mother.[9] A week before the deadline for prep players to sign letters of intent as to which college they will attend, the prison warden at Attica informs Jake that the governor of New York is an alumnus of Big State University, and would be "grateful" if Jake can convince Jesus to sign a letter of intent to play for the school. In return, the governor offers to commute Jake's sentence.[10] In the course of their conversation, the question of basketball operating in the lives of African-Americans is brought to light by the warden:

[Jake is seated in the desk chair opposite a white prison warden in his mid-50s.]

Warden: As you already know, you've picked the perfect recreation. Dr. James Naismith [basketball's acknowledged inventor] knew what he was doing. It's a great game, isn't it?

> Jake: Basketball, yes.
> Warden: You played some?
> Jake: Uh, yes, sir, when I was younger. You know, uh, I put in a little work.
> Warden: I coach my son's team,
> Jake: I ran a neighborhood center [flashback to coaching his son at night].
> Warden: You coached?
> Jake: Nah, nothing like that there. Just, you know, I see somebody out there, a little kid who needs some help [flashback to son], I work with you, you know, give him a few tips [flashback to son]. But nowadays, uh, Warden, they—these kids ain't gonna listen to nothin' you say, you know. They think they know it all. All they wanna do is dunk and—you know, everything like that. Their fundamentals is, uh—is, like, sorely lacking.
> Warden: That's strange. I haven't had that problem yet.
> Jake: Yeah, well, your kids—they smart. They know they don't listen to you, they end up in here with me.
> Warden: I never thought about it like that (Lee, 1998).[11]

It is crucial to understand this scene not only in terms of pointing out the disparities found between the life experiences of the warden and Jake insofar as involvement in sport (i.e., *of course* the warden had never thought about sport in those terms), but it also serves as an indictment of basketball—pro or otherwise—and the much-propagated theme of the day that the "fundamentals" (i.e., shooting and passing the basketball) of many younger players were weaker than in times past as the "dunk" had become a major preoccupation of the time, especially with Slam Dunk contests trickling down to the collegiate and high school. Moreover, the NBA was at the time (and continues to this day) experiencing an influx of highly skilled and fundamentally sound European players that "threatened" to take jobs away from American-born (read: African-American) players.[12] Their conversation also moves to equate being in prison as having to do with personal choices made free from any larger institutional constraints: in other words, disobey the rules-based social order and you end up in prison with black felons.

In one of the very next scenes, Lee reinforces the overdetermined belief that sport is the only way out of the "ghetto" for young African-Americans when he introduces the starting five on Jesus's high school basketball team, the Lincoln Railsplitters:

> [Each player speaks directly to the camera, one-on-one, breaking the fourth wall as if being interviewed, and states his reason for playing basketball.]

> Lonnie "Dub" Dukes: The game brings me love, peace, and happiness.
> Sip Rodgers: My name is Sip Rodgers. I go to Abraham Lincoln High School. I play the two-spot. We're the Railsplitters, and nobody's fuckin' with us.

Jesus Shuttelsworth: Basketball is like poetry in motion. Just comin' down the court, you got a defender in your way. You take him to the left, take him back to the right, and he's fallin' back, and you just "J" right in his face. And then you look at him, and then you say "What?"

Mance Littles: Basketball's the birthplace of all of my dreams, of everything that I wanna be, of everything I wanna accomplish, and what it is that I wanna do in life.

Booger Sykes: I feel handsome when I'm on the court. I feel like I'm somebody (Lee, 1998).

Unlike in, for example, *Menace II Society*, Jesus and his friends are not "scary, young, nihilistic black males" driving the film; instead, theirs is a world full of (possible) hope organized not around drugs or gang violence (though it does exist, in the background, outside of their immediate sporting lives, as Lee shows), but around sport and the much-hailed fiction of basketball as the only socially accepted avenue of success for African-American youth (Cole, 1996; Cole and Andrews, 1996).

One particularly graphic scene later in the film continues this theme, wherein Jesus is both dissuaded by a local Puerto Rican gang leader named Big Time Willie against drugs, gambling, and the possibility of HIV/AIDS (in what would be Lee's 5-minutes Public Service Announcement to the audience, since Jesus had already clearly experienced and rejected most of these temptations anyway), all the while being reminded he is being "looked after" and should be grateful. He states, "You know it's no coincidence motherfuckers don't be fucking with you, right? Starting beefs with you, starting shit with you … Look, the reason why nobody fucks with you is 'cause Big Time Willie put the word out, all right?" (Lee, 1998). Jesus, however, simply blows off/placates Big Time. But Big Time's oration continues undaunted, this time focusing on, and returning to, the "getting out" theme:

Big Time: You know, a lot of great ballplayers came out of Coney Island, but most of them didn't amount to shit.

Jesus: What about [current NBA star] Stephon Marbury? He made it.

Big Time: Oh, true dat, true dat. Yeah, but he's one of the few.

Jesus: (*With a grin on his face*) If he can make it out of here, so can I.

Big Time: Yeah, you're gonna make it?

Jesus: Yeah, I'm gonna make it.

Big Time: You're gonna make it out like the rest of these niggers out here, in a casket (Lee, 1998).[13]

Here, then, we see Lee integrating his environment in such a way that previous *hood/barrios* hadn't overtly done: the urban landscape of Jesus and his friends is harmoniously interracial, a pastiche of ethnicities all coexisting without incident.

The race-related violence that existed in Lee's early work, such as *Do the Right Thing* (Lee, 1989)—a film inspired by the Howard Beach killings in Queens, New York, in December of 1985—is nowhere to be found. Nor is the black-on-black violence of *Menace II Society*. Like an edgier version of a Gurinder Chadha film filled with commercialized multicultural longings, the utopian vision Lee strives for is hamstrung by its ideological position. While it is undeniable that Lee deserves praise within this film for starting the work of challenging long-standing colonial and patriarchal narratives of dominance and subordination—both within the urban center and with regard to African-American athletes—it is no longer sufficient, as Denzin (2002) reminds us, "to offer examples of good and bad films, including inventories of negative images. It is time to move away from the search for an essentialist (and good) black or brown subject" (p. 185).

As the build-up surrounding Jesus and his choice of college continues to grow, we see him tempted with the allure of "easy money" associated with signing with a (stereotypically sleazy) agent and declaring himself eligible for the NBA draft (a la Garnett, Bryant, O'Neal, and Iverson). He is offered a Lexus from his abusive uncle, who is explicit in his desire to get a kickback from having raised Jesus. He is offered $10,000 from his high school coach for inside information as to where he will attend college. He is offered a $36,000 platinum and diamond watch from the sports agent; and, on a recruiting visit to Tech University, he hears about the "benefits" of attending the school insofar as generous alumni and other such accoutrements of big-time college basketball. However, Jesus is immune to such (monetary) pressures, and is instead always framed as the hardworking, individualistic, young man taking care of his younger sister and aware of the larger world around him.

But back to Jesus and his father. After the two have several tense meetings—in which Jesus claims that he "doesn't have a father anymore"—the stage is set for the anti-climactic final scene. As Lee moves toward this eventual resolution, we see—via flashback—Jesus's childhood *vis-à-vis* interactions with his (present) father. On the last night of Jake's "freedom," the two play a game of one-on-one. Jesus, by now the better player, easily defeats his father, and the two police officers assigned to follow Jake come and take him away in handcuffs. However, Jesus decides to attend Big State University anyway, setting up a two-fold resolution. First, Jesus has gotten out of the projects via basketball. In doing so, he has also lived up to, and in accordance with, traditional notions of the (Reaganite) meritocratic America Dream—hard work, moral values, and commitment to family irrespective of socioeconomic status or larger systemic barriers. Second, his father is forever fated to his life in prison, as we see Jake back in prison—perhaps a bit wiser, but certainly no better off: the Governor having reneged on his promise of freedom.

Where Lee fails in his moralizing tale is in reducing the solution to the problems of the inner-city to simply "getting out," as Jesus leaves Coney Island for the greener pastures of big-time college basketball. As Denzin (2002) remarks, "Lee's Afrocentric aesthetic is not the radical or militant aesthetic of the Black Arts Movement of the 1960s and 1970s" (p. 156). Rather, Lee's Afrocentricism "is a conservative aesthetic that *appears* radical" (ibid., p. 156, my emphasis). While Lee clearly has on his agenda the positive representation of African-American men, no space is created within the film that allows for the community to be revitalized on its own (i.e., Empowerment Zones aside); Lee chooses to make it the site of a glossy, pop culture: Urban Decay *Lite*. Because of this move, as Stuart Hall (2000) points out, such a strategy depoliticizes the transgressive potentiality of the message, leaving us (only) with a commercialized multicultural vision that "assumes that if the diversity of individuals from different communities is recognized in the marketplace, then the problems of cultural differences will be (dis)solved through private consumption, without any need for a redistribution of power and resources" (2000, p. 210).

In enacting the realist apparatus of depicting allegedly lifelike struggles faced by coming-of-age, African-American, urban youth, *He Got Game* remains deeply ingrained in a discursive formation whose stereotypical imagery actively contributes to our recognition, consumption, and understanding of inner-city Americana. That the film is located in Coney Island is no surprise, as Lee takes full advantage of our visual sense. Using shots of Ferris wheels, boardwalks, and neon signs—combined with street corners busy with drug deals and graffitied walls—Lee portends to offer us a realistic glimpse into the everyday lives of his characters.[14] Moreover, and while Lee's film depicts a softer version of the urban condition—one that mirrors the changing view of it that many Americans perceived during the late-1990s (the neoconfederate far right wing not withstanding)—his depiction of, for example, women, is still disturbing. The females of *He Got Game*, including the sultry Milla Jovovich as a down-on-her-luck-yet-compassionate prostitute (but certainly not like the glamorous Julia Roberts of *Pretty Woman*), are cast as pawns for the male characters: the sex scenes are violent, gritty; the women are cast as manipulative; Jesus's Latina girlfriend Lala is presented as a pawn to rope him into signing with an agent (and thus forfeiting college in favor of the pros); two white college co-eds are "offered up" to Jesus on his visit to one college campus; and his mother (shown alive via flashbacks) is presented as wanting to "limit" Jesus in his quest for basketball greatness.

Despite the at-times-gritty realism of the film, it sees its mainstream success precisely because of its explicitly conservative message, couched as it is against a backdrop of urban slang and ghettoized popular references. As film critic Roger Ebert (1998) opined in his glowing review of the film for the *Chicago Sun-Times*,

"The father and son win, but so does the system" (para. 10) The "system," of course, consists of a double-fiction, one that endorses the police state and the white, capitalist order it protects, while at the same time offering itself as the authoritative answer to the very societal ills it (re)produces and (re)generates: Jesus leaves his community, Jake goes back to prison, and everyone (and everything) is safe. Of course, the popular appeal and reception of movies such as *He Got Game* remains

> intricately bound within an historical context that has shaped and has been shaped by America's fascination with and acquired literacy of "urban problems," particularly as those problems have been rendered visible through coming of age narratives of African-American male youth. (Cole and King, 1998, p. 51)

Thus, we are left with a film whose originary narrative erases political and ethical considerations that mark history as a site of struggle, producing what Giroux (1995) has called "a filmic version of popular culture" (p. 57), one that effaces the everyday hardships and ground-level struggles of daily life in favor of a faux-progressive vision of hope. Through it all, though, we are led to believe that this is just another (tragically hip) day in America's urban centers.

CONCLUSION

> "America" is an assumed relation, an explication of ongoing collective practices, and also an occasion for exploring what it means that national subjects already share not just a history, or a political allegiance, but a set of forms and the affect that makes these forms meaningful.
>
> —LAUREN BERLANT (1991, P. 5)

By its very definition, as Stuart Hall (1992) reminds us, (black) popular culture is a contradictory space, a site of strategic contestation. From the continued marginalization of urban American issues to the expansive forces of neoliberal capitalism, from the selling out of culture to the exploitation of cultural problems in the name of diversity, the (post)-Clinton/Bush era casts its shadow upon the masses in new and productive ways. Furthermore, the (black/urban/minority) body—as a floating racial signifier—has within this period come to assume a contested position within mediated (sport) culture. Andrews (2001), reflecting on the contextually specific racial signification of African-American athletes during the late-1980s, wrote of the clean-cut, All-American superstar Michael Jordan as representing

> the conjunctural appropriation and fleeting curtailment of the endless play of signifiers that have historically contributed to the violent racial hierarchy [...] of American popular culture in general, and that of the NBA in particular. (p. 119)

Our current era, however, has opened up new(er) doors while simultaneously closing them, creating, as Synthia Sydnor (2000) argues, liminal spaces "where the old rules may no longer apply, where identities are fluid, where meanings are negotiated" (p. 226). The undulating valleys of identity formation—and the constitutive instabilities both governing and challenging such formations—are evermore fertilely reproduced within popular (sporting) culture (e.g., stylish hybridity, flexible citizenship, and metro-sexuality). While policy intellectuals such as Anthony Giddens have been keen on developing new theoretical models of social democratic philosophy that can meet with the growing challenges of global economic interconnectedness, it is clear to us that, following Hall (1996), popular culture is where people go to learn about themselves most specifically. And, therefore, where *we* must go if we are to acknowledge the promise of multiple subjectivities and diverse cultural traditions.

From our perspective, those culture workers wishing to enter into any dialogue with sport must move beyond prosaic, uncritical dichotomizations that view sport—as an object of popular culture—as either "positive" *or* "negative," "global" *or* "local," and/or "cultural" *or* "economic." In foregrounding the topic of sport as part and parcel of the global popular, we must be committed to getting beyond the paradox of celebration and anxiety. Instead, we should consider the full complexity of its prevailing determinate forces, delving into its production of cosmopolitanism *as well as* its reproduction of unequal relations and uneven developments; its expression in movement and migration *as well as* its reinscription of old practices of colonialism, imperialism, and asymmetrical relations of domination; and its potential to yield progressive interventions into the social arena *as well as* perpetuate hegemonic understandings of race, class, and gender relations. In short, we must ask how popular culture can help us create a critical race and gender consciousness for the 21st century (Denzin, 2002).

NOTES

1. This chapter is closely based on an article by the same title and authorship, published in *Cultural Studies ↔ Critical Methodologies*, Vol. 5, No. 2, May 2005, pp. 145–173.

2. Part of the 1972 Educational Amendments Act, § 901 of Title IX, states in part that: "No person in the United States shall, on the basis of sex, be excluded from participation, be denied the benefits of, or be subjected to discrimination under any education program or activity receiving Federal financial assistance." Most frequently applied to sport in recent years, Title IX "has been, and is at best, unevenly instituted and enforced. Most universities have made minor and symbolic compromises while few have been penalized for persisting disparities" (Cole, 2000, p. 5). Despite such poor enforcement—and its highly controversial ramifications from the point of view of collegiate men's athletic programs—Title IX is still widely regarded as the turning point in women's athletics in terms of creating equal opportunities and increased funding.

3. In *Reading race: Hollywood and the cinema of racial violence,* Denzin (2002) challenges us to "undo a hundred years of racism and violence and injury, a hundred years of a racist cinematic order," (p. 190), by opposing, resisting, and ultimately changing the media's representations and interpretations of the popular racial order.

4. See Cole and Giardina (2003) for a discussion of how narratives of the NBA and the documentary *Soul in the hole* (Gardner, 1997) mediate between American identity and multinational capitalism, and, relatedly, how they shape racially codified ways of thinking about equality, freedom, power, leisure, and consumption within late-capitalist America.

5. Pushed to the fore of American politics by the Democratic Leadership Council (DLC)—a 501(c)(4) nonprofit organization dedicated to promoting centrist politics—Third Way political rationality within the US seeks "a new balance of economic dynamism and social security, a new social compact based on individual rights and responsibilities, and a new model for governing that equips citizens and communities to *solve their own problems*" (Progressive Policy Institute, 1998, italics added). While scholars have debated for years about what exactly Third Way philosophy is and how it applies to contemporary social democratic societies and global political machinations, its early deployment within the United States under Clinton was not that of a fully realized political philosophy. Rather, as Giddens (2001) suggests, Clinton's Third Way was, first and foremost, developed as a tactical response to Democrat losses in the 1980, 1984, and 1988 presidential elections.

6. In truth, however, it has never been abundantly clear as to what extent this rightward swing can be credited to Clinton himself. As has been recorded in the annals of American political history, Dick Morris was crowned as the prime architect for Clinton's 1996 reelection campaign, and has been credited with implementing the strategy of co-opting the Republicans' agenda—such as welfare "reform"—and deploying it as a New Democrat/centrist issue. Clinton, though obsessively concerned with reelection, seems to have been at odds from the start over such a rightward move. Bob Woodward (1994), for example, relays an exchange between Clinton and his senior staff that speaks to the personal discomfort Clinton sensed with the 'great moving right show' of even his *early* administration:

> "Where are all the Democrats?" Clinton bellowed. "I hope you're all aware we're Eisenhower Republicans," he said, his voicing dripping with sarcasm. "We're Eisenhower Republicans here, and we're fighting the Reagan Republicans. We stand for lower deficits and free trade and the bond market. Isn't that great? [...] We must have something for the common man [...] At least we'll have health care to give them, if we can't give them anything else." (Woodward, 1994, p. 84)

7. It should be pointed out that, as a figure operating within "pop" culture, Clinton himself would find unrivaled political favor within urban America, most notably by promoting himself through popular engagements with minority viewers. For all of his strategic political maneuvers as the Governor of Arkansas, it was playing the saxophone on *The Arsenio Hall Show* (1992) that first gained Clinton national pop notoriety (even though he had appeared on *The Tonight Show with Johnny Carson* some four years earlier, where he also played the saxophone for a national audience). This move, ranked by a *TV Guide/VH1* joint poll as *the* most historic moment in music television history (eclipsing the Beatles debut on *The Ed Sullivan Show*), not only thrust Clinton to a national stage outside of politics but also set in motion numerous appearances with, and assisted in cultivating celebrity credibility with, minority voters.

8. An Empowerment Zone is a Clinton administration initiative designed to "revitalize distressed communities by using public funds and tax incentives as catalysts for private investment" (Upper Manhattan Empowerment Zone Development Corporation, 2005). For a detailed analysis of the convergence of sport, black entrepreneurship, and Empowerment Zone initiatives within the Clinton era, see Giardina and Cole (2003).

9. During an argument over Jesus wanting to quit basketball, Jake pushes his wife down; she hits her head on the stove and does not regain consciousness.

10. As media critic David Edelstein (1998) reminds us, the plot of *He Got Game* (Lee, 1998) is standard Hollywood fare, last demonstrated in the 1981 John Carpenter vehicle *Escape from New York* (Carpenter and Castle, 1981), in which "a convict is sprung from prison, promised liberty by an untrustworthy government in return for accomplishing a morally ambiguous task that no one else can do, given a strict deadline, and ruthlessly monitored by his ex-captors" (p. 1).

11. All quotes from *He Got Game* (Lee, 1998) are taken from the DVD version of the film.

12 In the 2003 NBA entry draft, roughly one-third (19 of 58) of the players drafted were foreign-born, the largest percentage to date (see Entertainment and Sports Programming Network (ESPN), 2003).

13. It is worth noting that filmic narratives centering on (or framing) the use of physical exploits as a means of upward mobility throughout the 1990s—that is, getting out of the (housing) *projects*—are not unique to *He Got Game* (Lee, 1998). For example, *Blue Chips* (Friedkin and Shelton, 1994) deals with recruiting violations at the college level (high school players receiving monetary inducements to attend one school over another); *Love & Basketball* (Prince-Bythewood, 2000) inflects both race and gender into the storyline, in which "making it big" in the professional game is seen as the end, with a college education (i.e., playing collegiate ball) as the means to get there; and, obviously, we have the previous examples from *Hoop Dreams* (James and Marx, 1994).

14. The score also grasps the viewer, blending rap songs from the group Public Enemy (to give it some *street cred*) and, in an ingenious move, timely renditions of classic pieces by composer Aaron Copland. As a sensory *tour de force*, the film is made all the more real by combining such emotive elements that pass for everyday life in the mainstream.

REFERENCES

Andrews, D. L. (1998). Excavating Michael Jordan: Notes on a critical pedagogy of sporting representation. In G. Rail (Ed.), *Sport and postmodern times* (pp. 185–219). Albany, NY: State University of New York Press.

Andrews, D. L. (2001). The fact of Michael Jordan's blackness: Excavating a floating racial signifier. In D. L. Andrews (Ed.), *Michael Jordan, Inc.: Corporate sport, media culture, and late-modern America*. Albany, NY: State University of New York Press.

Andrews, D. L. (2001). Coming to terms with cultural studies. *Journal of Sport and Social Issues*, Vol. 26, No. 1, pp. 110–117.

Andrews, D. L. and Giardina, M. D. (2005). Sport without guarantees: Coming to terms with a cultural studies of sport. *Cultural Studies ↔ Critical Methodologies*, Vol. 5, No. 3, pp. 145–173.

Andrews, D. L. and Jackson, S. J. (2001). Introduction. In D. L. Andrews and S. J. Jackson (Eds.), *Sport stars: The cultural politics of sporting celebrity* (pp. 1–19). London: Routledge.

Andrews, D. L. and Silk, M. (2001). Beyond a boundary: Sport, transnational advertising, and the reimagining of national culture. *Journal of Sport and Social Issues*, Vol. 25, No. 2, pp. 180–201.

Bennett, T. (1995). *The birth of the museum*. New York: Routledge.

Bennett, T. (1996). Putting policy into cultural studies. In J. Storey (Ed). *What is Cultural Studies* (pp. 307–321). New York: Arnold.

Bennett, W. (1998). *The children's book of virtues*. New York: Simon Schuster.

Berges, P. M. (Writer) and Chadha, G. (Writer/Director) (2000): *What's cooking?* [Motion picture]. United Kingdom/United States: Trimark Pictures.

Berlant, L. (1991). *The anatomy of national fantasy: Hawthorne, Utopia, and everyday life*. Chicago: University of Chicago Press.

Berlant, L. (1996). The face of America and the state of emergency. In C. Nelson and D. Gaonkar (Eds.), *Disciplinarity and dissent in cultural studies* (pp. 397–440). London: Routledge.

Berlant, L. (1997). *The queen of America goes to Washington city: Essays on sex and citizenship*. Durham, NC: Duke University Press.

Bruce, T. and Hallinan, C. J. (2001). Cathy Freeman and the quest for Australian identity. In D. L. Andrews and S. J. Jackson (Eds.), *Sport Stars: The cultural politics of sporting celebrity* (pp. 257–270). London: Routledge.

Butler, J. (1990). *Gender trouble: Feminism and the subversion of identity*. New York: Routledge.

Butler, J. (1999). Revisiting bodies and pleasures. *Theory, Culture, and Society*, Vol. 16, No. 2, pp. 11–20.

Callinicos, A. (2001). *Against the third way: An anti-capitalist critique*. Cambridge: Polity Press.

Carpenter, J. (Writer/Director) and Castle, N. (Writer) (1981). *Escape from New York* [Motion picture]. Paramount Pictures.

Carrington, B. (2001a). Decentering the centre: Cultural studies in Britain and its legacy. In T. Miller (Ed.), *A companion to cultural studies* (pp. 275–297). Oxford: Blackwell.

Carrington, B. (2001b). Postmodern blackness and the celebrity sports star: Ian Wright, "race" and English identity. In D. L. Andrews and S. J. Jackson (Eds.), *Sports stars: The cultural politics of sporting celebrity* (pp. 102–123). London: Routledge.

Chideya, F. (1997) All eyez on us. *Time*, March 24, p. 47.

Clinton, W. J. (1996). *Between hope and history: Meeting America's challenges for the 21st Century*. New York: Random House.

Coffey, M. K. (2003). From nation to community. In J. Z. Bratich, J. Packer, and C. McCarthy (Eds.), *Foucault, cultural studies, and governmentality* (pp. 207–242). Albany, NY: State University of New York Press.

Cole, C. L. (1996). American Jordan: P.L.A.Y., consensus, and punishment. *Sociology of Sport Journal*, Vol. 13, No. 4, pp. 366–397.

Cole, C. L. (1998). Addiction, exercise, and cyborgs: Technologies of deviant bodies. In G. Rail (Ed.), *Sport and postmodern times* (pp. 261–276). Albany, NY: State University of New York Press.

Cole, C. L. (2000). The year that girls ruled. *Journal of Sport and Social Issues*, Vol. 24, No. 1, pp. 1–6.

Cole, C. L. and Andrews, D. L. (1996). "Look—It's NBA Showtime!": Visions of race in the popular imaginary. In N. K. Denzin (Ed.), *Cultural Studies: A Research Annual*, 1 (pp. 141–181). Stamford, CT: JAI Press.

Cole, C. L. and Giardina, M. D. (2003). From NBA to "Soul in the Hole": Black masculinity and the (racialized) consumption of (racial) consumption. Paper presented at the Founding Conference of the Cultural Studies Association (North America), Pittsburgh, PA, April.

Cole, C. L. and King, S. J. (1998). Representing black masculinity and urban possibilities: Racism, realism, and Hoop Dreams. In G. Rail (Ed.), *Sport and postmodern times* (pp. 49–86). Albany, NY: State University of New York Press.

Dean, H. (2003). Speech to the California Democratic Conference. Sacramento, CA, March 15.

Democratic Leadership Council (2001). About the third way. At: http://www.ndol.org/ndol_ci.cfm?
kaid=128&subid=187&contentid=895 (last retrieved December 5, 2007).

Denzin, N. K. (2002). *Reading race: Hollywood and the cinema of racial violence.* London: Sage.

Denzin, N. K. (2003). Screening race. *Cultural Studies ↔ Critical Methodologies*, Vol. 3, No. 1,
pp. 22–43.

Denzin, N. K. (2004). The war on culture. The war on truth. *Cultural Studies ↔ Critical Methodologies*,
Vol. 4, No. 2, pp. 137–142.

Ebert, R. (1998). He got game. At: http://www.suntimes.com/ebert/ebert_reviews/1998/05/050104.
html (last retrieved December 5, 2007).

Edelstein, D. (1998). He got balls: Spike Lee and the mythopoetics of hoops. At: http://slate.masn.
como/id/3252/ (last retrieved December 5, 2007).

Entertainment & Sports Programming Network (ESPN) (2003). NBA draft coverage. At: http://
sports.espn.go.com/nbadraft/d03/tracker/round?round=1 (last retrieved December 5, 2007).

Friedkin, W. (Director) and Shelton, R. (Writer) (1994). *Blue chips* [Motion picture].

Gardner, D. (Director) (1997). *Soul in the hole* [Documentary].

Giardina, M. D. (2001). Global Hingis: Flexible citizenship and the transnational celebrity. In D. L.
Andrews and S. J. Jackson (Eds.), *Sport stars: The cultural politics of sporting celebrity* (pp. 201–217).
London: Routledge.

Giardina, M. D. (2003). "Bending it like Beckham" in the global popular: Stylish hybridity, per-
formativity, and the politics of representation. *Journal of Sport and Social Issues*, Vol. 27, No. 1,
pp. 65–82.

Giardina, M. D. and Cole, C. L. (2003). The national fantasy of Harlem USA: Empowerment
zones, Clintonian neoliberalism, and racialized consumption in urban America. Paper
presented at the annual meetings of the British Sociological Association, York, England,
April.

Giardina, M. D. and Metz, J. L. (2001). Celebrating humanity: Olympic marketing and the homogenization of multiculturalism. *International Journal of Sports Marketing and Sponsorship*, Vol. 3,
No. 2, pp. 203–223.

Giardina, M. D. and Metz, J. L (2005). Women's sports in Clinton's America: Body politics and
the corporo-empowerment of "everyday athletes." In S. J. Jackson and D. L. Andrews (Eds.),
Sport, culture, and advertising: Identities, commodities, and the politics of representation (pp. 60–82).
London: Routledge.

Giddens, A. (1998). *The third way: The renewal of social democracy.* London: Polity Press.

Giddens, A. (2001). *The global third way debate.* London: Polity Press.

Gilroy, P. (1995). *The Black Atlantic: Modernity and double consciousness.* Cambridge, MA: Harvard
University Press.

Giroux, H. A. (1995). Innocence and pedagogy in Disney's world. In E. Bell, L. Haas, and L.
Sells (Eds.), From mouse to mermaid: The politics of film, gender, and culture, (pp. 43–61).
Bloomington, IN: Indiana University Press.

Hall, S. (1992). What is this "black" in black popular culture. In G. Dent (Ed.), *Black popular culture*
(pp. 21–33). Seattle, WA: Bay Press.

Hall, S. (1996). Introduction: Who needs identity? In S. Hall and P. DuGay (Eds.), *Questions of cultural
identity* (pp. 1–17). London: Sage.

Hall, S. (2000). The multi-cultural question. In Hesse, B. (Ed.), *Un/settled multiculturalisms: Diasporas,
entanglements, transruptions.* (pp. 209–241). London: Zed Books.

Hartmann, D. (2001). Notes on midnight basketball and the cultural politics of recreation, race and
at-risk urban. *Journal of Sport and Social Issues*, Vol. 25, No. 4, pp. 339–372.

Hay, J. (2003). Unaided virtues: The (neo)liberalization of the domestic sphere and the new architecture of community. In J. Z. Bratich, J. Packer, and C. McCarthy (Eds.), *Foucault, cultural studies, and governmentality* (pp. 165–206). Albany, NY: State University of New York Press.

Hirsch, E. D., Kett, J. F., and Trefil, J. (1993). *The dictionary of cultural literacy*. New York: Houghton and Mifflin.

hooks, b. (1990). *Yearning: Race, gender, and cultural politics*. Boston, MA: South End Press.

hooks, b. (1995). *Teaching to transgress: Education as the practice of freedom*. London: Routledge.

Horne, G. (1994). Race: Ensuring a true multiculturalism. In R. Caplan and J. Feffer (Eds.), *State of the Union 1994: The Clinton Administration and the nation in profile* (pp. 184–199). Boulder, CO: Westview Press.

Hughes, A. (Writer/Director/Producer), Williams, T. (Writer) and Bennett, M. (Producer) (1993). *Menace II society* [Motion picture]. United States of America: New Line Features.

James, C. L. R. (1993). *American civilization*. Oxford: Blackwell Publishers.

James, S. (Writer/Director) and Marx, F. (Writer) (1994). *Hoop dreams*. [Motion picture]. United States of America: New Line Features.

Jeffords, S. (1994). *Hard bodies: Hollywood masculinity in the Reagan Era*. New Brunswick, NJ: Rutgers University Press.

Kellner, D. (1995). *Media culture: Cultural studies, identity, and politics between the modern and the postmodern*. New York: Routledge.

Kincheloe, J. and McLaren, P. (2000). Rethinking critical theory and qualitative research. In N. K. Denzin and Y. S. Lincoln (Eds.), *The handbook of qualitative research* (2nd edition) (pp. 279–313). London: Sage.

Klein, J. (2002a). *The natural: The misunderstood presidency of Bill Clinton*. New York: Doubleday.

Klein, N. (2002b). *No logo: No space, no choice, no jobs*. New York: Picador.

Lee, S. (Writer/Director) (1989). *Do the right thing* [Motion picture]. United States of America: Universal Pictures.

Lee, S. (Writer/Director) (1998). *He got game* [Motion picture]. United States of America: Touchstone Picutres.

Lee, S. (Writer/Director) (2000). *Bamboozled* [Motion picture]. United States of America: New Line Features.

McCarthy, C. and Dimitriadis, G. (2000). Globalizing pedagogies: Power, resentment and the re-narration of difference. *World Studies in Education*, Vol. 1, No. 1, pp. 23–29.

McCarthy, C., Giardina, M. D., Harewood, S., and Park, J. (2003). Contesting culture: Identity and curriculum dilemmas in the age of globalization, postcolonialism, and multiplicity. *Harvard Educational Review*, Vol. 73, No. 3, pp. 449–465.

McMillan, T. (Writer) and Sullivan, K. R. (Director) (1998). *How Stella got her groove back* [Motion picture]. United States of America: 20th Century Fox.

Mirón, L. F. and Inda, J. X. (2000). Race as a kind of speech act. *Cultural Studies: A Research Annual*, Vol. 5, pp. 85–107.

Moallem, M. and Boal, I. A., (1999). Multicultural nationalism and poetics of inauguration. In C. Kaplan, N. Alarcon, and M. Moallem (Eds.). *Between woman and nation: Nationalisms, transnational feminisms, and the state* (pp. 243–263). Durham, NC: Duke University Press.

Ong, A. (1999). *Flexible citizenship: The cultural politics of transnationality*. Durham, NC: Duke University Press.

Pizzo, A. (Writer) and Anspaugh, D. (Producer) (1986). *Hoosiers* [Motion picture]. United States of America: Metro, Goldwyn, and Meyer (MGM).

Prince-Bythewood, G. (Writer/Director) (2000). *Love and basketball* [Motion picture]. United States of America: New Line Cinema.

Progressive Policy Institute (1998). The third way. At: http://www.ppionline.org/ppi_ka.cm?knlgAreaID=128 (last retrieved December 5, 2007).

Rowe, D. (1999). *Sport, culture, and the media: The unruly trinity*. Buckingham: Open University Press.

Silk, M. (2001). Together we're one?: The "place" of the nation in media representations of the 1998 Kuala Lumpur Commonwealth Games. *Sociology of Sport Journal*, Vol. 18, No. 3, pp. 277–301.

Singleton, J. (Writer/Director) (1991). *Boyz n the hood* [Motion picture]. United States of America: Columbia Pictures.

Sydnor, S. (2000). Sport, celebrity and liminality. In N. Dyck (Ed.), *Getting into the game: Anthropological perspectives on sport* (pp. 221–241). London: Berg Publishers.

Tillman, G., Jr. (Writer/Director) (1997). *Soul food* [Motion picture]. United States of America: 20th Century Fox.

Upper Manhattan Empowerment Zone Development Corporation (2005). At: http://www.umez.org (last retrieved December 5, 2007).

Wallace, M. (1992). Boyz n the Hood and Jungle Fever. In G. Dent (Ed.), *Black popular culture: A project by Michelle Wallace* (pp. 123–131). Seattle, WA: Bay Press.

Watkins, S. C. (1998). *Representing: Hip hop culture and the production of black cinema*. Chicago: University of Chicago Press.

Whal, G., Wertheim, L. J., Munson, L., and Yaeger, D. (1998). Paternity ward: Fathering out-of-wedlock kids has become commonplace among athletes, many of whom seem oblivious to the legal, financial, and emotional consequences. *Sports Illustrated*, May 4, p. 62.

Williams, R. (1961). *The long revolution*. London: Chatto and Windus.

Woodward, B. (1994). *The agenda*. New York: Simon and Schuster.

CHAPTER SEVEN

Governing doped bodies: The World Anti-Doping Agency AND THE global culture OF surveillance[1]

JIN-KYUNG PARK

University of Illinois at Urbana-Champaign

In *Foucault, Cultural Studies and Governmentality* (2003), Jack Bratich, Jeremy Packer, and Cameron McCarthy claim that governmentality studies, a recently emerging strain of Foucauldian work in cultural studies, breaks new ground in the analysis of culture, power, and governance. In this chapter, I attempt to extend recent cultural studies debates over governmentality to examining transnational cultural institutions by focusing on the evolvement of the World Anti-Doping Agency (WADA) and its regulatory practices. Through the study of WADA, this chapter calls attention to the rationalities and techniques of government of transnational cultural institutions upon which cultural studies scholars have shed little light. In what follows, first, I discuss the main themes of Foucault's theory of governmentality. Surveying contemporary scholarship, I illustrate how cultural studies scholars have engaged governmentality to discuss culture and government. Second, I document the background, structure, and policies of WADA to examine WADA in light of governmentality. Finally, I show how the rationalities and arts of governing doped bodies under the governance of WADA work to police athletic bodies. I also delineate how WADA impacts the Third World by suggesting that WADA embodies First World, technologically driven governance of doping in the age of globalization.

CULTURAL STUDIES, GOVERNMENTALITY,
AND TRANSNATIONAL CULTURAL INSTITUTIONS

To begin with, a serviceable definition of government is necessary in order to come to grips with governmentality. According to Mitchell Dean (1999), government is

> [a]ny more or less calculated and rational activity, undertaken by a multiplicity of authorities and agencies, employing a variety of techniques and forms of knowledge, that seeks to shape conduct by working through out desires, aspirations, interests and beliefs, for definite but shifting ends and with a diverse set of relatively unpredictable consequences, effects and outcomes. (p. 11)

Governmentality is referred to, here, as the rationalities and arts of government. In his 1978 lecture on "Governmentality," Michel Foucault (1991) suggests that with the rise of political economy in the 18th century, the problem of government began to emerge. Foucault stresses that modern governmentality began to focus on the population as its primary target and object of intervention, having the strategic management of the population as the ultimate end of government. In other words, governmentality primarily aims at securing "the welfare of the population, the improvement of its condition, the increase of its wealth, longevity, health, etc" (p. 100).

Within cultural studies, governmentality studies have revolved around the consideration of culture, government, and policy. Tony Bennett's essay, "Putting Policy into Cultural" (1992), which he presented at the groundbreaking cultural studies conference at the University of Illinois in 1990, inspired governmentality studies in the field. In this piece, Bennett draws attention to the processes by which culture becomes both the object and the instrument of government. More specifically, Bennett challenges the dominant approach that views culture as primarily signifying practices. He also problematizes Gramscian cultural studies' theoretical devotion to counterhegemonic politics that, he claims, ultimately fails to articulate the Foucauldian notion of power, government, and "police" in the formation of modern state-people relations (p. 27). In addressing these issues, Bennett provides a new definition of culture. According to Bennett:

> Culture is a historically specific set of institutionally embedded relations of government in which the forms of thought and conduct of extended populations are targeted for transformation—in part via the extension through the social body of the forms, techniques, and regimens of aesthetic and intellectual culture. (1992, p. 26)

Methodologically, this historical reconsideration of culture as the programmatic, institutional, and governmental relations compels us to critically assess policy that takes priority over the semiotic properties of cultural practices (see also Bennett, 1997). In his later work, Bennett (1995) takes up these theoretical issues and documents how the public museums as cultural technologies have functioned as parts of governmental programs and policy that regulate, monitor, and reshape the conduct of a citizenry and the general norms of social behaviors.

Following Bennett's work, a number of cultural studies scholars have reflected upon the relationship between governmentality and culture and extended the area of governmentality research. Toby Miller (1998) has examined the cultural formation of citizenship using the notion of governmentality. Jack Bratich et al. (2003) have attempted to shed light on culture and government in the context of the United States in which cultural practices, in opposition to the Australian and British cases, are seldom mediated by direct state sponsorship but rather deeply embedded in a privatized, corporate set of conditions (see "Introduction: Governing the Present," in J. Bratich et al., 2003). Bratich et al. scrutinized a range of cultural practices (e.g., volunteerism) in light of the liberal and neoliberal art of governing at a distance. In doing so, they refused to interrogate culture and government as primarily a policy issue. Bratich et al. instead brought into focus the intersection of policy and ethos (the practices of the self on the self and the technologies of subjectification). Clive Barnett (1999) has proposed that Foucauldian cultural studies scholars have to reconsider different spatialities of cultural institutions when shedding light on government and cultural institutions. Barnett asks us to critically question whether the Foucauldian model of Panopticon and disciplinary power, grounded in a particular conceptualization of spatiotemporal relations, can be a useful formula for understanding government and cultural institutions. Barnett thus warns that applying the Foucauldian model to all cultural institutions fails to take into consideration the spatial and temporal specificities of varying cultural institutions (e.g., electronic mass media) and their heterogeneous technologies of government.

Recent scholarship on governmentality stresses the importance of reconceptualizing the problematic of culture and government in the context of globalization (Barnett, 1999; McGuigan, 2001; Bratich et al., 2003, p. 18). In the globalized world, government is no longer circumscribed by the boundary of the nation-state. It is indispensable to come to terms with a new geography of culture and government in light of the political, economic, social, and cultural changes that globalization processes have brought to us. Considering the proliferation of transnational cultural institutions and newly emerging modes of government, it is timely to investigate how governmentality operates in these new settings of transnational cultural institutions. I argue that WADA can be explored as a useful case that helps us to understand the governmentality of transnational cultural institutions and to figure out how culture becomes the instrument of government that goes beyond the boundary of the nation-state in the age of globalization. Before I analyze the governing practices of WADA, I briefly discuss the connections between governmentality, sport, and doping.

GOVERNMENTALITY, SPORT, AND DOPING

Governmentality particularly concerns the political management of the bodies of the whole population and involves a set of techniques to achieve it. As Mitchell Dean (1994, pp. 171–185) argues, the rationalities, operation, techniques, strategies, and practices of governmentality are centrally associated with governance of the social body. Modern governmentality regulates the bodies of the whole population to ensure the population's health.

It is right to suggest that governance of the health of the social body in the form of sport is a prime instance of the arts of government. Like Toby Miller et al. (2001), I would like to emphasize that sport should occupy a pivotal place in the history of modern governmentality. Sport is a central cultural technology of governing the social body, a technology to help keep the population healthy, efficient, and productive. Sport as a "crucible of nation" (Miller et al., 2001, p. 102) became a core means to discipline the bodies of the population and construct a docile and healthy labor force (Brownell, 1995; Pfister and Reese, 1995; Vertinsky, 1995; Miller et al., 2001).

In particular, with the revival of the modern Olympic Games and other international sporting events like the *Fédération International de Football Association* (FIFA) World Cup, sport began to play a prominent role in demonstrating national power in international politics. As a result, many nation-states set the promotion of high-performance sport as a priority of state policies (Hargreaves, 1987). Beginning with the Cold War era, international sport events became a heated battleground of competing state ideologies. Wining international sporting games was often regarded as quintessential "proof" of the power of the modern nation-state. The athletic body that symbolizes the state has become a signifier of state power (Hargreaves, 1987). In this political milieu, a number of pharmaceutical products and methods (i.e., blood doping) became available that could boost athletic performances. High-profile athletes, trainers, and sport officials were readily drawn to them. In addition, in the latter half of the 20th century, sport itself became a gigantic and lucrative industry. It was evident that world-class athletes were hard to resist performance-enhancing drugs, as those drugs were considered effective in enhancing their athletic performances.[2]

The severity of the use of performance-enhancing drugs prompted major international sport organizations to solve the problem by institutionalizing drug-testing at international sport events. The International Olympic Committee (IOC) was the first organization to administer drug-testing in the 1960s. In 1967, the IOC created the Medical Commission to deal with the use of drugs among high-profile athletes. It carried out the first drug-testing in the 1968 Mexico Olympics. The Medical Commission illustrated three reasons for conducting drug-testing, which included protecting the health of athletes, preserving medical and sport ethics, and enhancing equality among all competing athletes. Agreeing on these rationales, leading international sport federations began to establish their own drug-testing system and run drug-testing.

WADA

In spite of the established doping control system, the use of illicit performance-enhancing drug has persisted. The 1998 Tour de France became a critical event that helped to launch a collaborative fight against doping on a global scale. During the Tour, there were widespread rumors about illicit drug use among Tour participants, and thus doping inspection was severe. Allegedly, almost half of the participants withdrew from the competition because of the severe doping inspection. After the Tour, the IOC took immediate action to cope with the drug crisis and alleviate pervasive panic resulting from the incident. In response, the IOC convened The World Conference on Doping in Sport in Lausanne in February 1999. The principal purpose of the conference, the IOC claimed, was to initiate a worldwide fight against doping. The IOC and other international sport federations, governmental, and intergovernmental representatives (such as those from the World Health Organization [WHO] and the United Nations [UN]), sport officials, and athletes pointed out the limitations of the existing doping control system and simultaneously discussed ways to effectively control the use of prohibited drugs. In particular, they proposed to create a transnational anti-doping agency that could independently and efficiently govern doping practices. Various organizations and the individual States stated that they would support the agency to be called "WADA" (the World Anti-Doping Agency). At the World Conference, the Olympic Movement, an IOC-affiliated group, announced that it would allocate US$25 million to found the transnational anti-doping agency. Barry McCaffrey, Director of the US Office of National Drug Control Policy at that time, claimed that the United States would contribute one million US dollars toward the founding of the agency (Schnirring, 1999).

Following the conference, the IOC took the initiative in establishing WADA. The IOC organized the Working Group on Doping in Sport, which was a major step toward founding WADA. Members of the Group included representatives from the IOC, the European Union, the Council of Europe, the Supreme Council for Sport in Africa, the Arabic Confederation of Sports, the WHO, Interpol, and the United Nations' Drug Control Program (IOC, 1999b). The framework of WADA was completed by July 6, 1999 (IOC, 1999c). Approximately 10 months after the Conference, WADA was officially established on November 10, 1999 (IOC, 1999d). The Board of WADA held its inaugural meeting on January 13, 2000 (IOC, 2000) and WADA headquarters were permanently housed in 2002 in Montreal, Canada.

WADA officials state that WADA is established to protect athletes' fundamental right to join in doping-free sport, promote fairness and equality for all competing athletes worldwide, and maintain their health. Richard Pound, chairman of WADA emphasizes that WADA was created to support and promote fundamental values in sport and to create completely doping-free sport.[3] To accomplish these objectives, WADA has established a highly developed and sophisticated organizational structure, and runs a series of programs. WADA has a Foundation Board, an Executive Committee, and three working committees, including the Ethics and Educational Committee, the Finance and Administration Committee, and the Health, Medical and Research Committee. The key programs and activities of the Foundational Board and related committees include: (a) conducting unannounced out-of-competition testing among elite athletes; (b) developing the World Anti-Doping Code; (c) funding scientific research to develop new detection methods; (d) observing the doping control and results management program of major events; (e) managing the Athlete's Passport program; (f) providing anti-doping education to athletes, coaches, and administrators; and (g) fostering the development of National Anti-Doping Organizations.

GOVERNMENTALITY, WADA, AND GLOBAL SURVEILLANCE CULTURE

Closer scrutiny of the above-mentioned programs and activities allows us to examine governmentality or the arts of government at work in WADA. WADA does not simply operate to detect who is doped and who is not by conducting drug-testing and penalizing doped athletes. Rather, WADA attempts to govern doping practices through the administration of a series of programs and the deployment of disciplinary mechanisms. In other words, WADA employs, as the arts of governing doped bodies, cultural as well as educational programs that seek to shape athletic conduct by working through athletes' desires, aspirations, and beliefs. Ultimately, WADA constructs a surveillance culture and aims at producing disciplined athletic bodies aware of the gaze of WADA.

Let me illustrate these points by examining core WADA programs. First, I would like to direct attention to the unannounced out-of-competition testing that WADA administers. In the past, international sport organizations usually conducted doping tests during the course of competitions, which is referred to as in-house and in-competition drug-testing. In contrast, WADA extensively implements out-of-competition drug-testing, along with in-house testing. The out-of-competition testing is meant to allow doping governing authorities to test athletes anywhere and anytime without any prior notice. Allegedly, WADA adapted this system to monitor athletes who manipulated the in-competition/in-house drug-testing system by using illicit drugs while they were away from testing sites.

The idea of the unannounced out-of-competition testing met with strong support even at the World Conference on Doping in 1999, which proposed to establish WADA. Conference participants like Barry R. McCaffrey, for instance, strongly advocated permanently establishing the out-of-competition doping control system, while stressing that the global drug agency would have to work not only at competitions but also all 365 days of the year, and that it must be free to choose which athletes to test and where (Montgomery, 1999). Currently, the established WADA system grants drug-testing officials administrative powers to test athletes without prior notice throughout the year.

Second, in tandem with effectively administrating out-of-competition testing and actively inspecting doped athletes, WADA attempts to develop sophisticated drug-testing methods for currently undetectable substances (e.g., the Human Growth Hormone).[4] From the beginning, WADA promised to fund large-scale research projects, stating that it would provide US$5 million per year to develop new and improved detection methods for the growing list of performance-enhancing drugs. For instance, in June 2001, WADA awarded more than US$4 million to twenty-one research teams working in these areas, and the rest of the US$5 million for 2001 was used to initiate a study on genetic doping. In January 2002, WADA began its second round of multimillion dollar research funding, while promising to award US$5 million in new funding.[5] In particular, WADA collaborates with international doping expert groups in developing innovative testing methods, and has subcontracted the Drug Free Sport Consortium (DFSC)—consisting of the Australian Sport Drug Agency, the Canadian Centre for Ethics in Sport, and the Norwegian Olympic Committee and Confederation of Sports—to implement large-scale research projects.

Third, in 2002 WADA initiated a program called "The Athlete Passport" (WADA, 2002a, 2002b, 2007a). The Athlete Passport program was designed to be a web-based, interactive program as well as a visible, tangible way for athletes to demonstrate their commitment to doping-free sport. The initial idea was that once athletes signed up for the Passport program, they would receive an ID and password that would allow them to access the Athlete Passport Web site (see WADA, 2007b). That would allow them to update WADA on their contact information and training schedules. WADA developed this program to serve several purposes. The Passport would serve as an educational tool for athletes to trace and examine doping control information. Comprehensive and up-to-date doping control information (e.g., the list of banned substances and methods, current rules, regulations, and the effects of doping) would eventually be located on the Passport Web site. The Athlete Passport program, according to WADA, was also designed to build a communication line between various actors involved in doping control and athletes. WADA was supposed to receive and sort all doping control results and related athlete information, and to record each subscribed athlete's doping control information in a secure database. This would allow authorized officials of international and national sports/testing bodies, along with the laboratories conducting the tests, WADA, and athletes, to access the data, including athletes' test results, longitudinal studies, and approved medications. Consequently, WADA officials assumed that a direct line of communication would be established among them through the Web site.[6] In addition, WADA officials strongly hoped that the worldwide database would enable WADA and the authorized officials to organize, harmonize, and link testing programs to share information about athletes' whereabouts for testing purposes (WADA, 2002a).

WADA stressed that the Athlete Passport program would be based on athletes' voluntary cooperation. It emphasized that the Athlete Passport program would be a voluntary program through which athletes could demonstrate the belief that "clean athletes are the most powerful force against doping in sport" (WADA, 2002a, p. 9). The Passport program was initially implemented at the 2002 Winter Olympic Games in Salt Lake City. According to WADA, around 700 athletes decided to sign up for the program at the WADA booth during both the Olympic and Paralympic Games. The Passport program was expected to be in full operation by the 2004 Olympic Games, although, according to information available on the newly updated WADA Web site, its full implementation is still under development due the complexities involved (see WADA, 2007a).

Based on these WADA programs, including the unannounced out-of-competition testing, the development of new testing technologies, and the Athlete Passport, it is possible to suggest that WADA embodies a surveillance culture. Under the governance of WADA, elite athletes become the objects of surveillance. For instance, consider out-of-competition testing. WADA highlights that unannounced out-of-competition testing is meant to "educate" athletes regarding the fact that they can be tested randomly. Yet we should assess this sort of testing method more critically. As previously mentioned, WADA's unannounced out-of-competition testing system allows doping officials to test individual athletes at will throughout the year, and high-profile athletes are required to be available for drug-testing at any time. This intensification of the unannounced out-of-competition testing has paved the way for sport authorities to intrude into the private and everyday life of athletes perennially. Legalizing this degree of inspection ultimately creates a global surveillance culture in which all athletes worldwide, whether athletes are on drugs or not, are the object of control under WADA.

Further, I would like to claim that the development of new and sophisticated drug-testing methods is closely linked to the culture of surveillance. It is useful to turn to the debates over developing new drug-testing methods underway at the first World Conference on Doping in Sport in 1999 in Lausanne, and to think about how technological innovation in drug-testing is tied to the culture of control. This case is symptomatic of what WADA has been attempting to achieve through the advance of new drug-testing methods. While conference participants discussed how to regulate doping practices, government representatives like Berry McCaffrey suggested that a new international testing agency (now WADA) would have to preserve urine and blood samples, from competing athletes for as long as twenty years for further investigations subject to the availability of new drug-testing methods. This meant that the ageny could potentially strip athletes of their medals following new testing results (Montgomery, 1999). Here, we may claim that the will to punish underlies the effort to preserve the blood and urine samples, and facilitate the effort to develop more innovative detection methods. Consequently, if out-of-competition testing works to police high-profile athletes at the current moment, a series of WADA projects on developing new drug-testing technologies may serve to regulate athletic bodies not only at the present time, but also beyond temporal constraints through the retesting of preserved blood/urine samples.

Finally, let me briefly comment on the Athlete Passport program, as it is a crucial instrument of government, which aims at disciplining athletic bodies. According to WADA, the Athlete Passport is expected to fully document individual athlete's doping history and to create a direct communication line between WADA and athletes. Further, the Passport program was originally claimed to be a campaign *by* athletes and *for* athletes to demonstrate their commitment to doping-free sport (WADA, 2002b). However, given that the program was designed, in part, to help pinpoint athlete's *whereabouts* for the unannounced out-of-competition testing, the Passport program does not simply tell us about a "voluntary" campaign by and for athletes. The database of bodily information from elite athletes helps testing officials conduct out-of-competition testing, thus creating more room for policing athletic bodies. Further, it can be claimed that the

Athlete Passport program naturalizes the process in which athletes become the constant object of WADA drug-testing officials by stressing the voluntary cooperation of athletes. To this regard, we may argue that it is a sort of cultural technology that enables WADA programs such as the compulsory out-of-competition testing, and that produces disciplined subjects willing to accept the rules and codes of conduct that WADA imposes, such as out-of-competition testing. We may also view the Passport program as an art of government that seeks to shape athletic conduct that conforms to WADA authority.

WADA, DRUG-TESTING TECHNOLOGIES, AND THE THIRD WORLD

In addition, I would like to bring into focus how WADA governs elite athletes by utilizing advanced drug-testing technologies from "advanced" countries, and how the arts of governing doped bodies by WADA rearticulates the divide between the First World and the Third World in the era of globalization. Note the following incident that occurred in the mid-1990s in China. It provides a clue as to how a First World agent, utilizing the drug-testing-technology system, inspects Third World athletes:

> In a quiet Beijing apartment, Lindstedt plots a war on steroids. As the only foreign drug tester permanently stationed in China, the 33-year-old Swede pores over training schedules and consults a map, planning his next attack. His most valuable weapon: a permit that grants him passage into everything from swimming pools in Guangzhou military compounds to high-altitude training centers among Tibetan herdsmen. By charting obscure competitions, Lindstedt aims to find unknown athletes who suddenly sweep golds in little-known contexts. New prodigies, as well as established superstars, should expect a visit. "I knock on the door and say hello, I want you, you, and you." Those so summoned urinate into two tamper-proof bottles, which Lindstedt dispatches by express mail to one of three European testing centers. He's been filling bottles since moving to Beijing in 1994 to represent International Doping Test & Management, a Stockholm based company specializing in out-of-competition testing for international sports federations. For Lindstedt, that means traveling upward of three weeks a month pursuing China's pre-eminent athletes in track and field, swimming, canoeing and rowing …"It would be suicide for a nationally ranked athlete to dope" [Lindstedt said]. (Forney, 1996, pp. 56–57)

Just as the international sport federations subcontracted the International Doping Test & Management in the above case to implement out-of-competition testing, WADA has appointed the Doping Free Sport Consortium (DFSC) to develop, conduct, and manage its drug-testing program (especially out-of-competition testing). According to WADA, DFSC is supposed to facilitate the effective delivery of worldwide drug-testing programs. WADA allows DFSC to partner with other national anti-doping organizations or service providers in the doping control field to assist DFSC by providing sample collection and analysis services through IOC accredited laboratories.

More specifically, to illustrate, for instance, how the out-of-competition testing coordinated by DFSC proceeds, international sport federations provide DFSC with a list of athletes' names and DFSC coordinates test distribution planning with the assistance of Eugene, a computer system developed by the Australian Anti-Doping Agency (one of the three anti-doping agencies that constitute DFSC). All samples collected on behalf of DFSC are sent to one of the twenty-seven IOC accredited laboratories. WADA and the concerned international sport federations receive all test results directly from the laboratory (WADA, 2002c). Here, an important aspect of DFSC is that it consists of three First World sporting agencies: the Canadian Centre for Ethics in Sport, the Australian Sports Drug Agency, and the Norwegian Olympic Committee and Confederation of Sports. Given that DFSC plays such a vital role in coordinating and carrying out WADA drug-testing programs, the composition of DFSC partly accounts for the nature and art of the WADA governance over doped bodies. It constitutes First World-driven governance of doping.

With this regard, we need to explore how discourses on the fight against doping work to differentiate the First World from the Third World based on the availability of advanced testing methods. "The International Summit: Drugs in Sport" held in 1999 in Australia is a good case for such a scrutiny. The Summit called for international collaboration among governments, international federations, the IOC, other anti-doping agencies, and WADA to maximize the efficiency and effectiveness of international anti-doping initiatives. Bilateral and multilateral anti-doping agreements were identified as important strategies to build an effective international network. In particular, in the process of establishing the global network, countries, unable to carry out their own drug-testing programs (because they had limited testing capacities, or were in the process of setting up national testing programs), were especially "guided" to implement national drug-testing programs through "resourcing" or subcontracting other governments/anti-doping agencies to conduct drug-testing on their behalf. These countries were further asked to establish testing agreements with other governments and international sport federations able to administer drug-testing, and to make their athletes available to be tested.[7] In light of the conference discussions, it would not be far-fetched to suggest that discourses on the global fight against doping in the form of establishing the worldwide drug-testing system strategically restructure the divide between the First World and the Third

World based on the capability of performing technologically sophisticated drug-testing. In such a case, technological developments required in drug-testing can serve as an indicator of national or regional power. Thus, further investigation is needed on how the worldwide drug-testing system initiated and run by WADA and the DFSC rearticulates and reshapes divisions and power relations between the First World and the Third World.

Finally, I would like to direct attention to how the administration of the World Anti-Doping Code, which WADA developed, may function as a new regulatory instrument that could reinforce the First World's technologically driven governance of doping.[8] At the World Conference on Doping in Sport in Copenhagen, Denmark in 2003, all major sport federations, and approximately eighty governments, approved the World Anti-Doping Code (version 3.0) as the basis for the fight against doping in sport. According to WADA, the Code is the first document to harmonize regulations with regard to anti-doping across all sport and all countries. It is set to provide a basic framework for anti-doping policies, rules, and regulations within sport organizations, and among public authorities, and to ensure harmonized, coordinated, and effective anti-doping programs for the detection, deterrence, and prevention of doping. The Code was put into effect prior to the Athens 2004 Olympic Games. With the birth of the Code, WADA plays a leading role in carrying out new sets of regulations and codes of conduct that can impose new technological as well as institutional standards on developing countries. At the 2003 World Conference on Doping in Denmark, IOC President Jacques Rogge insisted that no country whose government has neglected or refused to implement the Code should be awarded the organization of the Olympic Games, and that the same philosophy be applied to all international sport federations (WADA, 2003). With such stringent criteria in place, it may become mandatory that elements like the drug-testing programs or technologies available in First World countries be adopted in order to advance the global fight against doping. Third World countries may be compelled to make use of those testing technologies to respond to the new global standards that WADA sets. At this point, however, it remains to be seen how WADA governance based on the Code may serve to reinforce the divide between the First and Third Worlds.

CONCLUSION

In this chapter, I have demonstrated that debates on governmentality and cultural institutions in cultural studies can be enriched by paying closer attention to the politics of transnational cultural institutions and the different modalities of government that go beyond the arts of government contained within the nation-state. I have also attempted to shed new light on how the governance of anti-doping in the globalizing era can become a fruitful site of investigation for governmentality studies. As part of this attempt, I have analyzed the background, structure, and policies of WADA. In doing so, I have shown how an array of anti-doping policies undertaken by WADA fundamentally works to police athletic bodies, and how those ongoing projects in developing new drug-testing methods for currently undetectable drugs are implicated in this surveillance mechanism. It has been argued in this chapter that WADA embodies the First World, technology-driven governance of doping by illustrating how WADA and the governance of doped bodies rearticulate the Third World based on the availability of drug-testing technology. The WADA case, in the broad sense, helps us understand governmentality at work in transnational cultural institutions, and suggests the need for further research on various cultural institutions whose administrative and disciplinary powers are exercised beyond the boundaries of the nation-state.

Before I conclude, I would like to discuss the agency of the governed—in this case, high-profile athletes. That is to say, as governmentality concerns not only how to govern others but also how to govern oneself as well as how to be governed, we cannot leave behind questions about agency of the governed and practices of the self (Barnett, 1999). A new set of knowledge, truth, and obligatory rules produced through WADA consequently impose novel codes of conduct and ethics on high-performance athletes. Elite athletes are increasingly subjected to a wider range of doping inspection, and are expected to collaborate with the global fight against doping through such programs as the Athlete Passport program. Such collaboration, according to WADA, is a way for athletes to demonstrate sport ethics and commitment to doping-free sport.

In this regard, it is useful to turn to Eugene König (1995), who argues that doping is a constitutive part of modern sport and a natural evolution, considering the "nature" of elite sport. In other words, given the logic of modern sport, athletes are expected to push themselves to the limits of human performance capacity, reached even at the expense of exploiting one's own body.[9] These constitutive demands of modern sport discipline, in which athletes are pressured to reach human limits, is predicated upon the development of technologies that make this possible, including technologies like doping. Thus, König contends that the assumption of "pure," "natural," or "authentic" sport to be defended against doping remains a fiction. Taking König seriously, we can claim that WADA's governance, which is substantively oriented to address the "unethical" dimension of doping, "artificiality" of doped performance, and the protection of athletes' health, needs to be reconsidered.[10]

Therefore, in governing oneself, athletes should reflect upon this paradox of anti-doping governance. As Debra Shogan and Maureen Ford (2000) note, it may require elite athletes to attend to Foucault's ethics and technologies of the self. Shogan and Ford suggest that a proper consideration of ethics involves an "investigation not only of one's relationship to moral codes but a tracing of those standards or norms that shape one's actions and behavior" (p. 51). Further, the emphasis in ethics is less on the conformity to rules, the law, or standards than on "the relationship of the self to the code and on the methods and techniques through which this relationship is worked out" (p. 51). Perhaps the actions of athletes that refuse to passively accept the WADA's rules, codes, and standards can become a point of departure for reinventing one's athletic identity and producing counter-discourses that challenge WADA authority.

NOTES

1. This chapter is closely based on an article by the same title and authorship, published in Cultural Studies ↔ Critical Methodologies, Vol. 5, No. 2, May 2005, pp. 174-188.
2. Various attempts have been made to reflect upon this problem. Topics of research around the problematic of doping have included doping and its dehumanizing effects on sport (Hoberman, 1992); the regulation of doping practices through the punitive system (Lueschen, 1993); the logic of drug-testing and the "cyborg" athletic body in the postmodern era (Cole, 1998; Cole and Orlie, 1995); doping and the "antiquated view of sport ethics" (König, 1995); the role of sport medicine in the development of performance-enhancing drugs (Waddington, 2000); and the evolution of anti-doping policy (Houlihan, 1999). Despite the theoretical insights that these works provide, they fail to bring to the fore the policing aspects of anti-doping policy and doping inspection in global sport.
3. Based on information retrieved in 2005 from the "About WADA" and "Welcome Notes" sections of the former WADA Web site (http://www.wada-ama.org/en/t3.asp?p=41506).
4. In fact, developing new testing technologies is not a new project. Prior to WADA, the International Olympic Committee (IOC) had taken various measures to come up with new testing methods. The IOC's efforts to support projects for new testing technologies have been intensified in the last decade. Since 1990, the IOC has allocated a substantial amount of funds for developing effective testing technologies for frequently used illicit performance-enhancing drugs. For example, in 1994, the IOC, in conjunction with the European Union, launched research for detecting human growth hormones (IOC, 1999a).
5. Based on information retrieved in 2005 from the "Scientific Research" section of the former WADA Web site (http://stage.wada.netcomsus.com/index.phpsectional=programs_en).
6. Based on information retrieved in 2005 from the "Athlete Passport" section of the former WADA Web site (http://stage.wada.netcomsus.com/index.phpsectional=programs_en), and from various issues of the WADA *Athlete Passport Newsletter.*
7. For information about the Summit, see its official Web site at http://www.dbcde.gov.au/drugsinsport/sum_info.htm (last retrieved on December 7, 2007). For information regarding international cooperation and resourcing, read the Summit Theme Papers (Theme 2: Drug Testing and Theme 3: International Collaboration) at http://www.dbcde.gov.au/drugsinsport/them_pap.htm (last retrieved on December 5, 2007).

8. The current version of the World Anti-Doping Code can be consulted at www.wada-ama.org (last retrieved on December 5, 2007).
9. This is epitomized by the logo of the modern Olympic Games: "Faster, Higher, Stronger."
10. See Cole (1998) for a critical discussion of the logic of drug-testing.

REFERENCES

Andrews, D. (1993). Desperately seeking Michel: Foucault's genealogy, the body, and critical sport sociology. *Sociology of Sport Journal*, Vol. 10, No. 2, pp. 148–167.

Barnett, C. (1999). Culture, government and spatiality: Reassessing the "Foucault effect" in cultural-policy studies. *International Journal of Cultural Studies*, Vol. 2, No. 3, pp. 369–397.

Bennett, T. (1992). Putting policy into cultural studies. In L. Grossberg, C. Nelson., and P. Treichler (Eds.), *Cultural studies* (pp. 23–37). New York: Routledge.

Bennett, T. (1995). *The birth of the museum: History, theory, politics*. New York: Routledge.

Bennett, T. (1997). *Culture: A reformer's science*. Thousand Oaks, CA: Sage.

Bratich, J. Z., Packer, J., and McCarthy, C. (2003). *Foucault, cultural studies, and governmentality*. Albany, NY: State University of New York Press.

Brownell, S. (1995). *Training the body for China: Sports in the moral order of the People' Republic*. Chicago, IL: University of Chicago Press.

Clarey, C. and Abt, S. (1998). Drug scandals dampen cycling's top event, July 3. *The New York Times*, p. A.1.

Cole, C. (1994). Resisting the canon: Feminist cultural studies, sport and technologies of the body. In C. Cole and S. Birrel (Eds.), *Women, sport and culture* (pp. 5–29). Champaign, IL: Human Kinetics.

Cole, C. (1998). Addiction, exercise, and cyborg: Technologies of deviant bodies. In G. Rail (Ed.), *Sport and postmodern times* (pp. 261–275). Albany, NY: State University of New York Press.

Cole, C. and Orlie, M. (1995). Hybrid athletes, monstrous addicts, and cyborg natures. *Journal of Sport History*, Vol. 22, No. 3, pp. 229–239.

Dean, M. (1994). *Critical and effective histories: Foucault's methods and historical sociology*. New York: Routledge.

Dean. M. (1999). *Governmentality: Power and rule in modern society*. London: Sage.

Doping Control (2002). *WADA news: The official newsletter of the world anti-doping agency*, 1, February, pp. 4–5.

Forney, M. (1996). Proscription drugs: State-sponsored doping theory loses credit. *Far Eastern Economic Review*, No. 159, July, pp. 56–57.

Foucault, M. (1991). Governmentality. In G. Burchell, C. Gordon, and P. Miller (Eds.), *The Foucault effect: Studies in governmentality* (pp. 119–150). Chicago, IL: University of Chicago Press.

Hargreaves, J. (1987). The body, sport and power relations. In D. Jay and A. Tomlinson (Eds.), *Sport, leisure, and social relations* (pp. 139–159). London: Routledge and Kegan Paul.

Hoberman, J. (1992). *Mortal engines: The science of performance and the dehumanization of Sport*. New York: Free Press.

Houlihan, B. (1999). *Dying to win: Doping in sport and the development of anti-doping policy*. Brussels: Council of Europe Publishing.

IOC (International Olympic Committee) (1999a). The International Olympic Committee is maintaining its total commitment to the fight against doping [Press release, July 8]. Lausanne, Switzerland: Author.

IOC (International Olympic Committee) (1999b). Working group on doping in sport. [Press release, June 8]. Lausanne, Switzerland: Author.

IOC (International Olympic Committee) (1999c). Working group on doping in sport nears completion of agency framework. [Press release, July 6]. Lausanne, Switzerland: Author.

IOC (International Olympic Committee) (1999d). World anti-doping agency is established. [Press release, November 10]. Lausanne, Switzerland: Author.

IOC (International Olympic Committee) (2000). WADA sets program for 2000. [Press release, January 13]. Lausanne, Switzerland: Author.

König, E. (1995). Criticism of doping: The nihilistic side of technological sport and the antiquated view of sport ethics. *International Review for the Sociology of Sport*, Vol. 30, Nos. 3–4, pp. 247–259.

Lueschen, G. (1993). Doping in sport: The social structure of a deviant subculture. *Sport Science Review*, Vol. 2, No. 1, pp. 92–106.

McGuigan, J. (2001). Problems of cultural analysis and policy in the information age. *Cultural Studies* ↔ *Critical Methodologies*, Vol. 1, No. 2, pp. 190–219.

Miller, T. (1998). *Technologies of truth: Cultural citizenship and the popular media*. Minneapolis, MN: University of Minnesota Press.

Miller, T., Lawrence, G., Mckay, J., and Rowe, D. (2001). *Globalization of sport*. London: Sage.

Montgomery, P. (1999). IOC credibility questioned as drug meeting starts. *The New York Times*, February 3, p. D1.

Pfister, G. and Reese, D. (1995). Gender, body culture, and body politics in National Socialism. *Sport Science Review*, Vol. 4, No. 1, pp. 91–121.

Rail, G. and Harvey, J. (1995). Body at work: Michel Foucault and the sociology of sport. *Sociology of Sport Journal*, Vol. 12, No. 2, pp. 164–179.

Sandomir, R. (1999). IOC's plan criticized at hearing. *The New York Times*, October 21, p. A.29.

Schnirring, L. (1999). IOC conference produced plan for antidoping agency. *Physician & Sportsmedicine*, Vol. 27, No. 3, March, 21–22.

Shogan, D. and Ford, M. (2000). A new sport ethics: Taking König seriously. *International Review of the Sociology of Sport*, Vol. 35, No. 1, 49–58.

Vertinsky, P. (1995). The "racial" body and the anatomy of difference: Anti-Semitism, physical culture, and the Jew's foot. *Sport Science Review*, Vol. 4, No. 1, 38–59.

WADA (World Anti-Doping Agency) (2002a). The Athlete Passport program. *WADA news: The official newsletter of the world anti-doping agency*, No. 2, June, pp. 9–10.

WADA (World Anti-Doping Agency) (2002b). World anti-doping agency unveils "Athletic Passport" with doping control record and e-learning interactive program for athletes, coaches, and trainers [Press release, July 2]. Montreal: Author.

WADA (World Anti-Doping Agency) (2002c). Doping control. *WADA News: The Official Newsletter of the World Anti-Doping Agency*, No. 1, February, pp. 4–5.

WADA (World Anti-Doping Agency) (2003, Spring). A tough stand. *Play true: An Official Publication of the World Anti-Doping Agency*, p. 9. From the WADA Web site: http://www.wada-ama.org/rte-content/document/pt_may_03.pdf (last retrieved on December 7, 2007).

WADA (World Anti-Doping Agency) (2007a). Athlete's Passport Q&A: 3. How close is WADA to approving the widespread implementation of the Athlete's Passport? [Subsection of WADA Web site]. From http://www.wada-ama.org/en/dynamic.ch2?pageCategory.id=754 (last retrieved on December 7, 2007).

WADA (World Anti-Doping Agency) (2007b). *Wadapassport.org*. [Web site]. At: http://www.wadapassport.org/ (last retrieved on December 15, 2007).

Waddington, I. (2000). *Sport, health and drugs: A critical sociological perspective*. New York: E & FN Spon.

CHAPTER EIGHT

Pro(fits) OF A future NOT OUR own: Neoliberal reframings OF public discourse ON social justice

EMILY NOELLE IGNACIO

University of Washington Tacoma[1]

Peace is not the product of terror or fear. Peace is not the silence of cemeteries. Peace is not the silent result of violent repression. Peace is the generous, tranquil contribution of all to the good of all. Peace is dynamism. Peace is generosity. It is right and it is duty.

—ARCHBISHOP OSCAR A. ROMERO, THE VIOLENCE OF LOVE (1988, P. 127)

PEACE IS NOT THE SILENCE OF CEMETERIES

It has been twenty-seven years since Archbishop Oscar Arnulfo Romero's assassination, and, since then, remarkable things have occurred in El Salvador. First, 2007 marked the 15th anniversary of the signing of the historic Peace Accords, which ended a brutal civil war in which an estimated 80,000 people were killed and countless civilians disappeared or maimed (Peterson et al., 2001). In the United States, January 16, 2007 came and went with little or no coverage in mainstream news sources. But this is to be expected: after all, only seven years after the Peace Accords were signed, a *New York Times* reporter covered an amazing story about a man who—orphaned as a child when his mother was killed in the massacre at Sumpul River during the civil war—had recently been elected

Mayor of Zaragoza, the town in which his orphanage, COAR (Comunidad Oscar Arnulfo Romero), was, and still is, housed. What is most significant about his case, however, is that, as the first elected mayor representing the FMLN (Farabundo Martí de la Liberación Nacional)—the political party of former guerillas—Jose Isidro Rodriguez's election demonstrated to El Salvador and the world that peace had, indeed, settled on this small country in Central America (Navarro, 1999, p. 4).

Second, Monseñor Oscar Arnulfo Romero, who was a central figure in El Salvador, has surprisingly cleared several hurdles on his way to sainthood. A Jesuit archbishop, Romero urged both the Salvadoran and US governments, militaries, and even the Salvadoran guerrillas to end the brutal violence—especially that aimed against the poor—in this small country. Like other church leaders and catechists there, however, Romero was labeled a "political enemy," and severely criticized by both the political and ecclesiastical establishments for interfering with governmental, economic, and international policies (Martín-Baró, 2003).

Presently, Images of Romero abound in El Salvador: he is immortalized in various murals across the country and in posters and pictures displayed in family homes and institutions such as the University of Central America and the Museo de la Revolución. Similarly, on the way from Zaragoza to Santa Tecla, home of an ostentatious shopping mall and several beautiful, residential homes, one sees Romero's image on a billboard for COAR orphanage. This is noteworthy because, just prior to the escalation of the civil war, it had been considered subversive to listen to his homilies or, following his death, to attend his funeral. Fifteen years later, however, his image is now commonplace, which makes it appear as if peace and security are truly present in El Salvador.

Yet, while the massacres and civil war have officially ended, the massive economic, political, and social inequalities with which Romero was greatly concerned still persist. Peterson et al. (2001) have shown that neoliberalism has, in many ways, created and/or re-created tremendous disparities in El Salvador. This has had profound effects on Salvadorans—both in the homeland and the diaspora. El Salvador's Gross Domestic Product (GDP) is still highly dependent on remittances from its emigrants, who are largely located in the United States (Peterson et al., 2001). In addition, like other countries with significant emigration flows and corresponding policies, so-called "nostalgia" items (i.e., food and other cultural artifacts) comprise El Salvador's major exports, and are heavily marketed to these Salvadoran émigrés. Nonetheless, as has occurred in other developing countries that have grown dependent upon the economic dynamics of emigration, neoliberalism has exacerbated transnational inequalities, for life both in El Salvador and throughout the diaspora tends to be economically and politically unstable.

This instability also solidifies, rather than destabilizes, support for neoliberal economic policies:

> El Salvador is a particularly illustrative example here: Salvadorans abroad send $1.2 billion annually, a figure by far larger than what the country earns through coffee exports. This money has mitigated the social cost of—and thus reduced opposition to—neoliberal economic policies implemented by conservative administrations. (Peterson et al., 2001, p. 18)

There is no doubt that Salvadorans are suffering. The question now is: what is the best way to address the impact of these neoliberal economic policies on the quality of life in El Salvador? In the fascinating volume, *Christianity, social change and globalization in the Americas,* Peterson et al. (2001) critically assess the ties Salvadorans maintain to various churches and base communities that emphasize "stop-gap" measures that focus primarily on the betterment of individuals. In a similar vein, this chapter is intended to serve as another kind of stop-gap measure—a "mid-term" check, if you will—on the effects that neoliberal policies have had on the rearticulation of Romero. Specifically, I wish to show that co-opting various phrases from Romero's homilies and rearticulating their meaning in abstract, liberal terms serves to justify and reinforce neoliberal economic policies. In addition, it can also pave the way for misguided antipoverty policies (see Peterson et al., 2001) that place most of the onus on individual betterment rather than on restructuring society itself. As Gómez and Vasquéz (2001) argue:

> [W]hat kind of alternative subject and community is Pentecostalism constructing? Does Pentecostalism's emphasis on discipline and control produce docile subjects, ready to plug into any hegemonic project from above (by state)? After all, Jelín argues that the construction of citizenship also requires a critique of the "culture of domination-subordination" that is the legacy of authoritarian regimes and the violent movement that opposed them. While evangelical Christianity might be producing "peaceable," disciplined subjects, it may be less successful at eroding the larger culture of domination and subordination. Bastian (1993, 39, 50–51) argues that while historic Protestant churches in Latin America in the nineteenth century "arose from the political culture of radical-liberal minorities and questioned the corporatist order and mentality," contemporary Latin American Protestant movements are no longer vehicles for a democratic religious and political culture. On the contrary, they have adopted the authoritarian religious and political culture and are developing themselves within the logic of corporatist negotiation. (Gómez and Vásquez, 2001, p. 167)

Furthermore, I argue that it is imperative that we search for patterns in the ways in which the words of both Romero and the "Civil Rights Martyr" of the United States, Dr. Martin Luther King, Jr. have been similarly appropriated to promote neoliberal ideologies in the United States, El Salvador, and beyond. By comparing struggles over the memory and meaning of both Romero and Martin Luther King, Jr., not only can we better understand the pervasiveness of these neoliberal ideologies, but perhaps also uncover language or discourses that may help us illuminate the problematic repercussions of their influence.

Many scholars have argued that racial discourses are simultaneously formed within and across nations in relation to specific political and economic contexts (see, for example, Omi and Winant, 1994; Ignacio, 2005). It is therefore paramount that we always study racial formations as cultural, political, and economic contexts change. In this spirit, we must also examine how the emphasis on the success of the Civil Rights and other social movements, Peace Accords (such as that signed in El Salvador), and multicultural policies have been used to exacerbate racism and hide the negative impact of globalization and free market agreements on racially subordinated groups, as well as widening social class inequalities, within the United States and around the world. I contend that this emphasis on our supposed successes, coupled with inadequate discussions about the consequences of globalized neoliberal policies on social policies and the quality of life in general, in turn, make it difficult to talk about pervasive structural racism in the United States and across the globe (see also Crenshaw, 1998; Barlow, 2003; West, 2004; Ignacio, 2005), while it also exacerbates tensions between racial groups and immigrants in the United States, and fosters or maintains suspicions of the United States abroad.

For this reason, it is highly important to simultaneously unearth any patterns in the relationships among the cultural, political, and economic aspects of diverse societies for the sake of opening up avenues for coalition building. Using Michael Omi and Howard Winant's (1994) theory of racial formation, George Lakoff's (2002) theories about values and framing, Stuart Hall's (1996) theory of representation and articulation, and, more generally, Antonio Gramsci's (1997 [1971]) theory of hegemony, I focus on two specific communities and examine the parallels between the construction of "success" and the intended erasure of inequalities, particularly with respect to (1) Dr. Martin Luther King Jr. and affirmative action in the United States; and (2) Monseñor Oscar Arnulfo Romero and the Peace Accords in El Salvador, as well as neoliberal economic policies such as the Central American Free Trade Agreement (CAFTA).

I am primarily concerned with how traditional US values such as the "American Dream" and self-reliance permeate discussions within both the United States and El Salvador. I also focus on how relying on these particular values has made it difficult to truthfully talk about—and thus work towards seriously addressing—racial, social class, and other oppressions. With respect to Romero's homilies, I wish to show how ideas about self-reliance have overridden other ideas about interdependence, even as we celebrate two heroes who called for a reimagining of the interrelationship among peoples in today's world. I will shed light on the ways in which the words of these "martyrs"—Dr. Martin Luther King, Jr., and Monseñor Oscar Arnulfo Romero—have been similarly appropriated and effectively used to justify neoliberal economic policies that intensify inequalities and maintain the status quo.

My intent with this comparative analysis is to reveal how discourses about race, racism, social class, and poverty have been adeptly rearticulated to stifle "globalization from below." In uncovering these tendencies and exploring beyond mere national interests regarding race, class, and ethnic community, I believe it is possible to unearth hope and create coalitions organized through knowledge, empathy, and understanding.

FRAMING, RACIAL FORMATIONS, AND WORKING FOR OUR FUTURE: HOW DO WE MEASURE SUCCESS?

Linearity and progress still have a very strong place in narrative histories about race and racism in the United States. Even in thorough historical accounts of institutionalized racism, most social science textbooks on issues related to race still break history up into chunks that, purportedly, signify the beginning and end of specific racist policies, practices, and laws, such as those spanning from slavery to the Civil War or from the Jim Crow period to the "Civil Rights" movement. Although many social scientists have been very thorough in describing the interrelationship between the economy, politics, and cultural images and discourses which have given rise to, maintained, and helped put an end to institutionalized racist policies, I believe that we still have relatively few accounts which critically analyze what happens *in-between* these eras, particularly with regard to the specific changes in public discourse, and its use in the continuance of racism.

Although there are excellent studies that examine the *effects* of mainstream discourse on the rearticulation, or framing (Lakoff, 2002), of race and its use in implementing policies which uphold the status quo (see, for example, Omi and Winant, 1994), and while a corpus of rigorous research has revealed how the language of "color-blindness" has been used to blind people's understanding of how racism has been restructured in the United States (see, for example, Barlow, 2003 and Bonilla-Silva, 2006), I believe it is equally important to specifically examine the cultural *production* of these discourses, the values which underlie them, and their use in shaping current public policy. If we can spot rearticulation as it occurs, we can better counter future policies in the making. In following this model, I wish to continue Stuart Hall's (1996) approach to examining rearticulation, not for the sake of inquiring into the intricacies of this reframing *per se*, but so that scholars, activists, and concerned citizens can police the crisis of maintenance of institutionalized racism and other social oppressions.

THE PROBLEM OF SUCCESS: FOCUSING ON INDIVIDUALS

In *Moral politics*, George Lakoff (2002) argued that in the United States, both conservatives and liberals outline political positions by invoking ideas of the "Nation as Family." Specifically, he proposed that social issues are often written or talked about in relation to two major models for conceiving the role of social policy in society—the "nurturant parent" model and the "strict parent" model. For example, Lakoff (2002) contended that the two polar ends of this model would interpret affirmative action as follows:

> Conservatives have understood very well that their goals are not just political and economic. Conservatives want to change American culture itself. They want to change the idea of what counts as a good person and what the world should be like [...]

> Strict Father morality comes with a notion of the right kind of person—a self-disciplined person, one who can set his own plans, make his own commitments and carry them out effectively. It requires that competition between people not be impeded in any way if they are to continue to have incentive to be self-disciplined. Any policy that gives people things they haven't earned is seen as immoral, because it lessens the incentive to be self-disciplined. From this perspective, affirmative action looks immoral to conservatives, on the grounds that it gives preferential treatment to women and minorities. It is a relatively direct consequence of the Strict Father model. (Lakoff, 2002, p. 222)

Within this model, it is clear that affirmative action can be framed as "immoral" when interpreted as a policy through which individuals are not treated on the basis of their individual merit, but on that of their membership to a category. As Bonilla-Silva (2006) has noted, this kind of abstract liberalism exploits the end of King's "I Have a Dream" speech to promote color-blind racism. For example, conservatives have claimed that King, Jr. himself would argue that affirmative action is immoral, and that antiaffirmative action policies such as the brilliantly named "California Civil Rights Initiative" (Proposition 209)[2] are moral (Dyson, 2000). After all, one of the things King, Jr. had professed in his "Dream" speech is that people should be judged "by the content of their character, not by the color of their skin." Affirmative action, framed as above, clearly violates this provision argued by King, Jr. himself.

Dyson (2000), West (1993), Bonilla-Silva (2006), Barlow (2003) and others have found that part of the reason why this segment of the speech has been preserved as the perfect seven-second sound bite is because it represents the most palatable part, for it calls upon "universal" values of love, respect, and preserving dignity—actions all good citizens are capable of and are morally obligated to practice. Yet, this insistence on individual behaviors has its cost. In particular, the constant focus on changing individuals' actions and attitudes, combined with the historical erasure of King Jr.'s concerns with structural and institutional racism in the first half of the same speech, in effect, makes it appear as if the end of racism is held *solely* in individuals' hands. In addition, the corresponding erasure of the role of educators, union members, and students of various races and genders in the 1963 March on Washington, and the subsequent renaming of the Freedom Movement to the "Civil Rights Movement," limit our nation's understanding of the original goals of the Freedom Movement.

Lakoff (2002) further argued that proponents of affirmative action, and more broadly, those concerned with addressing and eradicating institutional racism, often depend on a different "family" metaphor, one which emphasizes fair treatment. He states that, in contrast to the "strict parent" model,

> [t]he Nurturant Parent model gives the opposite answer. It is the job of a nurturant parent to see that the children in the family treat each other fairly. In the Nation As Family metaphor, that becomes: It is the job of the government to see that its citizens treat each other fairly. Thus it is the responsibility of the government to guarantee fair treatment of people who have been subject to discrimination—women, nonwhites, and ethnic minorities.
>
> In a nurturant family, the issue of fair distribution concerns the whole family over its whole existence. When unfairness has existed in the past, some unfairness in the present may be needed to balance things out and make things fair overall. The Nation As Family metaphor makes that true of a nation. (p. 223)

Yet, even in this model, "individuals" are constantly highlighted:

> Liberals further adopt the common metaphor that a natural group is an individual, the metaphor that defines collective action and collective rights. It allows considerations of fairness to individuals to apply to groups. Thus, one must look not just at fairness to individual women at the present, but at fairness to the group of women considered as a unit, taking into account both the past and the present.
>
> The use of the Group As Individual metaphor is not arbitrary. Liberals offer two reasons for such a group focus. First, there is the phenomenon of stereotyping. People commonly reason in terms of stereotypes, judging all members of a class in terms of a stereotypical image. That image is usually based on a past cultural model … [Gendered stereotypes, for example] could result in a woman being judged less qualified than a man without the person doing the judging even being aware of his prejudice. The Group As Individual metaphor helps remedy prejudices, whether conscious or unconscious, by measuring fairness with reference to a group over time. Affirmative action is a means for remedying unfairness from whole groups over time […]

Under affirmative action, white men still have advantages they don't even know they have: stereotype-advantages and subculture-advantages ... and it will take affirmative action over a much longer time to overcome them. (Lakoff, 2002, pp. 223–225)

While Lakoff wrote these viewpoints in a very general, broad-sweeping manner, and although he acknowledges that people's attitudes toward affirmative action do fall between the "strict parent" and "nurturant parent" models, what is of importance is that in both models, *individuals* or *individual rights* are emphasized. Furthermore, much attention is directed to individual prejudices, stereotypes, and attitudes. In the legal realm, Kimberle Crenshaw (1998) wrote that even key Supreme Court decisions have been so heavily influenced by the neoliberal idea of "free, individual, market choice" that members of subordinated racial groups *must* resort to the language of "victimhood"—which implies that each victim represents a unique case—rather than address the structural or institutional inequalities that caused the negative impact in the first place.

On a macro-level, Bonilla-Silva (2006) has argued that framing arguments in this manner makes it difficult for people to understand not only affirmative action, but institutional racism in general. Indeed, by focusing on individual acts alone, the cumulative effects of such separate or disconnected actions can easily be overlooked. This is how "racism without racists" becomes possible. It is only when the aggregate impact of particular actions is examined that racist structures (in the form of legal or extra-legal policies, practices, and/or laws) come into plain view, such as when one or two racial groups are clearly and consistently favored over others in society. For example, discussions regarding the recent "Jena 6" case are just now beginning to focus more upon the differential legal treatment of whites and blacks in Jena, Louisiana, rather than decontextualized stories of the noose hanging from a tree or even the final cafeteria brawl within which six African-American teenagers were charged with the beating of a white teenager.

Moreover, because these general dynamics exert influence over, and are in turn partially reproduced by, social and economic structures and institutions, they come to constitute structural racism. Barlow (2003) has further argued that the tunnel vision of individualism makes it difficult to talk about shared responsibility and the possibility of working towards equality, especially since the current framing of affirmative action policies and efforts to eradicate past discrimination lend themselves to questions about "reverse racism" and/or about whether racism even exists in this color-blind, post-Civil Rights era.

If this constant preference for addressing individuals' actions, beliefs, and values is what keeps us from understanding how institutional and structural racism operates, then I argue that the racial project of framing antiracism and antiracist policies in terms of individualism is one of the greatest obstacles to teaching people about race and racism. Words do matter, which is why paying close attention to our discussions about race and how they are used to pursue policies which aggravate racial oppression—as well as exacerbate social class and/or gender inequalities—is so important. Furthermore, since structural racism operates through seemingly "race neutral" policies working in conjunction with legislation, judiciary practices, and institutional circumstances that were established, in many cases, when racism was overt, we must be constantly alert as to how specific discourses and rhetorical strategies that privilege individual actions and rights can and have impeded antiracist interventions, for no frame can (as yet) be called upon to immediately identify and articulate this tendency as it occurs. For example, in the wake of Hurricane Katrina, it would have been helpful to have had a frame readily available in order to promptly explain how racist and classist policies, practices, and laws converged to adversely affect thousands of poor African-Americans whose evacuation was, in effect, not even considered to be a viable option. But that frame had to have already been created and articulated through continuing discussions about the ways in which policies—both past and present—have converged to not only impede people's rights, but limit their freedoms. Centering our attention on stereotypes, prejudices, and attitudes, while important, is inadequate in that it rests upon the assumption that racism will be eradicated when individuals change the way they think about races and racism. The rationale behind this limiting, albeit pervasive, lens is that as individuals change, then so too will social practices, laws, and policies. This particular logic makes it appear as if combating institutional and structural racism merely entails removing "the bad seeds," or resocializing specific social actors. "Individuals make up institutions," as many of my students say, "so we have to focus on them."

Diversity and multicultural policies are often framed in terms of individualism as well. For instance, "promoting diversity," while important, is frequently interpreted to mean, and is represented as, increasing individual choice. But such framing of difference or variance among people easily marginalizes analyses of the underlying legislative processes and administrative policies that perpetuate or even exacerbate oppressions and thus hinder diversity in schools, neighborhoods, and the workplace.

If these issues are instead examined using Omi and Winant's (1994) theory of "racial formations," and more generally, Gramsci's (1997) concept of the processes of *absorption* and *insulation*, it is easy to see how institutional racism has been largely insulated from our language, again, primarily because "racism" is conceived of in terms of individual behavior. Since the period of the Freedom Movement, laws have subsequently been passed that make it seem as if the civil rights of African Americans have since been secured and preserved. When this belief or imaginary is coupled with explanations of institutional racism that emphasize the workings of a "a few bad apples" within the institution—rather than the problematic effects of systemic or structured policies—it is understandable that dreams of a perfect, race-less, or color-blind society of respectful individuals still stand.

Because attitudinal measures have shown that overtly racist attitudes have indeed lessened in the last fortyfive years, these measures are often used to proclaim the death of racism (Magubane, 2002). This practice obscures institutional racism, as does insulating parts of the speeches—or entire speeches, for that matter—of national heroes such as Martin Luther King, Jr., as mentioned earlier. Dyson (2000) showed that this racial project was in fact initiated during King's lifetime, when he was effectively "branded" as a saint, while Malcolm X and members of the Black Panther Party were simultaneously labeled as "dangerous Negroes." In the 1990s, this racially biased practice continued through the marketing of African-Americans' past, as well as the branding of those who attempted to address structural racism. For example, although the rap group Public Enemy and filmmaker Spike Lee were deemed in the late 1980s to be "militant" and dangerous to American society, by the 1990s, their works—as well as Malcolm X's image (although not his words, other than "by any means necessary")—came to be quite commercialized. Of course, Malcolm X's life and works could have been made more public as Spike Lee's film about this key 20th century figure hit the theaters, but the branding and consumption of the "radical" quality of Malcolm X's image, through "X" hats, shirts, and even stamps, stymied serious discussion about the structural racism he opposed.

Given that multiculturalism, and judging others by the "content of their character," had been so well socialized into the American public by then, cries of institutional racism were regarded as alien, and not fully taken seriously. Whereas emphasis on respect and multiculturalism were and are greatly needed, and although they have led to some positive changes in interpersonal relationships among races and ethnicities throughout the past few decades, this particular "use of culture" (to paraphrase Cameron McCarthy, 1998) can have pernicious effects, for it redirects analyses away from inquiring into institutional racism, now regarded as something "of the past." The reframing and marketing of Malcolm X, as well as the selective valorization of Martin Luther King, Jr., show "just how far our society has gone," particularly if the seven-second sound-bite regarding Malcolm X's contribution to history is that he was "the opposite of King, Jr." That is, whereas once Malcolm X was thought to be a "dangerous Negro," now his revolutionary ideas have been made palatable because they have either been re-packaged into a "cool image" ("X" hats were all the rage in the early 1990s) or transformed into piecemeal sound-bites (as with Martin Luther King, Jr.). Both these images were bought and sold. As discussed below, Archbishop Oscar Arnulfo Romero's message and image have been undergoing similar transformations.

By creating the illusion that discrimination against racially subjugated groups has been completely eliminated, and equal rights attained, prejudices lessened, and "political correctness," "diversity," or "multiculturalism" made the ultimate goal, the context has been shaped to the extent that any policy on the books that allows for the application of equal opportunity measures (when accessing various kinds of jobs and institutions of higher learning) is immediately labeled as "racist" and anathema to the American Dream. As Omi and Winant (1994) have asserted, the reframing of the "Dream" speech, as well as the renaming of the Freedom Movement to the Civil Rights Movement, made it possible for a racially regressive policy like Proposition 209 to be called the "California Civil Rights Initiative." Likewise, cries of "reverse racism" are only possible if open discussions about institutional and structural racism are inadequate or made invisible. Today, only thirty years after the Freedom Movement period, the California Civil Rights Initiative succeeded in cementing the reframing of King's speech and in retracting the goals and accomplishments of that important Movement.

The frame of individual racism only works because we have been socialized to take it for granted. But people cannot see these things unless patterns are pointed out to them. And, if the issues are framed solely in terms of individuals, this is how concerns about race and antiracism will be discussed. Thus, to remedy the situation, I argue that we must try as best as we can to isolate these rhetorical devices, and then actively challenge all discussions of issues ranging from diversity, multiculturalism, affirmative action, and racial inequality if they employ frameworks relying exclusively on notions of the "individual." This, of course, is a difficult task, as it entails adopting the viewpoint that race is embedded in institutions, and that racism can persist even when intent is pure. It would also involve creating metaphors (or alternative frames) that might work within the "Nation as Family" metaphor, but that, again, are not centered on individuals. These new metaphors could then be immediately recalled to unearth and denounce the individualistic reframing of both racism and efforts to end it. Although this will be difficult, for the above reasons, I believe it is essential for fighting against racial oppression.

PRO(FITS) OF A FUTURE NOT OUR OWN:
ARCHBISHOP ROMERO, NEOLIBERALISM, AND CAFTA

Hiking, Surfing, History—and not another tourist in sight.

El Salvador's name still evokes images of the brutal civil war fought throughout the 1980s. But the war is long over, and the most turbulent aspect of El Salvador today is its volcanic landscape.

—Lonely Planet Worldguide (2006)

> Kept pristine by conflict, even heavily populated El Salvador has more than its fair share of parks, protected areas, and privately owned reserves, crisscrossed with trails and laced with waterfalls just waiting to be experienced ...
>
> —PENLAND ET AL. (2006), P. 43.

In a similar vein, neoliberal ideology and abstract liberalism, I argue, have been and are being used to downplay the negative effects of economic globalization on El Salvador. El Salvador has had, to say the very least, a tumultuous 20th century. The assassination of Archbishop Oscar Arnulfo Romero occurred only a few months before the "official" beginning of the twelve-year Civil War.

In the 1970s, this state of affairs was not uncommon. Prior to Romero, Father Rutillo Grande, an ardent defender of the poor, was frequently targeted and eventually assassinated. In fact, many Catholic missionaries, nuns, priests, and *campesinos* were labeled subversive and faced threats and/or physical violence for merely carrying the Bible (Martín-Baró, 2003). Although the killings of priests and nuns had been reported in the United States' mainstream media, because the Civil War was couched as an anti-Communist war, many in the United States believed that the guerillas were funded by the Soviet Union (then, *the* quintessential enemy).

In El Salvador today, however, there are people who wish to preserve the memory of those who were assassinated and murdered during this tumultuous period: El Museo de la Revolución; the hospital chapel in which Romero was assassinated; the University of Central America (UCA); the church in which four Maryknoll catechists were raped and murdered; and El Mozóte: the site of one of the more well-known massacres. All are currently home to artifacts, monuments, or simple graves that remind all Salvadorans and their visitors of its martyrs. Each of these spaces clearly tries to keep the memory alive, not to dwell on the violence, but in hopes that future generations will remember the people—and the causes that they stood for or symbolized—who were sacrificed on the way to the historic Peace Accords. There is, thus, a tragic irony in these peaceful settings in that they are accompanied by reminders of the violence: in the UCA, a beautiful rose garden was planted at the site in which the bloodied bodies of six Jesuits and two workers were found; at the library, pictures of the Jesuits and women are prominently displayed. Similarly, at the small church in which Romero was assassinated, a room adjacent to an otherwise peaceful chapel displays Archbishop Romero's artifacts along with his bloodstained clothing.

As poignant as these museums are, there is yet another dimension to them, another reading which I wish to address here. It has to do with the lessons we must learn regarding racial formation and framing: that we must always be keenly aware of how images and words can be used. For example, one of the most visible orphanages in El Salvador, the COAR, proudly displays Archbishop Romero's portrait on a wall facing the highway which links Santa Tecla—a city complete with a super-mall and transnational textile and other manufacturing corporations which are dependent largely on a young, female labor force—to a small town within which many of these female workers reside. The image of Archbishop Romero stands out, and yet, I fear that with time, and in a neoliberal context, the fact that he was critical of policies that maintained or worsened wealth disparities will be erased and completely forgotten.

Without an understanding of the full, complex history of El Salvador's place in the global market and its effects on the present, daily lives of Salvadorans around the world, one of Romero's most famous quotes is bound to be distorted.

> And I want to say to all the people, to rulers, to the rich and powerful: if you do not become poor, if you do not concern yourselves for the poverty of our people as though they were your own family, you will not be able to save society. (July 15, 1979 homily, Romero quoted in Campbell-Johnson, 1989, p. 1361)

Peterson et al. (2001) have shown that some of Romero's church teachings have generally been used to promote individual efforts to reach out to the poor either through charity rather than a restructuring of society so as to eradicate poverty. Thus the above quote could be used *against* those who are critical of *maquiladoras*. The argument, using the individual framework is: *maquiladoras* pay almost double the wages per month of other local jobs. Thus, it is those who are critical of the *maquiladoras, not* those who support the *maquiladoras* who "do not concern [themselves] with the poor." In this context, Romero's overall message is thus highly vulnerable to being manipulated and reframed into obscurity.

Similarly, church leaders emphasize focusing on molding the actions and belief systems of those who live in poverty rather than those pertaining to government officials, business leaders, and other members of the ruling elite, who have created wealth disparities and their corresponding problems:

> These young men, many of whom have recently returned from the United States, are learning how to control themselves. They are taking control of their lives not through drugs but through the spirit of God. You see, a Christian person must live in brotherhood. That is what I preach to young people; they must walk in brotherly love. Just as Christ loved us so we must walk. A Christian home must persevere in love. Today when we get home we behave more like wolves. Speaking of the most pressing problems faced by Salvadoran youths today, Pablo states: "Young people need clubs or houses where they can learn an occupation. They need jobs and education. Instead of building more prisons, they [the government] could build spaces for recreation far away from the city and its contamination; spaces where one can teach young people how to conduct their lives without vices, without drugs, alcohol, and cigarettes." (Gómez and Vásquez, 2001, p. 178)

Prophets of a future not their own

Bishop Ken Untener once wrote a prayer about Monseñor Romero entitled "Prophets of a Future Not their Own."[3] In it, he reminds his listeners that:

> No program accomplishes the church's mission.
> No set of goals and objectives includes everything.
> This is what we are about:
> We plant seeds that one day will grow.
> We water seeds already planted,
> knowing that they hold future promise.
> We lay foundations that will need further development.
> We provide yeast that produces effects beyond our capabilities.
> We cannot do everything
> and there is a sense of liberation in realizing that.
> This enables us to do something,
> and to do it very well.
> It may be incomplete, but it is a beginning, a step along the way,
> an opportunity for God's grace to enter and do the rest.
> We may never see the end results,
> but that is the difference between the master builder and the worker.
> We are workers, not master builders,
> ministers, not messiahs.
> We are prophets of a future not our own.

Throughout the three years in which he was Archbishop of San Salvador, Monseñor Romero continually challenged people to think about interdependence and building a more just and equitable future. And while he did absolutely center his sermons on the plight of the poor, he did not do so to merely evoke feelings of charity. On the contrary, Romero consistently challenged various institutions (the Salvadoran military and government, as well as the US government) and implored them to dissolve policies which would further both violence and poverty in El Salvador.

This is one of the reasons why he was so dangerous to those who wished to maintain the status quo. In calling for a more equitable society, Romero made the following statement less than two months before he was assassinated:

> I am sure that so much blood and so much pain caused to the families of so many victims will not be in vain. It is blood and pain that will water and make fertile new and continually more numerous seeds—Salvadorans who will awaken to the respon-sibility [that] they have to build a more just and human society—and that will bear fruit in the accomplishment of the daring, urgent, and radical structural reforms that our nation needs. (Romero, quoted in Brockman, 2005, p. 223)

Perhaps even more pointedly, he once stated:

> It is not a matter of sheer routine that I insist once again on the existence in our coun-
> try of structures of sin. They are sinful because they produce the fruits of sin: the deaths
> of Salvadorans—the swift death brought by repression or the long, drawn out, but no
> less real, death from structural oppression. That is why we have denounced what in
> our country has become the idolatry of wealth, of the absolute right, within the capi-
> talist system, of private property, of political power in national security regimes, in the
> name of which personal security is itself institutionalized. (Romero, 1985, p. 183)

Prior to Romero's ascendancy, the government, security forces, and wealthy families of El Salvador had repressed Catholic Church leaders and their followers with
violence, or threats of violence, so much so that, in the late 1970s, merely carrying a
Bible, a copy of the Catholic weekly *Orientación*, or a picture of Fr. Rutillo Grande
(one of the church's most vocal critics of the Salvadoran oligarchy's economic and
political policies) was expressly prohibited as these actions were thought to foster
antigovernment, or worse, communist thoughts (Martín-Baró, 2003, p. 7). When
Romero was chosen as Archbishop on February 3, 1977, the ruling elite rejoiced
because they believed him to be conciliatory and conservative.

Nonetheless, especially after Grande's assassination, Romero never preached
that it was solely up to kind individuals to feed the hungry, serve the poor, or perform other acts of charity to alleviate repression in general. Instead, he *explicitly
named* the organizations and the legal dispositions, instruments, and interventions
that created and maintained hunger and repression.

In addition, it is worth noting that Archbishop Romero did not merely
describe the violence and repression Salvadorans experienced. Instead, Romero
suggested changes in policies that he felt would, at the very least, curtail some of
the violence. For example. in his February 17, 1980 letter to US President Jimmy
Carter, he implored the President to deny economic and military support to the
Salvadoran security forces because of widespread murders, massacres, and other
human rights violations of innocent peoples in El Salvador:

> Dear Mr. President:
>
> In the last few days, news has appeared in the national press that worries me greatly.
> According to the reports, your government is studying the possibility of eco-
> nomic and military support and assistance to the present government junta. [...]
> I am very concerned by the news that the government of the United States is plan-
> ning to further El Salvador's arms race by sending military equipment and advisers
> to "train three Salvadoran battalions in logistics, communications, and intelligence."
> If this information from the newspapers is correct, instead of favoring greater justice
> and peace in El Salvador, your government's contribution will undoubtedly sharpen
> the injustice and the repression inflicted on the organized people, whose struggle has
> often been for respect for their most basic human rights ...

For this reason, given that as a Salvadoran and archbishop of the archdiocese of San Salvador, I have an obligation to see that faith and justice reign in my country, I ask you, if you truly want to defend human rights:

– to forbid that military aid be given to the Salvadoran government;
– to guarantee that your government will not intervene directly or indirectly, with military, economic, diplomatic, or other pressures, in determining the destiny of the Salvadoran people;
– In these moments, we are living through a grave economic and political crisis in our country, but it is certain that increasingly the people are awakening and organizing and have begun to prepare themselves to manage and be responsible for the future of El Salvador, as they only ones capable of surmounting the crisis.

I hope that your religious sentiments and your feelings for the defense of human rights will move you to accept my petition, thus avoiding greater bloodshed in this suffering country. (Romero, 1985, pp. 188–190)

In light of Romero's underlying message in these various pronouncements, a key rhetorical move—as occurred in the case of King, Jr. as well—has been to remove the *actors* to whom Romero was referring in his speeches by constantly selecting a limited handful of quotes and taking them out of context. For example, Romero, as seen in the above quotes, *named* the security forces, the wealthy, business, and government leaders as actors who maintained—and benefited from—economic inequality and repression. Removing these highly relevant actors contributes to historical erasure and changes the tenor of his discourse from direct criticisms to general platitudes. It also shifts his emphasis from demanding structural change to simply supporting charitable actions and causes. The quotes below illustrate how this reframing can be achieved:

When we speak of the church of the poor.
We are simply telling also the rich:
Turn your eyes to this church
and concern yourselves for the poor
as for yourselves
As Puebla we said the poor are a concern of Christ,
who will say at the end of life,
"Whatever you did to one of these poor ones, you did to me."

—(Romero, 1988, p. 125)

Or, another:

A civilization of love
that did not demand justice of people
would not be a true civilization:
it would not delineate genuine human relations.

It is a caricature of love to try to cover over
with alms what is lacking in justice,
to patch over with an appearance of benevolence
when social justice is missing,
True love begins by demanding what is just
in relation to those who love.

—(Romero, 1988, p. 130)

If all of Monseñor Romero's speeches are taken into account, and if one has a clear idea of the historical, socio-political context in which he made them, then it is clear that his references to "social justice" (as in the second quote) involved critically thinking about, and reversing, the negative impacts of various national, institutionalized policies (i.e., heightened militarization, removal of people from arable lands, and the inaction of the United States on human rights abuses, among others).

Taken out of this context and couched within the current, dominant ideology of neoliberalism, the meaning changes. The first of the two quotes above is especially open to abuse, particularly in this age of promoting charitable causes rather than structural transformation. Thus, "demanding justice," "concerning oneself with the poor," and "spreading love" are, once again, couched in individual terms. Following Mahatma Gandhi's adage "be the change you wish to see in the world" entails changing one's belief system or, perhaps, just making wise consumer choices (via looking for "red" signs). At best, it would mean being more nurturing and viewing the nation or world as one, big family. Rarely, though, does it entail critically analyzing the origins and maintenance of oppression and inequalities—which is, ironically, what Gandhi, as well as Romero and King, Jr., constantly espoused.

BECOMING PROPHETS OF A FUTURE NOT OUR OWN

One of the lessons I learned from my previous research on the Filipino diasporic community formation is that despite all attempts to establish some sort of authentic, unchanging culture, our discrepant and evolving histories, coupled with ongoing struggles with various kinds of interlinked oppressions, are the real starting points for coalition building (Ignacio, 2005.) That is, when people are faced with really questioning—and witnessing—the boundaries of, and the boundary-making process of, identity formation and authenticity, people become more aware of the *socio-political* links existing *across* and, more often, *underlying* those boundaries. Identity-making is never a neutral process and very rarely is it entirely democratic; this is why uncovering the politics of identity, and then assessing the uses of identity is so important.

Knowing this, it is equally important that we make visible these otherwise invisible politics. Various scholars have long argued that post-Civil Rights racism uses racially "coded" or race-neutral language to maintain racism (see, for example, Omi and Winant, 1994). There is an equally voluminous amount of literature that focuses on the co-optation of phrases and/or cultural forms to maintain the status quo. However, it seems that we often see these things after the fact; thus, it is difficult to undo the damage that has already been done. In other words, although institutional and structural inequalities still abound, many people in our society focus on the role of individuals, their agency and intents, because we have lost the vocabulary, framework, and analytical tools to be able to recognize and, less yet, deal with structural oppression.

However, as I have argued in this chapter, perhaps one of the things we currently can do is to focus not only on the negative repercussions of these coded and/or co-opted discourses on subordinate communities or even on the positive benefits that the dominant groups may attain, but on the underlying ideologies themselves that remain intact. In this case, neoliberal ideology and its corresponding, self-legitimizing strategies (laws, policies, etc.) have been maintained through the rearticulation of the messages and meanings of both Martin Luther King, Jr. and Monseñor Oscar Romero. Thus, it is imperative that we replace this ideology and its corresponding frameworks with one which, again, directly addresses, as both Romero and King, Jr had implored, the necessity of restructuring a world that chooses to continually produce inequalities.

NOTES

1. I would like to thank Cathryn Teasley, Alice Marie Ritscherle, and Patrick Erker for their insights and constructive criticisms during the preparation of this article. In addition, this article was wholly inspired by Julieta Borja and Sonya Rice from International Partners in Mission; my adopted mother, Elena Dolores Aguilar, and her beautiful family; Dean Brackley, S. J. from the Universidad Centroamericana; Guillermo Aragon from Fundación Aragon; all the strong women at Mujer y Comunidad; *Horizontes*; and all those I met in El Salvador in the summer of 2005. Their past histories and their approaches to each present moment taught me much about the importance of infusing hope, love, and joy in all endeavors, large and small.
2. The California Civil Rights Initiative (CCRI or Proposition 209) became law on November 5, 1996. The law states that:
    (a) The state shall not discriminate against, or grant preferential treatment to, any individual or group on the basis of race, sex, color, ethnicity, or national origin in the operation of public employment, public education, or public contracting.
    (b) This section shall apply only to action taken after the section's effective date.
    (c) Nothing in this section shall be interpreted as prohibiting bona fide qualifications based on sex which are reasonably necessary to the normal operation of public employment, public education, or public contracting.
    (d) Nothing in this section shall be interpreted as invalidating any court order or consent decree which is in force as of the effective date of this section.

(e) Nothing in this section shall be interpreted as prohibiting action which must be taken to establish or maintain eligibility for any federal program, where ineligibility would result in a loss of federal funds to the state.

(f) For the purposes of this section, "state" shall include, but not necessarily be limited to, the state itself, any city, county, city and county, public university system, including the University of California, community college district, school district, special district, or any other political subdivision or governmental instrumentality of or within the state.

(g) The remedies available for violations of this section shall be the same, regardless of the injured party's race, sex, color, ethnicity, or national origin, as are otherwise available for violations of then-existing California antidiscrimination law.

(h) This section shall be self-executing. If any part or parts of this section are found to be in conflict with federal law or the United State Constitution, the section shall be implemented to the maximum extent that federal law and the United States Constitution permit. Any provision held invalid shall be severable from the remaining portions of this section.

Proponents of the law have argued that it merely restates the United States Civil Rights Act of 1964 and bans all discrimination—including so-called "reverse discrimination" (Wilson, Connerly and Lewis, as quoted in Volokh, 1997). Opponents, such as Retired General Colin Powell, argue that Proposition 209 actually undercuts protections against discrimination. Unless institutional discrimination has been eliminated entirely, they argue, strongly adhering to this law would severely limit the number of female and/or minority applicants to public schools and other employment opportunities. Often, they quote Colin Powell's address on May 25, 1996 to argue against the merits of the CCRI: "There are those who say we can stop now. America is a color-blind society. But it isn't yet. There are those who say we have a level playing field, but we don't yet."

3. "Prophets of a Future Not Our Own"

It helps, now and then, to step back
and take the long view.
The kingdom is not only beyond our efforts,
it is beyond our vision.
We accomplish in our lifetime only a tiny fraction of
the magnificent enterprise that is God's work.
Nothing we do is complete,
Which is another way of saying
That the kingdom always lies beyond us.
No statement says all that could be said.
No prayer fully expresses our faith.
No confession brings perfection.
No pastoral visit brings wholeness.
No program accomplishes the church's mission.
No set of goals and objectives includes everything.
This is what we are about:
We plant seeds that one day will grow.
We water seeds already planted,
knowing that they hold future promise.
We lay foundations that will need further development.

We provide yeast that produces effects beyond our capabilities.
We cannot do everything
and there is a sense of liberation in realizing that.
This enables us to do something,
and to do it very well.
It may be incomplete, but it is a beginning, a step along the way,
an opportunity for God's grace to enter and do the rest.
We may never see the end results,
but that is the difference between the master builder and the worker.
We are workers, not master builders,
ministers, not messiahs.
We are prophets of a future not our own.

—ARCHBISHOP OSCAR ARNULFO ROMERO

REFERENCES

Barlow, A. (2003). *Between fear and hope: Globalization and race in the United States.* Lanham, MD: Rowman and Littlefield Publishers.

Bonilla-Silva, E. (2006). *Racism without racists.* Lanham, MD: Rowman and Littlefield Publishers.

Brockman, J. (2005). *Romero: A life. The essential biography of a modern martyr and Christian hero.* Maryknoll, NY: Orbis Books.

Campbell-Johnson, M. (1989). Be a patriot: Kill a priest. *The Tablet,* No. 25 (November), p. 1361.

Crenshaw, K. (1998). Color blindness, history, and the law. In W. Lubiano (Ed.), *The house that race built* (pp. 280–288). New York: Vintage Books.

Dyson, M. (2000). *I may not get there with you: The true Martin Luther King Jr.* New York: The Free Press.

Gómez, I. and Vásquez, M. (2001). Youth gangs and religion among Salvadorans in Washington and El Salvador. In A. Peterson, P. Williams and M. Vasquez. (Eds.), *Christianity, globalization and social change in the Americas* (pp. 165–187). Piscataway, NJ: Rutgers University Press.

Gramsci, A. (1997). *Selections from the prison notebooks.* New York: International Publishers.

Hall, S. (1996). *Critical dialogues in cultural studies.* New York: Routledge.

Ignacio, E. N. (2005). *Building diaspora: Filipino community formation on the Internet.* New Brunswick, NJ: Rutgers University Press.

Lakoff, G. (2002). *Moral politics: How liberals and conservatives think.* Chicago, IL: University of Chicago Press.

Lonely Planet Worldguide (2006). Hiking, surfing, history—And not another tourist in sight. Article retrieved from the Lonely Planet Worldguide Web site at: http://www.lonelyplanet.com/worldguide/destinations/central-america/el-salvador (last retrived on December 1, 2007).

Magubane, Z. (2002). Black skins, black masks or "The return of the white Negro." *Men and masculinities,* Vol. 4, No. 3, pp. 233–257.

Martín-Baró, I. (2003). Oscar Romero: Voice of the downtrodden. In Archbishop O. Romero (Ed.), *Voice of the voiceless: The four pastoral letters and other statements* (pp. 1–21). Maryknoll, NY: Orbis Books.

McCarthy, C. (1998). *The uses of culture*. New York: Taylor and Francis, Inc.

Navarro, M. (1999). Zaragoza Journal: War orphan is Mayor, and at peace with himself. *The New York Times* (Monday, April 5, late edition, final, section A, column 3, foreign desk), p. 4.

Omi, M. and Winant, H. (1994). *Racial formation in the United States: From the 1960's to the 1970's*. New York: Routledge.

Penland, P., Chandler, G., and Prado, L. (2006). *Lonely planet: Nicaragua & El Salvador*. London: Lonely Planet Publications.

Peterson, A., Williams, P., and Vasquez, M. (2001). *Christianity, globalization and social change in the Americas*. Piscataway, NJ: Rutgers University Press.

Romero, Archbishop, O. A. (Ed.) (1985). *Voice of the voiceless: The four pastoral letters and other statements*. Maryknoll, NY: Orbis Press.

Romero, Archbishop, O. A. (1988). *The violence of love*. Rifton, NY: Plough Publishing House.

Sobrino, J. (2003). A theologian's view of Oscar Romero. In Archbishop, O. Romero (Ed.), *Voice of the voiceless* (pp. 22–51). Maryknoll, NY: Orbis Books.

Volokh, E. (1997). The California Civil Rights Initiative: An interpretive guide. *UCLA Law Review*, Vol. 44, No. 5, pp. 1335–1404.

West, C. (1993). *Race matters*. Boston, MA: Beacon Press.

West, C. (2004). *Democracy matters*. New York: Penguin Press.

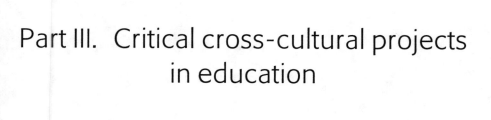

Part III. Critical cross-cultural projects
in education

CHAPTER NINE

School culture AND THE fight against exclusion: An optimistic curriculum

JURJO TORRES SANTOMÉ

University of A Coruña

Any amount of reflection on teachers' work in the classroom, or on curriculum planning and development, and how these might best be approached, compels us to stop and think about the meaning of knowledge itself and the purposes it has served in the past and present, in the specific historical moment we now find ourselves.

At this juncture, the production, dissemination, and use of knowledge becomes a primary concern—a process of inquiry to be actively engaged and guided by consideration for the type of society we wish to live in now, and in the future.

Social analysts largely agree that the productive world is undergoing sweeping transformations at great speed, a reality that is now being felt in all other spheres of society as well. Indeed, the heavy presence of new technologies has led Manuel Castells (1998) to assert that capitalism itself is experiencing a transformation or restructuring toward what he describes as *informational capitalism* (p. 44). Other authors, such as Kevin Robins and Frank Webster (1988) conceptualize these changes as the emergence of *cybernetic capitalism*, that is, as a system of social control based on the capacity of the state and corporate bureaucracies to collect, process, and use great quantities of personal data, on a scale that would have been inconceivable until but a few years ago. This is done in order to monitor, coordinate, and control the development of behavior in each and every citizen, and to have access to any and all data in this regard.

I believe these events demonstrate that we are moving toward a model of social organization based on highly developed technologies, through which the ability to generate, process, and transmit information is becoming the main source of productivity and power; hence the term *informational capitalism*. The difference between this and what others call the information society is that the emphasis in this last conception is on the importance of communicating knowledge perceived as inseparable from a particular society at any given moment in its history. There are, in fact, no societies that do *not* value the transmission of information, or that have not developed more or less sophisticated strategies to facilitate communication. However, the sort of societies now emerging at the onset of this new millennium are characterized by the power to control the production, circulation, and use of information. For instance, the speed and ability with which access to certain information is gained may help to increase the productivity, competitiveness, and power of a country, or, inversely, to leave it in the lurch.

Hence, we must not lose sight of the implications of the different ways knowledge is produced, organized, disseminated, and used.

In this sense, one of the lines of reflection we might pursue concerns the economic, political, and social functions of knowledge. The need for this focus becomes clear when considering the strong inclination existing throughout the second half of the 20th century toward greater professionalization and institutionalization of knowledge. In present-day neoliberal societies, the professionalization and institutionalization of knowledge entails control over who may have access to specialized learning; who may use it, and in what ways; whose interests it should serve; and the kind of sanctions that professional infiltration—or the heterodox use of such learning—might bring in their wake.

This institutionalization of knowledge also tends to involve a notable degree of oligopolization of discourses, which in turn favors the circulation of hegemonic perspectives alone. Given that this process occurs within the parameters of dominating power structures, it thus serves the interests of the most powerful social groups in society.

Specific forms of knowledge are generally institutionalized through structures providing the foundations from which hegemonic social groups may articulate and project their particular interests and visions of reality. It follows, then, that only select forms of knowledge can reach the mainstream when produced by institutions that are promoted, endorsed, and largely controlled by these same sectors of society. The fact that the bonds between university faculties, research groups, and major corporations are now growing stronger is clear proof of this trend. Such close intersectoral association is thus very likely to condition the ways in which certain lines of research—especially those serving the commercial interests of companies associated with the research circles in question—are financed and dynamically engaged. What is also becoming alarmingly more apparent by the day are the various tactics these groups employ in their attempts to control and exclusively exploit research findings that serve their interests and proceed from projects they themselves finance. One such strategy involves keeping the findings from becoming public knowledge for a number of years. Consider what is potentially at stake behind research findings concerning, for example, the human genome project or computer learning (in particular, that generated by and for the military field). Seen in this light, the interest in monopolizing knowledge becomes strikingly clear.

Moreover, when these diverse forms of knowledge eventually do attain a minimum level of public recognition, the institutions that monitor and foster learning play a fundamental role in the supervision of orthodoxies associated with such findings. That is, university departments and, more specifically, organizational structures based on differentiated areas of knowledge not only serve to select new members for the organization, but also to stimulate certain lines of research. And whether explicitly or implicitly, they further endeavor to hinder other such lines. A great number and variety of institutions watch over orthodoxy and function as border-guards or "gate-keepers" between disciplines and/or specializations, thus rivaling over exclusivity or even how to share certain spaces of knowledge and intervention. One of the main tasks of professional associations, for instance, is to protect their members' respective spheres of occupational activity and influence; we must therefore not overlook the fact that those vying for leadership in such organizations normally do so under the sway of particular ideological and/or corporatist interests as conveyed through discourses and programs that stress the practices of specific professions.

The same institutional actors who organize and promote each discipline or field of knowledge are those that approve the various specialized discourses as well, and issue the diplomas and certificates that authorize certain individuals to use and foster that specialized learning. With such legitimizations, all professionals, in turn, become supervisors of orthodoxies that prevent intrusions. They attempt to keep those who fail to hold similar credentials from making use of that specialized knowledge and taking part in the creation of it; they are primed to deny facilitating or supporting research projects presented by those who lack their same credentials or who do not share their scientific paradigm; nor will they admit such designated "outsiders" into teams and groups that assess practical experiences.

The institutionalization of knowledge also works to establish limits in relation to other fields or specializations of knowledge. This, however, cannot keep experts from various disciplines from disputing over who may lay claim to certain fields of intervention. In our society, there is abundant evidence of this struggle to occupy such parcels of symbolic space. Consider, for example, the way medical associations attempt to keep psychologists and psychiatrists from practicing their professions within the field of healthcare, not to mention the frenzied attacks aimed at so-called alternative medicine. We could provide similar examples for practically all the greater professions. Reinforcement of this monitoring role, which is so inherent to institutions that rely on defensive decrees and regulations endorsed by public administrations, is, moreover, the outcome of the ever and significantly growing number of specializations and professions now gaining a foothold in spheres that used to be the exclusive terrain of one specialization alone.

Thus, consideration of the kind of reflection on knowledge we want our educational institutions to promote is a question that raises numerous issues and queries. In this work, however, I will limit my focus to two such issues which I consider to be of primary importance to the central question at hand. One is the need to reconsider the dominating disciplinary approach to the organization of knowledge and learning—an endeavor that implies a corresponding commitment to seeking alternatives of a more interdisciplinary nature. The other concerns the need to stress curricular practices that allow students to "see" what is hidden behind the official knowledge provided at school, the aim being to generate, in this way, greater optimism in younger generations regarding their potential to eventually interrupt the dominant dynamics currently in control of the institutionalization of knowledge, for the purpose of building more humane, fair, and democratic models of society.

ON THE NEED FOR GREATER INTERDISCIPLINARITY

A commitment to deepening interdisciplinary approaches to knowledge and learning calls for some minimal excavation down to the root motives feeding into the dominating disciplinary approach. In so doing, my aim is to uncover the particular interests behind the current hegemonic division of knowledge into disciplines—a process that comports an ever-present risk of what we might call *babelization* (Torres Santomé, 2006).

One reason for this situation can be found in the struggle amongst scientific communities to impose particular or singular models of rationality on all sciences and fields of learning. Without aspiring to be exhaustive, I will suggest in this work where we might direct our gaze in an attempt to reveal some of the whys and wherefores of these tendencies. This will involve casting our gaze as far back as the 16th century, but fundamentally from the 18th and 19th centuries onward, to the historic conditions that gave rise to the initial motives behind the consolidation of an epistemological model which functioned to a great extent in a totalitarian manner when it came to approving what was considered to be valid and legitimate knowledge. Any knowledge that did not fit the mold—that is, that could not be neatly situated within the methodological rules and epistemology of the physical-natural sciences (which, in the aforementioned historic periods, were achieving notably efficient outcomes and relevancy in addressing the material needs of the people)—was rejected.

As far back as the days of Francis Bacon (1561–1626), one kind of knowledge was clearly privileged over all others: that which would contribute to the domination of nature by mankind. But in order for this domination to occur, the "deformation" of knowledge potentially resulting from diverse analyses and creations of the human mind had to be avoided, which was why even Bacon himself promptly sought to devise a new epistemological method capable of both minimizing such allegedly adverse effects and rectifying potential errors, all through a continuous construction of knowledge.

It so turned out, then, that mathematics would become one of the main languages used for constructing and verifying the validity of knowledge. Not only did mathematics function as a privileged instrument for investigating and formulating new and valid knowledge, but also as a language for representing and putting the adaptation of available knowledge to the test, inasmuch as its rigor and validity were concerned. Knowing would mean being able to represent that knowledge mathematically, treating it with numbers so as to quantify it. The kind of knowledge that could not be translated, however, into mathematical formulas would face great problems in being even initially considered for its validity, legitimacy, and usefulness for learning. More often than not, such non-quantifiable knowledge was associated instead with superstitious, religious, or popular forms of knowing.

This tendency to reduce reality and knowledge to numbers and formulas came to shape analytical perspectives to the point that researchers would focus almost exclusively on those aspects of reality that could be effectively quantified. The reasoning behind this approach was clear: it would allow for the comparison and possible convergence of different explanations of a particular phenomenon, this, in turn, further allowing for the classification and establishment of connections between explanations. That way, interventions into reality could also be carried out with greater precision and predictability as far as the outcomes were concerned. One of the main purposes of the construction of knowledge, then, would be that of gradually establishing regularities and laws in order to achieve better interventions and greater control over nature.

In a way, the aspiration to construct a kind of utilitarian and functional knowledge base somehow entertained an underlying image and idea of the world as a perfect and controllable machine. Hence the name "mechanism," which is how this epistemological paradigm used to be labeled.

This model was to enjoy great prestige as it echoed the aspirations of an incipient bourgeoisie that sought to break away from a reality until then constructed as controllable and interpretable solely in terms of religion, as through the exclusive will of some deity. But if nature was explicable and could be controlled by human beings, then privileges granted by way of blood line, the inscrutable will of God, or the social rank of one's descent, were no longer valid. Each and every human being regained control over his or her life, and would thus hold his own fate in his very own hands.

This development provided humankind with renewed optimism, an optimism that would prove, moreover, indispensable if this new model was to prosper. On criticizing medical learning for being careless and favoring situations of ignorance, Francis Bacon himself showed that he was fully aware of the need for a new epistemological paradigm. In one of his works first published in 1605, *The advancement of learning*, Bacon forcefully argued that

> [...] in the investigation of illnesses, the treatment of many is abandoned because such illnesses are claimed, in some cases, to be incurable due to their very nature, or because, in other cases, the opportunity to have cured the patient was missed, and this is practiced to such an extent that even Sila and the Triumvirs did not condemn as many men to death as do these [doctors] with their edicts of ignorance; nonetheless, many patients flee from them with less difficulty than from the Roman proscriptions. That is why I do not hesitate to point out that the failure to discover perfect remedies for many illnesses, especially in their extreme stages, is a deficiency; and so it is that [such illnesses] are sooner declared incurable and laws enacted that legitimate negligence and exonerate ignorance from discredit. (Bacon, 1988, pp. 123–124)[1]

Such hard sought control over physical phenomena and nature was to be developed and utilized to its maximum potential, its basic method therefore considered as desirable for application to social phenomena. The objective for the social sciences, then, would be to discover laws that would help explain, predict, and program the development of a given society. In order to accomplish this, the social sciences were to copy the universally valid models and methodologies of physics. It would therefore be a matter of aspiring to establish something along the lines of a "social physics," according to which social phenomena would be considered and treated through an approach replicating the methodology developed by physicists to understand and treat physical-natural phenomena. This would in turn imply having to frame reality in objective terms by dividing it into analytical units or plots, the various dimensions and social elements of which could therefore be "rationally" quantified and measured for analysis.

The difficulty of accomplishing this task is what led Thomas Kuhn (1980), in his work on scientific revolutions, to label the social sciences as "pre-paradigmatic," given that those researching in such fields of knowledge would be unlikely to reach substantial levels of consensus, not only concerning the methodologies but also the epistemologies upon which they might base their work. In keeping with Kuhn, this lack of consensus would account for the varying educational strategies engaged in these fields, as opposed to scientific strategies that may be referred to as paradigmatic. So it is, for instance, that in the spheres of both the fine arts (music, painting, and sculpture) and literature, textbooks play more of a secondary role. In fact, those who teach these subjects in primary and secondary education are likely to resort to a greater variety of resources and sources. "As a result," Kuhn (1980) writes, "students of any of those disciplines are always up to date on the immense variety of problems that the members of their future [professional] groups have attempted to solve over the years" (p. 254). Not only that, but such students will also learn that their areas of study constitute fields of expression and knowledge in which disputes are not easily settled, and from which arise numerous open problems and different groups of specialists with highly opposing stances.

In the sphere of education, on the contrary, the dominating scientific strategy would come to found teaching on textbooks. This occurred as a consequence of the high degree of historic consensus regarding what should be considered as rigorous and valid knowledge for the field, and regarding the methodologies used for constructing and evaluating that knowledge. In the so-called scientific subjects, "textbooks," Kuhn (1980) observes, "systematically substitute the creative scientific literature which makes them possible. Confidence in scientific paradigms is what makes this teaching technique possible, and few scientists would wish to change it" (p. 255).

Although there have been many attempts to apply such positivistic epistemologies to the social sciences, these attempts have long been challenged through strong disputes over the specific nature of the social fields of knowledge. In defense of the idiosyncrasy of these fields, the line of argument usually revolves around the fact that human beings' intentions behind their actions are not always easy to detect. Thus, in the social sciences, where *people* are the central objects and subjects of study, the methodologies derived from physical-natural research are not considered sufficiently comprehensive to address such subjectivities' expectations, nor to adequately interpret their personal and collective intentions behind certain decisions, habits, and routines, or behind their interpretations of the situations they take part in or choose to avoid. The commitment, then, to alternative methodologies of a more qualitative and interpretative nature has been on the list of demands since the early 20th century.

This situation has given rise to two broad spheres of learning which, until not long ago, appeared to be irreconcilable, not to say antagonistic: on one hand, that of the physical-natural sciences and, on the other hand, that of the social sciences.

Throughout the 20th century, moreover, a number of crises emerged from the physical-natural sciences. For instance, various researchers from the fields of physics and biology began to draw our attention to the fact that it was highly difficult to conduct research with complete objectivity—to measure without altering the conditions of what was being measured, without interfering. As a result, many of the laws currently formulated in the field of physics reflect a greater dose of caution intentionally factored into their discourse; that is, they are now presented as *probabilistic* laws.

The classification of physical phenomena into hermetic groupings that can be measured, counted, and analyzed independently, is also going through a crisis, while the conception of physical reality as a "continuum" is gaining ascendancy. In biology and medicine, for example, even living organisms now appear as more than simple conglomerates of cells, bones, and organs that can be analyzed and comprehended separately, without considering their networks of interdependence as organic wholes.

Yet, perhaps the one issue that has served as the greatest stimulus for developing interdisciplinary approaches to learning and knowledge has to do with recent revelations regarding the *uses* of the "objective" knowledge promoted by the physical-natural sciences.

THE DISCOVERY OF FRAGILITY

Throughout the second half of the last century, and in particular from the 1980s onwards, a profound revision took place concerning the way human progress was evaluated in all its spheres. Going back in modern history to the year 1798, this question had already been taken up by Immanuel Kant in his renowned essay "A renewed attempt to answer the question: 'Is the human race continually improving?'" (Kant, 1970 [1798]). Those were times when a clear teleology was overwhelmingly accepted as immanent in all historical processes. Kant reinforced this belief in that very work, wherein—as a result of a conflict that had arisen between the University Faculties of Philosophy and Law (a conflict further fueled by the effects of the French Revolution)—he dealt with the philosophy of history anew, attempting to reflect on human potential and the capabilities of social and moral beings, as well as the probabilities of humans improving their existential conditions. "However," Kant writes,

> [e]ven lacking prophetic spirit, and in accordance with the conditions and precursory signs of our times, I claim that I am in a position to predict that the human race will indeed accomplish that goal, and that its progress towards the best shall moreover

never again move backwards altogether. [...] Mankind has always been progressing towards the best and shall always continue to move forward in the future. (Kant, 1964, pp. 200, 202)

The enlightened reasoning which personalities like Kant were committed to was thought to be a construction that would facilitate more effective confrontation with the authority of the Church, so as to allow subjects to break free from a world of dictated truths that could neither be questioned nor denied, but only, in the very best of cases, subject to interpretation. The Enlightenment thus gave rise to the possibility of freedom of thought and criticism, and the exercise of so-called enlightened reason was meant to help transform the world and set human beings free.

This belief, which came to characterize modernity itself, was later to become one of the tenets singled out by the critics of modernity and challenged through perspectives that can be grouped together under the umbrella of postmodernism.

Numerous events taking place throughout the 20th century served to question the central tenets of modernity, which were founded on the belief that enlightened reason and technological progress (the latter perceived as the logical product of certain uses of the former) would result in the elimination of traditional beliefs and forms of knowledge that merely served to legitimize privileged ways of life for limited sectors of society, and consequently to justify and perpetuate oppression and domination. In the last two decades, however, those invested in the postulates of postmodernism have been attempting to reveal that the perceived relationship between reason and progress in modern thought is not always present. As Alain Touraine (1993) stresses,

[...] if modernization associated progress and culture by setting traditional cultures or societies against those modern, and by explaining all social and cultural realities in light of their place on the axis of tradition-modernity, postmodernism sets out to dissociate such previously associated notions. (pp. 239–240)

Indeed, when it comes to assessing the advancement of knowledge and the improvement of society, postmodern thought has been successful in highlighting the fact that economic success is not necessarily a symptom of progress, and all the more so when it is concentrated in very few hands. What is more, this same lack of correspondence is evident in the technological uses of knowledge forged, ironically, in accordance with the ideals of modernity.

Postmodern discourses, or perhaps to be more precise, the critics of modernity also denounce the inadequacy of rigid dualisms and polarities that hinder the understanding of more complex social dynamics. Binarisms of the kind oppressor/oppressed, white population/black population, working class (as progressive)/upper class (as conservative), limit our ability to perceive the more complex interplay of social dynamics operating on social beings at any given point in time.

Those critical of modernity point out the contradictions between, on the one hand, good intentions and commitment to the notion of progress—both so essential to the project of modernity—and on the other hand, some of the perverse forms and uses of modern knowledge, including the technologies it has given rise to. In this sense, the dramatic horror of Nazi extermination camps, epitomized in Auschwitz, has come to occupy the symbolic center of this line of postmodern critique. Nonetheless, Theodor W. Adorno (1998) had already formulated a similar critique early on, by questioning the kind of "technological personalities" emerging from 20th century research—personalities capable of mobilizing all available scientific knowledge for the sole purpose of developing a "a train system to take the victims to Auschwitz—one that was free of interference, and the fastest possible" (Adorno, 1998, p. 88).

The techno-sciences and their military uses; the impoverishment of the Third World through the pillaging of its natural resources; the human barbarity and genocide observable in numerous wars waged throughout the 20th and now the 21st centuries; the unemployment and poverty resulting from implementation of the most up-to-date business theories; etc.—all come to be seen by the critics of modernity as a certain failure of the ideas of progress and emancipation predicted since the Enlightenment.

According to Jean-François Lyotard (1992), modernity is characterized by "great tales" that legitimize a project of society founded on notions such as emancipation and certain forms of rationality considered to be socially powerful. These grand narratives, like long-standing myths, perform a

> [...] function of legitimization; they legitimize institutions, practices both social and political, legislation, ethics, ways of thinking, and symbolism. As opposed to myths, these tales do not find their legitimacy in original "founding" acts, but rather in an actively promoted future, i.e. in an Idea to be realized. This Idea (of freedom, of "light," of socialism, of general enrichment) inheres a legitimizing value because it is universal. It gives modernity its characteristic mode: the *project*, i.e. the will directed towards a purpose. (Lyotard, 1992, p. 61)

In any case, such teleological ideals are, as shall be argued here, the true motor behind the achievements of humankind, for they have most closely inspired the great social contracts that have led to universal values such as human rights, and thus embody what can and must continue to direct the actions of new generations.

This project should not prevent us, however, from attempting to detect the discontinuities, ruptures, and reappearances of practices and discourses—including the power relations that traverse them and their contexts—that contradict such goals. In fact, this determination is what was to become a central concern of Michel Foucault's (1990), which reached its maximum expression through his renowned genealogical-archaeological method.[2] On this epistemological undertaking, Foucault wrote:

> Archaeology does not attempt to define the thoughts, representations, images, issues or obsessions, hidden or visible, in discourses, but rather the very discourses themselves, discourses that, in their capacity as practices, obey certain rules. (1990, p. 233)

Thus, the aim is to examine not only the political aspects of the internal norms and regulations of discursive practices, but also the relationship these same political aspects sustain with practical discourses, which are reflected in the institutional practices that take place in schools, prisons, hospitals, and other social services.

Given that every society has its own set of rules for defining truth, genealogy is performed to trace the ways in which "truth" is constructed, and how its production conditions and explains the ways we govern ourselves and others.

In this context, it is important to understand Foucault's conception of power and learning because one of the idiosyncratic qualities of Foucauldian thought is that power is not necessarily a negative force, as would be the case with domination or coercion, which deprive, oppress, distort, and deceive through pure force, exploitation, lies, or false hopes. Power, on the other hand, does not necessarily have to be repressive; it may actually be positive and productive. Of equal importance in this portrayal of power is the fact that it is never the exclusive possession of any one person, but is wielded by many people through their diverse practices. So it is, for instance, that not only teachers exercise power in educational institutions, but so too do students and their families.

However, no sooner had such critical conceptions of knowledge emerged than frenzied attacks were unleashed against this new approach to researching and questioning the construction of social and scientific discourses—against any proposals to profoundly revise the dominant categories of analysis and systems of meaning.

On a deeper level, what the emergent form of criticism really highlighted was the difficulties involved in changing our way of looking at reality; it exposed the hegemonic traditions of knowledge that managed to compose a kind of commonsense: a rigid and routine way of dealing with the analysis and knowledge of reality. When alternative ways of knowing and acquiring knowledge are discovered, those invested in the exploration, production, and uses of knowledge do not always find it easy to manifest an openness of mind, a personal and intellectual flexibility that would allow them to discover just what it is that those new stances are really doing, and why.

What the emergent forms of deeply hermeneutic and poststructural analysis were actually doing was to perform the innovative and critical task of reviewing and, consequently, destabilizing interpretations of concepts and theories that had never been questioned before; they set out to historicize the validity of certain ways of thinking by focusing on other more novel, less established fields. They thus drew attention to a large contingent of human actors and cultural groups whose needs and interests had seldom ever been taken into account before.[3]

In this way, light has finally been shed on those conflicts and confrontations that are inseparable from the production of knowledge and, logically, from its applications and use. Given that the social sciences are designed to address the problems, issues, and conceptualizations of our world, they attempt to provide answers to the varied and manifold social realities and movements extant at any given point in history and in particular social contexts. It is therefore necessary to study this social epistemology in terms of the events, thoughts, and people that give rise to it, to situate it within the social circumstances such actors have had to manage and cope with, thus devising systems of rules that, in turn, impose the ways in which such circumstances may be brought to light and interpreted. Foucauldian genealogy is of great use in performing this task because, as a methodology, it facilitates "putting the categories of knowledge that have become established in the so-called scientific field, and more specifically, in the human and social sciences, to the test" (Varela, 1997, p. 37).

This call to pay special attention to those factors affecting the production and uses of knowledge is what has further led Pierre Bourdieu (1999) to assert that

> [...] the social sciences, as the only fields in the position to unmask and oppose the hitherto absolutely unheard-of strategies of domination, which they themselves sometimes help to inspire and deploy, will have to choose more clearly than ever between two alternatives: either that of offering their rational instruments of knowledge at the service of an ever more rationalized domination, or that of rationally analyzing such domination, in particular the contribution that rational knowledge can make to the *de facto* monopolization of the benefits of universal reason. The awareness and understanding of this logical political scandal of sorts, which the monopolization of universality represents, unmistakably indicates both the ends and the means of a permanent political struggle to universalize the conditions of access to universality. (p. 112)

Yet, there is one pressing need that the aforementioned collection of stances has made more evident than ever: namely, the need to establish and strengthen lines of interdisciplinary work, in particular those aimed at preventing and even undoing the exclusive dichotomies or divisions established between the social sciences and the physical-natural sciences. This is what will help to recover the human being as the *subject* of study, as the decisive factor affecting both purpose and orientation in the construction of knowledge. Furthermore, this need to break down the barriers between spheres of knowledge is what makes it easier to explain why, in nearly all such spheres, interdisciplinary lines of work have been opening up. So it is, for instance, that economists have begun to realize that much more than the traditional dimensions must be taken into account if they are to keep their interventions from producing negative outcomes or unwanted effects. Biochemists have come to understand that intervening to cure illnesses is much more complex than initially thought to be; that people have expectations and feelings that must be considered, not to mention additional social and material conditions affecting their health. If technologists wish to prevent irreparable damage to the environment, animal species, or human communities, they, too, are in need of cooperation and input from those practicing in other fields of the social sciences.

ON THE URGENT NEED TO REVIEW THE CULTURE OF CLASSROOM WORK

A similar philosophy needs to eventually penetrate not only institutions of higher learning but also the educational system as a whole, for mental habits are in fact already shaped to a great extent at the compulsory levels where ways of observing—which come to condition how citizens contemplate reality itself—are formed.

A commitment to these aims will require, moreover, teaching staff in possession of a much broader knowledge base and experiential background than those currently provided through university teacher education programs. The growing complexity of our societies, and the speed at which new knowledge is produced further contribute to this demand. If it is true that, in the past, the dissemination of information was more laborious and therefore much slower, today it may be said that one of the defining notes of our times is the enormous amount of information generated and disseminated at record speed.

The task facing teaching institutions, then, is to readily provide all learners with information commensurate with their age, level of development, and previous knowledge, while simultaneously seeing this function challenged by other media, such as electronic networks and communications technologies. Educators will increasingly find that their students can turn to an ever-growing array of alternative sources of information and learning such as television channels specializing in popular science and technology ("Documania," "Discovery Channel," "Cultura," "National Geographic Channel," etc.); the virtually all-encompassing realm of cyberspace; popular science magazines; information digitalized in disk formats; video tapes; science museums; and so on; not to mention the growing network of informal learning institutions. Newspapers constantly run advertisements from private schools offering in-person and/or distance learning, as well as advertisements from a great variety of associations offering all sorts of courses and training.

It is only realistic to acknowledge that, in certain fields, these alternative sources of learning have attained a more solid reputation than formal educational institutions themselves. This is the case, for instance, with language learning, music, computing, and the dissemination of popular science.

An essential consideration here is the fact that, in most conceptualizations about teaching and schoolwork, the role of the teacher as worker or professional is attributed a significant degree of ahistoricity or decontextualization. For instance, in teacher education programs, future teachers are rarely challenged to consider the social, economic, cultural, and political frameworks in which they will be practicing their profession. This is so because, among other reasons, such cultural content has never been considered an important part of the preparation of educators for early childhood and elementary level teaching; nor for higher levels, for that matter, because the disciplinary approach that so characterizes their formal preparation discourages these teachers from searching for root causes, deeper meanings, and broader connections. In other words, it does not foster levels of reflection that facilitate a more complete and critical understanding of what is really happening in the world we live in.

Teacher education developed in this direction for various reasons. However, one factor that serves to reinforce the current orientation is influence from the increasing number of conservative and neoliberal political options now in circulation throughout the world. These policies[4] stress the need to cut budget items earmarked for publicly financed social services such as educational systems, while simultaneously promoting a kind of commonsensical mistrust among citizens of all public programs and efforts to combat inequalities and forms of oppression such as racism, sexism, ageism, religious and political fundamentalism, or classism. Any formal attempts to reduce these injustices are instead construed as dangerous sources of trouble for the common good. As a result, escapism is turning out to be one of the most typical "solutions." Although these problems are considered to be very important, they are also thought to be too complex and conflictive to bring into classrooms and thus burden children, many of whom inherently face such problems on a daily basis.

For the vast majority of people who have attended school, and those who still do, curricular content is usually much too abstract and ahistorical, as it usually refers to vague, undefined, and abstract situations and contexts. There seems to be more of a concern about memorizing formulas, facts, and decontextualized generalizations than about attracting people's attention to concrete realities, both distant and near.

This idea of keeping young learners from having to see or perceive inequality and social injustice; this desire to supposedly shelter them within a kind of infantile limbo or artificial paradise, is what might account for the childish and insipid nature of most textbook contents intended for compulsory levels of schooling, particularly in early childhood and elementary education. I consider this advancement of a sort of "Walt Disneyfication" of life in general, and of schooling in particular, to be most worrisome because reality and scientific, historical, cultural, and social information are presented to children by means of fantasy beings, unreal characters, and anthropomorphic creatures that reduce such vital information to a collection of absurdly ridiculous and—more often than not—sugary-sweet, watered-down renditions of the world they live in. Many of the textbooks used in classrooms today include too many pictures and too much information of this kind, which subsequently hampers students' ability to learn how to clearly distinguish fact from fiction, fantasy from reality (i.e., the difference between a book of adventure stories and one that is factual in nature or scientifically rigorous from an informational point of view). Because these texts are aimed at children, it is implicitly believed that they should not reflect life the way it truly is; that it is best to keep these children immersed in a fantasy world for a few more years. Hence, the situations of everyday life reflected in these textbooks hardly differ from those appearing in the "twee" storybooks and comics, as far as treatment and form are concerned (this is not to underestimate the power of quality children's literature in treating reality in accessible, creative ways, without need for insipid distortions). This artificially puerile curricular material becomes powerfully attractive within the context of a world leisure and consumer culture immersed as it is in the conservative, classist, sexist, ageist, and racist values promoted by multinational corporations such as Walt Disney, Hanna Barbera or Mattel (i.e., the World-of-Barbie mold).

Where learning about real-life issues of a more specific nature is concerned, many children must rely on textbooks that address only highly superficial social and political problems, and whose publishers opt to present such information by reproducing advertising models of the kind employed by, say, Benetton. This particular model includes many images reflecting "difference," as well as social problems and injustices (AIDS, racism, poverty, wars, etc.), although it also chooses to depoliticize and reread these issues in a new setting full of colors (Benetton's emblematic periodical is entitled *Colors*), harmony, and world peace that is nowhere to be found in real life. In this framework, major social tragedies are often represented in a sensationalistic manner, through alternative images meant to inspire "compassion" and "pity" at an individual level, and that turn readers into "voyeurs." This same level of manipulation is clearly present in certain posters and paintings that represent grave human injustices or tragedies for decorative purposes alone;

such projects privilege the aesthetic qualities of "poverty" over all others: the look of a destitute and helpless person thus comes to displace the urgent, underlying political, economic, and other issues affecting his or her condition. Subsequently, observation of such images is not likely to lead to deeper analysis or fuller understanding of the situations they actually depict.

Information thus presented is characterized by a notable degree of decontextualization that neither reveals nor problematizes the structural causes underlying the cases it appears to denounce. Instead, it performs a recontextualization in the emotional sphere of the observer, who is most likely to initially experience a sentimental reaction to the particular case of suffering presented, and then perhaps a mixed sense of relief and guilt in knowing that his or her own situation is not half as bad. This is how highly dramatic images serve to overwhelm their observers to the point that the only solutions conceivable are direct individual actions such as donations. Assistance of a more structural nature—for example, the grassroots call for rich countries to allocate at least 0.7% of their GDP to sustainable development and the eradication of poverty in poorer countries—tends too often to fall to the wayside. While the so-called "0.7" campaign (a well-known issue in Spanish politics) is a useful and necessary strategy, policies that are more profoundly transformational by design, and global in scope, are absolutely essential if worldwide organizations such as the United Nations, the World Trade Organization, the World Bank and the International Monetary Fund are to be held accountable to populations across the globe for transnational activities that do not respect basic human rights. Such analytical perspectives are rarely reflected, however, in textbooks.

Thus, what is actually happening in school curricula and society at large is the reproduction of an assistance model for social welfare, in which poverty is automatically factored in as an *inevitable* part of our collective existence on this planet. To get people involved in ways that might lead to genuine solutions to poverty therefore necessitates a more complete analysis of the complex set of dynamics involved in the origins and perpetuation of the highly inequitable distribution of access to well-being throughout the world.

Conservative analyses only serve to reproduce the myth that each human being is entirely responsible for his or her own fate. So it is that, even in recent times, the state of need is increasingly associated with delinquency, as those who—at certain junctures in their lives—find themselves overwhelmed by urgent need are likely to be left with no other alternative than to obtain their essentials by illicit means. Zygmunt Bauman (2000) clearly denounces the easy condemnation of such desperation when he observes that "linking poverty to crime has yet another effect: it helps them [the most privileged of social groups] banish the poor people of the world from their moral own obligations" (p. 120). The only options left for the desperately poor, then, are either individual charity or purely coercive institutional measures, such as imprisonment (Wacquant, 1999).

It should be further noted that, at this stage in the development of the neo-liberal economy, those who might eek out a living as "unskilled workers" are finding the demand for their labor diminishing by the day. This greatly accounts for the fact that there is an ever rising legion of poor "left to their own fate." Let us also recall that phenomena such as homelessness amongst children are on the rise not only in the better known cases of Brazil, Argentina, Mexico, India, and Thailand, but in many other countries throughout the world. But how is it that we are periodically shocked by news about children soldiers, when we never seem to reach the point of analyzing how the weapons are supplied in the first place; which countries manufacture them and why; how they get into circulation; who the actual buyers and sellers are; how the weapons change hands so easily; which other countries are benefiting from those involved in armed conflicts; and so on?

The problem, once again, is that when injustices are denounced, the tendency is to treat each case on an individual basis, just like the solutions. This is a trap that even some nongovernmental organizations (NGO) fall into. Consider, for example, the sponsorship of children living in poverty-stricken countries. This kind of campaign misleadingly conveys that just a small personal donation each month to a particular cause will help put an end to child neglect and abandonment as a systemic social ill. Much worse than this, however, is an ever more visible marketing ploy that exploits charitable causes for the sake of increasing sales. That is, some multinational corporations and businesses announce that if people buy their products (e.g., Fortuna cigarettes of Spain, Pepsi, Nestlé and others), they are indirectly contributing to the development of Third World countries—a claim that is true, in a very superficial sense, because such companies indeed do commit to donating a negligible percentage of their profits (for instance 0.7% or 1.0%) to development programs managed by some NGO. In the process, however, they have also learned that the gains from this charitable activity far outweigh the losses thanks to the positive image it creates for the company in consumers' minds. Many people may even change brands in order to contribute—free of additional charge—to such "good deeds."

Similar forms of what we might call predatory charity are promoted under the umbrella of mega-shows, mega-gigs, and marathon TV-programs usually held in the wake of a particularly devastating crisis. Of course such benefic events do help, when help is urgently needed, but their mere existence speaks to the great void in national and international public policy where anticipating and mitigating human suffering is concerned.

A similar strategy, operating behind the guise of charity campaigns, repeatedly exploited the person of Princess Diana of Wales as well, even following her death, and always backed by a powerful publicity machine. The high media profile of the Lady Di charity missions throughout the world contrasted sharply, however, with the blanket of silence surrounding her country's involvement in, and responsibility for, a substantial part of the conditions leading populations to depend on charitable aid in the first place.

All of these tactics commercialize solidarity, thus allowing capitalist venture to mask its true face and appear before the general public as "more humane," ethical, and committed to the fight for social justice.

The point I wish to make here is that charitable donation approaches that mitigate people's guilty conscience, or that increase returns, may treat some of the *symptoms* but not the *causes* of oppression, inequality, and injustice across the globe. It is therefore crucial that people understand that, in order to effectively tackle such problems, sociopolitical measures are paramount. And one such measure involves *critically* addressing these issues in educational institutions in general, and in teacher education programs, in particular.

Based on research on how these controversial subjects are viewed in classrooms, we discern three general tendencies: (1) they are either omitted or silenced; (2) strategies that emulate those practiced by the most conservative of ideological groups are being used to justify policy decisions affecting these issues; or (3) solidarity is commercialized through means similar to those described above.

When the representation of southern-hemisphere countries (where the bulk of the world's poorest populations reside) in both advertising or curriculum materials sold by big publishers is analyzed according to the criteria suggested by Aquilina Fueyo Gutiérrez (2000, pp. 37–43), however, we see quite clearly how such representations lead people to conclude that the inhabitants of developing countries live the way they do because of a series of supposed reasons that, once again, mislead: "they are poor because they are lazy and do not work," "Latin Americans and black people are lazy" (attributed innate attitudes); "they have too many children" (reproductive practices and demographics); "there is not enough for everyone to eat" (economic development); "they are uncultured, they have no education, we have to educate them" (education); "they are poor due to natural disasters such as earthquakes or floods" (misfortune); "they are poor because they are always immersed in wars or have dictatorial governments" (political instability). When explanations of this kind are adopted, those thus convinced consider themselves to be exonerated from any sort of responsibility. In such circumstances, solidarity rarely surpasses the mere exercise of charity.

What is more, the world is generally presented in dualistic terms: whites/blacks; Christians/Muslims; the rich/the poor; and so on; and each polarity is assigned its prescribed location. Thus it is, for instance, that Africa is envisioned as "the black world," as though its lands were the exclusive territory of that imagined category of population, whereas the West (the world of wealth, modernity, progress, culture, and so on) is associated with white people. The fact that there is more than one race living in the West and in Africa alike is either forgotten or concealed.

When African populations are presented as "conflictive" "people of color" who frequently engage in more or less violent acts, this perpetuates the myths and prejudices associated with African immigration. It makes the perceived misery and ignorance of Africa—an erroneous perception fomented by Western ignorance—appear dangerously close, to the point that it might actually affect "us." This would account for the use of such unfair and racist expressions as "invasions" to represent the migration practices of African peoples. Meanwhile, the "push-factors" that motivate so many people to emigrate from their homelands are ignored. This stubborn refusal to comprehend the deeper causes of migration around the world has found expression, for instance, in Spain, where a pervasive silence envelops the historic circumstances causing considerable segments of the country's population to emigrate: people who saw—and in some cases still see—no other alternative than to attempt to "start over" mostly in Latin America and Central Europe (Torres Santomé, 2008).

More than this, a monolithic image of the world dominates our collective psyche, a world without cracks or possibilities for change. The dynamics that have actually helped solve social problems past and present, are simply not examined; open debates about the possible solutions are scarce.

When students around the world are presented with texts and images that do reflect misery and oppression, but that lack key information relevant to the historical genesis of such realities, such youth are being deprived of the tools they need to understand the whys and wherefores, or to begin to comprehend that there are solutions to the problems, many of which are contemplated by the inhabitants of their own societies. In rich countries, however, a notable degree of ethnocentric paternalism situates the First World as the sole bearer of explanations and solutions.

In reality, watered-down textbooks merely serve to perpetuate the myth that critical discussion and reflection is harmful to children, causing needless suffering and potential conflict at school. This popular belief is tantamount to a collective refusal to try to improve our human condition. Those who wish to shelter children from everyday life believe that certain aspects of our reality—aspects that may provoke too many questions or too much discomfort—are "inappropriate" and therefore expendable when it comes to educating the younger generations. Indeed, those who think this way must imagine that children's lives are overwhelmed by insoluble problems and constant failure. From my point of view, this disposition in educators is but one of the signs of a notable ignorance of history and the evolution of human culture.

On the one hand, this background pessimism favors strategies that marginalize childhood in the "protected" spaces of banal subjects and fairytale paradises, which keep young learners in a sort of limbo or "reserve" meant to defend their ascribed state of "natural innocence." On the other hand, it also serves to prolong the years that our society designates as the childhood phase. It thus extends childhood itself.

In fact, many adult productions aimed at children illustrate underlying erroneous suppositions about what it means to be a child, in the sense that they are artificially puerilized. Informative books or textbooks that indulge insipid contents and imagery do so because their authors equate childhood with *naïveté*, cheerful joy, carefree playfulness, and an inability to manage conflicts, mistakes, painful realities, or suffering. They believe that problems and difficulties are something that only adults should have to deal with and endure. Children must be pampered and protected from all that because they are thought to be insensible and irresponsible by nature. This false conception of childhood is ultimately responsible for the disproportionately high degree of twee drawings or caricatures that lack aesthetic values altogether. It is powerfully striking to witness the way so many textbooks, whose purpose it is to provide and facilitate knowledge about our sociocultural environment, incorporate so few photographs. On the contrary, they are plastered with drawings that give much less truthful, relevant, and significant information. Moreover, this imagery seems to serve the primary purpose of colorfully capturing children's attention, while it further serves to "fatten" such publications with filler-pages.

Preventing children from engaging more realistically with the world around them does them a great disservice as it perpetuates a negative image of the human potential for positive intervention and transformation of the world. A more just and realistic socialization of children compels adults to offer images of human achievements, of the ways in which societies have improved their living conditions. It calls for adults to underscore the strategies used by women and men to overcome conditioning factors of all kinds, the means by which they have successfully confronted instances of oppression and social domination.

One of the consequences of the eagerness to keep children in artificial paradises is the excessive silence, already mentioned above, in textbooks regarding reality itself. Such texts are based on the misguided premise that the only people in the world worth addressing are white adults (especially men), who live in cities, have jobs, belong to the middle class, and are fit, heterosexual Christians (please refer to Table 9.1). In such books, we are hard pressed to find information about issues such as: the everyday lives of most women; that of today's girls, boys, and teenagers; the daily realities of oppressed ethnic groups, of nations without a states, of unemployed people living in poverty, of those who live in agricultural and fishing villages, and of minimum-wage earners who endure poor working conditions;

Table 9.1. Present and Absent Voices in School Culture

School Culture	
Present Voices	*Absent Voices*
Men and androcentric perspectives	Women and their perspectives
Adults	Childhood cultures, youth and senior citizens
Healthy people	People with physical and/or mental disabilities
Heterosexual people	Gay, lesbian, bi- and transsexual people
Prestigious professionals and the world of the privileged	The working classes and the world of the poor
Urban populations	Rural and seafaring populations
Powerful nations and states	Nations without states
White people/powerful ethnic groups	Minorities /powerless ethnic groups
The First World	The Third World
Christian religions	Other religions and atheism

the lives of those with physical and/or mental disabilities, and of elderly and ailing people; the notions that practitioners of non-Catholic religions have about human beings and the world; or those held by atheists; etc.[5] These realities obviously do not tally well with the fantasy world of Disneyland, the prissy, privileged-class world of Barbie dolls, that of amusement parks such as Terra Mítica (in Alicante, Spain), or the distorted world of Asterix and Obelix.

Even today, when social movements and forms of resistance have succeeded in improving the conditions of traditionally silenced groups—for example, achieving due recognition of their rights, needs, realities, and potential forms of power; or fair representation of their role as active agents of change and/or creators of culture (art, literature, etc.)—some newfound label or other means are created to resituate these groups and their role in society as somehow inferior. This is what occurs with the use of the qualifier "popular culture" which, whether visibly or tacitly, is almost always placed in opposition to official "Culture." This latter concept is the one that gets the good reviews from official spaces; it is the kind of culture deemed compulsory in school curricula and the one that opens doors into the labor market, in today's neoliberal and conservative societies. Popular culture, by contrast, is the label used to strengthen the marginalization of all those experiences, cultural forms, artifacts, and representations produced by certain "powerless" groups which hegemonic social groups, from their institutional positions of power, define as less important or secondary.

Popular culture is always politics, in the sense of politics that Hannah Arendt (1997) asserts: "[...] politics is about togetherness, and about some with diverse others [...]. Politics emerge in the *amongst* and establishes itself as a relation" (pp. 45–46). Popular culture is produced and enjoyed from and in contexts of secondary power, and its existence generally proceeds from attempts to alter existing correlations of power. Many creators of popular culture, for example, make it exceedingly clear that the content of their creations is aimed directly at groups who dominate society from their positions of power. Thus, it may be stated that the most original and authentic creations such as proverbs, oral literature, popular humor, rock music, reggae, rap/hip-hop, bravú, comics, fanzines, and the like have no other meaning than that of being a reaction to so-called "official" or "prestigious" culture. This type of cultural production usually generates a great deal of solidarity from members of groups whose collective identity is questioned or threatened. This is why young people recognize themselves as such through their music and comics: they become aware that these representations capture their difference from adults. Groups who identify as nations without a state may resort to music, literature, and other creative forms to defend their languages, their ways of life, and their right to decide their own futures against the threats of colonization and the destruction of their collective memory.

Nevertheless, popular culture also generates its own contradictions and, under the pressure of certain historical and social conditions, it can give rise to political and social effects of a reactionary nature. But if there is a commitment to subjecting cultural and scientific productions to analysis, we can short-circuit their most perverse consequences.

DEFENDING AN OPTIMISTIC CURRICULUM

In a more pressing way than ever before, school institutions continue to play a central role in the cultural education of the citizens of a country as a whole. These institutions are privileged spaces where the youngest of society may be socialized and made aware of their necessary role in the greater community. We know that the work developed in schools is often not adequate and that the information pupils come into contact with in classrooms can be manipulated and distorted; yet we also know that school is a place where young people may acquire a critical approach to life, where they come to develop their ability to reflect and evaluate. This learning can only take place, however, when kids are allowed to analyze all information that comes their way, and to seek out different sources and kinds of information that may be useful. Although institutionalized education (Torres Santomé, 2005) may function in a reproductive manner, it can and should also be a space where people committed to the struggle against injustices are formed and educated.

The difference between the kind of informative contact that takes place inside schools versus that which occurs outside—through newspapers, magazines, radio and TV programs, family, friends, and so on—is that, in the former, the available data and facts can and should be checked and confirmed; in the latter, this procedure is not always assured. In schools, it so turns out that one of the top-priority tasks entrusted to teachers is that of awakening the reflexive and critical spirit in their pupils.

If culture can be understood as the set of tools by means of which we give meaning to life, it stands to reason that we must be alert to the fact that the cultural content selected by schools may not always be the most relevant, and that it might even come to be manipulated in order to serve the interests of the most influential social and business groups. Anticipating and alerting to this danger is what makes it feasible to correct these kinds of deficiencies. We must not forget that school is the place where the most disenfranchised social groups, in particular, can access potentially powerful information unavailable to them in their home environments.

Schools must offer the keys to understanding the whys and wherefores of social inequality. An educational system that does not offer all students access to such vital knowledge is unequal and unjust. When schools do not fulfill this basic function, one of the most likely explanations is that they lack either in rigorous and quality informational resources or in well-trained teachers who are committed to their work—or in both.

Upon exploring the cultural potentials of classrooms, one matter that is not given due attention is whether the materials used are relevant from a cultural and linguistic standpoint. Do some students have difficulty understanding them? Can they identify with them? Do the situations and examples reflected therein turn out to be strange and of no interest to them? Do the materials help the learners connect at an emotional level? Will it be possible to generate situations that favor significant learning? This is something that UNESCO (1997) itself points out when it declares that "[...] there is a need for children to have their culture, their experiences and their languages affirmed and reflected in school as well as in the media" (p. 112).

Curricular material must somehow offer the opportunity to awaken interest as well as generate enthusiasm; if not, we educators will only too often find ourselves faced with classrooms where problems will only increase, because boredom is the first step toward disruptive conduct.

This need to incorporate students' most immediate realities and experiences into the learning process should not lead us, however, to hinder them from feeling able and impelled to come into contact with other cultures, with more remote realities. On the contrary, school institutions constitute one of the privileged spaces through which it becomes easier for students to discover and approach realities of a very different kind, to develop solidarity and respect, as well as a commitment to this development.

Access to culture has to help us learn to see ourselves as people who need to interrelate with others so as to assume more collective, social, and political dimensions and commitments. To once more quote UNESCO (1997):

> It is essential to stress that children are the vectors of traditional cultures which link them to past generations, traditions which they must incessantly reinterpret and adapt to their own needs, thus laying the foundations for future cultural innovations. (p. 112)

We must remember that one of the *raisons d'être* of educational systems in democratic societies is that of preparing its citizens to defend their social rights and duties in a responsible, solidary and, logically, democratic way. Hence, even C. Wright Mills (1987) wrote that

> the main task concerning public education, the way it came to be understood in this country, is politics: to make citizens more aware and thereby more capable of thinking and judging public issues. (p. 295)

Nevertheless, when he wrote this book, *The power elite*, as early as the 1950s, he was very much aware of the most notorious deviations of modern educational systems: the ways in which they abandon political education—that which helps people participate in community matters—and submit to the requirements of ferocious capitalism, which does not demand educated people but "trained" individuals to fulfill posts with the best possible salaries.

The way I see it, the complaints many adults have about young people—especially about their individualism, not to say selfishness, or their isolation when it comes to overcoming individual problems—are in large part caused by the educational system in the sense that these children never come to understand how their individual and personal problems often have a more collective explanation: a large part of their fears, anxieties, and problems derive from the conditions of life affecting human groups that they themselves are part of. Consequently, some of the most effective ways to tackle and solve such problems depends on collective efforts that call on the cooperation of the rest of the members of their community.

Let us not forget that "[...] culture shapes the mind; [...] it provides us with the toolbox with which we construct not only our worlds, but also our own conceptions of ourselves and our power" (Bruner, 1997, p. 12).

Teachers indeed have an enormous amount of power in their hands because they count amongst the main cultural intermediaries society offers youth. They are the ones in charge of presenting history—the *past* of the human race itself— and, logically, that of the local school community. In accordance with their selection and narration of the past, as well as that projected through the curriculum, teachers must also attempt to explain the *present*. They thus turn to the past to search for the root explanations of developments occurring in the present. And as they embark on such explorations through time with their pupils, they are also engaging a highly significant and decisive form of intervention: *they are presenting a world of possibilities*. That is, their explanations about how the present is conditioned by the past function as stimuli and brakes with respect to what new generations may think about the future, about the chances of altering, or not, certain aspects of that historical moment, and of solving problems pertaining to the present (Bruner, 1997).

Educating in this sense means that

> [...] contributing to the birth of cultural, political and technical sensitivity in a group of people, in an attempt to form true members of a genuinely liberal public [not a mass], not only involves skills training but also educating in values [...]. It involves stimulating those capacities for controversy within oneself, which we call thinking, and within others, which we call debate. (Mills, 1987, p. 295)

The general refusal to pay attention to the daily experiences of those belonging to the unskilled working class, the younger generations, or to other nonhegemonic groups such as those classified according to certain racial and ethnic criteria, or rural and seafaring lifestyles, only strengthens the definition of reality and cultural productions promoted by the power elite, who are supported by a very closely knit mass media network (radio, television, the press, advertising, cinema, etc.).

By critically analyzing everyday life, we can put the academic content students work with at school to the test; by using the contents of daily realities, we can verify to what extent students come to understand the conditions of life experienced by silenced and marginalized groups; we can test students' ability to grasp the creative and diverse ways in which these groups have dealt with their harsh realities. The cultural content engaged at school must thus enable students to comprehend and confront everyday problems and injustices; to analyze and combat issues such as the destruction of collective identity; male-chauvinist forms of violence suffered by a great number of women; racist behavior and judgments suffered by certain members and groups of our societies; or the lack of job security due to precarious employment contracts or general unemployment, which condemns many to poverty and exclusion. Classroom work must challenge the classism, sexism, homophobia, and ageism prevailing in social and interpersonal relations, for when they are unreflectively internalized or taken for granted, they condition the decision-making processes that are important to all of us. Let us believe that no woman or man, upon reflection, would accept being made party to these negative aspects of reality.

Among other features, a democratic curriculum must allow children to understand how different groups of workers, adolescents, women, and men have come to defend and claim their rights; it must familiarize students with the history of achievements and other positive aspects of groups who have long faced unfair and unjust conditions.

If we believe that the school system should provide pupils with the skills they need to participate in society and to assume responsibilities, it cannot deny them information of such high educational value as the social, cultural, scientific, technological, and political achievements of people who have organized and resisted ongoing forms of oppression. If diverse social groups and peoples were, and still are, capable of coping with many forms of oppression and domination, this implies that we may rightly be optimistic about the future of our societies and humankind, in general.

It is indeed paradoxical to witness how the tensions between optimism and pessimism play out in an educational system whose agents occupy the important role of educating the younger generations for the future of humankind, and for the potential to either reproduce or transform the social realities their students will inhabit as adults. I find that there exists a state of confrontation amongst judgments about, and attitudes toward, the world in which we live—opposing views that are nonetheless constructed in classrooms. Thus, while a great, even excessive, degree of *optimism* toward the possibilities of scientific and technological knowledge is generated, an even greater degree of *pessimism* circulates around the human capacity to transform contemporary societies, and ways of life, that is, around our collective ability to overcome social injustices that are the fruit of today's means for organizing and distributing opportunities and resources. The great majority of the world's inhabitants are totally optimistic, for instance, about the probabilities of humans traveling to Venus or discovering vaccines against different types of cancer and other currently fatal diseases; they are convinced that soon there will be machines and robots for a full range of tasks, including those now carried out by specialists; and so on. People have been taught that it is all simply a matter of time, patience, and allocating sufficient resources to develop the type of research needed to meet such objectives. Yet, very few of these same citizens of the world are likely, by contrast, to hold high expectations regarding our collective ability to end poverty, to permanently prevent the resurgence of authoritarian and Fascist agendas for social organization, or to distribute available resources among all the world's people in a more equitable way.

It seems that the new generations feel impotent in terms of their potential to forge more democratic, solidary, and just future societies. There is a notable amount of intellectual nihilism, social skepticism, and political cynicism behind this negativism which, in reality, has already led many to celebrate the so-called "the end of history."

If indeed we continue to accept the notion that humans are rational beings, it is then reasonable to hope that humankind make a commitment to policies and social actions intended to transform all realities that constitute an outrage against humanity itself, and peoples' chances of building, and continuously improving, the world in which they live. As beings that are capable of observing, analyzing, and theorizing, we are also able to develop our capacity to imagine alternative ways of improving conditions we identify as deficient.

Thus, educating the younger generations compels us to convey this optimism. They need to know that social dilemmas have come to be solved, and will continue to be solved, when those who are affected get properly organized and committed to tackling them. Pupils need to learn, by means of positive examples, that social conquests do not occur merely because a political personage or a certain political party is able to muster enough support to get a particular bill passed into law. Students must instead realize that it is often thanks to the collective struggle of various affected groups that gets such legislative proposals on the agendas of political parties and trade unions that are most sensitive and responsive to their problems. This is how such concerns become pressing issues for governing bodies. Fostering this kind of awareness amongst pupils allows them to conceive of a world in which the transformation of unfair conditions no longer seems to hinge on prestigious or charismatic figures, or on solitary heroes. There is an urgent need to tackle the whole culture of personalization, itself a product of dominating individualistic models that attempt to isolate human beings in order to make them easier to dominate.

Sociohistorical issues that are not dealt with in today's classrooms may just become as educationally relevant as those currently deemed worth teaching, for ignorance about them is not equivalent to neutrality. Those issues that are not taught, or that are silenced, are bound to condition to a greater or lesser extent the analyses of many social concerns, and are bound to hinder taking some alternatives into account. They are also likely to limit the potential for social intervention and may even give rise to unfair situations or pressing issues whose immediate solution is nowhere to be found.

A concept and narration of history that either silences or offers poor explanations of the ways in which different groups have gone about—and go about—solving their problems is an alienating approach to history which can only promote alienating and frustrating forms of education. History thus represented, children will come to believe that nothing has changed since the human race came into existence, and that the unjust conditions to which they are now witness will never be overcome. What is often conveyed to them is that our world is ruled by a kind of law of the jungle, where it is every man for himself, at all costs. It is this kind of preselected and filtered information that is used in classrooms and is largely to blame for the diagnosis of the present-day human condition asserted by the philosopher Cornelius Castoriadis (1998):

> [C]ontemporary human beings behave as though life in society were an odious obligation that a terrible misfortune alone keeps them trapped within [...]; they behave as if they must endure society; yet, on the other hand (under the formula of the State, or of *the others*), they are always ready to hold it responsible for all their troubles and—at the same time—to ask for assistance or "a solution to their problems." They no longer nurture any projects related to society—neither those related to its transformation nor to its preservation/reproduction. (pp. 24–25)

When we state that a "selective tradition" (Williams, 1980) is employed in the educational system, what we really mean is that if, for example, pupils remain ignorant about the history of working-class struggles, or of the women's liberation movement, what is actually being cultivated in these children is an inability to confront the problems they themselves, as citizens and future adults, will most likely also face. When students repeatedly hear that "reality is unfair; it always has been and always will be," they are being subjected to a kind of education that silences the key factors that move and transform societies.

It is also in classrooms where those children belonging to the least favored social groups come to realize that their experiences, language, feelings, traditions, and families are not considered interesting. They further come to realize that what is truly valued and dubbed as worthwhile in society are the lives of "other people," the ones who belong to those social groups serving as models to educators, those who everyone envies and seeks to imitate or resemble. If teachers do not help their students to reflect on their own reality, such youth will experience their first big frustrations right there at school, where they will learn to see themselves as deficient or, even worse, as failures. It is through education that these young people can enable themselves to perceive their own virtues and, logically, their shortcomings as well, but also ways of coping with the latter.

If such important functions take place in classrooms, curricular materials must clearly become a priority, a focal point of our attention. Many studies attempt to make us aware of the strongly biased ways in which the information contained in these materials is construed.[6] Struggles over the control of their content, or over the perspectives deemed most valuable or appropriate for inclusion, is an aspect we must not only never lose sight of, but must also monitor much more closely.

UNESCO itself has for years accepted—albeit with notable caution—that there is no such thing as apolitical education, and that, in general, there are consequently no such things as apolitical textbooks or curricular materials either:

> [I]n relatively open political systems, textbooks often reflect delicate transactions between groups with different ideological positions, religious beliefs and practices, or ethnic origins. Inappropriate decisions [regarding these contents] may give rise to political conflicts or cause some groups to reject certain such texts. In one-party States [for instance], their contents are usually elaborated in such a way that they reflect the dominant ideology. (UNESCO, 1994, p. 56)

Nevertheless, and as we have tried to show elsewhere, apart from political interests, economic issues are also involved which deserve our due attention (Torres Santomé, 2007).

Schools and their classrooms must become spaces where children of diverse origins feel stimulated to criticize and to question the information they come into contact with, the attitudes and behaviors they experience on a daily basis. Such personal experiences must further become an active part of classroom interaction, and compared, assessed, and perhaps reconsidered.

To be realistic, we should acknowledge that academic institutions are no paradise, but they may nonetheless be made into interesting spaces where young people can feel optimistic about their chances of playing an active role in, and transforming, the society in which they live and will eventually work and perhaps come to enjoy. This call to foster hope and optimism in younger generations is a message bell hooks (1994) has repeatedly conveyed when she asserts that

> [...] classrooms, for all their limitations, continue to be places of possibilities. In this field of possibilities, we have the opportunity to work for freedom, to demand an openness of mind and heart from ourselves and our fellow teachers which allows us to cope with reality at the same moment as we collectively imagine ways of going beyond the limits, of overcoming them. This is education as the practice of freedom. (p. 207)

LINES OF ACTION FOR ANTI-DISCRIMINATION EDUCATION

If among their most idiosyncratic of aims educational agents prioritized mediating critically in the comprehension of social dynamics in the world today, this would compel them to develop their students' capacity to arrive at informed judgments and opinions about what goes on around them, to practice making decisions about what to do, and how and where to address the problems and needs that concern them. Optimizing pupils' ability to reflect and research is an essential part of this overall transformation.

Curricular work in this direction requires that careful attention be paid to the reality students are presented with, to the cultural content they are given access to. Children's motivation to learn is clearly related to the significance of what they are being taught. It therefore stands to reason that if the information students interact with also concerns them, they are more likely to be interested in trying to understand it and judge its value, to discover the whys and wherefores as well as the consequences of learning such information, in researching certain concepts, theories, or methodologies, or in understanding certain values promoted as valid and acceptable.

Regarding the pedagogical implications of this perspective, I might highlight the following:

(a) *The need to examine controversial issues.* Pupils need to examine controversial topics, including pressing issues for which no consensus has yet been reached as to how best to address them. Students must learn to debate and analyze the explanations of social conflicts and human difference offered in the past, for such differences have since become more explicit in many respects. This practice enables youth to attempt to uncover the implicit arguments involved in certain decision-making processes, or the reasons behind people's actions in their community and elsewhere. These factors are reflected in the diverse sources of information that students come across in their daily life: in films, magazines, newspapers, on the television and radio, and so on. A similar philosophy is endorsed by entities such as the Organization for Economic Cooperation and Development (OECD, 1989) when its members explicitly state that education must stimulate people to achieve a

> [...] rational understanding of the conflicts, tensions and processes at stake; [it must] arouse critical awareness of cultural interactions and offer a framework for conceptual analysis that can prevent us from accepting obscurantist, jingoistic and irrational explanations. Above all, school is, or at least it should be, the place for rational knowledge; thus its primary task is to offer information, explain and analyze problems, and subject them to criticism. (p. 68)

Introducing this philosophy into the curriculum engaged in classrooms and schools requires that we not become obsessed with the evaluation of academic achievement, the way most traditional schools are. As John Elliott (1993) highlights, "uniform achievement scores indicate that pupils are not developing their own comprehension abilities, but merely reproducing their teachers' understandings" (p. 169).

Working with controversial social issues, subjecting them to research and debate, implies creating conditions that do not interfere with students' freedom to defend their own ideas. This, in turn, requires promoting an atmosphere of trust and respect that makes taking risks possible, or speaking out and offering ideas and solutions without the threat of sanctions, as far as school performance evaluations are concerned.

Incorporating this perspective into a curricular project also involves revising and avoiding the obsessions so characteristic of our (Spanish) school tradition, such as filling children's heads with countless definitions, formulas, dates, and facts, most of which lack connection, and instead programming fewer subjects in order to give them more in-depth treatment. These changes would immediately redound in the significance of pupils' work. The more we know about a subject, the more likely it will become relevant to us, and vice versa; the less deeply we go into a subject, the more likely it will hold little meaning to us, thus becoming tedious and dreary. It is the latter of these cases that leads students to resort to copying and cribbing strategies in order to remember information they find hard to retain, but which they temporarily need to store in their memories for testing purposes.

Open and reasoned dialog does not have to lead to agreement on all fronts, or to total accord, particularly not if it concerns matters that occur and are ongoing outside classrooms.

(b) *The need to struggle for a fairer and more democratic world.* An anti-discrimination curricular project capable of convincing students about the need to struggle for a fairer and more democratic world, requires making it clear that society is permeated by distinct ideologies, values, and visions of the world. The perceptions we have, and the judgments we make, about our social environment and the people around us depend on the lenses through which we view them. Such lenses are formed by values and ideologies. The student body, as a whole, must understand how reality is filtered through the values that come into play as processes of cultural selection that take place in classrooms. By putting concepts such as justice, equity and impartiality into practice, pupils learn to analyze and assess human ideas and behaviors, the incidents and events that occur in everyday life, and not only those reflected in the media, but also those not likely to make the headlines.

Educational work that contributes to the elimination of discrimination must include well-informed debate, or dialogical strategies and deliberation, as the motor behind the construction and analysis of knowledge. Children need to acquire deliberative and analytical habits that facilitate their comprehension of the ways in which implicit assumptions, perspectives, and prejudices operating at the heart of scientific communities are the source of biases and assessments affecting the knowledge they work with at school, and whose origins can be traced back to the action proposals asserted by, and accepted from, certain social groups and not others. School tasks need to be programmed in such a way that children are able to identify and critically engage with dominant ideas and behaviors referred to as "common sense." Girls and boys must be made to systematically reflect upon the clichés and judgments that are taken for granted and circulate freely in their respective communities, to uncover their reproductive effects on the potential to transform the quality of life of society's least favored groups and peoples. This may also encourage students to get involved in real interventions in their communities that place them in direct contact with diverse social groups, especially those most disenfranchised. Such experiences, coupled with the curricular work outlined above, stand to offer these young people greater opportunities to reflect upon their own daily lives: their routines, consuming habits, social practices, beliefs, feelings, desires, and values.

It is up to teachers to help the younger generations understand the social dimensions of culture, to detect the biases operating through race, gender, social class, religion, and age, all of which influence the construction of knowledge.

Working in this direction means approaching the planning and development of teaching and learning processes as a moral practice. It means paying close attention to each student's cultural origins, and creating a climate of respect for, and protection of, difference, that is, a learning environment in which all cultural practices that do not violate people's most universally recognized human rights are duly embraced. Each and every child needs to feel that s/he is respected by the teaching staff and, more importantly, that teachers have faith in her/his human potential, and confidence in her ability to overcome the range of difficulties generally encountered in life.

Teaching as a moral enterprise is not limited, however, to paying careful attention the aims and objectives of education alone; educating in this way also involves focusing on teaching methods and strategies that help create and maintain a climate of dialog and respect in classrooms. Thus, the ends of education must not be separated from the means, for, when they are, educators are likely to think that merely establishing objectives is sufficient to justify using any means in classrooms to achieve such ends. This tends to occur with technocratic curricular proposals. When learning is thus perceived and structured, pupils become overwhelmingly obsessed with answering quiz and test questions correctly; their consideration for the actual contents they are supposedly learning becomes almost incidental, when not seen as bothersome and boring.

When such means and strategies for teaching and learning are not explicitly checked and revised, the necessary critical analysis of the ever-evolving moral dimensions of learning may never get beyond mere mention in well-intended official school documents and plans.

As early as the 1970s, Lawrence Stenhouse had already pointed out that when the ethical dimensions of knowledge development are left out, full knowledge formation does not take place (see, for example, Stenhouse, 1970). Even so, specific sets of values are almost never subjected to open debate among students. It is not until we attempt to critically analyze such teaching and learning methods and contents that we begin to perceive the existence of a hidden curriculum, which neither teachers nor students tend to be aware of (Torres Santomé, 2005).

One of the *raisons d'être* of antidiscriminatory education is to facilitate an understanding of human conditions and behaviors, and the values and justifications they are based on, to shed light on those who benefit from such realities, and those who are harmed or silenced.

The set of considerations addressed above make one aspect of education absolutely indispensable: the maintenance of reflexive attitudes regarding the nature of knowledge and the methods of teaching and learning, on the part of both teachers and pupils alike.

Commitment to such a philosophy is one way to convince fellow agents of teaching institutions to stop focusing on "official knowledge" alone, that is, conceptions of life that favor those who are already privileged. The struggle for social justice through school institutions calls for today's mistakes—such as defining and endorsing standardized conceptions of life and culture—to be acknowledged and rectified. Resistance to such acknowledgment merely serves to perpetuate the relentless attacks, both explicit and implicit, on the recognition of diversity, which in turn only furthers the hegemonic articulation of *mono-societies*: monocultural, monolinguistic, monoethnic, monoideological, and so on. These attempts to deny diversity and thus impose a homogeneous culture are publicly referred to, nonetheless, as "common," as "reached by consensus," as "valuable," or "historical," as in "the way things have always been."

Today's groups of intellectuals, researchers, investigators, artists, and educators all face the important task of reinterpreting and reconstructing the histories of societies, and, in the process, of making their societies respond to the perceptions and interests of those who have been left out or suffered injustices.

Supporting democracy through education means that concepts such as "social justice," "ethical responsibility," "participation," and "equality" must not be allowed to continue their course toward becoming nice-sounding yet vapid notions, devoid of meaning or importance; rather, they must be actively promoted as *ways of life*. In this sense, pedagogy itself has a dual function: that of helping to provide the means by which oppressed social groups become aware of their oppression, and that of serving as an instrument with which those same women and men may struggle to transform reality (Trend, 1995, p. 148).

Learning institutions that embody this commitment will pave the way for teaching and learning processes that encourage students to freely participate in society, and to feel optimistic about the potential of all human beings. Such a commitment will give rise to schools that generate dreams, not dismay.

NOTES

1. Translated from the Spanish-language edition of Bacon's *The Advancement of Learning* (*El avance del saber* [Bacon, 1988]). This, and all subsequent quotations taken from non-English source documents have been translated into English by the translators, authors, and editors of this volume.
2. Although the differences between these two concepts merit further discussion, to explore them here would exceed the focus of this chapter.
3. For an in-depth discussion of this void, see Torres Santomé (2006), chapter four.
4. For a more detailed discussion of these policies, see Torres Santomé (2007).
5. See Torres Santomé (2006), chapter four.
6. See, for example, Apple (1989); Blanco García (2000); Grupo Eleuterio Quintanilla (1998); Johnsen (1996); Subirats et al. (1993); or Torres Santomé (2005).

REFERENCES

Adorno, T. W. (1998). *Educación para la emancipación*. Madrid: Morata.

Apple, M. W. (1989). *Maestros y textos: Una economía política de las relaciones de clase y de sexo en educación*. Barcelona: Paidós/M.E.C.

Arendt, H. (1997). *¿Qué es la política?* Barcelona: Paidós/I.C.E. de la Universidad Autónoma de Barcelona.

Bacon, F. (1988). *El avance del saber*. Madrid: Alianza.

Bauman, Z. (2000). *Trabajo, consumismo y nuevos pobres*. Barcelona: Gedisa.

Blanco García, N. (2000). *El sexismo en los materiales educativos de la E.S.O.* Seville: Instituto Andaluz de la Mujer.

Bourdieu, P. (1999). *Meditaciones pascalianas*. Barcelona: Anagrama.

Bruner, J. (1997). *La educación, puerta de la cultura*. Madrid: Visor.

Castells, M. (1998). *La era de la informació:. Economía, sociedad y cultura. Vol.1: La sociedad red* (2nd edition). Madrid: Alianza.

Castoriadis, C. (1998). *El ascenso de la insignificancia*. Madrid: Cátedra.

Elliott, J. (1993). *El cambio educativo desde la investigación-acción*. Madrid: Morata.

Foucault, M. (1990). *La arquelogía del saber* (14th edition). Madrid: Siglo XXI.

Fueyo Gutiérrez, A. (2000). *Imagen publicitaria y representaciones sociales sobre el Sur. Implicaciones en la educación para el desarrollo*. Unpublished doctoral dissertation. University of Oviedo.

Grupo Eleuterio Quintanilla (1998). *Libros de texto y diversidad cultural*. Madrid: Talasa.

hooks, b. (1994). *Teaching to transgress: Education as the Practice of Freedom*. New York: Routledge.

Johnsen, E. B. (1996). *Libros de texto en el calidoscopio: Estudio crítico de la literatura y la investigación sobre los textos escolares*. Barcelona: Pomares/Corredor.

Kant, E. (1964). *Filosofía de la historia* (2nd edition). Buenos Aires: Nova.

Kant, E. (1970 [1798]). The contest of the faculties. In H. S. Reiss (Ed.), *Kant: Political writings* (pp. 176–190). Cambridge: Cambridge University Press.

Kuhn, T. S. (1980). *La estructura de las revoluciones científicas* (5th edition). Madrid: Fondo de Cultura Económica.

Lyotard, J. F. (1992). *La posmodernidad (explicada a los niños)* (2nd edition). Barcelona: Gedisa.

Mills, C. W. (1987). *La élite del poder* (9th edition). México: Fondo de Cultura Económica.

OECD (1989). *One school, many cultures*. París: OECD.

Robins, K. and Webster, F. (1988). Cybernetic capitalism: Information, technology, everyday life. In V. Mosco and J. Wasko (Eds.), *The political economy of information* (pp. 44–75). Madison, WI: University of Wisconsin Press.

Stenhouse, L. (1970). *The Humanities Project: An introduction*. London: Heinemann Educational Books.

Subirats, M. (Ed.) (1993). *El sexismo en los libros de texto: Análisis y propuesta de un sistema de indicadores*. Madrid: Ministerio de Asuntos Sociales/Instituto de la Mujer.

Torres Santomé, J. (2005). *El curriculum oculto* (8th edition). Madrid: Morata.

Torres Santomé, J. (2006). *Globalización e interdisciplinariedad: El curriculum integrado* (5th edition). Madrid. Morata.

Torres Santomé, J. (2007). *Educación en tiempos de neoliberalismo*. (2nd edition). Madrid: Morata.

Torres Santomé, J. (2008). Diversidad cultural y contenidos escolares. *Revista de Educación*, No. 345 (January–April), pp. 83–110.

Touraine, A. (1993). *Crítica de la modernidad*. Madrid: Temas de Hoy.

Trend, D. (1995). *The crisis of meaning in culture and education*. Minneapolis, MN: University of Minnesota Press.

UNESCO (1994). *Educación para todos: Las condiciones necesarias*. París: UNESCO.

UNESCO (1997). *Nuestra diversidad creativa: Informe de la Comisión Mundial de Cultura y Desarrollo*. Madrid: UNESCO-SM.

Varela, J. (1997). *Nacimiento de la mujer burguesa*. Madrid: La piqueta.

Wacquant, L. (1999). *Les prisons de la misère*. Paris: Editions Raisons d'Agir.

Williams, R. (1980). *Marxismo y literatura*. Barcelona: Península.

CHAPTER TEN

Educational change, cultural politics, AND social reinvention

MAR RODRÍGUEZ ROMERO

University of A Coruña

INTRODUCTION

The dominance of technical approaches in contemporary understandings and policies of educational change is well-acknowledged. The hegemonic presence of technical discourses at the level of practice has been revitalized by means of the recent neoliberal reforms which very successfully extend a way of perceiving education as if it were an exclusively private good, and therefore a matter of consumption and an object of business management. Various authors from differing intellectual positions have commented on this, criticizing these limited conceptual visions that have circumscribed contemporary thinking on educational change (Popkewitz, 1991; Hargreaves, 1994). Indeed, many others have warned of the debacle that will ensue in education as a consequence of neoliberal reforms and what they represent for the future of education, understood as a public good that might help to assuage social inequality (Cantor and Courant, 2003). But beyond this complaint, what are the alternatives?

Voices from critical approaches have considered the reconstruction of educational change through the use of postmodern and poststructural resources (Kemmis, 1995). This alternative, from my point of view, could be very productive because it works with seldom-used conceptions of educational change,[1] which nevertheless have great potential, precisely because of their inherent commitment to social transformation. Moreover, in the wake of a disruptive postmodernity, these conceptions seek to incorporate revitalizing perspectives from critical theory, and thus attempt to construct a postmodern critical project (Santos, 2003a). This last path could be very interesting in renovating conceptual categories, such as emancipation, which are so essential to educational change. By placing educational change within the framework of cultural politics, new possibilities emerge, both for renovating the conceptualization of educational change and for revitalizing its implementation. This is done by exploring the options arising from new social movements and alternative formulas, such as situated reform. This last strategy for change may help to bring together local commitment and social justice in education, and thus facilitate the development of reciprocal actions among social groups committed to the defense of particular identity differences.

EDUCATIONAL CHANGE AND THE REINVENTION
OF EMANCIPATORY INTENTIONS

Poststructural, postmodern, and feminist approaches explore a feature that is essential for educational change: the utopian dimension of pedagogical practices. They argue that this vital dimension is in fact weakened when taken for granted, or when it is not explicitly addressed through critical discourse. Hence, talking about educational change within the critical project means nothing less than problematizing utopian faith in emancipation.

Even so, I am not saying this utopian faith must be abandoned. As Tomaz Tadeu (2005) suggests, to question the point of reference of critical theories does not imply giving up thinking or acting in a critical mode; it is precisely this uncertainty and intellectual instability that inspires political action. Writing from a similar standpoint, Stephen Kemmis (1995), in his own efforts to reconstruct educational change, finds support in Stuart Hall (1986) who reasons that social theory must respond to theoretical challenges put forth by postmodernism, while simultaneously finding ways to keep faith with the emancipatory ideal of critical social theory. It seems essential, then, that the ideal of emancipation be separated from the universalizing desires that have accompanied conceptions of change undergirded by an epistemology of progress. These conceptions have been characterized by Thomas Popkewitz (1991) as expressed through various tendencies such as: the acceptance of a global dualism between oppressor and oppressed; the declaration, by some, of a direct relationship between the critical researcher and social movements of opposition; the idea that researcher knowledge necessarily produces progress; the description of all practices related to oppressed groups as progressive; and the definition of the social good as a universal notion of politics, morality, and aesthetics.

In present-day societies, the more fluid nature of identity, coupled with multiple forms of suffering complicate the nature of oppression, although the distinction between oppressor and oppressed remains important. A more sophisticated conceptual map of our societies is therefore needed, one that reflects a social topography in which there is no preferred marker of oppression and suffering, and one that shows it is not improbable that social actors may be, simultaneously, oppressors and oppressed. The importance and relevance of the practical value of emancipation as a contemporary aspiration cannot be dismissed when one observes the continuity of dependence, oppression, suffering, and irrationality, although these are now manifested in a plurality of ways that were at times underemphasized in previous analytical models. That is why since the 1960s the new left-wing social movements in the United States have created an updated description of oppression which includes its plural nature, as opposed to the Marxist perspective which attributed injustices to class domination and bourgeois ideology. Iris Young (1990) has taken on the task of clarifying this concept, which is so central to the political discourse of these movements, her aim being to persuade people that the discourse of oppression makes sense in light of most of our social experience. Oppression refers to the injustices that emerge from relations between social groups, and does not always coincide with the premeditated subordination of one group by another. It has a structural sense, and is not eliminated by substituting rulers or laws because it is systematically encouraged by key cultural, economic, and political institutions. In a broader sense, structural oppression refers to sweeping and profound injustices suffered by some groups as a result of certain forms of thinking and acting that other people project, often unconsciously, onto everyday interactions. These injustices are also caused by stereotypes spread by the media, by cultural stereotypes, and by the structural aspects of bureaucratic hierarchies and market mechanisms; in short, they are the fruit of the normal processes of everyday life (Young, 1990). It is necessary then, to redefine emancipation in such a way that multiple forms of oppression can be confronted, and the totalizing vision of emancipation associated exclusively with social class oppression overcome. Redefined emancipation does not announce a particular program; it is a critical concept whose power resides in critical negation; that is, it enables us to condemn structures of oppression, but is not conceived in such a way so as to offer a clear, positive, and universal vision of the nature of liberation from suffering, irrationality, injustice, or from the lack of equality in a specific historical moment and for any particular group (Kemmis, 1995). Set out in this way, emancipation would be adapted to the various forms of oppression and their multiple points of contact, and thus give rise to specific proposals for social and educational transformation. This is essential because, as Sandra Harding (1996) asserts, each form of domination makes use of other forms, and so they become mutually reinforced in extremely complex ways. For instance, Cameron McCarthy (1990) has shown that the dynamic relations among race, social class, and gender have contradictory effects at the level of everyday practices in the school, producing a "non-synchronous" context in which the three dynamics constantly configure, and are (re)configured by each other.

To reinvent the emancipatory intentions of educational change, it is also necessary to regain the stand point of commitment, which is so integral to radical formulations. The type of commitment most appropriate for responding to the plural quality of emancipation, one that is in tune with a multiplicity of identities and social struggles, is that which possesses a local, contextualized character, and which is sensitive to revision. Local modes of emancipatory commitment engage alternative means for repoliticizing human interaction, as promoted by postmodernism and poststructuralism (Bernstein, 1992 in Biesta, 1995). The potential of local commitment is endorsed by Jennifer Gore (1993), who finds that the Foucauldian perspective offers a means of abandoning the pessimism frequently associated with poststructural positions on the specific relations of power and technologies of the self in local contexts.[2] Despite arguments to the contrary, the standpoint that emphasizes local positions does not oblige one to reject visions of different societies, but rather proposes that these be carried out at the local level.

But neither multifaceted emancipation nor local commitment has put an end to our problems. On the contrary, they constitute a source of new setbacks. Although analysts acknowledge that there exists a multiplicity of fields in which human beings struggle for liberty, justice, dignity, and more fulfilling lives, it is clear that these fields overlap and intertwine, producing a complex social map of aspirations and human struggles. On the one hand, it is understood that different forms of oppression have their own dynamics; on the other hand, it is accepted that, at the same time, the respective forms usually interact. Taking as a point of reference the intersection between race, gender, and social class oppression at the local level of the school (McCarthy, 1990), one finds that there are interruptions, discontinuities, and rises and falls in the original effects of any of these dynamics, which are produced in tandem with both internal relations of the school and social organizing principles around which inequality is articulated. Group differences permeate people's lives in multiple ways, and this may imply both privilege and oppression for the same subjects, depending upon different facets of their lives and institutional contexts. This is so because the mixture of history, subjectivity, interests, and abilities that people bring to an interaction, as well as their means for negotiating and establishing relationships, determine the direction that inequality will take.

In this setting, the creation of a program for educational change that is as inclusive as possible and can accommodate the widest spectrum of human struggles and preoccupations, only makes sense when projected onto the local sphere. It is only possible to consider the dynamics of antagonism and solidarity, as produced through different forms of oppression, if innovation is located in a specific institutional context. The main obstacles to the achievement of inclusive policies for change are related to the ways multiple facets of oppression interact or are given priority in the everyday practices of schools, and to the ways innovation will influence and be influenced by these internal differences. This problem becomes especially crucial when we consider that the production of inequality at school is, in itself, a very contradictory and nonsynchronous phenomenon that does not guarantee fair or definitive results for the school's actors—regardless of whether they represent the majority or minority groups (McCarthy, 1990). If we decide to struggle for political, civil or social rights, or for the expansion of a democratic culture as the cohesive element in proposals for inclusive change, it will be difficult to articulate this engagement with more local efforts related to emotional damage and lack of cultural respect. This is why local experiences with injustice must play a primary role in broader struggles around civil rights.

Regarding the problems associated with local commitment, one must first consider the fundamental vulnerability of all forms of commitment, which derives from the potential oppression involved in any liberating effort. This intrinsic fragility in commitment is related to the tension produced between contingency and commitment; a tension which could either be resolved by tending toward contingency—which then leads to nihilism—or by leaning toward commitment, and thus toward fundamentalism. Perhaps the only solution, then, is to maintain the tension in order to see the possibilities for carrying out the emancipatory potential of educational change, while also attempting to be fully conscious of the uncertainty of this attempt (Biesta, 1995). In order to sustain this tension without falling into the extremes of nihilism or fundamentalism, emancipatory commitment should involve examining whatever means are employed to attain the ends, while not forgetting that such means are applied in circumstantial contexts. Reflection on the ends of this commitment is also necessary, as it is in our interest not to forget that no emancipatory aspiration, however fair it seems, can be achieved without producing undesired consequences. Moreover, the area of action for local commitment is usually quite narrowly defined. On the one hand, attention is focused on silenced minorities, and, on the other hand, it is applied to small political narratives that are localized in the domain of human intersubjectivity. However, the snag associated with this peculiarity is fairly clear: it causes a loss of influence in the general social and political context and also leads to the fragmentation of emancipatory initiatives; it may even increase rivalries between projects for local change. But this is the price to be paid when researchers, educators, and other social agents try to work at the level of human action and everyday practices in schools.

In order to reconstruct emancipatory commitment without losing the capacity for social influence, projects for inclusive change could attempt to strike a balance between local commitment and attention to issues that unite the suffering of different groups of human beings, without losing sight of the contradictory relations among specific dynamics of oppression. This in turn involves broader social struggles concerning issues that affect most people.

In this setting of tension between local commitments and global social battles, we must further consider the renewed forms of oppression that are generated through transnational capitalism and hegemonic mercantile logics, and, by virtue of these, through the increasing transfer of power relations from the state to the sphere of private property. This circumstance is leading to the relocation of emancipation associated with gender and race differences within the framework of social class processes. It is not a matter of considering the latter as the referent of the former, but rather of understanding that social class oppression, as expressed through the social relations produced by global capitalism, should be taken into account when defining gender and race oppression.[3] Peter McLaren and Ramin Farahmandpur (2001) venture to criticize the postmodern left for not having sufficiently problematized the social universe of capital. And, in a fairly unpredictable twist, they have declared that they are beginning to recognize the potential of Marxist theory to invigorate our understanding of political resistance to commercial exploitation and corporatism in schooling. Addressing social differences, and without renouncing identities related to race, gender, and sexual orientation in the process of highlighting class identities, these authors assert the need to locate all such identities as features of a social reality and a life experience that requires an understanding of the global context, one of a historical and materialist nature. According to these authors, in the present situation, the most important social ability to develop would be that of acting politically as a class, as a collective class of workers, whereas the corresponding pedagogical option would imply defending a revolutionary citizenry, a sociopolitical praxis which involves a form of proletarian solidarity. Nevertheless, this vision, which prioritizes such a notoriously homogenizing affinity, clearly does not fit easily into the analyses or the strategies of today's oppositional groups (Klein, 2000).[4]

In the search for links between local commitments and global social battles, the conciliatory proposal offered by Nancy Fraser (1997) stands out. Her main contribution here lies in her description of the dimensions of social justice that demonstrate the close relationships between the global and the local. Her work initially centered around the tension between the critical project of redistributive policy, as supported by socialist and social democratic formations, and the policy of recognition of difference, promoted by multiculturalist postures. More recently, she has analyzed the problem of social justice within a globalized context, thus adding a third dimension to her analysis. But let us consider the implications of her work, step by step. First, addressing social justice nowadays demands a simultaneous consideration of the redistribution of goods and the recognition of difference. But both facets of social justice (redistribution and recognition) can only be reconciled once we identify the forms of oppression that result from the intersection between economic inequality and a lack of cultural respect. It is therefore essential to coordinate emancipatory efforts to interrupt the kind of oppression derived from both socioeconomic and cultural injustices.

In order to overcome the bifurcation of the critical project, social agents would have to recognize the legitimacy of both types of emancipatory programs while embarking on a process of harmonization among the various programmatic and synergetic fields within the political plane (Fraser, 1997). The dominant aspiration in this process is two-fold: (a) reconciliation of the most productive contributions from seasoned socialist politics and from the political agendas emerging from current social movements; and (b) restoration of the truly valuable tendencies within neo-Marxist criticism of capitalism, the objective being to integrate these into the most intelligent currents of critical postmodern theorization.

Without a doubt, this mediation effort constitutes one of the main challenges to emancipatory educational change, and it can only be produced on the basis of the illuminating tensions between critical perspectives and postmodern and poststructural intellectual traditions. This situation of generalized interpellation between different intellectual positions could be very useful in redefining the direction of educational change, and mobilizing around alternatives.[5]

But Nancy Fraser's analysis goes further to include a third dimension of social justice associated with both globalization and the vulnerability that groups and subjects feel when faced with transnational forces: the political dimension of representation. This dimension is related to the question of who participates and how they participate in debates about social justice. These are metalevel questions because they refer to the absence of an adequate framework in which to apply social justice. This type of injustice becomes most apparent when problems concerning social justice are framed in such a way so as to impede the consideration of certain issues affecting particular individuals, and thus deny these actors the possibility to defend their first-order transnational demands concerning economic or cultural injustices. This problem persists because the global nature of the new forms of oppression is generally ignored, and because there is no established space to hear the voices of the millions of people affected. Metalevel questions open up a very fruitful path for the conciliation of demands among groups affected by both economic and cultural injustices. This possibility for meeting is not merely intellectual, but has been made evident by the behavior of social groups themselves, who have created spaces for debates on social justice where previously there were none—the World Social Forum is the main example, as Fraser states—and by creating alternative channels for representation and debate.[6] It is precisely this general strategy which inspires the direction taken by Fraser's (2005) proposal when she associates the political dimension of representation with the democratization of the process through which the different categories of justice, which she refers to as democratic justice, become established and modified.

Taking as a source of inspiration the social interventions put into action by oppressed or oppositional groups constitutes a sign of identity of a new intellectual attitude which rebels against "the indolence of instrumental reason." That is to say, against the systematic waste of knowledge contained within the multiple resistance initiatives carried out by anonymous actors who fight to have a dignified and decent life here and now, however unfavorable their conditions for survival are (Santos, 2003a). This particular type of intellectual disposition is present in cultural politics and is a very productive channel for reinventing emancipatory intentions for educational change, and for seeking to strengthen coalitions and shared resistance.

THE POSSIBILITIES OF EDUCATIONAL CHANGE AND CULTURAL POLITICS[7]

Educational change emerges with special force when linked to a form of intellectual inquiry and practice characteristic of cultural studies, known as cultural politics, because it allows for the exploration of possible innovations that can contribute to social transformation. Such practices are informed by certain poststructural and postmodern theoretical resources, and they make simultaneous use of strategies associated with new social movements.

As an intellectual undertaking, cultural politics deploy theoretical intervention and educational action by focusing on power and the pursuit of social change to broaden an emancipatory culture. When educational change is conceived as a form of cultural politics, its central concern consists of articulating reform proposals that increase the possibilities of overthrowing unequal social relations in schools, and thwarting the arrangements of the official culture.

Educational reform is perceived as a combination of the rhetoric and practices of individuals involved in struggles between social groups, and situated in the sphere of contradictory political, cultural, and economic dynamics at local, national, and global levels. The social content in which the dynamics of these three different levels are interwoven includes conflict and cooperation within and among actors; from state elites—transnational organizations and capitalists—to political parties, workers, and other groups based on gender, race, ethnicity, or religion, among other markers of collective identity. The relations among these different groups are typically characterized by inequalities related to size of membership, level of welfare, and amount of cultural representation and power. Thus, processes of reform generally appear as clusters of contradictions and conflicts because what could be seen as constructive change for one group may be perceived as a setback, or even as a threat to existence for another. The struggles, as well as the alliances, are produced through shifting terrains that make it difficult to anticipate the direction the reforms will take and the influence the various groups will exert in this process. In a certain sense, these contradictions provide a space for contestation and counterhegemonic action, but, at the same time, they restrict these possibilities. This contradictory context of reform offers educators, as subjects of different genders, ethnic backgrounds, and social classes, the possibility of daring to develop alternative ways of working and creating dissident subjectivities. These alternatives are directly related to the intellectual and strategic challenges the new social movements pose to educational change, through their diverse proposals for policy and action.

As social action, cultural politics are linked to new social movements that are more than mere contemporary versions of former emancipatory aspirations; they are an original expression of recent social, political, cultural, and economic conditions that have arisen in tandem with ideas from the New Left. These new movements not only address traditional issues concerning the social production and distribution of goods, and promote new modes of consumption, production, and work; they also extend their claims beyond the level of everyday life and into the global arena of challenges facing humanity today, in their search for alternative ways of living and interrelating. Although they lack an "all-encompassing ideology", it is evident that feminism, pacifism, environmentalism, and other social movements are ideologically related (Reichmann and Fernández Buey, 1994).[8] They all share a humanist critique of the current system and dominant culture; a determination to improve the world in the present; and a refusal to equate progress with static material and moral development. These movements also share a dual orientation. On the one hand, their actions lead them toward power as they aspire to gain political influence, to obtain recognition for their demands, or to increase the power of civil society through projects aimed at developing counterhegemonic forms of standing and influence. On the other hand, their initiatives are guided by a cultural orientation directed at transforming social subjectivities and their sociocultural relationship with the politicization of everyday life and private space. This ideological affinity explains how these activists come to coincide in the ways they contest many of the issues of so-called consensus in Western societies, and in their use of nontraditional political tactics and new organizational structures.

The defining character of these new movements is the effort to reconcile specific thematic interests into a unique sociopolitical force while maintaining the autonomy of such interests. One could say that there is a mixture of a general radical agenda and very specific demands. The contents of these struggles are focused on particular matters and, at the same time, are very general in nature. Values such as autonomy and identity are central to these causes, identity— regarded as a creative process which reappropriates everyday life and liberates it from subjection to instrumental reason—playing an essential role.

The most distinctive premise these movements share, however, is the recognition of difference, which acts as a mobilizing force. Considering that the potentially oppressive use of the notion of difference could easily give rise to stigmatization and exclusion, an egalitarian and inclusive concept of difference is a necessary starting point for work in this arena (Young, 1990). From an emancipatory point of view, social difference is conceived in a fluid, relational way, as a social process. Social differences are relational; they are not delimited by substantive categories and attributes; they spring from relations among social groups, and from interactions between social groups and institutions. Social groups have similar attributes, experiences, and objectives. They construct their identity through social processes of interaction and differentiation, during the course of which people come to acquire certain affinities. Affinity implies a way of sharing proposals, of generating affective connections, and establishing social networks. The relevant characteristics of people's group affinities may vary according to their social situation, or to each member's development throughout her or his lifetime. Such differences allow new affinities to form, which in turn establish bridges between social groups, thus allowing for new alliances and coalitions to form.

Understood in these terms, social difference does not refer to exclusion, but to variety, specificity, and heterogeneity, which are constructed in an ambiguous, changing, and relational way (Young, 1990). Difference is linked to diverse circumstances that allow distinctions to be made between social groups, according to, for instance, class, ethnicity, sexual preference, religion, ability, age, lifestyle, occupation, and so on. These circumstances may open up spaces where individuals and groups can share their experiences with repression and/or exclusion, thanks to the multiple levels of identity that converge on the life experiences of each person and each group. In this sense, it would be misleading to represent such social categories as if they were clearly different. On the contrary, one must take into consideration the diversity present in any of these classifications, and recognize that in each category interests and life experiences are interwoven.

Nonetheless, uniting equality and difference in this way is far from unproblematic, given the tensions that can arise from the conciliation of local commitments and more general social struggles. Nancy Fraser (1997) considers that social movements addressing these transversal axes of difference are in the process of establishing a kind of global resistance to a set of injustices produced in spheres both cultural and economic. However, considering that identity struggles are prevailing over struggles for equality, a complex political terrain with little programmatic cohesion is also arising. From Fraser's point of view, it is necessary to produce a critical theory of recognition that promotes different versions of cultural policy on difference, along with social policies for equality. This would be achieved by applying a transformative perspective to issues of economic inequality and cultural domination. Such a shift would in turn imply making profound changes in the ways we perceive the relationship between the material production and distribution of goods, and the cultural recognition of existing groups—and not only through affirmative action.

Although some of Fraser's claims here may contain weaknesses—which are fully acknowledged—or may lack generalizability, they represent an interesting attempt to find more balanced methods for tackling the two most important aspects of social justice: cultural recognition and redistributive equity. Fraser's proposal in this essay is to highlight the possibility of bringing together specific initiatives from contemporary social movements while establishing channels for articulating links between local and more general struggles in pursuit of social justice. Jorge Reichmann and Francisco Fernández Buey (1994), who attribute the weak convergence of the new social movements' projects to their short lifespan, consider that it is still only a question of time before we see the appearance of more deliberate, structured initiatives to achieve a wider antisystem movement through coalition-building policies.[9]

Indeed, one can observe some kind of convergence through the development of participatory democracy (Santos, 2005), or democratic justice (Fraser, 2005). Different social movements, such as ecology and indigenous movements, international feminist groups and global solidarity activists, are applying the moral principle of intervention on behalf of all those affected by matters of justice in a globalized world scene. Moved by this principle, they have championed the vindication of new democratic spaces where the framework for defining justice can be debated; that is, the who and the how. Various initiatives are now under way to construct alternative democratic channels. For example, cities and communities all over the planet have witnessed the formation of different forms of promoting participatory municipal management. They are strategies that combine electoral voting with referenda, popular consultations, public policy councils, advisory conferences, round tables, and public debates.[10] This way of working has been introduced into the world of ideas to the extent that one notices progress toward dialogic approaches to the theory of justice. The idea that matters related to the concept of justice should be discussed through deliberative, collective processes is becoming ever more widespread (Fraser, 2005).

SITUATED REFORM AND THE REINVENTION
OF SOCIALLY RECOGNIZED PRINCIPLES

Situated reform is an approach that may prove very productive in responding to diversified emancipation, as it works with local commitments and thus allows for consideration of the multiple facets of oppression suffered by different groups in their particular educational contexts. Yet, this proposal for change has not been sufficiently explored.[11] Recently, however, it has demonstrated its potential through educational initiatives for change applied, for instance, in indigenous communities of Australia, in rural and remote areas where situated pedagogy is a decisive conceptual reference that allows education to be based on the respective communities' social, historical, and spatial localizations (McConaghy, 2002). Given that all classroom practices are situated—meaning that they take place in institutions, historical moments, and cultural and social fields, and constitute a response to individual and unique social constraints—situated reforms seek to locate education in the dense particularities of the specific circumstances of teaching and learning (Miller, 1996).

Situated change circumscribes innovation to the peculiarities of the specific teaching and learning situations and to particular settings. For this reason, it is especially conducive to consideration of the diversity of cultures and identities at hand, and their relations to particular settings, periods of time, and other social groups. Situated reform seeks to construct ways of organizing innovation that makes differences visible, fostering the creative alteration of educational institutions through the meaningful inclusion of differences based on age, sexual orientation, abilities, ethnicity, language, social background, gender, and so on. Given the proliferation of difference, and its companion, radical pluralism, what is needed are versatile models for change that can adapt to the complexity involved in addressing the claims of various non-static groups and categories. Given that identity categories are configured in ways that are multiple, fluid, and often contradictory—both internally and externally—only the initiatives for change that include indeterminacy as part of their essential features will be able to take on educational contexts in which, for instance, gender is at times the determining factor for change, while at other times, the most influential factor may be social class or race. In the latter context, the reform may need to further address biracial or transsexual identities, or dynamic localizations between social classes.

Moreover, there may be situations in which situated change is aimed at meeting the rights and needs of groups and individuals experiencing multiple forms of difference resulting from the intersection of life circumstances and identity formation. This approach to change is perhaps the most desirable, as it would prevent situated reform from becoming diluted into fragmented and disconnected initiatives. On the contrary, it would bring these initiatives together, creating spaces for shared change. It is this sense of the versatility of situated change that responds to the possibility of interchanging identities or combining them in varying ways: given that identities are not fixed and constantly move around, it follows that fluid and adaptable reform initiatives are paramount. The need for flexible change in education becomes particularly evident considering that it is best forged through the collective efforts of those who participate in schooling and keep teaching institutions alive. Commitment to a situated perspective on school reform, then, necessarily involves approaching pedagogical, curricular, and organizational change by adapting, even transforming, our intentions and responses to different educational settings and social circumstances (Miller, 1996), and by systematically subjecting our forms or strategies for channeling such change to context-sensitive scrutiny and revision.

Situated change thus rejects a fixed model of development. It adapts to the ways of being and proposals foregrounded by diverse groups in accordance with their particular settings and circumstances. The versatility of situated change offers more lucid ways to respond to the variable, contextual, and complex nature of teaching contexts, in order to articulate specific social relations in the everyday life of schools. Moreover, situated reform seeks to use the potential of daily institutional interactions by making local commitment central to the change process, and by fostering a critical reflexivity that reconciles the recognition of both the contextual relevance of the educational processes and the political dimension of the local commitment. According to Patty Lather and Elizabeth Ellsworth (1996), proponents of situated change need to consider the lived experiences of the classroom, as well as the particular social relations that inform and condition the theoretical and practical work of teachers, researchers, and other institutional actors. They must also weigh the structural and historical forces converging on school life. Finally, situated change promotes the creation of pedagogical responses and initiatives in the emergent space between personal histories and the legacies of oppression and privilege that educators consciously and unconsciously engage in the classroom.

Given that domination has many faces, and that there are also many forms and agents of resistance, there is therefore no single principle for social transformation. In light of this reality, situated change serves to optimize the potential offered by the multiplicity of resistances, and to diversify the principles of educational transformation without increasing antagonisms. In order to produce coalitions of identity groups that do not adhere to exclusive forms of circumstantial unity, reforms based on the most shared of social interests must be encouraged. A focus on educational matters of such a transversal nature—those located in the intersections between specific social differences—would pave the way for promoting convergence among the various politics of difference. But for these common concerns to emerge in a meaningful way, a "theory of translation" would be in order, one that makes such struggles mutually understandable, and allows collective actors to discuss the oppressions they are resisting and the aspirations that inspire them (Santos, 2005). Or, as McConaghy (2002) argues, there is a need to develop theories of complementarity and similarity that allow for more refined understandings of strategic or significant difference.

The use of these theoretical approaches would enable a radically contextualized means of grasping educational change without renouncing the convergence of strategies and efforts. Through the deployment of these conceptual tools, initiatives for change would foster understanding rather than antagonism among groups mobilizing around economic equality and cultural recognition. Even if circumstantial, this understanding would promote collaborative projects, and, above all, help steer a "paradigmatic transition."[12] This search for mutual intelligibility among the multiple agents of transformation may be considered according to different approaches, with greater or lesser amounts of potential according to the context, and the aspirations and desires of the groups involved. What follows is a brief summary of some key options for the construction of agglutinating principles.

For Nancy Fraser (1997), affirmative solutions to injustices related to cultural recognition, which are characteristic of certain variants of multiculturalism, indeed do serve to rectify the unjust effects of a particular social system, but without disrupting the foundations that continue to generate such recurrent ill effects. Affirmative action policies thus attempt to reevaluate the identity of unjustly discriminated groups without addressing either the contents of such identities or the social differentiations underlying them. By contrast, what Fraser calls "transformative solutions" seek to neutralize these shortcomings by modifying the underlying cultural value structure. As a strategy for analysis in this arena, deconstruction may help to blur the differences between existing group identities, for its utility lies in its focus on questioning received significations and constructions, in this case, the very meanings that individuals attach to ideas of belonging, affiliation, and self. This strategy may be deployed, for example, to destablize and then transform the homo/hetero dichotomy by simultaneously disrupting all static conceptualizations of sexual identity while constructing a new sexual field composed of multiple, fluid, and variable differences. In the case of economic injustice, transformative actions tend to counteract the unjust distribution of goods by converting the underlying economic-political structure. A transformative redistribution of material and symbolic goods can foster solidarity as it serves to break down fixed, hermetic understandings of identity, and to contest problematic and stigmatizing forms of recognition, such as that resulting from redistribution based on affirmative action policies, which leave intact the undervalued identities of the social groups receiving social assistance and recognition.

Moreover, Fraser argues that it is possible to boost multiple and simultaneously interlinked resistances because the axes of injustice are interwoven and, as a result, so too are the tensions between redistribution and recognition. Above all, the confluence of social class, race, gender, and sexuality in social beings makes the need for transformative solutions all the more compelling. It also makes the combination of socialism (the transformative option that Fraser associates with the construction of economic equality) and deconstruction, which is linked to issues of cultural injustice, appealing. In the final analysis, and as aforementioned, the metalevel questions—the who and the how—would play a crucial conciliatory role by promoting deliberative strategies that would help to adjudicate among contending interventionary agendas, and elaborate appropriate frameworks for justice.

The recognition of socialism as a strategy for cohesive change is presented as a valid option for education by Peter McLaren and Ramin Farahmandpur (2001). Both authors suggest the socialist imagination is helpful for understanding the symbiosis between neoliberalization and globalization, and for constructing an alternative revolutionary pedagogy, one which challenges the view of education as an industry focused on achieving profits. Transforming education along these lines would help educators understand the mutual relations between work and capital in order to challenge the current direction educational institutions are heading—toward corporatism and privatization—and to redirect them instead toward satisfying human needs. These authors remind us that education is directly involved in the production of a good that generates the social universe of capital, with its dynamic and multiform existence: the work-power couplet. A reform focused on social justice should redesign education so that a socialist perspective, rather than a human capital approach, orients the work-power relationship. For this to take place, the relationship between race, class, and gender oppression must be examined in the global context of capitalist relationships (McLaren and Farahmandpur, 2001). These authors' proposal for a revolutionary pedagogy rests, moreover, on the praxis of a revolutionary citizenry: a sociopolitical form of praxis which challenges—in the classroom, the workplace, and the social setting—the ownership of the means of production as well as the sites of participation in the public sphere, where people struggle to redefine the meaning of a social, democratic life. This proposal implies, however, reformulating the goals of a socialist utopia by moving them away from changing the world, and toward changing our place in it. The struggle for educational reform thus implies resistance to capitalism at local and global levels, and requires that educators cultivate conflictive and critical attitudes that may help them confront the simplistic conceptualization of education promoted through mercantile interests, with their attendant privatizing practices.[13]

Another option for promoting convergence among resistance movements advocating social justice would involve regarding educational change as a contribution to democratic cultural pluralism. This would mean organizing school life in accordance with a concept of public space as heterogeneous, so that group differences are neither eliminated nor transcended; on the contrary, public and political differences between social groups are actively recognized and guaranteed as a means of assuring the participation and inclusion of all people in social and political institutions. With that goal in mind, claims to group rights and policies need also address general rights and policies of participation and inclusion, but in a strategic, circumstantial, and situated way. Policies that bring together group awareness are also necessary as a means of achieving social equality—as an objective of social justice—because they guarantee, on the one hand, the full participation and inclusion of all people in the major social institutions, and on the other, the social recognition of the opportunity to develop and use specific capabilities, and to pursue particular choices (Young, 1990).

It is clear that diverse intellectual positions and struggles have emerged around the issue of convergence among resistances; nonetheless, they all coincide in their pursuit of a redefinition of emancipatory intentions. We must recognize that deploying a politics of coalitions that connects general interests, such as social justice and critical democracy, with individual and local components of change, is intellectually uncomfortable. It is an aim that will challenge us to take on practical issues in order to avoid falling once again into the trap of abstraction that fails to influence life in our schools. Coordinating the fulfillment of rights and demands originating at both general and local levels of expression, becomes possible when we bear in mind that the setting for general action is not inevitably separated from local and individual spheres. Versatile strategies for meeting such diverse expressions of rights may promote the open and fluid nature of change targeted here, for it is this kind of change that contains a possibility of return, modification, and circularity. Collective rights would represent the general form, but the process through which they influence all members of society would occur at the local level, because individual experience is always unique. In this way, access to collective rights could be pursued through local routes and in varied forms. Socially recognized principles, upon which our intersubjective collective memory is based, would make interpersonal communication and solidarity among different social groups possible. Singularity and generality would be regarded as reciprocal terms. A more articulated attention to these different levels would offer the possibility of crossing various dimensions and promoting diversified, multidimensional and polysemic change initiatives. Educational change would thus have a common stamp while simultaneously maintaining its local tone, in response to specific circumstances and differences. However, would it not also be necessary to reconstruct recognized social principles in order to begin to create an alternative and intersubjective collective memory?

If we were able to recreate a politics of coalitions in the everyday practices of our educational institutions, we would be in a position to reinvent socially acknowledged and accepted principles so as to include new forms of coexistence that replace social relations of domination with social relations of emancipation. If our schools were pioneers in experimentation with alternative forms of sociability they would create the conditions to produce an avant-garde common sense (Santos, 2003a). In this way, education would fulfill its transformative role, successfully interfering with the mere transmission of experience—just what we need to challenge the narrow life horizon in which market pragmatism places us—and responding creatively to the demands of a world characterized by interracial coexistence, technocultural complexity, and social reinvention.

This is Boaventura de Sousa Santos' (2003a) message; he defends the reconstruction of the notion and practice of emancipatory social transformation, with an aim to changing how people are socialized, educated, and come to work, and to promoting rebellious subjectivities capable of identifying possibilities for transformation, and extending these beyond what is considered as possible. This transformation involves commitment to an explicitly utopian position and to recovering hope. This position would not be defined, however, as a general principle that would guide us toward a common future, but as a commitment to creating fields of social experimentation where it would become possible to "resist locally the evidence of what seems inevitable, to promote successful alternatives which seem utopian at all times and in all places except those in which they are in fact produced" (Santos, 2003a, p. 38; translated from the Spanish). This attitude concurs with the utopian realism of oppressed groups who relentlessly strive to construct local alternatives, and to achieve dignified and decent life conditions. These multiple, radical actions and experimental initiatives would allow for the creation of reciprocal complicities among alternatives in different places, and for the configuration of translocal networks that could offer new visions of cosmopolitanism. Indeed, a primary aspiration of situated reform would be to transform schools into spaces of social experimentation for the promotion of radical subjectivities that dare to reinvent socially recognized principles, and explore alternatives that can inform our social life from everyday experiences with solidarity, understanding, and local democracy.[14]

When local commitment to education is situated in the setting of struggle for civil liberties and human dignity, dissidence arises as an option against indifference, against the destiny of millions of individuals who—deprived of cultural, social and economic capital—are treated as less than human beings, and denied what they rightfully deserve: a decent education. Such an education would not only facilitate access to the goods that social, cultural and economic development can provide; it would also acknowledge the potentials of all individuals as human beings, as well as the peculiarities that shape their experiences as members of diverse social groups. Finally, it is, most of all, a pledge to uphold the dignity of women and men such as ourselves, who have indeed benefited from a decent education, for if our enjoyment of such a collective right remains as restricted as it now is, and has long been, then our condition will continue to amount to a mere simulacrum of human dignity.

NOTES

1. The scarcity of innovative proposals coming from radical approaches is partly due to the systematic marginalization suffered by critical discourses in the field of public affairs, but also to the amount of abstraction embodied in these proposals, as they remain remote from the field of human actions (McCarthy, 1990).

2. We could summarize the main aims of Michel Foucault as encouraging us to think in "an other way." Attempting to show that we are freer than we feel, he constructs the concept of "technologies of power," by which he means those strategies and mechanisms that influence people's behavior and imply a kind of domination; and "technologies of the self": those used by the subject to achieve a certain level of happiness or pureness. People accept as truth some "way of being," that has nonetheless been socially constructed in specific historical moments, and whose foundations could be criticized, taken apart, and reimagined from the possibility of alternatives.

3. Curiously, this rediscovery is being promoted by authors such as Peter McLaren, who stands out for his unconditional support for the most political aspects of postmodernism, and for his contribution to the creation of pedagogical engagements with the politics of identity and difference in educational institutions. An explanation of his return to Marxist origins can be found in Paraskeva et al. (2005).

4. According to Nancy Fraser's most recent analysis (2005), the proposal these authors make would not prove very successful given that they center on first-order questions of social justice. It is the metalevel matters that can have much more cohesive effects because they reflect issues related to representation, that is, questions about who can participate and how matters of social justice are resolved in a transnational context. These two aspects typically concern any social group.

5. Ben Agger (1992, p. 110) demonstrates the connections between these traditions by pointing out that the critical theory of the Frankfurt School has provided a sense of dialectical continuity between capitalist modernity and a possible socialist and feminist critical postmodernism. It is also worth remembering that intellectual instability, far from being negative or debilitating, seems to be an essential condition for the advancement of the critical project (Pinar et al., 1995).

6. For example, in his research project "The reinvention of social emancipation," Boaventura de Sousa Santos (1999–2001) tracked down in various countries the base initiatives connected to alternative globalization. He concluded that the rich social experience of alternative actions discovered through that project were nonetheless never given the necessary attention or projection

they deserved in order to influence a broader public. It is this kind of active absence-making, or *sociology of absences* (Santos, 2005), that in turn perpetuates the pessimistic belief that alternatives to neoliberal globalization are impossible. The project may be consulted at: www.ces.uc.pt/emancipa (last retrieved on December 12, 2007).

7. This topic is also explored in Rodríguez Romero (2003), in two of its chapters.

8. One must not forget the antiglobalization or alternative globalization movement, which in fact comprises myriad movements, and coalitions of coalitions that are united in their resistance to the privatization of all facets of life, and the conversion of all activities and values into (marketable) goods. They coincide in a "radical reclamation of common goods" through multiple campaigns and very distinct movements aimed at pursuing alternative modes of life, here and now. These movements are often in opposition, however, over the degree to which local communities may influence decisions about the ways their resources are used, in order to ensure that the inhabitants of their respective geographical spaces will benefit. What situates the multiple local disputes of these movements on a global ideological scale is the demand for an alternative participatory democracy which would bring power and decision-making closer to the citizens and strengthen their organization and self-determination in the local sphere. For Naomi Klein (2001) this global political "brand" should stimulate, celebrate, and fiercely protect the right to diversity: cultural, environmental, agricultural and, clearly, political diversity—the different ways of doing politics. Local communities should have a right to plan and manage their schools, services, and their natural environment according to their own conceptions. Obviously, this is only possible within a framework which establishes national and international guidelines related to public education, non-renewable energy emissions, and so on. Nevertheless, the objective should not be that the rules of remote rulers be improved, but that closer, groundlevel forms of democracy be forged.

9. If the intent is to promote solutions that are transformative and not affirmative, we should question the revolutionary potential of the recognition of difference. According to Reichmann and Fernández Buey (1994), the positions represented by the new social movements could be described as self-contained radicalism, or radical pragmatism, because they do not encourage a revolutionary offensive against the system, but rather a mobilization toward the transformation of democracies. Their strategies have also been called radical reformism because they fight for long-term change, are organized in actions of varying scope, and tend to maintain experimental, nonviolent dispositions toward political action; that is, their orientation is mostly characterized by revision and criticism. According to this author, this orientation embodies a clear paradox, the result of a radical critique of the existing order, as conditioned by *de facto* integration into the current social and political system.

10. Participatory budgets have a special place among these. See Santos (2003b).

11. See the 1996 special edition of the journal *Theory into Practice*, Vol. 35, No. 2.

12. Paradigmatic transition is the conceptual key that Boaventura de Sousa Santos (2003a) uses to refer to the present moment from which new theoretical and social horizons emerge and are imagined, albeit through the use of epistemological keys from former paradigms.

13. The desire to turn socialism into a meeting point for the politics of difference is not easily accepted and is being refuted by authors who see, behind proposals such as the aforementioned, a revitalization of Marxist orthodoxy that hinders any possibility of diversified emancipation (Butler, 1998). In particular, discourses such as that of Peter McLaren and Ramin Farahmandpur's (2001) reopen questions already dealt with from the field of critical pedagogy (Gore, 1996). For instance, these authors fail to recognize the destructive consequences that the pursuit of the good could cause when presented as a flawless option. Moreover, they have no interest in the practical

application of a pedagogy that they are demanding, and they speak for social groups to which they do not belong.

14. A classic example of education for democracy can be found in Goodman (1992). More recent studies can be consulted in Apple and Beane (1997); Fields and Feinberg (2001); and Goodman (2006).

REFERENCES

Agger, B. (1992). *Cultural studies as critical theory.* London: Falmer.

Apple, M. W. and Beane, J. A. (1997). *Democratic schools.* Alexandria, VA: Association for Supervision and Curriculum Development (ASCD).

Biesta, G. (1995). Postmodernism and the repoliticization of education. *Interchange,* Vol. 26, No. 2, pp. 161–183.

Butler, J. (1998). Merely cultural. *New Left Review,* Vol. I, No. 227 (January–February), pp. 33–44.

Cantor, N. and Courant, P. (2003). Scrounging for resources: Reflections on the whys and wherefores of higher education finance. *New Directions for Institutional Research,* No. 119, pp. 3–12.

Fields, A. B. and Feinberg, W. (2001). *Education and democratic theory.* New York: SUNY Press.

Foucault, M. (1988). *Technologies of the self: A seminar with Michel Foucault.* Amherst, MA: University of Massachusetts Press.

Fraser, N. (1997). *Justice Interruptus: Critical reflections on the "postsocialist" condition.* London: Routledge.

Fraser, N. (1998). Heterosexism, misrecognition and capitalism: A response to Judith Butler. *New Left Review,* Vol. I, No. 228 (March–April), pp. 140–149.

Fraser, N. (2005). Reframing justice in a globalizing world. *New Left Review* No. 36 (November–December), pp. 69–88.

Goodman, J. (1992). *Elementary schooling for critical democracy.* New York: SUNY Press.

Goodman, J. (2006). *Reforming school.* New York: SUNY Press.

Gore, J. (1993). *The struggle for pedagogies: Critical and feminist discourses as regimes of truth.* New York and London: Routledge.

Hall, S. (1986). History, politics and postmodernism: Stuart Hall and cultural studies (an interview with Lawrence Grossberg), *Journal of Communication Inquiry,* Vol. 10 (Summer), pp. 61–77.

Harding, S. (1986). *The science question in feminism.* Ithaca, NY/London: Cornell University Press.

Hardt, M. and Negri, A. (2004). *Multitud: Guerra y democracia en la era del Imperio.* Barcelona: Debate.

Hargreaves, A. (1994). *Changing teachers, changing times: Teacher's work and culture in the postmodern age.* London: Casell.

Kemmis, S. (1995). Emancipatory aspirations in a postmodern era. *Curriculum Studies* Vol. 3, No. 2, pp. 133–167.

Klein, N. (2000). *No logo.* New York: Harper and Collins.

Lather, P. and Ellsworth, E. (1996). Introduction. *Theory into Practice,* Vol. 35, No. 2, pp. 86–92.

McCarthy, C. (1990). *Race and curriculum: Social inequality and the theories and politics of difference in contemporary research on schooling.* New York: Taylor and Francis.

McConaghy, C. (2002). Situated pedagogies: Researching quality teaching and learning for rural New South Wales schools. (Position paper prepared for the ARC Linkage 2002–2004, NSWDET). Sydney.

McLaren, P. (1999). Pedagogía revolucionaria en tiempos posrevolucionarios: Repensar la economía política de la educación crítica. In F. Imbernón (Ed.), *La educación en el siglo XXI: Los retos del futuro inmediato* (pp. 101–120). Barcelona: Graó.

McLaren, P. and Farahmandpur, R. (2001). Educational policy and the socialist imagination: Revolutionary citizenship as pedagogy of resistance. *Educational Policy*, Vol. 15, No. 3, pp. 343–378.

Miller, J. L. (1996). Teachers, researchers, and situated school reform: Circulations of power. *Theory into Practice*, Vol. 35, No. 2, pp. 86–92.

Paraskeva, J., Gandia, L., and Hypólito, A. (Eds.) (2005). *Diálogos educacionais e curriculares a esquerda. Fúria e esperança: A pedagogía revolucionária de Peter Mclaren.* Lisbon: Plátano Editora.

Pinar, W. F., Reynolds, W. M., Taubman, P. M., and Slattery, P. (1995). *Understanding curriculum: An introduction to the study of historical and contemporary curriculum discourses.* New York: Peter Lang.

Popkewitz, T. S. (1991). *A political sociology of educational reform.* New York: Columbia University, Teachers College.

Reichmann, J. and Fernández Buey, F. (1994). *Redes que dan libertad: Introducción a los nuevos movimientos sociales.* Barcelona: Paidós.

Rodríguez Romero, M. M. (2003). *Las metamorfosis del cambio educativo.* Madrid: Akal.

Santos, B. d. S. (1999–2001). Reinventing social emancipation (Research project, Centro de Estudos Sociais, School of Economics, University of Coimbra, Portugal). See http://www.ces.uc.pt/emancipa/(last retrieved on July 12, 2007).

Santos, B. d. S. (2003a). *Crítica de la razón indolente: Contra el desperdicio de la experiencia.* Bilbao: Desclée de Brouwer.

Santos, B. d. S. (2003b). *Democracia y participación: El ejemplo del presupuesto participativo de Porto Alegre.* Barcelona: El Viejo Topo.

Santos, B. d. S. (2005). *El milenio huérfano: Ensayos para una nueva cultura política.* Madrid: Trotta.

Tadeu da Silva, T. (2005). Mapeando a (complexa) produção teórica educacional. In J. Parakesva, L. Gandín and A. Hypólito (Eds.), *Diálogos educacionais e curriculares à esquerda. Fúria e esperança: A pedagogía revolucionária de Peter Mclaren* (pp. 36–50). Lisbon: Plátano Editora.

Taylor, S., Rizvi, F., Lingard, B., and Henry, M. (1997). *Educational policy and the politics of change.* London: Routledge.

Young, I. M. (1990). *Justice and the politics of difference.* Princeton, NJ: Princeton University Press.

CHAPTER ELEVEN

The challenges OF migration: Anthropology, education, AND multiculturalism[1]

DOLORES JULIAÑO

University of Barcelona

INTRODUCTION

From an educational perspective, the schooling of children of foreign-born immigrants, frequently classified in Spain as second generation immigrants, is generally considered to be a challenge, or indeed a problem. How is it possible to follow a curriculum while respecting the students' right to their own specific cultural origins? What sense of identity should the children of immigrants develop? Do members of the host society respect practices which clash with their own customs or which diverge from their own moral values? Is the alternative to cultural assimilation necessarily segregation or marginalization? More specifically, how can we as educators and scholars overcome differences in education and assure that all children perform at school on an equal footing, regardless of cultural origin? These are key issues, especially considering how easily racism and xenophobia can become contributing factors. For example, is it possible to prevent families from gradually drifting away from a school community as the number of immigrant children on roll increases? And how can we keep these immigrant students themselves from being marginalized, bullied, or unnecessarily targeted by their peers?

In order to address the challenges these issues pose we turn to work from anthropology and the social sciences; although what we find is often far from satisfactory. In order to understand why this is so, let us first consider the issues that anthropologists tend to focus on within this realm of educational concerns, the main features of which would include the following:

- The children of immigrants are not a fixed and permanent part of any one source culture, but bearers of a multicultural experience that allows them to move fluidly between the world of their forebears and their host society. As a survival strategy, they tend to develop versatile identities, and with these they can give priority to certain spheres of belonging and enrich their lives with culturally diverse experiences. The aim of education, according to this view, should therefore be centered not on trying to imitate or reproduce the parents' original culture at school (nor on separating the children from it) but instead on creating a framework of respect in which these children do not feel stigmatized, and are free to develop their own identity.

- Respect for difference might serve to hide the wide variety of similarities shared by different cultural groups. In terms of fostering coexistence, highlighting common ground tends to be more productive than emphasizing difference.

- Every culture, including our own, has within it practices with which some will disagree. Coexistence implies dialogue and respect for these practices, not an indiscriminate acceptance of the same.

- Foreign students whose parents' languages differ from that or those spoken in the surrounding community tend to suffer difficulties with comprehension and communication. If given support in this area, however, an acceptable level of learning can be attained. These students' multilingual experience is, in fact, a helpful resource to be tapped, rather than a hindrance in their schooling.

- Problems faced by particular schools tend to exist long before the arrival of immigrant children. These problems might include a lack of equipment, the poor condition of buildings and infrastructure, and a generally low economic and social standing among students. The newly arrived thus become visibly associated with a set of circumstances that they have not themselves created.

In what follows, I will deal with some of these issues whilst analyzing the reasons for difficulties in achieving free-flowing communication between teachers and social scientists, beginning with what I believe to be a crucial point: individual and ethnic identity.

Single or multiple identities

Baroness Blixen (1999), who lived in Africa for many years and acquired in-depth knowledge about the ways in which distinct identities can coexist within individuals who move between different worlds, suggested in her short story *The Dreamers* that various advantages can be had by adopting different personalities throughout one's life:

> You have to be more than just one person; you must be as many as you can bear. I believe that all of the world's people should be more than one. In so doing they stand to enjoy much more freedom, joy and happiness in life. (p. 314)[2]

Creating multiple identities and blending them together, she suggests, can help overcome the self-centered distortions that emerge from knowing only one way of life. In this way, one achieves a greater acceptance of others, whilst bringing into perspective one's own concerns and problems.

The Nicaraguan writer Gioconda Belli (2000) deals with similar concerns in her memoirs, which conclude with a story of immigration and exile illustrating the need to

> live not one but several lives at the same time. To accept oneself as a being that exists on multiple planes of space and time; this is part of modernity and of the current possibilities available to those living in an age where technology can be used as a source of freedom instead of being rejected as a source of alienation. Human aspirations have lost their geographic restraints. (pp. 408–409)

This same idea is dealt with by Agustín (2002) from a more academic and less personal perspective, through the concept of "cosmopolitism," by which she means enrichment as a consequence of having access to diverse cultural experiences. She points out that the experience of migration—even when it occurs in poor and difficult conditions—allows for a broadening of the boundaries of existence and a better understanding of diverse realities, usually denied to those tied to a single way of life and to a stable cultural universe.

The status of having changed country or culture would not then be seen as the (aberrant) result of having no fixed place of residence, but rather as a valid and even desirable alternative. As Sutcliffe (1998) points out, rather than asking ourselves why 2% of the world's population leave their place of origin, we should ask ourselves what limitations and deficiencies prevent the remainder of the population from doing the same. He notes that

> [i]t is an error to assume that the actions of the majority require no explanation. By concentrating theories on the characteristics of minorities we are very subtly contributing, albeit unintentionally, to the notion that their conduct is not normal. (p. 15)

Discussions of this kind serve to devictimize the concept of immigration, and to refute the opinion that every person has a unique and permanent identity, which forms them, and lends them structure as a person, and at the same time provides a link to their forebears. Thus, the problem faced by second generations ought not be characterized as one of having to choose between being part of the group of their forebears or assimilating, in a depersonalized way, into the host society. Further, schools need not attempt to resolve this dilemma, as it is essentially a false one. Children can make multiple and complex choices regarding their identity, sometimes even contradictory ones, as part of their social interactions, without these generating excessive anxiety (except for the inconvenience of having to respond to external demands relating to this situation).

The hypothesis that fluid identity options are normal is based on theoretical analysis from scholars such as Mary Douglas (1995), who notes that the apparent unity and continuance of an essential individual identity is in fact a social construct, and as such responds more to the maintenance of structural order than to people's experiences and desires. At the international level, such alternative interpretations have a long tradition, ranging from the work of Amir Maalouf (1999) to that of Zygmunt Bauman (2005) and García Canclini (2002), as well as work from Abou (1981), Barth (1994), and Calhoun (1994).

Nevertheless, the cultural assumption that people have a fixed identity throughout their lives—one that is taken even further by those who believe in the permanent continuity of all eternity—comes from an equally long academic tradition, and is generally supported by a strong social consensus in Spain. This deeply rooted notion leads to the perception that those who change certain aspects of their identity throughout their lives are somehow lacking or aberrant, as is also thought of those who change their names or cut their ties with the past. Moreover, this sense of lives that are lacking serves as a model against which those identities accepted as legitimate can be valued as such, namely sexual, ethnic, and national identities. As a result, those who would choose to modify their sexual tendencies, or change their nationality or ethnic allegiances, are regarded with suspicion. Such fixed and exclusive models, especially where sexual dichotomies are concerned, have been critically deconstructed and challenged by Rich (1986, 2001), Kitzinger and Wilkinson (1994) and Butler (2001), while similarly essentialized constructions of ethnicity have received equally critical analyses from those subscribing to Barth's insights (Vermeulen and Govers, 1994).

THE SCHOOL OF IDENTITY AND ITS DEMANDS

We have already seen, however, how the arbitrary nature of the concept of individual identity as necessarily stable and cumulative has constituted no obstacle to its general acceptance and geographical scope. Taking the construction of nation-states as a starting point, efforts have been made to create imaginaries from which such fixed and homogeneous identities become desirable (Verdery, 1994), and schools have been charged with the task of turning each of these imaginaries into reality.

The advent of the industrial revolution brought with it a period of social restructuring, which in turn engendered the development of new forms of control (Foucault 1980), based on new models of attachment. Emerging national states were erected upon two pillars: the idea that homogeneity in conduct and values (through an assumed joint national identity) was a prerequisite for social organization; and the conviction that this could be achieved by implementing an efficient educational system.

In response to this demand, models of fixed and exclusive identity, on the one hand, and educational institutions, on the other, have become mutually complementary. If the mission is to produce "good citizens" who favor patriotism over other identity options, and who exclude foreigners from their system of solidarity, then people must be inculcated with such values. Schools were designed as the means to achieve this objective.

Given that this aim is neither natural nor indeed necessary, various approaches have been explored and negotiated, as well as specific techniques developed, to destabilize its naturalization. The methodological approach asserted by Barth (1976) involves considering identity options as strategies constructed at different levels (micro, mid, and macro) which bear fruit in different spheres. In simple terms, the micro level represents individual options, developed through interaction with others and through influences received; the midlevel involves social and political movements; and the macro level involves state regulations.

If we apply this analytical approach to the dominant model for developing identity through schooling, what becomes immediately evident is that schools provide the cornerstone for each of the three levels. In addition to being the site for primary interaction with regard to the first set of identity options, schools are also the place where ideological models take form and where specific policies implement these models. Considering that the objective of schooling is to achieve the "normal" development of students, this necessarily involves reaffirming the use of symbols that represent immobile identity, as well discouraging change and innovation. Of course, the more efficient this dominant model is, the farther it will be from creating an environment of freedom and satisfactory individual options, as Le Guin (1980) has pointed out:

> It is of no use to have an answer when the question is wrong in the first place. (p. 68)

Indeed, if theoretical questions are not adequately formed at the outset, and if the conception of identities as fixed and exclusive is taken as the starting point, then technical and methodological applications can only serve to exacerbate the problem, for they engender purely dualistic or binary responses: that "newcomers" either be compulsively assimilated into the host country's culture, or contained, immobilized within the cultural system of their forebears, inevitably seen as *different*.

One can but wonder what has gone wrong, especially considering cases of countries such as France—among the most developed inasmuch as the schooling of the children of immigrants is concerned—yet which is experiencing the gravest of problems with "second generation" immigrants. When such conflicts arise, schools are overwhelmed and tend to respond by offering more of the same. This occurs when former assimilationist models are rejected because the problem is thought to reside in the system perhaps not being sufficiently multicultural or respectful of difference. But far from transforming the institution, a vicious circle instead arises in which the same recipe is reasserted (one which appears dangerously similar, moreover, to the theoretical basis of South African apartheid) as a sign of supposedly progressive values, in the belief that the only solution is yet another version of assimilation/containment, which in fact is neither wanted nor advocated by anyone.

The victims of this confusion are the children who, labeled as *second generations*, are often uncomfortable with the pressure of being categorically identified with the essentialized cultural universe of their forebears, as highlighted by Franzé (1998) in her study of this phenomenon in Madrid. Educational agents tend to consider the shift in identity in these children as a "dangerous rejection of their origins"—an idea that nonetheless serves to alienate them from a diverse range of experiences that can potentially lead to the construction of an enriched, mobile, complex, and ever-changing individual identity.

DEMANDS FOR SUPPORT

In Spain, there is unease around the persistence of problems originating from inadequacies in the educational system. This is considered a pressing social issue, and has led, over recent decades, to the demand for input from anthropologists. Anthropology has thus been seen as offering a possible source for solutions to the problems arising from multicultural coexistence in schools.

However, this demand has two sides to it. Spanish society—still in the early stages of its multiethnic reality—is faced with the dilemma of how to transmit its dominant cultural foundations while questioning the very basis of this cultural project of self-reproduction over time. This situation implies a constant demand for theoretical support from social scientists, and delimits the scope for research, not to mention additional demands from the technical sphere for research technologies supporting participatory observation and other methods.

Indeed, the anthropology of education can satisfy both demands here. In many places, such as English speaking countries and their areas of influence, this kind of work has a long-standing tradition, with a great many anthropologists contributing to a broad corpus of literature. Outstanding names in this field include Margaret Mead and Jules Henry, and, more recently, Elliot, Giroux, and Ogbu. Much work in this vibrant field, though, remains to be done. As Bruner (1997) noted, sadly:

> Frighteningly little systematic study has been dedicated to the institutional anthropology of education, given the complexity of its social character and its role in the ever-changing social and economic climate. (p. 51)

The situation is even worse in Spain. Our universities, so often overly dependent on the North American model, have, in this case, followed the French tradition of assigning such work to the area of sociology, a tradition which in the French case has led to a prestigious body of research ranging from Durkheim (1989) to Bourdieu (Bourdieu and Passeron 1970; Bourdieu 1992). Studies concerning the interaction between schools and society in Spain have, then, been undertaken chiefly by sociologists, ever since the pioneering work of Carlos Lerena Aleson (1989). Notwithstanding the great increase in the number of departments of sociology of education, anthropology has also shown much interest in this issue. Theoretical work is abundant (Garcia Castaño 1991; Jordán 1992; Campani 1993; Velasco et al. 1993; Garcia Castaño and Pulido Moyano 1994; San Román 1996; Garcia Castaño 1997; Malgesini and Gimenez 1997; Velasco and Diaz de Rada 1997; Escandell 2002), and I myself have worked for a number of years in this area (see Juliano 1987–2004). However, the academic response to the demand for work here remains clearly insufficient.

MISUNDERSTANDINGS

There are reasons which might serve to explain why in Spanish universities anthropology has become relatively distant from the study of the educational system, despite demand from schools for work in this camp. One might say, at a simplistic level, that because this demand has not been correctly formulated, it has been poorly answered. The fact is that educational agents have long considered anthropology as a discipline focused on the study of the "other," the foreign. Hence, its research focus, offering, and production have only been deemed necessary since Spanish society began to consider its social body as an essentially plural group, that is, since the initial arrival of foreign immigration. Consistent with the view that anthropology specializes in faraway worlds, the cooperation of anthropologists is eventually sought when members of the social majority begin to perceive of immigrants from developing countries as too "exotic." Although this is nothing more than a mental construct, or an imaginary reality which tends to broaden cultural distances and obscure similarities—one that automatically qualifies immigrants as "others" regardless of their level of Westernization—it is nevertheless irrefutable that, since the 1980s, the demand for anthropological involvement in schools has risen in tandem with increasing reports of problems related to multiculturalism and immigration.[3]

This understanding of the primary work of anthropologists is, in fact, erroneous. Anthropology no longer prioritizes the study of distant societies, but for decades has redirected its attention toward complex societies, the study of institutions and urban anthropology: areas in which social complexity and mutability converge.

On the other hand, today's society—which so urgently demands the services of anthropology—is in fact little more multicultural than it was thirty years ago. The main transfer of cultural models in Spain during this period has mainly taken place as a result of internal migrations, with large masses of the population moving between different metropolitan areas, and from the countryside to the city. A survey carried out in 1997 by the Spanish Sociological Research Center (CIS)[4] found that nearly 90% of the young people interviewed had been born in the same region where they currently resided, whilst six years earlier only 60% could say the same. This illustrates a process of increasing social homogenization that the current population of foreign origin, which is rapidly approaching 10% of the total population of Spain,[5] does little to change.

For this reason, one might argue that multicultural awareness today, rather than describing adequately the current situation, is in effect more the result of the emergence of a social imaginary based on differentiation. If one also considers that these allegedly "different" immigrants tend to come from areas such as the Mediterranean, which shares a long history with Spain, or regions such as Latin America, where Spanish colonial expansion imposed common cultural values, it is not difficult to see that such imagery of difference incorrectly identifies cultural divergences when in fact the differences have more to do with race and social status. An example of this can be found in the above-mentioned survey, in which it was found that the most culturally distant groups are thought to be those that have the darkest colored skin (e.g., the Senegalese).

The idea that the children of immigrants from Third World countries (not rich countries) present problems at school can also be considered as derived from the construct of differentiation. Studies such as those carried out by Franzé (1998) in the poorer suburbs of Madrid, or by Serra in the province of Girona (Serra i Salamé 2001 and 2002) show that cause and effect are inverted in these cases. Children of immigrant families normally go to schools located in the suburbs where they live, and due to their families' lack of economic resources, these suburbs tend to be underprivileged, with few services and a high degree of social conflict. Whilst not necessarily aggravating this already negative situation, the presence of these newly arrived people tends to make it more visible. As Franzé (1998) notes:

> The phenomenon of the concentration of minorities is only one aspect of a much wider process of differential distribution, from which social differences become significant as regards education. (p. 118)

Even at the macrostatistical level, there is no correlation between the worsening of performance at school and the presence of immigrant populations. In fact, according to recent reports,[6] the communities that, due to their wealth, attract the most immigrants are those that show the lowest rates of failure at school.

For all of these reasons, the popular assignment of negative associations to the increasing presence of immigrants in Spain is misguided. Yet even as this tendency continues to serve as the basis for soliciting anthropological interventions, it has not been sufficiently discussed or reformulated by Spanish academic anthropology. That said, other factors have likely contributed to this silence. One is that involvement in the educational system is seen as an extreme departure from the traditional image of the anthropologist as an explorer of far-off worlds. Although this model is no longer considered to be valid or current, it nevertheless continues to exert a certain degree of influence on anthropologists. The irony of this situation is that the institution of education, by its very nature as an integral part of Western life, occupies a central space in the meaning of the "homeland," of place, indeed, of the realm in which researchers themselves have set up their homes and established their roots. If Margherite Yourcenar (1977/1951) could say, in *Mémoires d'Hadrien*, that the true homeland is in books, then for professional intellectuals who are the heirs of the Enlightenment, the educational sector has constituted a very central source of their intellectual and political pursuits, a privileged field of systematic development and, of course, a major target for criticism and the expression of frustrations. Involvement in such an institution is a character-building experience. In this sense, Elena Achilli is right to point out that one of the obstacles faced when carrying out ethnographies of the classroom is the difficulty in moving away from this very reality, so naturalized in our minds that it poses a real problem for objective research in this area. Another obstacle here is the feeling of guilt for spying on a world to which we ourselves deeply belong (Achilli 1988, 1993, 1995).

Other obstacles appear to be less immediately significant, and have to do with the image of the social scientist as devoted to pure research, with little or no commitment to practice. This posture—which in the past constituted a healthy reaction among anthropologists to administrative dependence through applied anthropology during the colonial era—is perversely reinforced in teaching establishments through a similar rejection of critical social science attendant to the 70s mold. These establishments had to undergo change, whether cosmetic or suprastructural in nature, as institutions became increasingly cataloged and ordered. Thus, the ongoing pedagogical demands for active measures were equally sidelined from anthropological research, either to avoid political commitment, or indeed because they were considered insufficiently political.

Some further obstacles arise from the poor communication between different academic spheres, as well as from anthropologists' inadequate grounding on the difficult theoretical issues related to social pedagogy. This leads to information gaps in the area of critical trends in pedagogy, and as a result, work in the aftermath of reproductivism—particularly theoretical productivist trends and the methodological proposals for research/action here—tends to remain ignored, even in research on this issue.

Reality, however, is stubborn. The school sector (for reproductionists, a key site for social conservation; for constructivists, an essential element in its renovation) needs theoretical models with which educational agents might best understand its own functioning and develop methodological tools to unravel its secrets. Those who conduct research in the educational system, particularly sociologists, already draw on a number of strategies from anthropology to carry out institutional analysis and participatory observation. Thus, contemporary anthropological commitment to the analysis of complex societies can only complete the puzzle if its practitioners gain a deep understanding of an institution that, for more than two centuries, has been identified as a specially equipped arena for providing cultural continuity and ethnic belonging. If one also bears in mind that the concept of education covers not only institutional practices (including the largely invisible practices that make up the so-called hidden curriculum) but also informal practices (including those generated through the mass media), one can see that education as such spans a broad horizon that is essential to understanding social strategies and the ways in which power is organized and legitimized.

THE RESPONSIBILITY OF ANTHROPOLOGY

The convergence of both fields of interest here can only be fruitful. Given that it has been decades since the "exotic" gaze of anthropology was replaced by inquiries into less remote environments, and given that complex societies are the basis of current research in Spain, it seems that the moment has come to focus on societal institutions of self-reproduction and social control. This way anthropologists can close the gap with respect to sociologists, historians, and philosophers.

Anthropology, as a field that retains historical connections and moral commitments to the institution of schooling, is thus owing to this institution just as it is partially accountable for some of the demands emerging from schools. Consider, for instance, that some of the most complex and problematic concepts tackled within anthropology today originated, in fact, from the arsenal of concepts circulating within the educational field. The clearest example here is the incorporation of the concept of "multiculturalism" into schools during the last decades, which was based on a simplified interpretation of the anthropological notion of cultural relativism. This conceptualization of multiculturalism in school contexts implies that cultures have come to be understood there as delimitable, homogeneous, permanent, and agreed-on through consensus, and that people remain unproblematically linked forever to their original cultural environments. It is therefore anthropology that must adopt the task of substituting this essentializing conceptualization for current critical ideas on culture and identity (seen as fluid, varying, and internally contradictory).

The adaptation of the anthropological concepts of multiculturalism and "respect for difference" in schools came about as a means of focusing on cultural content, of homogenizing the image of all cultures of origin, and of assigning the students a single sense of belonging; and has tended to marginalize the possibility of choice. This worrying issue is discussed by Barth (1994), and can lead to situations that scholars such as Jordán (1992), Grignon (1993), Franzé (1998), and others have alerted us to in Spain.

LIMITED CONCLUSIONS

The concepts under discussion here have a political background and social repercussions. In this sense, anthropologists have an inherent responsibility to clarify and update theory in this area, and a need for all those involved in today's problems to remain current as well on their theoretical approaches.

As a result of neoliberal globalization and its systematic exploitation of human beings and resources, large masses of people emigrate to richer countries in search of new and better opportunities. Upon arrival, these people are labeled, illegitimated and, in many cases, expelled. We compulsively try both to assimilate their children into our schools and at the same time to urge them to remain true to the ethnic identity we have assigned to their parents. As Bruner (1997) points out, this is a significant source of problems:

> Should schools simply aspire to reproduce host cultures, or assimilate—to use this odious word—the young into small Americans or Japanese? Nevertheless, assimilation was commonplace as recently as the beginning of the past century. Would schools perhaps not find more success in preparing the young for the ever-changing world in which they are to live? And how are we to even decide how this world will be, and what it will demand of them? (p.11)

Anthropologists need to work together with the agents of educational institutions to design and spread the theoretical approaches that will allow for the development of innovative strategies. A multiple world must not be regarded as a patchwork of different cultures, but as a complex field of interrelations and mutations, where diverse experiences enrich us all. A world that accepts mutating identities and spatial movement as values. A world where we feel that we learn from life as the social landscape around us changes.

There remain many loose ends, but maybe it is best this way. Anthropology offers no answers to the problems but rather the opportunity to see them in a different light. The change from strong to weak paradigms that goes hand in hand with postmodernism does not provide stand-alone answers, but opens the door to trial and error as well as to individual thought. This is how the most productive form of coexistence can be accomplished. As Maalouf noted (1993):

> I have always believed that heaven created the problems and hell the solutions. Problems manhandle us, mistreat us, disaffect us, completely change the way we are. This strikes a healthy imbalance, for such problems lead species to evolve, whereas solutions lead them to become petrified and extinct. Is it a coincidence that the worst crime ever remembered goes by the name of the final solution? (p. 12)

NOTES

1. An initial version of certain parts of this chapter was presented at the conference *IX Congrés d'Antropología FAAEE* in Barcelona, in September of 2002, under the title "*Antropología, educación e interculturalidad: Una historia de encuentros y desencuentros*" (Anthropology, education and cross-culturalism: A story of encounters and misencounters).
2. All citations have been translated from Spanish-language source publications.
3. This so, only a fifth of all research to date on multiculturalism that is financed through the Ministry of Education and Culture has been headed by anthropologists, a reality which shows that there is still much to be done in this field.
4. See Moral and Mateos (1999) for a detailed discussion of the 1997 report *Estudio CIS 2.214: "Actitudes hacia la inmigración."*

5. Information based on the latest demographics report from the National Statistics Institute of Spain (see INE, 2007).
6. The findings from a study carried out by the Department of Education and reported in the national newspaper *El País* on September 7, 2002 show that the autonomous regions with the lowest school failure rates are Aragon, Asturias, Cantabria, Castile-Leon, Galicia, and Madrid. These regions are closely followed by Andalusia, Catalonia, the Canary Islands, and the Basque Country, all of which fall under the national average rate for school failure. Nonetheless, immigrant populations are highest in Madrid and Catalonia.

REFERENCES

Abou, S. (1981). *L'identité culturelle: Relations interethniques et problemes d'aculturation.* Paris: Anthropós.

Achilli, E. L. (1988). Práctica docente: Una interpretación desde los saberes del maestro. *Cuadernos de Antropología Social: Antropología y Educación*, No. 2, pp. 5–19.

Achilli, E. L. (1993). *Profe… ¿No quiere que cambiemos la escuela?* Rosario: Universidad Nacional de Rosario.

Achilli, E. L. (1995). Escuela, pobreza y multiculturalismo (De la práctica docente y las políticas educativas protagónicas). Unpublished paper presented at the V Reunião de Antropologia Merco-Sul Cultura e Globalização, held in Tramandaí, Brazil.

Agustín, L. M. (2002). Cuestionar el concepto del "lugar": La migración es algo más que una pérdida. *Development: Society for International Development*, Vol. 45, No. 1, 110–116.

Barth, F. (Ed.) (1976). *Los grupos étnicos y sus fronteras.* México: Fondo de Cultura Económica.

Barth, F. (1994). Enduring and emerging issues in the analysis of ethnicity. In H. Vermeulen and C. Govers (Eds.), *The anthropology of ethnicity* (pp. 11–33). Amsterdam: Het Spinhuis.

Bauman, Z. (2005). *Identidad.* Buenos Aires: Losada.

Belli, G. (2000). *El país bajo mi piel: Memorias de amor y guerra.* Barcelona: Plaza and Janés.

Blixen, K. with Dinesen, I. (1999). *Siete cuentos góticos.* Madrid: El Mundo Millenium.

Bourdieu, P. (1992). L'ecole et la cité. *Actes de la recherche en Sciences Sociales*, pp. 91–92, 86–96.

Bourdieu, P. and Passeron, J. C. (1970). *La reproduction: Eléments pour une theorie du systeme d'enseignement.* Paris: de Minuit.

Bruner, J. (1997). *La educación, puerta de la cultura.* Madrid: Visor.

Butler, J. (2001). La cuestión de la transformación social. In E. Beck-Gernsheim, J. Butler, and L. Puigvert (Eds.), *Mujeres y transformaciones sociales* (pp. 7–31). Barcelona: El Roure.

Calhoun, C. (1994). *Social theory and the politics of identity.* Oxford: Blackwell.

Campani, G. (1993). La educación intercultural: Una perspectiva pedagógica en Europa. In J. García Castaño (Ed.), *Educación multicultural: Hacia el reconocimiento de la diversidad en la educación* (pp. 45–62). Granada: Universidad de Granada.

Caravantes, C. (1992). Análisis institucional de un establecimiento educativo. *Revista de Antropología*, No. 2 (marzo), pp. 85–105.

Demo, P. (1987). *Investigación participante: Mito y realidad.* Buenos Aires: Kapelusz.

Douglas, M. (1995). The cloud god and the shadow self. *Social Anthropology*, Vol. 3, No. 2, pp. 83–95.

Durkheim, E. (1989/1922). *Educación y sociología.* Barcelona: Península.

Durkheim, E. (1990). *L'evolution pédagogique en France.* Paris: PUF.

Elliot, J. (1989). *Pràctica, recerca i teoria en educació.* Vic: Eumo.

Escandell, V. (2002). *Inmigración y escuela. La escolarización en España de los hijos de los inmigrantes africanos.* Alicante: Universitat d'Alacant.

Foucault, M. (1980). *Microfísica del poder.* Madrid: La Piqueta.

Franzé Mundanó, A. (1998). Cultura/culturas en la escuela: La interculturalidad en la práctica. *Ofrim suplementos: publicación especializada en inmigración*, No. 2, pp. 43–62.

Franzé Mundanó, A. (2002). *"Lo que sabía no valía": Escuela, diversidad e inmigración.* Madrid: Consejo Económico y Social, Comunidad de Madrid.

Garcia Castaño, J. (1991). En busca de modelos explicativos del funcionamiento de la transmisión/ adquisición de la cultura. In Díaz de Rada (Ed.), *Antropología de la Educación* (pp. 76–81). Granada: F.A.A.E.E.

Garcia Canclini, N. (1999). *La globalización imaginada.* México: Editorial Paidós.

García Canclini, N. (2002). *Latinoamericanos buscando lugar en este siglo.* Buenos Aires: Paidós.

García Castaño, J. and Pulido Moyano, R. (1994). *Antropología de la educación.* Madrid: Eudema.

Garcia Castaño, J., Pulido Moyano, R., and Montes del Castillo, A. (1997). La educación multicultural y el concepto de cultura. *Revista Iberoamericana de Educación*, No. 13. Retrieved from the journal's website: http://www.oei.es/oeivirt/rie13a09.htm (last retrieved December 1, 2007).

Giroux, H. A. and Flecha, R. (1992). *Igualdad educativa y diferencia cultural.* Barcelona: El Roure.

Giroux, H. A. (1992): *Border crossings: Cultural workers and the politics of education.* London: Routledge.

Giroux, H. A. (1994). *Disturbing pleasures: Learning popular culture.* London: Routledge.

Grignon, C. (1993). Cultura dominante, cultura escolar y multiculturalismo popular. *Educación y Sociedad*, No. 12, pp. 127–136.

Henry, J. (1963). *Culture against man: England.* London: Penguin Books.

Instituto Nacional de Estadística (INE) (2005). Padrón de Población de España, 1º de enero 2005. Madrid: Instituto Nacional de Estadística (INE).

Instituto Nacional de Estadística (INE) (2007). Anuario estadístico de España. 2007. Madrid: Instituto Nacional de Estadística. Report retrieved from the following INE web site: http://www.ine.es/ prodyser/pubweb/anuario07/anu07_02demog.pdf (last retrieved on November 30, 2007).

Jordán, J. A. (1992). *L'educació multicultural.* Barcelona: CEAC Editores.

Juliano, M. D. (1987). El discreto encanto de la adscripción étnica voluntaria. In R. Ringuelet (Ed.), *Procesos de Contacto Interétnico* (pp. 83–113). Buenos Aires: Búsqueda.

Juliano, M. D. (1988). La educación sistemática en situaciones de fricción interétnica. Las opciones de las comunidades indígenas americanas. In Universidad de Alicante (Eds.), *IV Congreso de Antropología* (pp. 12–22). Alicante: Universidad de Alicante.

Juliano, M. D. (1989). Estrategias de elaboración de la identidad. *Realitat*, No. 13, pp. 9–23.

Juliano, M. D. (1991). Antropología pedagógica y pluriculturalismo. *Cuadernos de Pedagogia*, No. 196 (octubre), pp. 8–10.

Juliano, M. D. (1992a). Educación y pluriculturalismo. In Escola d'Estiu sobre Interculturalitat (Ed.), *Sobre interculturalitat: documents de treball de la segona* (pp. 69–72). Girona: Escola d'Estiu sobre Interculturalitat.

Juliano, M. D. (1992b). Multiculturalisme a les escoles. *Debats de l'Aula Provença*, No. 13, pp. 13–23.

Juliano, M. D. (1993). Educación intercultural: Escuela y minorías étnicas. Madrid: Eudema.

Juliano, M. D. (1994a). La construcción de la diferencia: Los latinoamericanos. *Papers*, No. 43, pp. 23–32.

Juliano, M. D. (1994b). Educación y pluriculturalismo. In Escola d'Estiu sobre Interculturalitat (Ed.), *Sobre interculturalitat 2: Documents de treball de la tercera i quarta Escola d'Estiu sobre Interculturalitat* (pp. 159–165). Girona: Fundació Servei Gironi de Pedagogia.

Juliano, M. D. (1994c). Migraciones extracomunitarias y sistema educativo: El caso latinoamericano. In J. Contreras (Ed.), *Los retos de la inmigración: racismo y pluriculturalidad* (pp. 147–161). Madrid: Talasa Editores.

Juliano, M. D. (1996a). Antropología de la educación. In J. Prat and A. Martinez (Eds.), *Ensayos de antropología cultural: Homenaje a esteva fabregat* (pp. 278–286). Barcelona: Ariel Antropología.

Juliano, M. D. (1996b). Un lugar en el mundo: identidad, espacio e inmigración. Khora = Historia + Cosmos, No. 1 (International Symposium on Architecture and Semiotics, Barcelona), pp. 25–40.

Juliano, M. D. (1998). Inmigrantes de segunda: la adscripción étnica asignada. In E. Santamaría and F. González Placer (Eds.), *Contra el fundamentalismo escolar: Reflexiones sobre educación, escolarización y diversidad cultural* (pp. 125–138). Barcelona: Editorial Virus.

Juliano, M. D. (1999). No todos los caminos conducen a la nacionalidad, o como transformar "ilegales" en ciudadanos. Nova Africa. Barcelona. Centre d'Estudis Africans, No. 5, pp. 15–25.

Juliano, M. D. (2001). Integración, exclusión y movilidad social: Los difíciles caminos de la educación. In A. Valencia Gutierrez (Ed.), *Exclusión social y construcción de lo público en Colombia* (pp. 387–401). Bogotá: Cidse/Cerec.

Juliano, M. D. (2002). Los desafíos de la migración. Antropología, educación e interculturalidad. *Anuario de psicología*, Vol. 33, No. 4, pp. 487–499.

Juliano, M. D. (2004). Cultura y exclusión. Polémica teórica. *Quaderns de l'Institut Català d'Antropologia (Sèrie monogràfics)*, No. 19, pp. 55–69.

Juliano, M. D., Bergalli, V., and Santamaría, E. (1996). Global and local identities in Catalonia: Towards an anthropology of identity processes. In D. Provansal and C. Szanton Blanc (Eds.), *Identities, transnationalism and cultural reterritorialisation* (pp. 89–123). Barcelona: Universitat de Barcelona.

Juliano, D., Caba, A., Hidalgo, E., and Roset, M. (Eds.) (1997). *Enseñar Ciencias Sociales desde valores no-androcéntricos*. Madrid: Akal.

Kitzinger, C. and Wilkinson, S. (1994). Virgins and queers: Rehabilitating heterosexuality? *Gender and Society*, Vol. 8, No. 3, pp. 444–463.

Le Compte, M. and Preissle, J. (Eds.) (1992). *Handbook of qualitative research in education*. San Diego: Academic Press.

Le Guin, U. (1980). *La mano izquierda de la oscuridad*. Barcelona: Minotauro.

Lerena Aleson, C. (1989). *Escuela, ideología y clases sociales en España*. Barcelona: Círculo de Lectores.

Maalouf, A. (1993). *El primer siglo después de Béatrice*. Madrid: Alianza.

Maalouf, A. (1999). *Identidades asesinas*. Madrid: Alianza.

Malgesini, G. and Gimenez, C. (1997). *Guía de conceptos sobre migraciones, racismo e interculturalidad*. Madrid: La Cueva del Oso.

McLaren, P. (1986). *Schooling as ritual performance*. London: Routledge.

Mead, M. (1972). *Educación y cultura*. Buenos Aires: Paidós.

Moral, F. and Mateos, A. (1999). Opiniones y actitudes 26. La identidad nacional de los jóvenes y el estado de las autonomías. Madrid: CIS. Centro de Investigaciones Sociológicas.

Muñoz Molina, A. (2001). *Sefarad*. Madrid: Santillana.

Ogbu, J. (1985). La etnografía escolar: Una aproximación a nivel múltiple. In H. M. Velasco, F. J. Garcia, and A. Díaz de Rama (Eds.), *Lecturas de antropología para educadores: El ámbito de la educación y de la antropología escolar* (pp. 145–174). Madrid: Trotta.

Provansal, D. (1998). La domesticación del otro: Enseñanza y colonialismo. In E. Santamaría and F. González Placer (Eds.), *Contra el fundamentalismo escolar: Reflexiones sobre educación, escolarización y diversidad cultural* (pp. 37–50). Barcelona: Virus Editorial.

Provansal, D., Juliano, M. D., Bergalli, V., Muñoz, M., and Santamaría, E. (1993). Identité nationale et production sociales de l'étranger en Catalogne. Paper presented at the Colloque International Sur l'Image de l'Autre in Tunisia.

Rich, A. (1986). Notes toward a politics of location (1984). In A. Rich (Ed.), *Blood, bread and poetry: Selected prose 1979–1985* (pp. 210–232). New York: Norton.

Rich, A. (2001). *Sangre, pan y poesía: prosa escogida 1979–1985*. Barcelona: Icaria.

San Román, T. (1995). *Los muros de la separación: Ensayo sobre heterofobia y filantropía*. Barcelona: Ediciones de la Universidad Autónoma de Barcelona.

San Román, T. (1996). La educación ante la marginación y la diferencia cultural. In Escola d'Estiu sobre Interculturalitat (Ed.), *Sobre interculturalitat* 3 (pp. 127–135). Girona: Fundació SERGI.

Serra i Salamé, C. (2001). Violència, racismes i identitat: Les relacions interètniques en un institut català. [Doctoral dissertation].

Serra i Salamé, C. (2002). *Antropología de l'educació: L'etnografía i l'estudi de les relacions interètniques en l'àmbit de l'educació*. Girona: Publicacions Docents 32.

Sutcliffe, B. (1998). *Nacido en otra parte: Un ensayo sobre la migración internacional, el desarrollo y la equidad*. Bilbao: Hegoa.

Velasco, H., Garcia Castaño, J., and Diaz de Rada, A. (1993). *Lecturas de antropología para educadores*. Madrid: Editorial Trotta.

Velasco, H. and Diaz de Rada, A. (1997). *La lógica de la investigación etnográfica: Un modelo de trabajo para etnógrafos de la escuela*. Madrid: Editorial Trotta.

Verdery, K. (1994). Ethnicity, nationalism, and state making. In G. Vermeulen and C. Govers (Eds.), *The anthropology of ethnicity* (pp. 33–59). Amsterdam: Het Spinhuis.

Vermeulen, G. and Govers, C. (Eds.) (1994). *The anthropology of ethnicity*. Amsterdam: Het Spinhuis.

Yourcenar, M. (1977/1951). *Mémoires d'Hadrien*. Paris: Gallimard. [First published in 1951].

CHAPTER TWELVE

Ethnic group, class, AND gender: Paradoxes IN THE education OF Moroccans AND Roma IN Spain[1]

MARIANO FERNÁNDEZ-ENGUITA

University of Salamanca

The panorama of the Spanish educational system has recently been completely transformed by the progressive incorporation of two previously absent groups: the Romani people and immigrants. The dominant note in referring here to both groups is ethnicity. This is so because, on the one hand, the Roma—who in Spain also refer to themselves and are referred to as Gypsies—tend to strongly differentiate themselves ethnically from the rest of the population (*Gadges*), and are also strongly differentiated by the latter. On the other hand, while immigrants may come from anywhere in the world and any cultural background, in the case of Spain, the majority have emigrated either from the Maghreb (and are therefore mainly Arab or Berber, as well as Muslim), or from Central and Andean America (and are thus generally indigenous or *mestizos*). Beyond the expected difficulties and effects produced by the encounter between the school culture and the cultural identities and practices of each of these groups, other more specific challenges may arise from the articulation of ethnic group and class, or ethnic group and gender, in the specific environment of the school institution. It is to these unforeseen effects that this study is dedicated.

Considering that the Roma have lived in Spain for more than half a millennium, referring to them as a new phenomenon in the Spanish school environment may seem quite surprising for anyone not familiar with this situation. Nevertheless, it is very real, for, in addition to the Roma's long history of social exclusion, the national education system of Spain bears its own set of weaknesses. Regarding the first of these problems, historic edicts aimed at expelling the Roma from national territory were established and applied during the period spanning from the end of the 15th century to the end of the 18th century, and then replaced, as in the rest of Europe, by a fiercely enlightened assimilationism that included massive internments, the separation of children from their parents, and, by the 20th century, the systematic persecution of their way of life. However, because these laws and policies were never entirely effective, the Roma came to inhabit the margins of society, segregated, where they kept to themselves and did not participate in the dominant institutions of social life, such as guilds, industry, urban centers, politics, school systems, and the like. What concerns us here in particular, however, is that the Roma stayed away from school, or attended very infrequently, and they did so for three related reasons: because of their own rejection (understandably, they saw schooling as an aggression on their culture and a reminder of the conditions of past internments, which they have never forgotten); because of the inadequacies of the school system itself (which rarely served rural areas and new settlements in the urban periphery where the Roma concentrated); and because of certain incompatibilities with the academic calendar or with the *Gadge* majority. Of course, some of the more economically buoyant groups were incorporated in schools more quickly (especially in Madrid and Barcelona), and some schools were more disposed than others to attending to their children (e. g. the Catholic schools of Andrés Manjón in Granada).

However, this situation changed radically at the beginning of the 1980s. On the one hand, the Socialist government of Spain was determined to establish universal, compulsory schooling through to age 16, and indeed managed to do so. On the other hand, rapid demographic growth, coupled with the urbanization of the population, industrialization, and transformation into a tertiary economy, caused a great part of the Roma's traditional niches and economic opportunities to disappear, this forcing them to migrate massively to the outskirts of cities, or to degraded inner-city districts. This meant that the Roma were subjected to strong pressure from Social Services, which offered them economic aid, but demanded in return that their children attend school. Thus, what until then had been a slow process of incorporation—one continually subordinated to the very gradual modernization of the ethnic group itself—gave way to an accelerated incorporation that was to a great extent forced, in accordance with the demands of the Social Services in ferment, and educational policy at that time, which favored universal and egalitarian schooling (and which was also declaredly assimilationist at the beginning). This claim to egalitarian schooling was one of the main mottoes of the left, and it was also taken up in part (at least in its universalism) by the right. From that moment on, the Roma minority became the most problematic student group from the point of view of the school, as well as the main failure in the quest for educational equality, particularly in public schools.[2]

The case with immigrant groups is clearly different. Until very recently, Spain was a country of emigrants, their numbers reaching two and a half million at the beginning of the 1970s (somewhat more than half went to Latin America, and somewhat less to Europe). However, since the end of the 1980s, immigration has been increasing rapidly, and could even be termed exponential following 1997 (between 1996 and 2004, the yearly count of foreign-born immigrants increased by the following units of a thousand: 17, 36, 57, 99, 331, 394, 443, 430, and 646) (INE, 2007). Within this general growth pattern, however, there have been important related changes in the internal composition of immigration. For example, in the period from 1996 to 2004, immigration from European countries wealthier than Spain (immigration which is essentially linked to multinational corporations, international institutions, and senior citizens looking for a benign climate), has dropped from 26.7% to 12.3%. Likewise, Moroccan immigration slowed from 21.9% to 9.1%. The contrary occurred, however, with immigration from Romania, which rose from 0.5% to 7.7%, and from Ecuador, which rose from 1.3% to 1.8% (in 2000, it reached 27.5%). In short, there have been two great changes within the general rise in immigration flows: the entries from poor countries have over-whelmingly overtaken the entries from rich countries, and among the poor countries there has been a subsequent displacement of those from Northern Africa by those from Latin America and Eastern Europe.

These immigrant populations, which were initially comprised mostly of adults, have quickly become an issue for schools, now that they are settling and initiating the process of family reunification. And most significantly, birth rates among immigrants are higher than the host population's.[3] Thus, between the academic years spanning from 1995 to 2005, the number of foreign-born students enrolled in formal nonuniversity education in Spain grew by the following figures in the thousands: 57, 63, 72, 81, 107, 141, 207, 309, 401, 457 (MEC, 2005a).

It almost goes without saying that this was a huge jolt for the Spanish educational system and teaching profession, which as in many other countries, were forged from the *ethos* of a culture of self-styled and unquestionable universal validity, and in particular, from an apparent homogeneity and the naïve conviction that there was only one possible direction for progress in education and teaching: one born in the forgone context of a society in its first stages of modernization, following forty years of dictatorial rule.

It is in this context that the focus here will be on Moroccan immigrants in Spain because of this group's economic, cultural, and social distance with respect to the native population, this making Moroccans the most problematic immigrant group from the perspective of the school. By contrast, East European immigrants have similar ways of life to Spaniards (at least on the level of industrialization, technology, and education) and Latin American immigrants share both the language as well as a cultural legacy, both of which notably facilitate their incorporation into the Spanish system. The Moroccans, on the other hand, come from largely subsistence, agrarian, economic backgrounds; they speak a foreign language; and they practice a different religion. In the 2003–2004 academic year, Moroccans comprised 14.8% of all foreign students,[4] and in 2004–2005 African students (most of whom were Moroccan) constituted an estimated 19.1% of the total (MEC, 2005c).

ETHNIC GROUP, CLASS, AND GENDER IN SCHOOL: FROM PARALLEL BEGINNINGS TO DISPARATE OUTCOMES

Ethnic group, class, and gender represent the three great sources of fracture among individuals in today's societies. They are not the only sources, however, for they coexist with others associated with disabilities, sexual orientation, political affiliation, religion, and so on. These categories are easily perceived and understood as they are inherent to both modern and traditional societies, although in the latter they take on a more radically ascribed form to the extent that ethnic group is often regarded as a caste; social class as an estate; and gender as another kind of estate-like division. And while these inequalities may pale in comparison to inequalities among different national societies, the latter, logically, are not readily apparent within the context of a single school system. Within any one society, then, ethnic group, class, and gender represent the great divisions, and it is worth taking the time to look at certain parallelisms and divergences among them and, above all, at the various effects of the policies that address them within the school environment.[5]

What all three factors have in common is the fact that the groups they place at a disadvantage (class, through exploitation and possibly class discrimination; gender and ethnic group, through discrimination and possibly exploitation) have been successively excluded, segregated, and finally incorporated at a disadvantage into educational institutions. At first, disadvantaged groups were simply excluded from schools that served the bourgeoisie, and could only be attended by men from the dominant ethnic group. While it is impossible to offer a detailed account of this reality here, a broad idea can be provided. In Spain, schools came into being as an urban phenomenon that was limited to the wealthy bourgeoisie and to a sector of the petit bourgeoisie associated with (or aspiring to be associated with) ecclesiastical, bureaucratic, or military functions. The rest of the population, comprised of peasants, artisans, and the proto-proletariat of the cities, which possessed neither land nor trade, were excluded either *de jure* or *de facto* from schools. In this scenario, women were also excluded *de facto*. They were either brought up by their mothers, or incorporated into "schools" where they were not even taught the alphabet, but rather discipline, piety, and good manners. Similarly, ethnic minorities experienced a long history of exclusion until very recently. For example, the Roma were historically and initially excluded *de jure* from dominant activities—they were not admitted to guilds and other institutions—and later, their exclusion was *de facto*, as they tended to reside in pockets of the urban and rural landscape that either lacked schools or whose schools were greatly lacking (i.e. in the poorest of rural areas, the most marginal of urban peripheries, etc.)—a situation that echoes the historic experiences of African Americans in the United States, or, in fact, those of most of the world's greater minorities, although certainly not all.

Contrary to what is sometimes argued or assumed, the Enlightenment—that wave of thought to which we can justly attribute the origins of pedagogy in the contemporary age—was not an unequivocally favorable movement as far as the education of workers is concerned, or that of women, ethnic minorities, or colonized peoples, for that matter. Indeed, it was quite the opposite. Most of the *philosophers* of the 18th century French Enlightenment, including Voltaire, Mirabeau, or Destutt de Tracy, were openly hostile to public education, while some were only concerned about the education of the nobility and the bourgeoisie. This meant that, for them, the civilized world was limited to these two social classes, as was the case with Rousseau's nobiliary model of education in *Emile*, or in his disquisitions on whether the lower nobility should or should not be educated in the same physical and intellectual learning environments as the upper nobility, in *Considerations on the Government of Poland*. Of course, the other major current of enlightened thought represented by the economists (and with them, the English philosophers), never doubted that the lower classes should be educated, but for the sole purpose of disciplining and training them for work. As for women's education, only Condorcet firmly advocated for their education on an equal footing with men. Finally, the doctrines on education that were based on human reason were not applicable to the so-called "savage" peoples of the world. For instance, Jules Ferry—an illustrious French minister who was highly experienced in colonial administration—claimed that the Declaration of the Rights of Mean had not been written for colonized peoples.

At a later stage in history, these groups came to be schooled, albeit in segregated environments. Workers and the lower classes were educated in "German schools" (the term used in Italy), in *petites écoles, escuelas populares, Volkschülen*, and so on., which in the beginning were not the primary level of a unified system, but the only level and type of education they had access to, while their contemporaries from the privileged classes attended institutes, *lycées*, *Gymnasia*, public schools, and the like, which had their own preparatory levels for the younger students. This dualism is strongly present today in the language used to describe schools, not only in the preservation of some of the terms mentioned, but also in terms of other dualisms, some of which have since lost part of their meaning, but they nonetheless remind us that the current degree of distinction between elementary and secondary school was, in the past, a difference of class: teacher/professor, school/college, pupil/student, instruction/teaching, and so on. For their part, women were schooled for a long time in separate institutions—a situation that in many countries lasted until quite recently. If there were enough material and economic resources, and sufficient population density, separate schools were created for each gender, even at the elementary level. If this was not the case, boys and girls were separated into different classes within the same school, or at a minimum, a male teacher taught the boys, a female teacher the girls. In many cases, the latter teacher was the former's wife, and was not necessarily a qualified teacher. This was accompanied by partially different curricula at the elementary level, and even more so at the secondary level.

Ethnic minorities experienced a similar situation. Initially, the segregation was *de jure*, as occurred with the segregation of schools for African-Americans in the United States. But later, such state sanctioned policies were replaced by *de facto* segregation, as occurred with schools in black neighborhoods in the US North (it is therefore not surprising that the civil rights movement had its *tour de force* in busing). In Spain, in the 1970s and early 1980s, the Roma were concentrated into so-called "bridge" schools, which were located in Romani communities and designed to be a first step toward the subsequent incorporation of Gypsy children into mainstream schools. In reality, however, the bridge school was the first and last step for most Gypsy students. Even today, the compulsory inclusion of these youth in mainstream schools is not paralleled by their full incorporation into the dominant economy as adults. This situation is producing a new social phenomenon known as "public schools with Gypsies," that is, public schools attended by a large proportion of Romani and other ethnic minorities (the latter of immigrant origins) due to their location in poor neighborhoods and/or shanty towns from which the *Gadges* or the dominant Spanish students have been fleeing. This process, which is similar to the *white flight* practiced by American whites when blacks enroll in "their" schools, makes the situation even more complicated, as it gives rise to ethnic school ghettoes.

In the third and most recent stage of their history in Spain, at the advent of the 21st century, all of these groups are being mainstreamed into what we can call regular schools. Three reforms were established for this purpose and have taken on different names: comprehensiveness, coeducation, and integration. These "regular" schools, though, were also the schools of the petit and middle bourgeoisie, comprised of males from the dominant ethnic group. We can thus say that workers were incorporated into bourgeois schools, women into previously all-male schools, and the Roma into *Gadge* schools.

Yet, no conspiracies or perverse plans mapped out this development; no one proposed that schools be made hostile to the new groups. Rather, schooling had simply been tailored to the socially and culturally dominant groups. After all, the middle and upper classes, males, and the ethnic majority had not only participated actively and prominently in all spheres of social life for a long time, but had also comprised the pool of teachers, not to mention the authorities with the power to make decisions both in schools and in the administration of education. But, above all, their culture, attitudes, values, their characteristic forms of behavior and views about themselves, others, and the world, were, as they still are to a great extent today, those that prevail in global society, particularly among its elite. What is more, it can be said that schools had been founded and promoted in order to propagate these preferences—to disseminate and legitimize "cultured culture" (i.e., the values, symbols, discourse, and knowledge base of the middle and upper classes); to socialize according to the demands and criteria set by economic and political institutions located beyond the domestic sphere, or by that half of the world that was then predominantly male; in effect, to construct a national identity that was differentiated from the outside, and free from internal differences; and to foster the progress and advancement of "civilization," and thus deepen its distinction from pre-industrial cultures.

However, the results of these reforms have been uneven. The most successful has without a doubt been the incorporation of women. For instance, at all levels of education, current access, retention, and promotion rates for women are higher than for men, although there are certain branches and specializations in which women do not yet (or rarely) participate. Even when a more detailed treatment of the topic would demand greater differentiation according to competencies, branches of education, and so on., it can generally be argued that women obtain better outcomes than men both in formal terms (grades, credentials) and real terms (on "objective" tests and other performance measurements outside regular assessments). Overall, women are achieving educational levels comparable to those of men of their same class and ethnic group (although certain male bastions remain, and access to the labor market is an altogether separate issue). What this means then is that the results of the reform have in general been positive for all women, regardless of class and ethnic group.

On the other hand, the overall effects of comprehensive reforms aimed at compensating class differences have been middling or mediocre, despite long periods of application or the emphasis placed on such reforms. Even when it can be claimed that these reforms have both improved the education of those who receive the least, and broadened the opportunities for educational mobility, class origin still weighs heavily on educational opportunities (as it eventually does, too, on the effects of educational outcomes in terms of access to the labor market). It must be noted, moreover, that these reforms have not had the same impact on all workers as they have on all women, *urbi et orbi*. Here, the impact has varied proportionally to people's social class. The reforms have indeed done more to improve the performance and opportunities of urban petit bourgeoisie and service workers than it has those of rural or industrial workers.

Regarding the impact of the reforms on ethnic minorities, attention should first be drawn to achievement rates, or educational outcomes, which have been hugely uneven and poor. These disparate outcomes can be explained by the dimension of ethnic group, which by definition is much broader than that of social class or gender, as we are dealing with the achievement of diverse ethnic minorities. Some minorities' educational achievement, for instance, is spectacular, as occurs today in the US with many students of Asian origins, or with Jewish students worldwide. The successful achievements of these groups has been linked to their predominant role as *middleman minorities* with good economic standing (as is generally the case with part of the Jewish diaspora, Indians in free ports, or the Chinese in other Asian countries), to their learned and book-oriented cultural tradition, or to their coming from societies which can be very different from our own, but are already highly structured and function distinctly from traditional societies with subsistence economies (this is mainly the case with Asians immigrating to Western countries, particularly the Japanese, Chinese, and Indo-Chinese). However, the outcomes for other minority groups, such as African and Mexican Americans in the US and the Roma in Spain, have been disastrous. Given that these groups outnumber the other minorities, as a whole, one can argue that ethnic minorities have not benefited from the reforms.

I have analyzed elsewhere and in greater detail the possible causes of these dissimilar effects (Fernández-Enguita, 1997). They can be attributed in part to economic factors when the minority group in question is marginalized and/or heavily exploited (the degree of which can vary greatly from group to group) because poverty marks the exploited classes, albeit not necessarily school-aged women as a whole. The causes are also cultural because, while the differences between women and men in terms of proximity and familiarity with the school culture are null, these differences are appreciable between classes, and are often greater among ethnic groups. There are also strategic causes, because while women have every reason to identify with the school institution (for the reasons mentioned earlier, and more, as we shall see), ethnic minorities may have reason to reject or resist it, while the lower classes may find themselves in a more ambivalent position. This brief overview on the differing outcomes of educational reform according to gender, class, and ethnicity should suffice to help situate the analyses that follow.

SCHOOL, ETHNIC GROUP, AND CLASS:
THE TRANSITION TO WORK AND ADULTHOOD

Returning to ethnic group and education in Spain, one effect on Moroccans in particular is that immigration has lengthened their overall period of education. This is not necessarily true however for all foreign born students, as some have immigrated from highly modernized societies and are well educated. But it is the case for most immigrant populations, as the social circumstances in their countries of origin have unfortunately been lacking in terms of educational opportunities. According to UNESCO statistics, the net schooling rate in Morocco is 53% for early childhood education (4 to 6 years of age); 88% for elementary education (International Standard Classification of Education [ISCED] 1); 57% for lower secondary (ISCED 2); and 41% for all of secondary (ISCED 2 and 3). By contrast, the net schooling rate in Spain reaches 93% in early childhood (3 to 6 years of age, noncompulsory); 100% in elementary (ISCED 1) and compulsory secondary education (ISCED 2); and 94% for all of secondary (ISCED 2 and 3). Although Spanish official statistics do not offer a schooling-rate breakdown according to immigrant vs. native status, nor a fortiori according to national origin in particular (i.e., schooling rates for Moroccans), one may argue that the compulsory nature of schooling in Spain is generally effective; and one may therefore also assume that the rates are notably higher for the noncompulsory levels as well, at least for early childhood and vocational studies. A recent survey of Moroccan immigrants in Madrid and Barcelona revealed rates of 87.5% for the 3–5 year old group (early childhood education); 98.4% for ages 6–15 (elementary); 67.9% for 16–17 year olds (upper-secondary and lower level vocational training); 34.6% for 18–20 year olds; and 18.2% for 21–24 year olds (Colectivo IOÉ, 2003, p. 93). It must be said, however, that the schooling rates achieved among immigrants residing in large urban centers are not necessarily equaled outside of these urban areas, given the probable differences in economic activity, living conditions, and availability of, or proximity to, schools, at least for the noncompulsory levels.

The first effect, then, of immigration on the children and adolescents of most immigrant groups is the reinforcement of schooling, in particular the prolongation of the schooling years. This should not be taken as an unequivocal indicator of a rosy panorama, considering that another side to schooling exists, which involves experience with failure. According to the survey mentioned above, this failure rate affects 28.3% of Moroccan students in Madrid and Barcelona—a percentage that is twice as high for males (38.3%) as it is for females (19.4%), and which shoots up to 40.5% among the former in compulsory secondary education. But what seems to be even more decisive is the age in which these youth are first enrolled in school in their destination cities. This is so because the percentage of Moroccan youth who experience failure rises sharply among those who arrive in Spain at ages corresponding directly to the secondary level (13 or older).

This is not surprising, but does call for some reflection. It should not surprise us because we can expect that language can be a greater problem at this age, and because the new environment may cause a certain degree of shock (maturity levels working to compensate such effects). Furthermore, the best students may not always be the first to be pulled out of school in the middle of their studies in order to emigrate. There remains, as well, another likely cause: adolescents migrating to Spain may not come to study, but to work. They arrive, in other words, at an age in which they must be schooled, whereas in their country of origin they would already be working, and thus contributing to the family economy. They are what we might call the *first-and-a-half generation*: an age group caught between those who emigrate as adults and those born or arrived to the destination country in their early childhood. This gap between one's desires (or expectations as internalized in one's place of origin) and the new reality, is most likely more radical for boys than for girls. This could be due to boys' relatively lower academic performance and stronger orientation toward the extra-domestic economic sphere (paid work), as well as the relatively higher degree to which this orientation, on the one hand, corresponds to eventual working realities for boys, and on the other hand, reinforces these boys' gendered sense of self-representation.[6]

At issue here is the role of the deproletarianization of youth (meaning simply the process of postponing their entrance into the labor market). The universalization of schooling had this effect on most European populations in the 20th century, and today the effect is similar for certain immigrant groups, although it is condensed in time. The constant concern with education as a right often leads to overlooking its other dimensions: as a duty and an imposition. Historically, schooling was not only a way to protect children from industrial exploitation and introduce them to "culture," but it also served to keep them out of the labor market (as occurred with women, who were redomesticated, or sent back to the domestic sphere) for the benefit of adult male workers who feared their competition. The notion that phylogeny (the evolution of society) should be repeated in education as ontogeny, (as the evolution of the individual), is evident in the schooling of many immigrants, who experience in the host society a kind of sudden abduction by the school which, in their societies of origin, would only have taken place throughout several generations, or in any case, not in their own. That is, in the name of the universality and equality of education, adolescent work is replaced in the destination country with a prolongation of schooling which, in the country of origin, would probably only become universal in future cohorts or generations. And the protagonists of this process, or the victims—depending on how it is perceived—are those youth who emigrated to work, to partake in what was for them perhaps a desired transition to adulthood, but who instead, found themselves faced with more schooling. This lack of correspondence between expectations and realities could thus contribute to the failure rate of this group in compulsory schooling.

It must be highlighted that what comes into conflict here with the school institution and its ability to institutionalize a population is a characteristic of class, not of ethnic group. That is, it is not inherently Arab or Islamic to expect earlier participation in the workforce than is permitted in Europe (the children of sheiks do not seem to be in any more of a hurry to transition to the workplace than do their Western or Christian cultural counterparts). Rather, this expectation proceeds from the conditions of an agrarian and proto-industrial society, today in Morocco, yesterday in Spain, and the day before yesterday in central and northern Europe. That is, this expectation once existed everywhere, but changed with the advance of industrial capitalism, the historic development and impact of which differed among the world's societies. Unlike the Roma, whom we shall address below, most Moroccan immigrants do not migrate to Spain with any other purpose than to become proletarians, just as, or even more than, Spaniards themselves do.

In the case of the Roma, there is also a clear mismatch between the demands of the educational institution and the group's own prevailing norms for participating in the economic sphere. The Roma's economic way of life continues to revolve around self-employment. Even today, their livelihood retains elements of a subsistence economy, but above all, it has responded to what some anthropologists call, euphemistically, *structural pluralism*: a framework through which the ethnic group relates to others, in this case to the rest of society, but only through the market. This only deepens the evasion of interethnic relations, which are already discouraged in consumption and leisure activities, in marriage, and so forth. (Basically *connubium* and commensality constitute, according to Weber, the basis of community life, but also through regular salaried work). This framework, needless to say, operates to the detriment of the Roma because it implies a loss of independence and, what is worse, almost always having to work for a *Gadge* (a non-Roma). Even working for a Roma employer implies breaking with the solidarity of the endogroup, for salaried work is synonymous to exploitation for most Roma. Thus, self-employment, or even more, being in business for oneself, is the characteristic economic model for the Roma (and if this can be achieved without working, even better).

However, the *Gadge* school—i.e., simply "school"—has basically been designed as a function of the dominant cooperative work model, more precisely the wage labor model, which organizes work into complex production schemes requiring a high degree of cooperation and discipline from workers, and it is assumed that most students will enter the workforce in varying hierarchical positions (albeit mainly lower ones). Current educational jargon, which has, since its origins, undergone transformations and acquired autonomous meanings, obscures all too easily the extent to which the demands of the transition to industrialized society—in particular, the demand for the socialization of a submissive, collective workforce—has come to inform schooling, as well as the degree to which these demands have proven effective (Callahan, 1962). It is likewise true that education today is evolving toward greater attention to individual initiative, toward active participation in cooperative groups, and so on., although undoubtedly much more slowly than businesses are moving toward network structure, *adhocracy*, or worker autonomy. In any case, the school is still basically a homogenizing and authoritarian institution, a carbon copy of the model of bureaucratic organization characterized by the large company with salaried workers. And for this very reason, it is hardly disposed to, or even capable of, training students in the direction of entrepreneurial initiative or self-employment.

What Roma children need, if they are to participate in the forms of economic activity that are valued within their own ethnic communities, is precisely that: to develop a sense of initiative and the skills needed for successful interaction in the market, as well as the bonds of solidarity and the practices of collaboration that are both encouraged and operative within the endogroup, without feeling the need to leave the community in order to "get ahead." But school not only does not offer them this opportunity; it hinders them from acquiring such initiative wherever and however they can (e.g., by accompanying the adults of their community in their domestic chores, craftwork, peddling, street markets, public entertainment work, shady dealings, etc.). The school, in other words, prepares them for a type of work which neither the children nor their group seem especially interested in pursuing, and which they rarely access because society both limits their opportunities to, and impedes them from preparing for, the kind of work they will probably be engaged in later on. A real achievement!

Again, we find an imbalance here between the demands of the school and those of work, which are now dictated by the ethnic singularity of the group rather than by their class position. Nonetheless, it is the reciprocal closure of the respective ethnic groups (Roma and *Gadge*) that reduces their relationship to the market. The Roma opt for mobility as the basis of their economy, partly because they are forced to (since they are the object of discrimination and hostility), and partly because they opt to (because of the specific opportunities it entails, as well as its good fit with the extended family structure). This reduces their labor options to small craft production or trade, and to a traditional, petit-bourgeois class configuration for which the school is not very functional, since it was inspired by the factory model of production (or in the best of cases, the office).

The question that arises with both immigrants and the Roma is whether it is absolutely necessary to impose *tout court* a schooling formula derived from, and adapted to, other economic and sociocultural demands, conditions, and standards set beyond the group in question. Would it not be more reasonable, at least in the short run, to offer these groups the option of a mutual adjustment, not a unilateral one, between the educational institution and its audience? Would it not be possible, for example, to adapt the curricular pace and school calendar to the mobility needs of the Romani economy, thus allowing the Roma to make school attendance compatible with participation in the productive family economy, or, in the case of Moroccan immigrants, to allow them to combine work and school (both being part time, the former in controlled conditions and the latter adapted to the circumstances), and at an earlier age than that contemplated for students who have attended the destination county's schools from the very beginning? These proposals, even when posed as mere ponderings, will undoubtedly clash with the iron-clad universalism promoted by the educational institution, a situation that only confirms the suspicion that the issue is as much a matter of bureaucratic standardization as it is a case of genuine universalism. For, if we do not pay more attention to these students' perspectives and interests in this sense, we are in effect closing our eyes to the lacerating inequality of educational outcomes, or ends, while soothing our conscience with the formal egalitarianism of the means— another case of what Merton referred to as *bureaucratic ritualism*.

SCHOOL, ETHNIC GROUP, AND GENDER: FROM THE OPPRESSION OF PATRIARCHY TO UNEXPECTED EQUALITY

The interactions between ethnic group and gender in the school context can be even more complex. The first effect of schooling on these is unquestionably egalitarian. In the case of the Roma, it involves equal treatment of male and female students when, in their family and community contexts, they are already learning the norms of a strict segregation of roles, and a no less strict subordination of women to men. Roma boys will often learn early-on to order their sisters around, and in full adolescence may begin giving orders to their mothers in matters of daily life, although this is accompanied by certain veneration. In the case of Moroccan immigrants in Spain, the schooling rate for girls quickly surpasses that of those who stayed in Morocco, and comes close to the boys' rates. Thus, in the 2003–2004 school year, the percentage of female Moroccan students was 45.5 in early childhood education; 46.5 in elementary school; 43.7 at the compulsory secondary level; 43.6 in upper secondary; and 54.8 in vocational training. Overall, female students still participate less in the educational system (the only exception occurring at the secondary level). The lower participation of Moroccan women in schooling is the object of much discussion, and needs further analysis. But at first glance, it can be interpreted as the effect of a certain resistance on the part of Moroccans to the schooling of women, or of discrimination. However, as some authors have pointed out (e.g., Colectivo IOÉ, 2003), this lower presence of females in school becomes notably conditioned, however, by the ratio of women to men in immigration statistics as a whole. Table 12.1[7] shows the distribution of the population of Moroccan nationals in Spain by school age and gender. These more general statistics point to a lower presence of females across the various school age levels,[8] so what also becomes apparent is that school attendance among Moroccan girls deviates from the theoretical equality of genders not only because their presence at school is lower, but also because their overall presence in the various age groups within the Moroccan youth population as a whole is lower. The percentages of females in school are indeed well below 50%, but they are only somewhat lower (and not always) than their proportion in the general school age population. This small difference may indeed be reflecting the presence of family educational strategies that are biased according to the child's gender, but above all, what it reveals is the existence of biased migratory strategies. It is not so much a matter of whether Moroccan parents restrict their daughters' access to school once in Spain

Table 12.1. Composition by Sex of Moroccan Immigrant Students in the Various Levels of Nonuniversity Education

Age	0–4	05–09	10–14	15–19
Both sexes	30110	23870	21196	29359
Women	14178	11226	9645	11954
% Women	47.1	47.0	45.5	40.7

Level	Preschool	Elementary	Compulsory Secondary	Upper Secondary
All students	14143	25779	15503	3901
Women only	6575	12197	6755	1457
% women students	46.5	47.3	43.6	37.3
Diff. % women–50%	−3.5	−2.7	−6.4	−12.7
Diff. % women–% Cohort	−0.6	0.3	−1.9	−3.4

than it is of restricting their access to Spain in the first place. Moreover, as long as adult women immigrate to a lesser extent than men, it can be expected that minors will remain to a greater degree with their same-gender parent.

What is more, migratory plans are not unrelated to educational expectations, for if Moroccan immigrant parents tend to leave more daughters than sons behind, they do so regardless of the possibilities for schooling in the destination county, or, perhaps, precisely because of such possibilities. If, on the one hand, they emigrate in search of improved living conditions, then they have more reason to take their daughters than their sons because, if we compare schooling rates for each gender in the respective countries of origin (Morocco) and destination (Spain), the girls would benefit. If, on the other hand, it is a matter of finding employment, it would once again be more reasonable to take the girls than the boys because the supply-demand relationship is more favorable in the domestic service sector and other jobs frequently occupied by women than it is in construction, agriculture, and other typically male jobs. But if the girls are going to have to be in school until age 16 and share classrooms, desks, recreation grounds, and so on with males, it may be precisely this possibility of a more egalitarian education that determines this migratory strategy marked by gender selection. In fact, if we look at the composition by gender of the age cohorts in Table 12.1, one notices how the female school attendance steadily decreases from 47.1% in the 0 to 4 year old population bracket to 26.4% in the 25 to 29 year old bracket, and then increases in an equally continuous way to 59.4% for ages 75–79. In the younger age brackets, which are what interest us here, it seems clear that girls born of Moroccan parents in Spain largely contribute to the proportion of females in the youngest group.[9] Yet, due to the effects of patriarchal migratory strategies, this proportion falls steadily as girls approach the age of fertility, and rise again as they move away from this age. In other words, the possible existence of a gendered schooling strategy among Moroccan immigrants in Spain cannot be dismissed merely because a pervasive migratory strategy—one that may wrongly be perceived as merely instrumental or gender-neutral—limits the number of Moroccan girls actually entering Spain. Schooling for Moroccans in Spain may indeed still be gendered to the extent that the patriarchy or sexism of Moroccan culture is what gives rise to this gender-selective migratory strategy in the first place (i.e., girls are kept back in Morocco so that they will not be schooled).

This said, Moroccan girls that do enter and remain in the Spanish school system obtain notably better outcomes than do their male counterparts, as occurs with the native population. In fact, this pattern is repeated in many other societies that offer universal education (for all), as well as universalist education (equal for all, despite gender bias in their structures and contents, which may be irrelevant in this case). As can be seen in Table 12.2, within the Moroccan student population that remains in school beyond the compulsory period, there is a greater proportion of women going into the "noble branches" of upper secondary education (academic tracks, but also the arts and languages), while the men are more likely to pursue either vocational training (the secondary branch with lesser relative value, both academically and symbolically, in the job market) or, above all, the so-called "Social Guarantee" programs, which are generally considered to be the "trash can" of the system.

This phenomenon is not limited to secondary education; it affects the entire educational system. In a specific study carried out by Colectivo IOÉ in 2002,[10] the Moroccan female students had a general success rate of 78.2% as opposed to 57.7% for their male counterparts. Even more noticeable is how this difference increases the higher the level: 95.5% as opposed to 84.6% at the elementary level; 77.1% as opposed to 58.5% in compulsory secondary education; and 79.4% versus 51.2% in the postcompulsory level; although this last figure reflects the sum of Moroccan and Dominican students. It is therefore not specific to the Moroccan minority but extends to others, although it is particularly acute in the case studied.

As regards the Roma school population, statistical information that would allow us to contrast educational outcomes by gender is lacking. However, there is some partial and anecdotal evidence available. Those who are in contact with Roma children at school soon perceive that Roma girls usually do much better than Roma boys. The same can be said about Roma access to higher education: more women enroll (almost always in majors related to the social sciences) than men. A recent report from the Andalusian regional government concluded that

Table 12.2. Composition by Sex of Immigrant Moroccan Students in the Various Levels of Nonuniversity Education

Level	Upper Secondary	Vocational Training	Social Guarantee	Arts	Languages
All students	871	1440	1289	16	285
Only women students	477	587	230	8	155
% women students	54.76	40.76	17.84	50	54.39
Diff. % women–50%	4.76	−9.24	−32.16	0	4.39
Diff. % women–% cohort	14.0	0.0	−22.9	9.3	13.7

very few Roma went to the University—scarcely 1%—but that of these, eight out of ten were women.[11]

Qualitative studies on schooling processes in Spain point in this same direction. These studies emphasize the relatively better performance of girls and, more importantly, the extent to which studying is satisfying for them, in particular, how it represents an immediate experience of equality and an instrument of liberation for the future: the possibility of getting a job, and a better job—as is equally the case for all women—and of postponing marriage or not being confined to marrying within the limits of their own ethnic group (see, for example, Abajo and Carrasco, 2004).

Let us recapitulate. A quarter of a century ago, it was taken as a certainty that men fared better than women at school, and this according to any indicator considered: performance, grades, promotion, area of study, and so on. For some, this was a manifestation of male superiority, for others, a sign of discrimination against women; but for everyone it was simply expected. Later on, this scenario began to change: women caught up with and surpassed men in most indicators of educational success. Of course, exceptions could always be found: women did better than men in language but not in mathematics; and while more women reached upper-secondary education, and in better conditions than men, they pursued mainly lesser university degrees because employment was less of a determining factor for them than for men (women also attended vocational training in much fewer numbers than men). When women did pursue higher degrees, these tended to be in the so-called "female" majors. All these *buts* have nonetheless been discredited one after the other, just as the corresponding male bastions have. On the other hand, these developments have not kept a *male chauvinist interpretation of female success* from spreading. According to this reading, when boys get better grades it is usually attributed to their supposedly greater abilities, stronger ambition, and so on. But when it is the girls' turn to be successful, other explanations are found: they conform better; they are better adapted to work routines; they are more disciplined; and so on. These attributes contrast sharply with the independence, rebelliousness, and other heroic virtues ascribed to young males. What is at work here, then, is a peculiar form of *critical male chauvinism* regarding schooling, not gender *per se*.

Years ago, however, another interpretation had already been put forth. Neither smarter nor slower, more submissive nor more rebellious, girls simply had every motivation to identify with school (Fernández-Enguita, 1990). They have come to identify with school in expressive terms because no other institution treats them as equitably in that age bracket. The educational institution is able to broadly articulate their experiences in long-lasting ways, and in ways that neither the family nor the work sphere have proved capable of accomplishing. In other words, for women, it is better to continue studying than to procure what will most likely be a subordinate and possibly servile job; or to help their mothers with the housework; or to take on similar tasks in their new family homes. Girls also identify with schooling in instrumental terms because, knowing that they will often enter the job market at a disadvantage with respect to men, they feel it is best to obtain additional educational credentials in order to compensate for the *stigma* of their gender. Furthermore, success in school leads to occupations that are generally less discriminatory, as occurs with professions linked to the public service sector. And in the *worst case* scenario, continuing one's studies has also been a way to access the best educational institutions, which are often perceived as offering some of the best marriage markets, as well as opportunities to improve one's competitive edge within that market. The differential success of women could thus be interpreted as the result of fully conscious and understandable individual strategies within given social conditions.

Yet, a paradox is particularly evident in the articulation of ethnic group with gender, in the case of the Moroccans and the Roma who, as minority groups, are nonetheless differentiated in an important way: the former is *voluntary* (the product of immigration) and the latter *involuntary* (with half a millennium of presence in Spain). The two groups are similar, however, in that they are both strongly patriarchal cultures, and because, through contact at school, not only do they encounter the same phenomenon—women's higher school success—that their *Gadge*/native counterparts have already experienced, but they do so to an even greater extent. In both groups, the women surpass the men academically, and spectacularly so.

The fact that the women benefit from schooling should and can be celebrated if for no other reason than as a simultaneous triumph of both the universalization of schooling (at least some sectors of the minority groups are successful here) and greater gender equality, or the emancipation of women (i.e., that sector which is precisely female). What must be lamented, however, is the tremendous price that these women will pay. Even within the native/*Gadge* population, a whole generation of women who have known educational success and become actively involved in the workforce have found that gender equality in the domestic sphere has not evolved as fast as it has at school, or even at work. They have had to combine their newly acquired equality outside of the home with the traditional inequality in the home: the *double-work day*. And, as members of the ethnic minorities dealt with here—Moroccans and the Roma—these women not only face a double workload but also a twofold moral breach. For many of these women will have to pay the heavy price of incomprehension, and even rejection, from their families and communities; or perhaps that of the not necessarily desired life as single adults; as well as the accompanying alienation from both worlds: from the minority community they come from and the mainstream society that has yet to fully accept them. They will be among those who, to paraphrase Bertoldt Brecht, having struggled all their lives, are the only ones who are indispensable.

NOTES

1. I want to thank Cathryn Teasley for her thoughtful revision of my English and her comments on a former draft of this chapter.
2. For a more detailed analysis, see Fernández-Enguita (2000).
3. For a more detailed analysis of this process, see Fernández-Enguita (2003).
4. Calculated from data reported in MEC (2005b).
5. The argument that follows in this section is developed in more detail in Fernández-Enguita (1997).
6. To explain this briefly, I believe that the strong link between obtained masculinity and the successful transition from school to paid work that Paul Willis found to be established by white, British, working class, and anti-school youth, is not necessarily limited to these particular youth because the tendency to link these aspects constitutes a patriarchal trait of all traditional cultures existing within market and/or industrial economies: the wife as homemaker and the husband as breadwinner (see Willis, 1978).
7. Based on data taken from INE (2005) and from MEC (2005b).
8. These statistics do not always concur with those of other sources, but they are provided by the most reliable sources available for such information: the Spanish National Institute of Statistics (INE) and the Ministry of Education (MEC). See note 7 above.
9. The fact that the immigrant population of Spain (Moroccans included) has contributed significantly to Spain's overall birth rate is another relevant factor here.
10. A survey was taken in 2002 of 322 Moroccan and Dominican students of both sexes in Madrid and Barcelona. Their schooling was understood as "successful," or not as a failure, if they answered the question: "How are you doing in your studies?" with "Well. Outstanding student" instead of "Fair, so-so" or "Badly, with difficulties." The sample was very limited; the response rate, low; the conditions of administration, dubious; and the formulation of the question rather debatable. But, in any case, it was the same for boys and girls, and no other studies of this kind have been carried out.
11. These estimates from the Regional Government of Andalusia are imprecise; however, they coincide with those of the Roma General Secretariat Foundation (Fundación Secretariado General Gitano). See the article "La mujer, motor del cambio gitano" in *El País*, May 22, 2005 (retrieved December 22, 2007 from http://www.elpais.com/articulo/sociedad/mujer/motor/cambio/gitano/elpepisoc/20050522elpepisoc_1/Tes/).

REFERENCES

Abajo, J. E. and Carrasco, S. (2004). Gitanas y gitanos en la encrucijada: Éxito académico, relaciones de género y cambio cultural. In J. E. Abajo, S. Carrasco, and Equipo de Investigación sobre el Éxito Escolar del Alumnado Gitano (Eds.) (2004), *Experiencias y trayectorias de éxito escolar de gitanas y gitanos en España: Encrucijadas sobre educación, género y cambio cultural.* Madrid: Instituto de la Mujer (MTAS)/CIDE (MEC), Colección Mujeres en la Educación. (A copy of this chapter was retrieved on September 21, 2007 from: http://www.loce.concejoeducativo.org/docu/enmarcar/enmarcar.htm).

Callahan, R. (1962). *Education and the cult of efficiency.* Chicago, IL: The University of Chicago Press.

Colectivo IOÉ (Pereda, C., de Prada, M. A., and Actis, W.) (2003). *La escolarización de hijas de familias inmigrantes.* Madrid: CIDE/Instituto de la Mujer.

Fernández-Enguita, M. (1990). La tierra prometida: La contribución de la escuela a la igualdad de la mujer. *Revista de Educación*, No. 290, pp. 21–41.

Fernández-Enguita, M. (1997). Los desiguales resultados de las políticas igualitarias: Clase, género y etnia en la educación. In M. Fernández Enguita (Ed.), *Sociología de las instituciones de educación secundaria* (pp. 107–122). Barcelona: Horsori.

Fernández-Enguita, M. (2000). *Alumnos gitanos en la escuela paya*. Barcelona: Ariel.

Fernández-Enguita, M. (2003). La segunda generación ya está aquí. *Papeles de Economía Española*, 98 (Special issue on "Inmigración en España"), pp. 238–262.

INE (Instituto Nacional de Estadística—Spanish National Institute for Statistics) (2005). INEBASE. Revisón del Padrón Municipal 2004. Madrid: INE. At: http://www.ine.es (last retrieved on November 9, 2005).

INE (Instituto Nacional de Estadística—Spanish National Institute of Statistics) (2007). Estadística de variaciones residenciales. Madrid: INE. At: http://www.ine.es (last retrieved on September 20, 2007).

MEC (Ministerio de Educación y Ciencia—Spanish Ministry of Education and Science) (2005a). *Las cifras de la Educación en España*. Edición 2005. Madrid: MEC. At: http://www.mec.es (last retrieved on June 12, 2006).

MEC (Ministerio de Educación y Ciencia—Spanish Ministry of Education and Science) (2005b). *Estadística de las Enseñanzas no Universitarias*. Resultados Detallados del curso 2003–2004. Datos Provisionales. Madrid: MEC. At: http://www.mec.es (last retrieved on July 5, 2005).

MEC (Ministerio de Educación y Ciencia—Spanish Ministry of Education and Science) (2005c). *Datos y cifras. Curso escolar* 2005–2006. Madrid: MEC. At: http://www.mec.es (last retrieved on June 12, 2006).

Roma General Secretariat Foundation (Fundación Secretariado General Gitano) (2005). La mujer, motor del cambio gitano. *El País*, May 22, 2005. At: http://www.elpais.com/articulo/sociedad/mujer/motor/cambio/gitano/elpepisoc/20050522elpepisoc_1/Tes/ (last retrieved on December 22, 2007).

Willis, P. (1978). *Learning to labour: How working class kids get working class jobs*. London: Gower.

CHAPTER THIRTEEN

New racisms
IN Spanish society

JUAN JOSÉ BUENO AGUILAR

University of A Coruña

Racism is based on the distrust, even the deprecation, of those with physical and cultural characteristics that differ from our own.[1]

—TAHAR BENJELLOUN

If you want to know the world, all you need to do is listen. What people see when they travel is never more than an illusion. Shadows chasing other shadows.[2]

—AMIN MAALOUF

A debate is opening up in Spain as to how best the "other," or alterity, might be represented in contemporary society: Which key elements promote communication between different cultures? How do discrimination and segregation actually operate? Where, fundamentally, lies the core of the challenge to coexistence among diverse groups? When does conflict arise? These are some of the key questions that have guided the present examination of the realities of racism in an ever more multicultural and cosmopolitan Spanish State. A central concern with this process of reflection and understanding is to inquire into exactly how new forms of racism are emerging, the ultimate goal being to contribute to the growing corpus of pedagogies aimed at unlearning racism.

Attempts to answer such questions are often fraught with difficulties, and sometimes with fear. Education, however, can play a vital role in combating this pervasive sense of unease. I refer not to a visceral kind of panic, but to a fear of the unknown, the arcane, the uncertain—apprehension of the future, which is manifested in irrational and defensive behavior and, on some occasions, even in outbreaks of violence. It is perhaps in these moments of irrationality and indetermination that this apprehension of the "other" as distinct—this feeling of "What will come next?"—is felt most palpably. In some cases it can take the form of hatred and racist alarm, which we might understand as a new expression of latent racism in contemporary Spanish society.

Faced as we are with this horizon of uncertainty or "crisis," education may indeed serve as a great asset, but only if decidedly approached as a powerful tool for confronting these ever more frequent and problematic contingencies, for it stands to provide individuals and groups with the means to create strategies to intercept racism and prevent its multiple forms of recurrence. Nonetheless, any action in the educational sector is clearly conditioned by myriad circumstances and infinite small details, which need to be taken into account in the formulation of specific educational proposals.

Prior to exploring such proposals, however, we must first establish what exactly is entailed in these new expressions of racism. A useful preliminary exercise, then, involves clarifying the meaning of racism in its most broadly applicable sense. Racism establishes a necessary correlation, a causal relationship between physical features and those of an intellectual, psychological or cultural kind. Racism is derived from the theory of a hierarchy of races based on the belief that one's social condition depends primarily on one's racial characteristics. This ideology, in turn, further prevents interracial association of any kind in its intent to preserve a supposed racial purity (D'Appollonia, 1998). In this sense, racism can be seen as a body of ideas that rationalize and legitimize those social practices that strengthen the hierarchical distribution of power amongst groups identified through physical or culturally selected characteristics. According to this system of values, only some individuals and groups benefit from their membership in certain collectives, while others pay the price of exclusion.

Despite this unjust situation, racism is a universal phenomenon which arises from historical processes occurring in specific contexts and conjunctures. It can be defined as synonymous with discrimination or exclusion, as stereotypes and dogma are mobilized against the object population or individuals, in rejection of their alterity. As Michel Wieviorka (1992) notes, racism represents an ideology marked by prejudice, which comports attitudes, values, and beliefs that serve to project the superiority of one group over another. However, an overriding feature of racism is also its complexity. For this reason, only a detailed exposition of each of its many facets and manifestations can shed light on the kinds of arguments deployed to justify its existence, and on its possible consequences and interceptions. Racism does not operate solely as a product of an individual's subjectivity, but rather, as a result of collective processes of interaction among groups, in which the status of minorities is defined in relation to the dominant group. These attitudes are not arbitrary but, on the contrary, are further conditioned by gender, social class, ethnicity, and other variables.

Current research perspectives on racism from the field of the natural sciences—especially those based on recent findings from the human genome project—draw attention to the great degree of genetic proximity, similarity, or equality among human beings, this despite the diversity of their physical attributes.[3] Although this corpus of research indicates that the existence of race cannot be securely grounded scientifically (see, for example, Anderson and Nickerson, 2005; Omi and Winant, 2005; or Smedley and Smedley, 2005), the problem of racism persists, as it inevitably finds expression through the attitudes and prejudices of some groups with respect to others. Racism, in addition to an ideological construct, thus constitutes the development and use of the concept of "race" as a category of social organization for systematic oppression.

Racism and xenophobia are resurfacing in modern industrial societies such as Spain with a renewed violence, and in very tangible ways. The sporadic nature of their appearance thus far, however, does not diminish their significance. In fact, it would be a gross error to attempt to explain these new expressions of racism simply in terms of the current social context, or to see them as a product of isolated events in time. The roots of racism run deep and must be thoroughly disinterred if we are to comprehend the full extent of its dimensions and power. As Nelson Mandela once asserted, "Racism is a very grave problem because it is not based on logic, but on prejudice and emotions, and for this reason we can never beat it with mere arguments" (Valenzuela, 1995, p. 55).

A rigorous characterization of racism thus requires careful analysis that rejects simplistic or essentializing explanations. Such analysis must also be based on a close reading of racist discourses and their complex manifestations so that they may be clearly and effectively confronted, and lines of dialog and understanding opened up that address the potential challenges and consequences. There are distinct stages and forms in the emergence of racist attitudes and behaviors which must be identified, as should also any changes in points of view regarding racism. In this way, the social thinking underlying racism can be brought to the surface, and the development of relations among cultures made more transparent. Researchers have attempted to depict cross-cultural relations in general modes or types of interaction. For example, Adam Kuper (2001) has identified the four modes of competition, conflict, assimilation, and conciliation (see also Suárez-Orozco and Suárez-Orozco, 2002), while John W. Berry et al. (1986) prefer to characterize these general forms of contact and interaction in terms of marginalization, separation, assimilation, and integration. But even the most essential elements of racism, such as discrimination, segregation, prejudice, and violence, can provide us with some of the most valuable points of access in our attempt to untangle and deconstruct its meaning.

A privileged site from which to take on this challenge is from the field of education, especially higher learning institutions, for such institutions are among the most equipped to comprehend the phenomenon of racism in all its complexity. But mere comprehension is clearly not enough. It should serve as a springboard for the elaboration of interventions designed to transform unequal racial relations, and promote interventions such as global educational policies that encompass the social, economic, and cultural spheres, as well as that of education. A critical, curricular form of multicultural education can help to articulate these lines of intervention, the most natural developmental context of which can be found in university settings and schools of education, but also in professional development programs for active teachers, as well as the various levels of educational policy production throughout the social institutions. What follows, then, is an exploration of the possible contents for this particular project of curricular intervention.

NEW RACISMS: A CURRICULAR APPROACH

Although we are living in an era in which new expressions of racism are constantly emerging, these more recent forms are not grounded in biology; neither do they necessarily use biology as a point of reference. Instead, they work relentlessly through culture, as van Dijk has pointed out in this volume. Racism, understood in this way, is a perpetually nuanced ideology, as it is regularly interrupted and reconstructed to reemerge in unpredictable forms. It thus works in diverse and sometimes contradictory ways. For this reason, the new expressions of racism must be studied in the concrete sociocultural contexts in which they occur.

These novel articulations of racism, which will be described in detail ahead, can present challenges of interpretation to the uncritical observer. They often work tacitly, and for this reason can be more pernicious than the more familiar earlier examples of overt racism, such as apartheid in South Africa, antiblack racism in the United States, the pogroms of Nazi Germany, or discrimination in Spain against the Gypsy population. It is therefore important to identify the mechanisms through which these new forms of racism hide their intentions through false appearances of "normality," "common sense," and other essentialisms.

Hence, we should ask ourselves where these new, everyday forms of racism come from, and how they emerge in our daily lives, often to our unawares. Why do they reappear in new ways, and at times with added vehemence and violence? What is the best way to deconstruct these new expressions of racism? How might they be contested, disrupted, and ultimately eliminated? All of these questions are worthy of ongoing investigation. Some researchers stand out for their efforts in this terrain, not only because they raise the necessary questions but also because they rigorously explore diverse angles from which to combat the new forms of racism.

Before inquiring further into such pedagogies, however, the new modalities of racism must first be carefully identified and clearly described to make their implicit modus operandi much more visible. The ultimate aim here is to offer an analysis of a synthetic nature that will support the ongoing development of curricular and more general educational interventions intended to actively confront racism in its multiple manifestations.

The various forms of racism described below are closely connected and interrelated. Hence, each of the general types or classifications can overlap with others, given that—as pointed out earlier—racism is often expressed in complex and heterogeneous ways. Nonetheless, drawing from the many different instances of new racism, one might identify as particularly salient types the following:[4]

As one of the most violent forms of racism, *xenophobia* involves a complete rejection and hatred of all foreigners and immigrants. Melding extreme and heightened elements of nationalism and territorialism, xenophobia also functions as a general rejection and stigmatization of groups based on their location or origins, their culturally distinctive practices, language, religion and so on. Further, xenophobia maintains a very close relationship with fundamentalist expressions of a polis's patriotic values, as set off against "the others." Considering, however, that this form of hatred is not expressed in uniform or straightforward ways, its nuances must not be overlooked (Perceval, 1995; Calvo Buezas, 2000).

Xenophobic attitudes toward those of other cultural origins are often accompanied by an exacerbated form of *ethnocentrism*, through which the world is viewed exclusively from an ethnically familiar and closed point of view. In the case of Western ethnocentrism, Western culture becomes the only paradigm for civilization, while the contributions and values of other cultures are disregarded. Some examples of this perspective can be found in Silvio Berlusconi's assertion that Western society is superior to Islam,[5] or in Oriana Falacci's article, "The Sons of Allah," in which she effectively totalizes and demonizes Islamic cultural identity, claiming that the set of values it allegedly inscribes cannot be imposed on Western nations.[6] These are just two examples of this kind of ethnocentrism, but there are many others that illustrate the unconscious, collective sense of superiority adopted by one group *vis à vis* those regarded as different. Similar discourses are proliferating in the aftermath of the September 11 attacks. Racism of this Eurocentric kind, moreover, has at times been ascribed the scientific aura of objective knowledge, as if free from the supposed impurities of subjectivity and contingency attributed to other cultures. This stance is all too closely linked, however, to biological determinism, which we shall examine in detail ahead.

Institutional racism can be defined as a set of practices in which the state, or given social institutions, promulgate laws, edicts, or policies that discriminate against certain racial and ethnic groups, and impede the equitable coexistence and integration of such groups. Legal, administrative, and social systems serve to restrict plurality and diverse identities in working environments, or indeed, hinder intercommunication among culturally diverse inhabitants. Perhaps the clearest example of this form of racism in the case of Spain can be found in the so-called Foreigners Act (*Ley Orgánica 4/2000* or *Ley de Extranjería*), which has been found to violate some fundamental civil rights. The Supreme Court has since annulled eleven articles from the law, including those concerned with freedom of movement, deportations, and work permits; and in 2003 the Act was heavily reformed. One might say, with respect to the Foreigners Act, that the government is experiencing a kind of *Penelope syndrome*, which has done little to palliate the *Ulysses syndrome* that so many immigrants are prone to suffer.[7]

Another example is provided by two Amnesty International (2002, 2006) reports, which denounce over 300 cases of racial violence and discrimination against immigrants perpetrated by various Spanish State security personnel assigned to police stations, detention centers, and prisons. Additionally, one might cite the Ombudsman's report of 2003 (Defensor del Pueblo, 2004), which reveals, among other violations, that immigrant children are concentrated in fully public (state) schools, this in part due to the fact that state-financed private schools regularly reject such students even though such selective practices are illegal.

A related form of racism on the rise today is *cultural* or *lifestyle racism*, which consists of the rejection of certain cultural practices simply because they are different, as well as the absence of any attempt to create forms of understanding or points of contact with those who value such practices and live other cultural realities. In such cases, a greater emphasis is placed on ethnocultural markers of difference between groups and individuals, whilst no attention is paid to political, socioeconomic, or gender-related issues, or to the racialization of diverse human beings. The concepts of "cultural minority" or "ethnicity" thus stand in as proxies for the category of race, broadly encompassing the same attributes. At the same time, there are no serious attempts to redefine "ethnicity" or to qualify its meaning. The negative connotations of the term "race" has proved convenient for some who practice unjust social selection according to racial criteria, but who now largely justify their selective attitudes and actions by resorting to disqualifications based, so they claim, not on race but on ethnic and other criteria (e.g. some students are disqualified because of "limited linguistic abilities in the standard language" or "poor intellectual development"). What is more, there is no consideration of the concept of marginalization in this monolithic conceptualization of human difference. The result is an exclusively culturalist reductionism in the reading of relations and interactions among different collectivities.

Close to this type of racism is *differentialist* or *separatist racism*, as a discourse of difference which focuses on the supposedly insurmountable obstacles to coexistence among groups, rather than on the possibility of establishing common ground, exchange, and integration. This type of racism thus leads to an absence of dialog, each group seeking its own development separately and independently of the others. The discourse of differentialist racism is readily evident in the debate set off by the publication of Giovanni Sartori's (2002) book, *La sociedad multiét-nica. Pluralismo, multiculturalismo y extranjeros* (The multiethnic society: Pluralism, multiculturalism, and foreigners), in which he expresses the impossibility of inhab-itants of certain ethnic origins coexisting as one civic body in the context of a single state, and refers to some groups as "inassimilable" in Western societies. Given that the conditions for assimilability, according to Sartori, are reciprocity and adapta-tion, for him, "integration" occurs only among those who are able to assimilate or adapt to other, dominant cultural norms and ways of being, even if this implies the renunciation of long-held cultural values and practices. For instance, he cites Latino immigrants as more capable of integrating in Western countries than immigrants of Islamic origins (2002, p. 114). Such a discourse inscribes a kind of latent racism based, on the one hand, on the establishment of a close, albeit clearly problematic, parallel between the notions of assimilation and integration, and on the other, on a unidirectional sense of integration: the minority group must adapt or assimilate into the majority group, while other directionalities of adaptation are not considered. This ideological bias works off the premise that certain kinds of dialogue and coexistence in multicultural societies are not possible, and thus precludes striving toward such goals. Nonetheless, this type of discourse is on the rise in Spain, especially where cultural identities related to the Islamic world are concerned, and in the aftermath of the March 11 terrorist attacks in Madrid.

A noteworthy example of what is promoted, again problematically, as "inte-gration policies," or even as "anti-racist education," are those recently adopted in France, designed to eliminate from educational and other institutional settings all references and symbols considered to either represent or potentially encour-age racist, ethnic, and other forms of discrimination, conflict, or oppression. Such policies extend into the absolute prohibition at school of all religious symbols and referents—such as the Islamic veil—a practice that writer and intellectual Mario Vargas Llosa has come out to defend.[8] Yet one might ask: is it possible or even advisable to eliminate all such representations from educational practice if our goal is to integrate? As will be discussed ahead, certain currents of multicul-tural and antiracist education seek instead to promote alternative processes for *un*learning racism, which, contrary to supporting such prohibitive and segrega-tional measures, attempt to foster unity through diversity.

A person of Gypsy origins once stated to the author that "we will only inte-grate when you *payos* (non-Gypsies) want to integrate us." The truth is that mainstream culture plays a fundamental role in this process, although most members of that culture remain unaware of the degree to which they themselves are implicated. What is clearly needed is for all members of society to make many more attempts to place themselves in the perspectives and circumstances of "others," and reflect on their experiences, outlooks, and feelings.

As scholars such as Pierre-André Taguieff (1995) or Teun van Dijk (2003) have pointed out, the conceptualizations that have historically characterized racist arguments have changed and moved away from biologically based inequality toward an emphasis on cultural difference. Ariane Chebel D'Appollonia (1998) has further argued that such differentialist racism can involve *racism without race* as well, in the sense that the racialization of difference is euphemistically reframed as alterity. This emphasis, however, on differentiation, as opposed to commonality among cultures, is articulated in a fundamental way—as an invariable phenomenon. As with cultural racism or the emphasis on difference based on ethnicity, the concept of alterity now supplants the need to refer to race, or racial difference, given that scientific research has been unable to differentiate human beings along clearly racial lines. In any case, although "races" may not exist as such, racism does. And while the evasion of the notion of race has led to significant controversy over race-based positive discrimination policies (or affirmative action) in the United States and elsewhere,[9] in Spain it has significant implications for those who regularly suffer the effects of racism, as do many members of Gypsy or immigrant populations. Compensatory measures for such groups are usually articulated around socioeconomic criteria, not the fact that racism itself can play an important role in their significantly greater experience with social marginalization.

A variant on this form of racism is observable in some educational proposals that suggest practicing *color blindness* in relation to "others." This would involve eliminating all racial references from any perception or analysis, the idea being that people's behavior toward others should be based on an assumption of equality, regardless of race. Even if perceivable as a commendable objective, such a posture ignores the fact that racist phenomena continue to exist and emerge independently of one's best intentions, or at times even one's skin color (Delgado Ruiz, 2002). For instance, while discriminatory behavior can respond very directly to variables such as social class, gender or ethnicity, when the race factor is added to any of these variables it can either exacerbate or weaken the degree of discrimination experienced, depending on which "color" comes into play (McCarthy, 1990). Turning a deaf ear to color or race, then, is obviously not a solution (Cochran-Smith, 1995).

Another new form of racism entails the more recent revival of *biological determinism*, (in addition to the new cultural expressions of racism), as evidenced in the racialized discourses of neo-Nazis and other white supremacist groups. The resurgence of this form of racism is observable in Europe through the electoral successes of Jean Marie Le Pen in France and Pim Fortuyn in Holland, and in the

United States in growing white supremacist movements. These expressions of racism obey an extreme logic of differentiation that is also xenophobic in nature, and is played out through various new configurations of the superiority attributed to white populations over other racialized groups. Moreover, European or Western culture—its arts, sciences, technologies, and intellectual legacy—is projected in a deterministic way as synonymous with culture in general, as if European cultural production were the only valid kind worthy of the term. This Eurocentrism can be understood as a subtle variant of biological determinism in that it often rests on, as mentioned earlier, an alleged scientific objectivity (read intellectual superiority) that other cultural groups are not considered to have developed to the same degree. Some researchers, such as Richard Hernstein and Charles Murray (1994) or J. Philippe Rushton (2000), have even attempted to justify this racist stance through what they construe as "objective" explanations of socioeconomic differences between races, classes, and genders. They thus attempt to establish correlations between inherited genetic attributes and social status, as if the latter were merely a higher-order reflection of the former. This racist philosophy, otherwise referred to as "social Darwinism," posits that some races or peoples are more fit for survival than others. It bolsters ethnocentric and xenophobic thinking, and establishes a hierarchy among groups, denying the possibility of conversion or transformation (Fraser et al., 1995; Omi and Winant, 2005).

It is worth recalling the great impact that Antonio Salas' book "*Diario de un Skin*" (Diary of a Skinhead) (2003) had in Spain. In this book, written under a pseudonym, Salas describes how he infiltrated the violent world of skinhead groups in order to uncover the ideological underpinnings of their actions. He found to be highly significant, for instance, the fact that members of such groups often express a *negation* of all racist atrocities committed in the not-too-distant past by denying, for example, any evidence of the genocide missions carried out against the Jews and Gypsies by the German Nazis. Another of their tactics is to *trivialize* these events, conceding them very little historical relevance. In relation to this tendency, it seems important to reflect on Alberto Manguel's (2001) words:

> (I)f there is in Judaism a central mandate, it should not be to question identity, but memory; it is not a matter of imitating persecution or of theatricalizing the Holocaust, but of honoring the victims so that the Holocaust is never underestimated, so that the Jews do not see themselves condemned to a double death, through murder and then through oblivion. (p. 36)

In other words, the negation and the trivialization of racist acts are tremendously dangerous, as they can lead to a kind of collective amnesia that perpetuates the lies and prejudices that have proved so difficult to overcome, and through which history has come to repeat itself.

Racism through deception—or the false expression and appearance of anti-racist sentiments in discursive contexts—occurs when a person declares that s/he is explicitly opposed to racism, but at the same time uses expressions of a some-times subtle, sometimes marked, racist or xenophobic character. Such rhetorical discourse is typified by phrases such as "I have no problem with immigrants," or "Some of my best friends are Gypsies!" and so on., only to be qualified immedi-ately thereafter by riders such as "... but I wouldn't want to have them as neigh-bors," or "... but I'm not sure whether I'd like my daughter to marry one." Such qualifications, needless to say, significantly alter the underlying sense of the initial declarations. This kind of racism extends into the exclusionary discourse of certain school textbooks, and into some educational projects that reflect a disconcertingly clear and persistent tendency to represent the racialized "other" in negative terms. This kind of racism draws its motivation from prejudice and operates as a form of symbolic violence.

A *racist lexicon* refers to terms and expressions that serve to reproduce or per-petuate an invidious color hierarchy—white and black serving to book-end differ-ence at the high and low extremes of this discursive racial structuration. In Spain, for instance, derogatory and stereotypical connotations often inhere to the terms that refer to immigrant and Gypsy populations. Descriptions of minority groups tend to convey a negative vision of these others, which in itself contributes explic-itly to the propagation of terminology replete with prejudices. Perhaps one of the clearest cases of such damaging connotations is the word *moro* (Moor), so deeply rooted in Spanish society that it is initially difficult to deconstruct its subtly dis-qualifying significance.[10] Indeed, some people defend its use as a general and thus inoffensive term, but they overlook its derisive connotations and the existence of other more neutral synonyms that are more suited to conveying its meaning (e.g., the term *magrebí*—Maghrebi or North African).

Racism in the media deserves special attention considering that the informa-tion society reproduces racism in very particular ways, and is gradually establish-ing new norms for communication which in turn affect reactions to, and reflection about, such communication in all spheres of public life, including, inevitably, edu-cation. How and why the new racist realities of today's largely globalized mass media are influencing education is thus a central concern.

As is evidenced, for example, through media images portraying the South to audiences in the North, new forms of racism are articulated through both the presence and absence of certain visual information thus conveyed. Not only is there relatively more absence, or underrepresentation, of racial minorities and marginalized groups in general (as compared to majority groups), but there is also a demonstrable silence when it comes to critical visions about their reali-ties, and virtually no serious debate on how to improve communication itself and education for the purpose of promoting deeper understandings of racism, and how it emerges and is propagated in today's society.

The ways in which Gypsy, Muslim, and Eastern cultures are represented in the mass media of Spain—or of the West, for that matter—is key, and can be explored through the straightforward (and highly useful) tracking of newspaper headlines and information from the Internet and television. Some examples of headlines and other forms of discourse from *El País* are very instructive here: "One out of every three Spanish schoolchildren opposes immigration" (January 23, 2003); "Racism on board an airplane" (March 29, 2003); "The Ministry of the Interior agrees to create 'a network for alerting and reporting' to detect 'the undocumented'" (illegal residents) (April 16, 2003); "Aznar defends the family before the European Popular Party and opposes multicultural society" (April 23, 2003); "The president of the Popular Party in New York seeks votes with a xeno-phobic letter" (April 23, 2003); "Immigrants in court" (May 25, 2003); "Three youths arrested in Huelva for the homicide of a Moroccan immigrant" (May 30, 2003). These are just a few examples of the kinds of discourse that could be ana-lyzed for their potential stereotypes, absences, and other forms of racism and dis-criminatory representation.[11]

Critical discourse analysis (see Teun van Dijk 2003 and this volume) can help us to better understand the complex sociolinguistic context in which the contemporary media operate; it also allows us to uncover some of the less obvious significations that mass communications give rise to. Critical discourse analysis focuses on the conditions of discourse, and on the components and consequences of the abuse of power exercised through the narratives of dominant elite groups and institutions, whose access to, control of, and authority over context, genre, text, speech, and its properties are critically examined, including the rhetorical strategies of persuasion. In sum, this type of analysis is centered on the forms and contents of communication, and its function in society: how discourse expresses, represents, legitimizes, and reproduces realities.

The curricular proposal pursued here aims not only to identify the various manifestations of new racisms in Spanish society, but to inquire into the role of the mass media, and the extent to which they function to both perpetuate and disrupt racism. A related objective is to explore the construction of discourses spe-cifically deployed to support and promote peaceful and respectful coexistence in multicultural societies such as Spain. In order to deepen the democratic nature of this cultural project, an essential element is the creation of strategies for *audio-visual literacy* that are capable of challenging the silences, absences, and biases currently observable in the media. Additionally, this type of literacy may instill the idea that a conscious, reflective, and ongoing search for information, which allows for a greater sense of awareness and a more critical view of these issues, is a necessary part of democratic life itself. And yet, such awareness does not come easily, for, ideally, it must leave one with a great sense of personal responsibility and commitment to analyzing, reflecting, and searching for alternatives.

This is where educational proposals play a key role: to initiate and consolidate policies that pave the way for social integration—not assimilation—for there is a significant difference between the two. To clarify this point, assimilation is a one-directional process of cultural adaptation that minority groups assume in their attempt to gain acceptance from the majority, and it involves a renunciation not only of certain cultural values and practices by the minoritized groups, but also of cross-cultural communication in general. Integration, by contrast, has as much to do with ethnic minorities as it does with the ethnic majority of any one state, and should be based on equality, communication across cultures, and respect for difference. Multicultural education, therefore, is not, nor should it be, identified merely with the education of immigrants or minority collectives. Rather, it should be regarded as education relevant to *all* social actors as cultural citizens of the demographically pluralist modern states that now properly characterize all countries in Western Europe and North America.

Putting multicultural education into practice in a media-driven world is becoming more indispensable by the day. It requires a critical, reflexive study of racism—particularly the new forms of racial essentialism, whose influence can be greatly intensified through the mass media—as well as the study of other forms of discrimination, and broader issues (such as immigration) related to the nature of coexistence in today's culturally diverse societies. Such an inquiry must include the analysis of European, and specifically Spanish, communications media in their various forms, with special attention to the particular registers and uses of language through the larger media (television, the press, the Internet). This would include an ongoing and exhaustive examination and disruption of the clichés and stereotypes presently in circulation, which continue to misrepresent populations from, for example, developing countries, and in terms that often translate into racist images and messages, especially when utilized for commercial ends such as advertising or attracting a greater readership in the case of sensationalistic headlines and images in periodicals. In the same way, critical engagements with key documents such as the *Code of conduct: Images and Messages relating to the Third World*[12] should become an integral part of the kind of multicultural and antiracist curricular contents and practices set forth here.

Novel forms of questioning and contestation are emerging in the new millennium in response to policies formerly taken for granted, as well as new approaches to the development of multicultural educational projects. The contribution of nongovernmental organizations (NGOs) in this arena, for instance, is noteworthy in Spain. Antiracist organizations and NGOs are making headway in establishing important links with immigrant, Gypsy, and other minority collectives of the Iberian Peninsula, giving them voice to articulate their views and resist racisms both new and old. This road toward encounter and dialog can offer some very useful means for opening a traditionally closed educational system to new sociocultural contexts, groups, and processes, and to innovative educational approaches.

At a broader level of curricular development and intervention, some orientations and initiatives from international scholars of educational policy and multicultural education can serve as general guides or frameworks for situating and facilitating the lines of curricular work proposed here. The analytical strategy of *nonsynchrony*, for instance, as elaborated by postcolonial scholar Cameron McCarthy (1990/1993), can provide future and practicing teachers with an essential tool for understanding the complex interactions among various forms of oppression and discrimination (racism, sexism, classism, etc.), and how they intersect and converge on human subjects, affecting their lives and identities in nonsynchronous ways. In addition to this, McCarthy and Dimitriadis (2000) find that processes such as *racial simulation* (invented versions of supposed racial purity) and *resentment* (redefining one's identity at the expense of "other" sense[s] of identity) work together through educational policy and curricula to further exacerbate racial exclusion, and that awareness about these tendencies will help those of us wishing to embrace a politics that is opposed to their proliferation. The antiracist project of Barry Troyna is another source of curricular inspiration for intervention. For Troyna (1993), antiracist education is inscribed in an emancipatory agenda for educational change which extends into teachings styles, organizational strategies, and exhaustive revisions of curricular contents that optimize the cognitive, social, and emotional development of youth, and expand the social and cultural contexts for learning beyond those most familiar to such learners.

The multicultural stances represented in scholars of critical pedagogy, such as Joe Kincheloe and Shirley Steinberg (1999), offer additional valuable insights into the curriculum, and actions for combating new cases of racism. For example, they argue that without commitment to emancipation, social justice, and egalitarian democracy, theoretical multiculturalism is nothing more than an apology of the status quo. Commitment to a transformative multicultural pedagogy, then, necessarily involves (in the case of Western nations) targeting the white middle-class majorities who have traditionally remained indifferent to, or even unsupportive of, social justice movements. As addressed earlier, critical discourse analysis (see van Dijk, 2003 and this volume) can also help to reconcile the transversal realm of media and institutional discourse with critical curricular commitments to resisting racism. As for Iberian scholarship on multiculturalism, Juan Luis Alegret (1992) emphasizes equality over diversity through an inclusive curriculum, while Javier García Castaño and collaborators (García et al., 1999) conceive of multicultural education as the development of cultural critique through its polyse-mic expressions.

Guided by such valuable multicultural and antiracist scholarship, educators will be better equipped to address curricular areas which are directly affected by, and intricately related to, the new forms of racism. These areas would include: cultural integration in cosmopolitan societies characterized by growing immigrant populations; the uses of discourse and the valuation of the symbolic codes and lin-guistic practices of minority groups; the study of diverse cultural realities and their social representations; concrete pedagogical proposals against racism, discrimi-nation, and segregation; the nature of new racisms and their impact on today's multicultural societies; interethnic learning environments in both university and compulsory education settings; and finally, the influence of the globalized com-munications media on the (re)production of racism.

In conclusion, the concise words of Tahar Ben Jelloun (1998, p. 22) put into perspective the significant challenge to educators wishing to unlearn racism: "The racist is not born, but made."

NOTES

1. See Ben Jelloun (1998). This quotation, as well as all subsequent quotations from Spanish-language sources, have been translated into English.
2. See Maalouf (1999).
3. See International Human Genome Sequencing Consortium. (2001); Venter, J. C., Adams, M. D., Myers, E. W., Li, P. W., Mural, R. J., Sutton, G. G., et al. (February 16, 2001). The sequence of the human genome. *Science,* no. 291, pp. 1304–1351; or the Human Genome Project Information web site at: http://www.ornl.gov/sci/techresources/Human_Genome/faq/faqs1.shtml (last retrieved on December 6, 2007).
4. Adapted from Bueno (1998).
5. See *"Berlusconi: La civilización occidental es superior al islam","* in the electronic version of *El País,* September 28, 2001, last retrieved December 6, 2007 from the Comunidad Europea Web site at: http://www.ucm.es/cgi-bin/show-prensa?mes=09&dia=28&ano=2001&art=29&tit=b.
6. See *El Mundo,* October 1, 2001, http://www.elmundo.es/2001/10/01/mundo/1054491.html (last retrieved December 6, 2007).
7. The Greek mythological figure of Penelope was said to weave fabric during the day only to undo her work at night so that she could resume weaving the next day as she awaited the return of her errant soul mate. The Ulysses syndrome refers to a recently identified pathology affecting one's emotional state, and is caused by separation from family and loved ones; experience with danger in travels abroad; poor living conditions; or awareness of abruptly diminished social status. Symptoms include separation anxiety, stress, depression, aches and pains, fear, and loneliness, among others. See Anchotegui (2002).
8. See *"El velo islámico"* in *El País,* June 22, 2003. Retrieved December 2, 2007 from the Web site: http://www.sepv.org/observatorio/religion/vargasllosa.htm.

9. The debate on affirmative action in education in the United States, for example, is addressed in detail and from various angles in a special issue of *Educational Researcher* (Vol. 27, no. 9, December 1998). See Linn (1998).

10. The term retains remnants of its original reference to "barbarian" invaders from the south.

11. These citations have been selected and translated from a collection of headlines and other press-related discourse originally written in Spanish and cited in Aierbe (2003); S.O.S. Racismo (2004, 2005).

12. Jointly elaborated by a group representing hundreds of European nongovernmental development organizations (NGDOs), this code of conduct for the mass media was accorded in 1989 during the General Assembly of the Liaison Committee of European NGDOs, known by the French acronym CLONG, before the then-European Commission. The group disbanded in 2001. Source: http://www.deeep.org/english/code/index.php (last retrieved on December 11, 2007).

REFERENCES

Aierbe, P. M. *et. al* (January, February, and March, 2003). Inmigración, racismo y xenofobia: Análisis de prensa. *Mugak*, No. 4, pp. 1–60.

Alegret, J. L. (1992). Educación y racismo. In P. Fermoso (Ed.), *Educación intercultural: La Europa sin fronteras* (pp. 91–110). Madrid: Narcea.

Amnesty International (2002). *Amnesty International Report 2002*. Online report from http://web. amnesty.org/report2002/home/home (last retrieved on December 11, 2007).

Amnesty International (2006). *Amnesty International Report 2006*. Online report from http://web. amnesty.org/report2006/index-eng (last retrieved on December 11, 2007).

Anchotegui, J. (2002). La depresión en los inmigrantes extracomunitarios: Características del síndrome del inmigrante con estrés crónico y múltiple (Síndrome de Ulises). In J. Anchotegui, *La depresión en los inmigrantes: Una perspectiva transcultural* (pp. 46–56). Barcelona: Editorial Mayo.

Anderson, N. B. and Nickerson, K. J. (2005). Genes, race, and psychology in the genome era: An introduction. *American Psychologist*, Vol. 60, No. 1, pp. 5–8.

Ben Jelloun, T. (1998). *Papá, ¿qué es el racismo?* Madrid: Alfaguara.

Berry, J. W., Trimble, J. and Olmedo, E. (1986). Assessment of acculturation. In W. L. Lonner and J. W. Berry (Eds.), *Field Methods in Cross-Cultural Research*, Vol. 8, (pp. 291–324). London: Sage.

Bueno, J. J. (1998). Controversias en torno a la Educación Multicultural. *Heuresis: Revista Electrónica de Investigación Curricular y Educativa*, Vol. 2, No. 1. At: http://www2.uca.es/HEURESIS/heuresis98/v1n2-3.htm (last retrieved December 1, 2007).

Calvo Buezas, T. (2000). *Inmigración y racismo: Así sientan los jóvenes del siglo XXI*. Madrid: Cauce.

Cochran-Smith, M. (1995). Color blindness and basket making are not the answers: Confronting the dilemmas of race, culture, and language diversity in teacher education. *American Educational Research Journal*, Vol. 32, No. 3, pp. 493–522.

D'Appollonia, A. C. (1998). *Los racismos cotidianos*. Barcelona: Bellaterra.

Defensor del Pueblo (2004). Summary of the report to Parliament for 2003. *The Ombudsman* (June), pp. 1–64.

Delgado Ruiz, M. (2002). Anonimato y ciudadanía. *Mugak*, No. 20, pp. 7–14.

Fraser, S. (Ed.) (1995). *The Bell Curve wars: Race, intelligence, and the future of America*. New York: Basic Books.

García Castaño, F. J., Pulido Moyano, R. A., and Montes del Castillo, A. (1999). La educación multicultural y el concpto de cultura. In J. García Castaño and A. Granados Martínez (Eds.), *Lecturas para educación intercultural* (pp. 47–80). Madrid: Trotta.

Hernstein, R. and Murray, C. (1994). *The Bell Curve*. New York: Free Press.

International Human Genome Sequencing Consortium (2001). Initial sequencing and analysis of the human genome. *Nature*, Vol. 409, No. 6822, pp. 860–921.

Kincheloe, J. and Steinberg, S. (1999). *Repensar el multiculturalismo*. Barcelona: Octaedro.

Kuper, A. (2001). *Cultura: La versión de los antropólogos*. Barcelona: Paidós.

Linn, C. (December 1998). Affirmative action in the 1990s: Perspectives from Willystine Goodsell Award Winners. *Educational Researcher*, Vol. 27, No. 9, pp. 4–5.

Maalouf, A. (1999). *Identidades asesinas*. Madrid: Alianza.

Manguel, A. (2001). *En el bosque del espejo: Ensayos sobre las palabras y el mundo*. Madrid: Alianza.

McCarthy, C. (1990). *Race and curriculum: Social inequality and the theories and politics of difference in contemporary research on schooling*. London: The Falmer Press [Spanish Edition: *Racismo y curriculum*. Madrid: Morata, 1993].

McCarthy, C. and Dimitriadis, G. (2000). Globalizing pedagogies: Power, resentment, and the renarration of difference. In R. Mahalingam and C. McCarthy (Eds.), *Multicultural curriculum: New directions for social theory, practice and policy* (pp. 70–83). London: Routledge.

Omi, M. and Winant, H. (2005). The theoretical status of the concept of race. In C. McCarthy, W. Crichlow, G. Dimitriadis, and N. Dolby (Eds.), *Race, identity and representation in education* (pp. 3–12). New York: Routledge.

Perceval, J. M. (1995). *Nacionalismos, xenofobia y racismos en la comunicación: Una perspectiva histórica*. Barcelona: Paidós.

Rushton, J. P. (2000). *Race, evolution, and behavior*. Port Huron, MI: Charles Darwin Research Institute.

Salas, A. (2003). *Diario de un skin: Un topo en el movimiento neonazi español*. Madrid: Temas de Hoy.

Sartori, G. (2001). *La sociedad multiétnica: Pluralismo, multiculturalismo y extranjeros*. Madrid: Taurus.

Smedley, A. and Smedley, B. D. (2005). Race as biology is fiction, racism as a social problem is real: Anthropological and historical perspectives on the social construction of race. *American Psychologist*, Vol. 60, No. 1, pp. 16–26.

S.O.S. Racismo (2004). *Informe anual 2004 sobre el racismo en el Estado español: S.O.S. Racismo*. Barcelona: Icaria/Antrazyt.

S.O.S. Racismo (2005). *Informe anual 2005 sobre el racismo en el Estado español: S.O.S. Racismo*. Barcelona: Icaria/Antrazyt.

Suárez-Orozco, C. and Suárez-Orozco, M. (2002). *Children of immigration*. Cambridge: Harvard University Press (Spanish Edition: *La infancia de la inmigración*. Madrid: Morata, 2003).

Taguieff, P. A. (1995). Las metamorfosis ideológicas del racismo y la crisis del antirracismo. In J. P. Alvite (Ed.), *Racismo, antirracismo e inmigración* (pp. 143–204). Donostia: Gakoa.

Troyna, B. (1993). *Racism and Education*. Buckingham: Open University Press.

Valenzuela, J. (1995). Nelson Mandela. *El País Semanal*, No. 242, pp. 50–57.

van Dijk, T. (2003). *Dominación étnica y racismo discursivo en España y América Latina*. Barcelona: Paidós.

Wieviorka, M. (1992). *El espacio del racismo*. Barcelona: Paidós.

CHAPTER FOURTEEN

Roma youth AT school: Instituting inclusion FROM A legacy OF exclusion[1]

CATHRYN TEASLEY

University of A Coruña

INTRODUCTION

The decades that directly followed Franco's death in 1975, which marked the end of 40 years of dictatorial rule in Spain, represented a watershed for the country's educational institution. In the 1980s and early 90s, the then Socialist Party majority-government instituted a number of educational reform laws, the most comprehensive of which is known as the LOGSE.[2] This law established, among other substantive reforms, the extension of compulsory education by two years, to age 16, which meant that for the first time in the history of Spanish schooling, all youth would be required to attend secondary schools. Consequently, since the mid-1990s, high school teachers have been receiving students that do not fit the traditional, privileged mold—a change that is especially evident in those schools where students of Roma or Gypsy[3] and immigrant origins have since enrolled. This historic event, while packed with opportunity, has nonetheless constituted an important challenge to the Spanish educational system inasmuch as it elicits institutional response to the ever more present effects of popular cultural forms on the dominant cultural politics and social environments of modern institutions such as schooling. In this case we witness the meeting of an institutional context steeped in elitist and exclusionary cultural tradition (Varela and Álvarez-Uría, 1991) with youth whose cultural identity formation has largely evolved on the periphery of Spanish society, and through diasporas that transcend what numerous scholars argue are the monolithic identity politics characteristic of nation-states and their institutions (Hall, 1996; Benhabib, 2002; Young, 2002).

Two decades after the transition from the dictatorship to the current parliamentary monarchy, however, the social and political institutions of Spain came to echo the conservative restoration that emerged in the 1980s and affected contemporary politics throughout the world (McCarthy, this volume; Torres Santomé, 2001). In fact, no sooner had the LOGSE been fully implemented—the process was completed in 2003—than it was significantly modified by a neoconservative counterreform: the Quality in Education Act (*Ley Orgáncia 10/2002, de 23 de diciembre, de Calidad de la Educación*), or LOCE.[4] This law was approved at the end of 2002 by an administration led by the Popular Party, which had come to power in 1996. The LOCE contained new measures related to streaming at younger ages; ability-grouping or tracking; tightening cultural controls over the base curriculum; restricting access to grade-promotion; and reinforcing the privatization of public education. Nonetheless, when the Socialists regained parliamentary majority two years later, in 2004, they placed a moratorium on the implementation of the more controversial aspects of the LOCE—such as streaming, the subject of Religion, and grade-promotion—and went on to establish yet another educational reform: the LOE of 2006.[5]

It was the LOGSE of 1990, however, that introduced structural changes substantial enough to inspire the ethnographic inquiry represented in this chapter, which is fundamentally concerned with the ways in which students who, since the turn of the millennium, have ostensibly been newly included or "integrated" into the educational system as a result of mandated reforms, enter into an interplay of ideologies, cultural constructs, and practices at school that—while ideally allowing for the emergence of promising educational opportunities—may, on the contrary, have engendered new forms of discrimination.

By honing in on a particular site of "recontextualisation" (Bernstein, 2000) of the LOGSE reform, we gain insight into some of the ways that top-down educational policy—as official knowledge discursively constructed and issued beyond the institutional contexts in which it is to be applied—combines with material and symbolic forces to be channeled, filtered, and reconstructed through the disputed professional space of local teacher agency. This process is of crucial relevance to Gypsy youth, whose hitherto overwhelming exclusion from secondary education in Spain warrants approaching this historic conjuncture with the utmost concern for cross-cultural comprehension and social justice. Yet, how has the initial

LOGSE reform actually played out since its implementation at the compulsory secondary level was finally completed in the 1999–2000 academic year? And what have the implications been for students and educators alike?

THE INSTITUTIONAL CONTEXT OF INCLUSION

Before these questions can be answered, the LOGSE reform must be further situated in its larger sociopolitical and historical context. When the reform was approved in 1990, nearly fifteen years had elapsed since the termination of four long decades of fascist rule in Spain. The Spanish State had recently attained full membership in the European Economic Community, and to meet the demands of a rapidly changing society, the then-Socialist administration set out to develop comprehensive social institutions premised on democratic principles. The LOGSE "updated" and overhauled the educational system, setting precedents with the establishment of Compulsory Secondary Education (for ages 12 through 16, followed by two noncompulsory years of Secondary Education for ages 16 and older), as well as Early Childhood Education (for ages 0–6), counseling departments, tutoring periods, class-size reduction, and, among other important measures, curricular adaptations for the "compensation of inequality in education" (according to the heading of Title Five of the LOGSE).

Yet the decentralization of educational administration in Spain, as stipulated in the Constitution of 1978, has meant that the responsibility for the application and implementation of the LOGSE's statewide mandates corresponds to the seventeen, locally elected regional governments (Autonomous Communities). A specific set of policies developed by one such Community, Galiza (or Galicia),[6] is central to the present analysis, for it served as a central institutional reference through which specific aspects of the LOGSE reform relating to compensatory and special education would be channeled, reinterpreted, and eventually converted into local practice at a particular school site. This regional set of policies, the product of legislation advanced by a conservative Galizan administration, was broadly termed "Attention to Diversity," and was designed to regulate the incorporation of nontraditional students into mainstream schooling in Galiza.[7] The particular Attention to Diversity policies reflected in this study are currently in effect (in the year 2007), and are comprised of measures such as diversifying instructional approaches within the "regular" curriculum and classroom contexts, adapting the curriculum through individual learning plans, or tracking students into self-contained behavior-management programs for up to two years per referral (see Consellería de Educación e Ordenación Universitaria, 1999).[8] Specifically, under examination are the ways in which this regional policy was received by a group of experienced teachers at an urban, public, secondary school—one affected by the aforementioned transformation in student enrollment.

Given, then, this brief overview of the political, social and institutional factors affecting the implementation of educational equity policy at the local level, our attention will be centered primarily on the teachers themselves as key—albeit structurally conditioned—agents in the recasting of public policy; but also on their Gypsy students, as members of what many researchers consider to be the most disenfranchised population of Spain (see, for example, Calvo Buezas, 1990; Asociación Presencia Gitana, 1992; San Román, 1997; or Fernández-Enguita, 1999a). Through the critical analysis of a limited selection of observations, interviews and conversations collected during a two-year ethnography at the teachers' workplace (1999–2001), another aim is to bring to the forefront the "politics of representation and difference" (McLaren, 1994) at the school, as revealed through the specific ways in which these educators responded to the new "demands" (according to the LOGSE) for student integration and inclusion.

Finally, the paper will explore some alternative means, especially through ethnographic action research, for producing "pedagogy as a performative practice" (Giroux with Shannon, 1997)—one that is conducive to more socially just and culturally responsive educational processes. The transformative potential of this method is explored in the paper's conclusions.

A LEGACY OF EXCLUSION IN PERSPECTIVE:
THE ROMA OF SPAIN

Beyond merely informing professional practice, the ethnography reflected in this paper is ultimately meant to serve the Gypsy people, which is why an additional overview of their experiences with social and educational injustice will facilitate a better understanding of the degree of marginalization at issue. The collective works of historians, sociologists, and activist groups in Spain and beyond, retell a history of severe oppression and persecution of a once nomadic people: the *calé*, the *rom*, the *sinti*, and other ethnic and linguistic groups within the Roma diaspora of Europe. Since their arrival to the Iberian Peninsula in the fifteenth century, the Gypsies have long suffered often brutal injustices such as genocide missions, torture, incarceration, and exile simply for practicing a nomadic lifestyle, speaking an unfamiliar language, or living in relative independence (Asociación Presencia Gitana, 1992; Fonseca, 1996; San Román, 1997).

In the more recent past, incorporation of the Roma into public schooling in Spain occurred as late as the 1970s, through compulsory primary education and the creation of experimental "bridge-schools." These latter institutions were largely located in Roma settlements and neighborhoods, and managed separately from mainstream schools, although their purpose was ultimately to make mainstream schooling more accessible to Gypsy youth (see Fernández-Enguita, 1999a). Official intentions aside, this policy turned out to nonetheless exacerbate preexisting forms of segregation, and was largely abandoned in the late 1980s when legislation concerning compensatory education was instituted. Nonetheless, Spain is today riddled with similarly marginalized schools, or educational ghettos, concentrated especially in and around urban centers (many immigrant students now experience this reality as well). In the year 2000, nearly one million of the approximately 40 million inhabitants of Spain were Roma, and over half of this group was 16 years old or younger; but according to the advocacy group Asociación Presencia Gitana (2000), only 30 percent of that age group was fully schooled. Another Roma organization, Asociación Secretariado General Gitano (2000), further confirmed that, even within this limited percentage of schoolgoing Gypsy youth, the majority experienced significant degrees of school failure. In fact, in 2001, a young Roma woman was interviewed and presented on Galizan television as the first of her ethnicity to attend a Galizan university—a poignantly revealing circumstance.

Finally, scholars have pointed out that the Gypsy people continue to receive some of the harshest forms of racist, xenophobic, and classist discrimination in Spanish society (see, for example, Calvo Buezas, 1990 and 2000; Jover and Reyero, 2000; or Vargas and Gómez, 2003). It is not so uncommon to read in the press about incidents of vehement parental protest against the first-time enrollment of Roma children in schools traditionally attended by non-Gypsy youth. Yet one of the most enduring injustices suffered by the Roma of the Iberian Peninsula has been attributed to historic linguistic repression, which impeded the development of a literary tradition in the Gypsies' root language, Romani (or Romanes; see Torrione, 1994 or Fernández-Enguita, 1999a.). Transnational Roma advocacy groups are now working to overcome this legacy, but as a general rule it can be said that, in Spain and throughout Europe, schooling has never been *for* the Roma (Liégeois, 1998). Nonetheless, since the LOGSE, Gypsy youth are now attending high schools in more significant numbers, as was the case at the school where the ethnography described below was conducted.

A SCHOOL IN TRANSITION

The secondary school chosen as the object of our analysis will be referred to as *Instituto Central*. A selection of a few key encounters at this institution will offer a contextualized view of the changing educational reality for Gypsy youth and teachers alike. To begin with, there is the portrait of the school prior to the initial implementation, in 1998, of the LOGSE's Compulsory Secondary Education (hereafter, CSE). Instituto Central was the second of its kind to be erected in the city in the 1940s, near one of the wealthiest neighborhoods, and has long held a position of prestige in the greater municipality. Perhaps not surprisingly, most of the staff members were mature and tenured. Since the LOGSE reform, however, the school not only began to receive Roma students—twelve in total—but there was also a sharp increase in the number of ethnic-majority youth from blue collar origins, as well as a first-time enrollment of four differently abled students (physically and cognitively challenged). And more generally, grades seven and eight were adjoined to the high school, as part of the new, four-year CSE, which brought in students ages 10–12 (to a school setting that formerly only admitted students ages 13–14 or older).

These student groups, however, were not the only new faces at the high school; a cohort of eleven, experienced, primary school teachers was transferred to Instituto Central from a local feeder school to help attend to the newly enrolled younger pupils. Thus, the presence of both new students and transferred teachers was cause for some stir among the high school's original staff members. One of the teachers from this original group expressed his opinion about the transformation by exclaiming, "We've been cheated, defrauded!" and then adding, "This isn't teaching; this is baby-sitting! It's not what *we* were educated to do." He later clarified that this "we" referred to the original staff cohort. And comments from most of the transferred teachers conveyed their general perception of a less-than-warm reception at the high school. Nonetheless, the school principal or "director"—himself an original-staff member—was highly critical of his peer group's rejection of the incoming teachers.[9]

In these ways and more, then, the educators at Instituto Central could not be treated as a homogeneous group with the same professional or ideological persuasions. On the other hand, none were of Roma descent, and it would later become apparent that the very premise of the LOGSE reform—that is, the extension of the comprehensive nature of a basic education—was fundamentally questioned, especially by the original staff members.

These professional concerns, tensions, and frustrations elucidate not only the teachers' complex situatedness in the reform, but some of the ways in which they would come to fit the nontraditional students into their working world. And the Gypsy collective indeed captured a great deal of their attention. Significantly, the staff's main interest in these students stemmed from the problems perceived in their schooling, particularly those related to lesson disruption, exceedingly low achievement levels, and chronic absence. Moreover, most of the teachers commented that the Roma students generally manifested "problematic" or "conflictive" behavior that "disrupt[ed] the peaceful coexistence" and "lower[ed] the overall academic performance" at the school. As regards the frequently absent half of the Gypsy students (usually six), a common comment to this regard was, "They don't *want* to be here," although there was also a tendency to blame the newly formed Counseling Department for a lack of coordination and commitment to addressing this issue.

Nonetheless, given the vehemence of the staff's complaints regarding the nonconformist attitudes attributed to most of the Gypsy students, the analysis that follows will focus on the teachers' reactions to, and representations of, these students in particular. And perhaps most importantly, it appears that their common concerns with respect to these pupils served to channel the design of the school's specific Attention to Diversity program. But before addressing that policy, let us first consider some ways in which the Roma students came to be constituted as a problem.

"PROBLEM STUDENTS": CONSTRUCTION OF A CATEGORY

Certain students' names repeatedly arose during assessment meetings, interviews, and informal conversations with staff members. Of the approximately twenty mostly male youth identified as "problem" students, most were of working class origins, and seven were Roma. This meant that Gypsy students were patently overrepresented in this problem grouping. Further, the tendency to categorize these students as misbehaved or disruptive reflects an implicit correlation between the teachers' employment of signifiers—those that signify the conflictive with those that signify the ethnically and/or racially different in students.

Whereas blatantly racist discourse *per se* was not directly observable amongst the teachers through this field study, several interviewees were quick to clarify that their perceptions of the Roma students "did not stem from racism" but from their "specific disruptive behaviors." As further "proof" of this, a few of these teachers noted that "not all Gypsies are dark," and that one of the Roma boys was "blond haired and blue eyed." The mere need to make these remarks, however, necessarily involved race. Moreover, if we consider this confluence of comments and perceptions conjointly with the aforementioned emergence of Roma ghetto schools throughout Spain, or with documented cases of mainstream racism and xenophobia toward Gypsies at school (see especially Calvo Buezas, 1990 and 2000; San Román, 1997; Jover and Reyero, 2000; or Vargas Clavería and Gómez Alonso, 2003), we may, at a minimum, acknowledge that the correlation between the signifiers "Gypsy students" and "conflictive behavior" may indeed help pave the way for the local emergence of institutionalized or *de facto* forms of discrimination, be these a result of racism, ethnocentrism, classism, sexism—or a mixture thereof.

ATTENDING TO INCLUSION THROUGH DIVERSITY: POLICY VERSUS PRACTICE

Focusing in on a particularly significant instance of teacher agency at Instituto Central, in November of 1999, a special meeting had been convened to review and assess the school's plan for addressing the "conflictive" students. Toward the end of the previous year, one of the school's classrooms, Room 10, had been designated as the site for a remediation program established in response to the Galizan Attention to Diversity mandate, and was coincidentally called *Atención á Diversidade* (Attention to Diversity). The original purpose of Room 10 was two-pronged: on the one hand, it was conceived as a space where individual students could go during class hours to receive tutoring on their work; on the other, it would also serve as a detention/punishment center. In this way, the teachers in charge would each serve in the dual capacity of tutor and disciplinarian, thus enacting a perhaps more defined version of the Janus-type role most of them claimed to already experience in the regular classroom. This said, all eight teachers present at the meeting acknowledged that, in practice, Room 10 functioned nonetheless almost exclusively as a disciplinary measure.

With the exception of the school principal, all those present were women. They were assigned weekly duty in Room 10 either because they had gaps in their teaching schedules, or because they ranked low on the seniority scale. Two of them remarked that they had accepted the assignment voluntarily, but the rest, along with most of the high school teachers, considered this responsibility as wholly undesirable. As for the principal, during his presentation at the meeting, he clarified that Room 10 indeed did not constitute a "complete" program of "attention to diversity," but that it was "surely better" than what a nearby high school had developed: there, a self-contained classroom, popularly known as "the dummies' class," represented the kind of tracking and segregating program that this principal would not have at Instituto Central. His professed rejection of such a program is significant because the Attention to Diversity policy, as mandated by the Galizan educational administration, indeed allowed for partial tracking (in some subjects), as well as separate ability- or behavior-management groupings organized into one- or two-year cycles (see Consellería de Educación e Ordenación Universitaria, 1999).

The principal's words set off a fairly intense debate amongst the teachers present, who did not directly oppose his stance, but who did question the general effectiveness of Room 10, including everything from handling recurrent visitors ("the regulars"), to the paucity of engaging learning materials in the room. Eventually the group proposed applying some stricter rules and consequences within the program; however, the conceivable latent tension between the tasks of tutoring and punishing in the same space remained unchallenged, just as, more importantly, the group failed to transcend the dominant conceptual framework for this program: that of attending to "diversity"—understood primarily as misbehavior—by means of discipline. What is more, the formal name of the Room 10 program, "Attention to Diversity" remained unquestioned, despite the contradictions.

THE DISRUPTIVE AS *DE FACTO* DIVERSITY

While the intent here is not to discredit the legitimate establishment of norms meant to promote mutual respect and viable coexistence in institutional settings, the intent *is* to point out that disciplinary sanctions serve as selective, negative deterrents in the absence of broadly based positive interventions that address the roots of the perceived problematic behavior. As the punitive consequences accumulate, along with the general feeling, in the case of the teachers interviewed, that one's role is more that of oppressor than of mentor—or in McLaren's (1999) terms, that of *hegemonic overlord* than of *liminal servant* (as shall be explored in further detail below)—the tendency to equate sociocultural diversity with misconduct becomes all the more apparent. In this sense, it is therefore crucial to examine how this tendency emerges from everyday institutional practice. What is it about this educational institution and the dynamics occurring within its realms that can lead to this form of discrimination?

In the case of Instituto Central, the 20 teachers interviewed (eleven transferees and nine original staff members) reacted similarly when faced with the challenge represented by the problematized students, locating the sources of their perceived behavior problems in four main causation factors: (1) the specific students and their "deficient" social environments; (2) the "unrealistic" structuring of schooling; (3) the "elitist mentality" of some of the teachers themselves; and (4) ineffective teacher education. Each one of these perceptions has its implications for attending to diversity in the teaching profession, but as we shall see, some of them held more sway than others at Instituto Central.

BLAMING THE VICTIM, OR THE CULTURAL OTHER
AS A PROBLEM

As an example of the first causation factor cited above, one major complaint shared by the teachers interviewed was that—in addition to the observable stress many experienced in their interactions with the nonconformist students—they were concerned that the academic achievement of "the rest of the students" was being adversely affected by the "troublemakers." This attitude, in which a minority collective or individual is perceived as more or less directly responsible for harm suffered by the majority, has been characterized in the research as "blaming the victim" (see, for example, Sue and Padilla, 1986). In other words, nonconformist students—many of whom are themselves victims of sociocultural disenfranchisement and accumulated school failure—receive the burden of the blame for conflicts arising in the multicultural educational setting. The failure on the part of institutional agents to deindividualize conflict, or to situate it in its broader social context—a reality documented by ethnographers such as Paul Willis (1981) or Douglas Foley (1990)—results in a failure to address the underlying and interrelated sources of conflict, and in a tendency to repress through a "discourse of legitimation" (Foucault, 1980), in an institutional culture and structure that is upheld against the essentialized cultural Other.[10]

It is also worth recalling here Foucault's insight that institutional structures of control are continually met with both intended and unintended manifestations of resistance and/or compliance on the part of all participants subject to such control. Blaming the nontraditional students can be conceived as one such manifestation of teacher resistance to change—a resistance resulting, as Apple (1995), Hargreaves (1994), McLaren (1999), and others have pointed out, in part from ideology, in part from context rituals and constraints, and in part from greater historical socioeconomic dynamics. As for the students, they too continually challenge the authority vested in the hegemonic culture of schooling. Through an ethnography at a Toronto Catholic secondary school, for instance, Peter McLaren (1999) documented the ways in which working class Portuguese immigrant students resisted conforming to behavior norms derived from middle class Anglo-Saxon culture by frequently attempting to impose what this researcher refers to as their "streetcorner state" (characterized by any student's spontaneous *modus operandi* outside of institutional settings). Likewise, Laurie Olsen (1997) has depicted how Latino immigrant students at an urban high school in California initially attempted to resist internalizing the racialized definitions of themselves imposed by schoolmates, teachers and US society at large, but eventually felt the need to position themselves within one or another dominant racial category in order to "fit in," while being simultaneously marginalized from the center. According to McCarthy and Dimitriadis (2000), this process of negative assimilation often involves some dose of Nietzschean "resentment" or negation of the ethnic or racial Other in oneself.

A couple of Roma students whom I interviewed and observed at school, at home in the settlement, and at a local community outreach center, seemed to be struggling with this very process. In what can be considered a significant instance of student agency and resistance, one of these boys practically pleaded with me to have him and his friend transferred to a nearby high school because, at Instituto Central, he said, "We've been figured out" (*pillados*). That is, he felt the two of them could no longer "start over" because they had become "regulars" in Room 10, and been preemptively pigeon-holed as "bad" (*malos*), as he saw it. He thus seemed to view their current school identities as immutable and reified, each identity having developed a kind of life of its own. He added that, "Here, they treat us Gypsies like dogs," whereas his impression of the other school—an impression in part derived from Roma acquaintances there—was clearly more favorable.

Curiously enough, that neighboring high school was the same one the principal had described as maintaining a segregated, remedial ("dummy") class for students behind grade level, most of whom were also Gypsies. Thus, this student's hopes of gaining "a second chance" there may unfortunately have already been thwarted in important ways, given the dominant-culture educators' disqualification of said program. Whereas a range of international scholars of ethnic, racial, class- and gender-related antagonism in education acknowledge that members of oppressed collectives can often find support in contexts of culturally homogeneous educational groupings—in what might be referred to, in a broader sense, as a "war of manoeuver" (Gramsci, 1971; also see Hall, 1996)—these same scholars also denounce the limits of this support.[11] Such programs become counterproductive when they discourage social integration by addressing one group's needs over all others, or when they emerge as mere by-products of social exclusion. This last dynamic is most visible in the formation of school ghettos, where educational expectations remain low and *de facto* segregation high. In any case, the bleak state of affairs for these boys at Instituto Central drove them to envision an alternative institutional existence elsewhere. This desire can be interpreted as an attempt to regain control over their own identity formation, and to escape institutional control mechanisms requiring that they conform to unfamiliar—and at times hostile or repressive—cultural norms. It is a situation that bears a strong resemblance to the experiences of minority students at another high school as far away as Texas. Ethnographer Douglas Foley (1990) offers a vivid overview of the strikingly similar dynamics occurring there:

> In this case, the vast majority of Mexicano youth were not getting ahead, escaping the sting of class and racial prejudice, or developing a well-articulated class consciousness. They were tracked into practical sections of semi-literates and passed on through social promotion policies until more than 50 percent dropped out. The vatos ended up being a thorn in the administration's side and amusing entertainers that enlivened the deadening routine of academic work—and school failures. (p. 203)

As Rizvi (1998) has observed, the practices of so-called integration in education have tended to promote mere access to schooling for traditionally excluded students, while they have done very little to challenge the actual culture of schooling or to make learning itself more accessible:

> Pedagogic and curriculum practices have remained largely unchanged with respect to the need to cater for a wide range of differences which are now acknowledged to exist in schools. [...] Schools are still based on the assumptions of homogeneity and uniformity. They still require conformity and obedience to rules that are based on the requirements of administrative convenience rather than moral principles. (Rizvi, 1998, p. 55)

Which brings us back to the first perceived causation cited above: the cultural-Other-as-problem. How might these boys indeed resist such a reductive and essentializing label which denies the organic, dynamic nature of cross-cultural contact, learning, and identity formation, while reproducing ethnocentric, even racist, forms of discrimination at school? Some light must therefore be shed on the deeper issues underlying the predominant reaction among teachers when challenged by nonconforming students such as the two cited above—whose ethnicity, gender, and social class are overrepresented in programs throughout Spain such as that of Room 10 (Fernández-Enguita, 1999).

IDENTITY, IDEOLOGY, AND REPRESENTATION IN SCHOOLING

As a digression from our discussion about the teachers' four perceived causes of nonconformist behavior in these and other students, several facets of a dominant practical ideology can be identified in the staff's practices that operate to the detriment of the students concerned. Ideology is understood here in the Althusserian (1971) sense as not primarily produced within the conceptual realm of mere ideas and knowledge, but as formed, conditioned, and exercised within a concrete, material world of daily social practices, including the context of professional activity. Ideology, in this sense, represents a "subjective slant on the world [that] is a matter of lived relations rather than controvertible propositions" (Eagleton, 2007, p. 152). This practical basis for the formation of ideologies thus serves to legitimate and reinforce particular ideological adherences. The problem is that, as Kickbusch and Everhart (1985) have argued, educational interventions that—due to this "practical ideology"—are assumed to be necessary (such as that of Room 10) can contribute to the reproduction of the very problems they aim to solve.

The first facet of this dominant practical ideology consists of a conception shared especially by the original staff, and concerns the particular intellectual/

academic and cultural standards that "most students" should attain through curricular contents that *have been* successfully transmitted and assimilated in the past—a ritual reference based on a relatively privileged student body that has now become more heterogeneous and less privileged overall. And although this conception was openly censured by the school principal, by several of the transferred teachers, and by some original staff members, it was nonetheless considered to inform the prevailing ideological stance regarding educational priorities at the school.

Secondly, in interviews, the teachers agreed more or less on what constituted a minimally acceptable social climate in the classroom, one necessary for acquiring the desired curricular standards: the students should be attentive and obedient *vis-à-vis* the teacher's authority, although there was observable variation as to how much and what kind of student talk was permitted. Even so, in the five regular classes observed, verbal interactions and learning dynamics were teacher-centered, and student participation individually oriented. In two of these classrooms, however, the four Roma students (two boys per class) tended to count amongst the most vocal and active of pupils.

Lastly, and as previously indicated, nearly all 19 of the regular-program teachers commented in interviews that what the traditional majority students stood to lose in a "disrupted" classroom environment lay at the heart of their concerns over the nonconformist students, in addition to their own discomfort when working with the latter. In other words, the *fundamental* injustice was that the problems attributed to one or two students affected the rest. Likewise, what the "problem" students lost by being dismissed from class did not figure directly into the teachers' discourse on this matter. When asked to consider the rights of the nonconformist students, the teachers mainly associated these with a hypothetical "right to not have to attend school." This perceived right, expressed by over half of the respondents, in turn justified further comments suggesting the separation of such students from the majority, either through the alternative behavior- or ability-based groupings permitted by the Galizan Attention to Diversity policy, or through more substantial structural modifications of the basic legislation (the LOGSE)—an option that soon became a reality through the conservative LOCE counterreform (the Quality in Education Act of 2002) and the most recent LOE of 2006.[12]

What was evident in these educators' ideologically informed discourse and actions was the centrality of historically contextualized and ritualized cultural points of reference. That is, what was missing in the majority of the staff was a professional disposition or a practical ideology leading to performance rituals favorable to the nontraditional students, as opposed to the majority. Amongst the roles teachers adopted through their performance as professional educators, at best I observed that of "teacher-as-entertainer," and at worst, that of "teacher-as-hegemonic-overlord," but rarely that of "teacher-as-liminal-servant" (McLaren, 1999). McLaren describes the liminal servant as

> both a convener of customs and a cultural provocateur—yet she (or he) [...] does not subordinate the political rights of students to their utility as future members of the labour force. [...] Whereas the teacher-as-entertainer is intent upon conditioning for sameness; the liminal servant nurtures counter-hegemonic forces through the formation of an alter-ideology. [...] She is closer to her students than to her profession. (ibid., pp. 115–116)

The cumulative effects, then, of the institutionalized conditioning of dominant performance types and the formation of practical ideology requires that we critically reconsider the role of ritual in teacher agency.

The structure of schooling

The significance of ritual is further visible in the second source factor cited by nearly all the interviewees as partially responsible for, on the one hand, the perceived conflicts related to student diversity, and on the other, the failure of Room 10 to diminish their occurrence. "Modifying the entire system" made up this most frequently cited means for solving these problems. Not surprisingly, the types of changes suggested had much in common with a return to the ritually familiar, precompulsory system. While many of those interviewed rejected the possibility of establishing tracks for specific students, as outlined in the Galizan Attention to Diversity policy, they were instead inclined to suggest streaming or "itineraries" of study applicable to the entire student body. For example, such streams might commence at age 14 (when noncompulsory secondary education used to begin). One stream might be oriented toward terminating all schooling at age 16; another toward continuing on to Vocational Education; and another toward entering the two-year College Preparatory Program. In fact, similar streams were established in 2002 as a result of the LOCE counterreform (but never implemented due to the shift toward Socialist Party leadership in Spain in 2004). Many of the interviewees suggested that general streaming or tracking would not stigmatize the students as much as the Attention to Diversity schemes were. However, the suggested streaming mirrored past rituals in that all students would be presorted according to "choice" or to qualifications. After all, and significantly, a common lament among the original staff was the fact that, in the previous secondary school system, the pupils were "manageable," so why not presort the current student body as well?

Colleague "mentality"

A third set of responses regarding the purported causes of behavior problems reflected an ideological disposition that competed with those oriented toward blaming the students or restructuring schooling. At least six interviewees—including two from the original cohort, and four newcomers from the primary school—considered that the "elitist mentality" of many of the traditional staff members constituted a significant source of conflict at the school. According to this view, a general "snobbiness" reigned amongst the senior staff, as well as a lack of willingness to collaborate and pool efforts for the benefit of the nontraditional students. But those who the six respondents claimed received the brunt of this "corporatism" were the pupils, who were also said to be labeled by the "elitist" teachers as "hopeless cases," "not worth investing in," or "incapable of attaining the 'high' academic standards" traditionally maintained at the school. As a possible solution to this problem, the informants suggested not only "recycling" the staff (through the retirement of older members), but also improving professional development and restructuring secondary education in the ways outlined earlier. In any case, care must be taken not to accept at face value this critique of class-related discrimination and practical ideology, as it may simultaneously constitute a kind of evasion tactic, or "passing the hot potato" on to one's colleagues. For instance, the Resource Specialist (from Special Education) considered that there was a "generalized lack of contact and collaboration with the students' families," which, as she saw it, was more serious than the division amongst the staff.

Professional development

Finally, the "mentality" issue also extended into a fourth cited cause of perceived misbehavior in students: that of inadequate professional preparation and development. A great majority of the teachers considered themselves and the rest of the staff to be poorly prepared to "deal with" the nontraditional students at the school. This position was presented and qualified, however, more as a critique of the system than of their own commitment to ongoing professional development. It extended into preservice teacher education, but was mainly centered, on the one hand, on deficient inservice preparation for the LOGSE reform (including CSE), and on the other, on the actual design, once again, of the LOGSE itself, and the perceived lack of teacher involvement in its development.

This last critique is especially noteworthy in that it may just reveal that these teachers assumed the stated reform goals were indeed contingent not only upon certain organizational constructs supposedly beyond their control, but also upon their own professional backing of the reform. For this very reason, the importance of the interpretive and ideological framework of these educators, as generative or "artistic" (Elliott, 1991) mediators of educational policy, cannot be downplayed or ignored (as has also been argued by Ball, 1987 and Hargreaves, 1994). By extraction, nor can their role in the politics of representation and difference—including the reproduction of bias—be overly attributed to institutional constraints. After all, education as an institution, as Bourdieu and Passeron (1977) have asserted, is part-product and part-producer of hegemonic culture. This notwithstanding, it became clear that the Galizan education authorities had indeed made little organized effort to facilitate access to professional development associated with the reform (e.g., nonteaching days allocated for professional development, or a series of cohesive inservice sessions at the teachers' work-site, etc.).

POLICY, PRACTICE, AND PARADOX
IN THE REPRODUCTION OF SOCIOCULTURAL BIAS

Theoretical perspectives on injustice in education have tended to set symbolic or cultural agency off against material or structural determinants. However, the teachers' combined comments and actions attest to the interrelatedness, and yet *nonsynchronous* (McCarthy, 1990) or contradictory dynamics, in and between cultural and structural tendencies. Competing ideologies were continually played out, disputed and negotiated among the staff. Some indications of this competition with the dominant ideology—which locates conflict in the cultural Other—are reflected in teachers' comments related to: reportedly desiring improved teacher education; resisting certain tracking procedures; denouncing "elitist mentalities"; desiring a greater degree of collaboration amongst educational professionals; and, as observed in a few cases, making some attempts to adapt instruction to individual learning needs through modified paper-and-pencil activities in the regular classroom, in Room 10, and for homework.

Contrary to these potentially critical stances, however, most staff members also tended: to send more Roma students to Room 10 (in proportion to their number at school) than any other ethnic group; to associate student diversity—most notably that involving Gypsy students—with behavior problems; to treat the symptoms of conflict with disciplinary means instead of seriously investigating the causes or exploring more culturally informed and global pedagogical responses; and to envision segregational streaming measures in order to ensure, and to favor, the academic "rights" of the majority students. Moreover, they generally failed to establish ongoing contact with the most disenfranchised sectors of the school community, or to collaborate with colleagues and other professionals in productive ways. They also avoided interactions with the "disruptive" youth (most teachers were assigned to Room 10 against their will), and they tended to blame either the students, "the system," or their colleagues as opposed to their own actions.

Clearly, multiple forms of discrimination—especially those involving ethnocentrism, class bias and racism—were at work in the teachers' interactions with the Gypsy students. We must not forget, however, to *totalize* (McLaren, 1994) this problematic portrayal of professional agency, by situating it in its larger context. The teachers' perceptions, imaginings, decisions, and actions—as components of their practical ideologies—were clearly conditioned not only by institutional constraints, but by underlying sociocultural factors as well. Concerning institutional constraints, the interviews revealed that none of the teachers suggested, for example, to increase the number of educators available to students in the regular classrooms as a viable response to the perceived behavior problems. Such an option was later described as institutionally "impossible" given the administration's hiring record. Moreover, as regards the reported lack of staff cooperation, the interviewees did not transcend the personal-attitude level. For instance, no references were made as to the negative effects of the Balkanization of schooling—for example, isolated disciplines and the nonintegrated curriculum, single-teacher classrooms, separate departments, strict scheduling requirements, etc.—none of which are conducive to collaboration or to a more relational and responsive learning environment (Hargreaves, 1994; Torres Santomé, 1998).

Along these same lines but on a larger scale, educational ethnographer Barry Troyna (1995) revealed, through a study conducted in 1992, the negative repercussions of institutional arrangements applied in England and Wales, where Local Education Authorities were disbanded by a 1988 reform act and replaced by Local Management of Schools schemes. This process of decentralization in turn led to the weakening of the already minimal antiracist education enacted under the auspices of the Local Education Authorities.

In addition to the influence of these kinds of institutional constraints, some latent sociocultural factors must also be considered. The ethnic and generational homogeneity of the staff constitutes an important source of cultural difference *vis-à-vis* their new students, as do the teachers' ritual notions of behavior norms and "high standards" in their workplace. The conflicts arising from perceived hierarchies between the original and transferred teacher-cohorts are also significant to the extent that they attest to the hegemonic and exclusionary tendencies associated with social class. That is, the perceived sociocultural disparities between professional groups may lead to corporatism, a lack of coordination amongst the staff, weaker commitments to serving specific students, and, ultimately, an unequal distribution of cultural capital throughout the educational system (Bourdieu and Passeron, 1977). Moreover, teacher engagement with the Roma community surrounding Instituto Central was nearly nonexistent: teachers and students were separated not only physically through material living conditions (place of residence), but also symbolically through differences in cultural (including racialized) identity.[13] And nonconformist behavior on the part of some Gypsy students only seemed to widen the gap. One teacher, drawn to tears during an informal gathering, expressed her frustration with some of these students by remarking, "For years I've had no problems; but now, suddenly, I have to deal with *this*!"

We must nevertheless once again be careful not to target teacher agency alone (or individual manifestations of practical ideology) as the sole factor(s) at work in this form of professional rejection and disengagement from the students served. And here is where the additional factor of gender enters into these discriminatory dynamics. For instance, regarding the feminization of the teaching profession in Spain, Mariano Fernández-Enguita (1999b) has criticized what he perceives to be a growing tendency amongst women teachers toward minimizing their professional commitments by demanding reduced hours or abandoning the school site during noninstructional working hours. The fact, however, that women teachers as workers generally attend to higher levels of daily unpaid labor at home than male workers do, helps explain the formers' desire for more time off from work. To this respect, researchers have argued that the gendered division of labor, as a structural concern, indirectly contributes to the formation of practical ideology in schooling (see Weis, 1988). It also implicates these teachers—just as it does their students—in a nonsynchronous interaction of sexist, classist, racist, and cultural biases in the reproduction of inequality through professional agency. On this point, we should recall that the staff members at Instituto Central who were placed in direct charge of Room 10 were all women, many of whom ranked low on the seniority scale. Moreover, additional gender-related antagonisms between teachers and Roma students complicated matters: they involved both the disproportionate abandonment of schooling amongst adolescent Gypsy girls (as compared to boys), as well as the perception amongst many women teachers that Gypsy boys tended to disregard teacher authority more in women than in men. As we have seen, perceptions such as these can become generalized and ritualized, operating both tacitly and organically through individuals and institutions alike.

Lastly, international scholars of educational reform have pointed out that teachers have not only traditionally received societal blame for the perceived failure of reform efforts initiated outside their conventional (and ritual) realms of professional practice (Apple, 1995; Martínez Bonafé, 1998; Popkewitz, 1991), but they have also come under attack from today's growing corporate culture in education (Torres Santomé, 2001; Whitty et al., 1998). Neoconservative reformers and parents alike treat standardized achievement scores as quality indicators of educators and schools, as if these were mere products, production line workers, and factories to be managed and selected according to neoliberal market logics and patterns of consumption and investment. In these cases, there is a blatant disregard for civil liberties, equal rights, or variations among the sociocultural circumstances of the respective school communities. Such institutional and structural dynamics must therefore be factored into critiques of teaching professionals themselves.

This is not to let teachers off the proverbial hook, but rather to locate their reproductive tendencies within the larger, multiple-sited, structural, cultural, and often nonsynchronous processes of educational exclusion. This will aid our attempts to deconstruct the biases and to envision some ways out of the cycles of oppression.

IMPLICATIONS FOR A TRANSFORMATIVE CROSS-CULTURAL PEDAGOGY

With this account of the ways in which the teachers at a Spanish secondary school incorporated the novel presence of Gypsy students into their professional lives, the aim has been to reveal how institutionalized expressions of bias can be reproduced through local teacher agency, even when top-down equity policy, such as the LOGSE reform, is enacted to provide students who do not fit the ideal-typical cultural mold with greater access to education. When we consider teacher agency at Instituto Central within a broader historical, political, and transnational context, we see how it is part-product of a very particular confluence in Spain of cultural, political, and economic dynamics both local and global: in the local sense, political sentiments during the postdictatorship were ripe for change and open to the progressive investment in social welfare and democratic process. In the more global sense, this openness—as represented through the Spanish mass media of the 1980s—reflected a kind of generalized anxiousness to "catch up" economically and socially with so-called developed nations throughout Europe and the West. Subsequently, as the decade of the 1990s unfolded, influences from global dynamics such as immigration, neoliberal market forces, and neoconserva-tive backlash became familiar in the still newly reformed Spanish State. Thus, some of the teachers from the study observed that whereas student heterogeneity resulting from rapidly growing immigrant populations in Spain, as well as the LOGSE's instating *compulsory* secondary education, may have helped some edu-cators to perceive old prejudices toward the Gypsies in new ways, it is clear that more conservative reactions to such global trends were gaining a foothold—the move toward streaming procedures serving as an example. It is through this larger lens, then, that this study is also meant to serve as a call to educators such as those at Instituto Central to reflect upon their own agency within these broader dynamics, and to challenge the potentially harmful ritual and global references that inform their practical ideologies.

Given the complex confluence and interplay of structural and cultural factors that figure into the discriminatory teacher practices described above—that is, blaming the students, the system, one's colleagues, or professional preparation for their continued marginalization—a potentially powerful approach to the disruption of such ritualized bias in schooling would require that educators at all levels, but especially those working in the schools, attempt to transcend the traditional divide between theory, policy, and practice. Through the development of action research projects in their respective school communities, teachers who are themselves overwhelmingly treated as the mere technicians of policy-makers might thus reclaim pedagogies from the experts, who frequently lack direct experience with—and thus adequate knowledge about—most levels of institutional conditioning of school-site practice. Teachers would in this way participate in the reconstruction of schooling that pedagogical activist groups in Spain have long pursued through their conception of school as a key site for democratic participation and deliberation (see also Castoriadis, 1991).[14]

Carr and Kemmis (1986), and Atweh, Kemmis, and Weeks (1998) approach action research in ways that are particularly amenable to this end, as they embrace an actively promoted exchange and development of critical pedagogic inquiry and intervention in and between all spheres of pedagogical knowledge production, including that pertaining to students, parents, scholars and other community members. If we consider that this process has ethical and political implications, and that ethics—in keeping with Bakhtin's (1993) understanding of it—cannot exist in theory but only in practice, the performative in action research becomes highly significant: educators may become not only more reflective, but also more deliberative and collaborative as researchers, practitioners and community agents. In the process, the participants' moral commitments to actively contesting the complex manifestations of bias in their own workplace are potentially enhanced through the diverse perspectives brought to the collective negotiation of meanings.[15]

Opening up institutional spaces to more relational, inclusive and deliberative forms of professional communication offers a kind of "dialogical hope" (Benhabib, 1992) for overcoming the seemingly hopeless (e.g., discriminatory) realities of schooling. By contrast, the traditionally closed and hierarchical institutional realms of cultural production in education have conditioned the prioritization of ideologically informed decisions in practice (Carr, 1995). The teachers of this study have demonstrated this tendency through their performance of contradictory, potentially critical, but predominantly oppressive practical ideologies. In this sense, and in keeping with Zeichner's (1995) recommendations, planting the seed of critical action research in preservice teacher education is paramount to empowering teacher agency. Above all, forging stronger links between teaching, research, policy, and socially responsible action is most promising when approached not only collectively but in tandem with the needs and participation of otherwise disenfranchised school community members, or as a kind of social movement (Sleeter, 1996). In this lies one of the means for promoting the kinds of cross-cultural exchanges so crucial to the fair participation and representation in education of subaltern groups such as the Roma.

Educators willing to transform ideologies, actions and the institution itself—one that is historically steeped in bias toward specific cultural and economic preferences and selection processes (see Ladwig, 2000 or Varela and Álvarez-Uría, 1991)—might further stand to gain from reenvisioning their role at work as that of McLaren's "liminal servant," and as that of "critical public intellectual" (Giroux with Shannon, 1997). The first of these might involve, for example, a cross-cultural commitment to transgressing racist, classist, and sexist ideologies reflected in the curriculum. According to McCarthy (1993), a multicultural focus on racism, for example, would entail, among other engagements, critically examining the construction of school knowledge and the centering of Western (dominant) culture in the curriculum; pursuing not only the cultural diversity of school knowledge, but the inherent "relationality" of that knowledge; developing a much more "nuanced" discussion of the racial identities not only of the minority groups, but also of the majority; and promoting democratic initiatives in the curriculum, in pedagogical practice, and in social relations at school. As for the teacher as public intellectual, taking on such a role may ultimately influence not only public opinion but policy-making itself, especially if such intellectual activity is approached, once again, as a collective effort.

Some of the staff at Instituto Central have already viewed an earlier version of this analysis. A forthcoming broader analysis will be presented to all participating educators, students, their families, and community agents as well. It is further hoped that this process serve to inspire the teachers to not only reflect more critically on their praxis in a prebiased institution, but to actively promote collaborative, community-based, cross-cultural pedagogical alternatives, so that it can be said, at least in their case, that schooling is for the Roma ... as well.

NOTES

1. This chapter is closely based on Teasley (2005).
2. The Organic Law for the General Ordering of the Educational System (*Ley Orgánica 1/1990, de 3 de octubre, de Ordenación General del Sistema Educativo*) can be retrieved from the Web site: http://wwwn.mec.es/mecd/atencion/educacion/hojas/E_SistemaEduc/e-1-4.htm (last retrieved on November 2, 2007).
3. Such students and their parents generally refer to themselves in Spanish as *gitanos*—meaning Gypsies—as opposed to *romà* or Roma. This latter term has emerged of late primarily amongst

activists and scholars as a means of promoting a historically informed, transnational ethnic identity. Out of respect for both postures, the terms Gypsy and Roma will be used interchangeably in this chapter.

4. To view the contents of the LOCE, see Ministerio de la Presidencia (2000): http://www.boe. es/boe/dias/2002-12-24/pdfs/A45188-45220.pdf (last retrieved on November 2, 2007).

5. *Ley Orgánica 2/2006, de 3 de mayo, de Educación* (Organic Law on Education). This law may be consulted at the Web site: http://www.mec.es/mecd/gabipren/documentos/A17158-17207.pdf (last retrieved on November 2, 2007).

6. This autonomous community is commonly referred to as "Galicia", although "Galiza" is also officially recognized. In recent years, certain sectors of Galizan society and government have been promoting the use of "Galiza" as more coherent with this polity's linguistic legacy (the persecution of which was rampant during the dictatorship).

7. The manual *Atención á diversidade: medidas organizativas* offers an overview of this policy. See Consellería de Educación e Ordenación Universitaria (1999), or the pdf version at the *Xunta de Galicia* Web site: http://www.edu.xunta.es/portal/mostrarfile?tipoRecursoCampoID=6f78dc5f-c0a8fd03-006e7a5b-393b5b95&recursoID=0d38412c-4532174a-01e7a26c-23042b46&lleng=gl (last retrieved December 6, 2007).

8. Due to space limitations, a detailed overview of these measures cannot be included here. See Consellería de Educación e Ordenación Universitaria (1999).

9. At the time, school principals were (and still are) elected into office by staff, student, and parent representatives. This particular principal assured me that he "owed his election" especially to the voting parents.

10. As for the construction of the Other as an essentialized, static being, Bhabha (1994) has pointed out that while the *object* of identification is always ambivalent, the *agency* itself in identification is, more significantly, "… never pure or holistic but always constituted in a process of substitution, displacement or projection" (ibid., p. 162). Likewise, Hall (1992) has denounced the myth of ethnic and cultural absolutism, and underscored the undeniable, historical processes of ethnic "hybridity" of national cultures in the West.

11. McCarthy (1998) has argued that the forms of cultural resistance pursued by African Americans through alternative institutions of learning can be characterized as a kind of "war of manoeuver," but that a "war of position" (challenging dominant ideologies and institutions *from within*) has also been instrumental and necessary. See as well: Freire (1970) on the need for indigenous literacy programs to transcend the sole use of local linguistic and cultural knowledge; hooks (1994) on her own experience in US educational contexts of varying degrees of racial homogeneity; Fernández-Enguita (1999a) on the problems with the bridge-school experience at Gypsy settlements in Spain; Willis (1981) on the false resistance implied in students' retreating into (or over-identification with) certain more restrictive practices associated with subordinated social-class cultures; McCarthy and Dimitriadis (2000) on the negative effects of the essentialized space of racial origins; and Nieto (2002), Grant et al. (1999), Sleeter (1996), and many others on the tragedies of ghetto schools and the benefits of multicultural education.

12. See Teasley (2002) for a critical overview of the Quality in Education Act (*Ley Orgánica de Calidad de la Educación* - LOCE, 12/2002).

13. One teacher arriving toward the end of my presence at the school took charge of Room 10 in part because he had worked for years with Roma communities through a local Christian charity organization. But his is a story apart.

14. See, for example, the agenda of the State Confederation of Movements for Pedagogical Renewal ("MRPs"), at: http://cmrp.pangea.org/ (last retrieved January 10, 2008).

15. Not all approaches to action research escape positivist influence (Kincheloe, 1993). Moreover, although I concur with most of the premises set forth by John Elliott, I beg to differ with him on the role of consultation: while Elliott rejects teachers' resorting to "experts" at any cost, I do not believe that all aspects of consultancy should be thus disqualified. On this point, Zeichner (1995) argues a strong case for closing the gap between university- and school-based realms of research.

REFERENCES

Althusser, L. (1971). *Lenin and philosophy*. London: New Left Books.

Apple, M. (1995). *Education and power* (2nd edition). Boston, MA: Routledge and Kegan Paul.

Asociación Presencia Gitana. (1992). *La escolarización de los niños gitanos e itinerantes en España: Investigación-acción y coordinación*. Madrid: Editorial Presencia Gitana.

Asociación Presencia Gitana. (2000). See declarations made by the Association, as cited in the daily journal *El País*, December 4, p. 34.

Asociación Secretariado General Gitano. (2000). Unpublished information presented at the conference: Social Services and Intervention with the Gypsy Population: Access to Normalized Resources, November 10 and 11. A Coruña, Galiza, Spain.

Atweh, B., Kemmis, S. and Weeks, P. (Eds.). (1998). *Action research in practice: Partnerships for social justice in education*. London: Routledge.

Bakhtin, M. (1993). *Toward a philosophy of the act*. Austin, TX: University of Texas Press.

Ball, S. J. (1987). *The micropolitics of the school*. London: Methuen/Routledge and Kegan Paul.

Benhabib, S. (1992). *Situating the self: Gender, community and postmodernism in contemporary ethics*. New York: Routledge.

Benhabib, S. (2002). *The claims of culture: Equality and diversity in the global era*. Princeton, NJ: Princeton University Press.

Bernstein, B. (2000). *Pedagogy, symbolic control and identity: Theory, research, critique*. New York: Rowman & Littlefield.

Bhabha, H. (1994). *The location of culture*. London: Routledge.

Bourdieu, P. and Passeron, J. C. (1977). *Reproduction in education, society and culture*. Beverly Hills, CA: Sage.

Calvo Buezas, T. (1990). *¿España racista?: Voces payas sobre los gitanos*. Barcelona: Anthropos/Ilustre Colegio Nacional de Doctores y Licenciados en Ciencias Políticas y Sociológicas.

Calvo Buezas, T. (2000). *Inmigración y racismo: Así sienten los jóvenes del siglo XXI*. Madrid: Cauce.

Carr, W. (1995). *For education: Towards critical educational inquiry*. Buckingham: Open University Press.

Carr, W. and Kemmis, S. (1986). *Becoming critical: Education, knowledge, and action research*. London: Falmer.

Castoriadis, C. (1991). *Philosophy, politics, autonomy: Essays in political philosophy*. New York: Oxford University Press.

Consellería de Educación e Ordenación Universitaria (1999). *Atención á diversidade: Medidas organizativas*. Santiago de Compostela: Xunta de Galicia. Available in digital format at the *Xunta de Galicia* Web site: http://www.edu.xunta.es/portal/mostrarfile?tipoRecursoCampoID=6f78dc5f-c0a8fd03-006e7a5b-393b5b95&recursoID=0d38412c-4532174a-01e7a26c-23042b46&dlleng=gl (last retrieved on December 6, 2007).

Courthiade, M. (1998). Estructura dialectal de la lengua romaní. *Interface*, No. 31, pp. 9–14.

Eagleton, T. (2007). *Ideology: An introduction*. London: Verso.

Elliott, J. (1991). *Action research for educational change*. Milton Keynes: Open University Press.

Fernández-Enguita, M. (1999a). *Alumnos gitanos en la escuela paya: Un estudio sobre las relaciones étnicas en el sistema educativo*. Barcelona: Ariel Praticum.

Fernández-Enguita, M. (1999b). ¿Es pública la escuela pública? *Cuadernos de Pedagogía*, No. 284, pp. 76–81.

Foley, D. E. (1990). *Learning capitalist culture: Deep in the heart of Tejas*. Philadelphia, PA: University of Pennsylvania Press.

Fonseca, I. (1996). *Bury me standing: The Gypsies and their journey*. New York: Knopf.

Foucault, M. (1980). *Power/knowledge: Selected interviews and other writings 1972–1977*. New York: Pantheon.

Fraser, N. (1995). From redistribution to recognition? Dilemmas of justice in a "post-socialist" age. *New Left Review*, Vol. I, No. 212, pp. 68–93.

Freire, P. (1970). *Pedagogy of the oppressed*. New York: The Seabury Press.

Giroux, H. with Shannon, P. (1997). Cultural studies and pedagogy as performative practice: Toward an introduction. In H. Giroux with P. Shannon (Eds.), *Education and cultural studies: Toward a performative practice* (pp. 1–9). New York: Routledge.

Gramsci, A. (1971). Problems of Marxism. In Q. Hoare and G. Nowell Smith (Eds.), *Selections from the prison notebooks of Antonio Gramsci* (pp. 378–472). New York: International Publications.

Grant, C. A. (1999). Personal and intellectual motivation for working from the margin. In C. A. Grant (Ed.), *Multicultural research: A reflective engagement with race, class, gender and sexual orientation* (pp. 157–167). London: Falmer Press.

Hall, S. (1992). Our mongrel selves. *New Statesman & New Society*, 121/88 (4089/1530), 6 (in "Borderlands" supplement), no page numbers present.

Hall, S. (1996). Gramsci's relevance for the study of race and ethnicity. In D. Morley and K.-H. Chen (Eds.), *Stuart Hall: Critical dialogues in cultural studies* (pp. 411–440). New York: Routledge.

Hargreaves, A. (1994). *Changing teachers, changing times: Teachers' work and culture in the postmodern age*. London: Casell.

hooks, b. (1994). *Teaching to transgress: Education as the practice of freedom*. New York: Routledge.

Jover, G. and Reyero, D. (2000, Fall). Images of the other in childhood: Researching the limits of cultural diversity in education from the standpoint of new anthropological methodologies. *Encounters on Education/Encuentros sobre Educación/Rencontres sur l'Éducation*, 1. Web site: http://educ.queensu.ca/publications/encounters/volume1/jover_reyero.pdf (last retrieved on December 15, 2007).

Kickbusch, K. W. and Everhart, R. B. (1985). Curriculum, practical ideology, and class contradiction. *Curriculum Inquiry*, Vol. 15, No. 3, pp. 281–317.

Kincheloe, J. L. (1993). *Toward a critical politics of teacher thinking*. Westport, CT: Bergen & Garvey.

Ladwig, J. G. (2000). World institutions, world dispositions: Curriculum in the world-cultural institution of schooling. In R. Mahalingam and C. McCarthy (Eds.), *Multicultural curriculum: New directions for social theory, practice, and policy* (pp. 56–69). New York: Routledge.

Liégeois, J. P. (1998). *Minoría y escolaridad: El paradigma gitano*. Madrid: Editorial Presencia Gitana.

Martínez Bonafé, J. (1998). *Trabajar en la escuela: Profesorado y reformas en el umbral del siglo XXI*. Madrid: Miño y Dávila Editores.

McCarthy, C. (1990). *Race and curriculum: Social inequality and the theories and politics of difference in contemporary research on schooling*. London: The Falmer Press.

McCarthy, C. (1993). After the canon: Knowledge and ideological representation in the multicultural discourse on curriculum reform. In C. McCarthy and W. Crichlow (Eds.), *Race, identity and representation in education* (pp. 288–305). New York: Routledge.

McCarthy, C. (1998). *The uses of culture: Education and the limits of ethnic affiliation*. New York: Routledge.

McCarthy, C. and Dimitriadis, G. (2000). Globalizing pedagogies: Power, resentment, and the renarration of difference. In R. Mahalingham and C. McCarthy (Eds.), *Multicultural curriculum: New directions for social theory, practice, and policy* (pp. 70–83). New York: Routledge.

McLaren, P. (1994). Multiculturalism and the postmodern critique: Toward a pedagogy of resistance and transformation. In H. A. Giroux and P. McLaren (Eds.), *Between borders: Pedagogy and the politics of cultural studies* (pp. 192–224). New York: Routledge.

McLaren, P. (1999). *Schooling as a ritual performance: Toward a political economy of educational symbols and gestures* (3rd Edition). New York: Rowman & Littlefield.

Nieto, S. (2002). *Language, culture and teaching: Critical perspectives for a new century.* Mahwah, NJ: Lawrence Erlbaum Associates.

Olsen, L. (1997). *Made in America: Immigrant students in our public schools.* New York: The New Press.

Popkewitz, T. S. (1991). *A political sociology of educational reform: Power/knowledge in teaching, teacher education and research.* New York: Teachers College Press.

Rizvi, F. (1998). Some thoughts on contemporary theories of social justice. In B. Atweh, S. Kemmis, and P. Weeks (Eds.), *Action research in practice: Partnerships for social justice in education* (pp. 47–56). London: Routledge.

San Román, T. (1997). *La diferencia inquietante: Viejas y nuevas estrategias culturales de los gitanos.* Madrid: Siglo XXI.

Sleeter, C. (1996). *Multicultural education as social activism.* Albany, NY: State University of New York.

Sue, S. and Padilla, A. (1986). Ethnic minority issues in the United States: Challenges for the educational system. In California State Department of Education (Ed.), *Beyond language: social and cultural factors in schooling language minority students* (pp. 35–75). Los Angeles, CA: Evaluation, Dissemination and Assessment Center, California State University.

Teasley, C. (2002). Perdidos en la batalla: El tratamiento del alumnado socioculturalmante diverso en la reforma de la LOGSE. *Revista Educar,* No. 29, pp. 67–90.

Teasley, C. (2005, May). Ambiguous legacy: Instituting student diversity at a Spanish secondary school. *Cultural Studies ↔ Critical Methodologies,* Vol. 5, No. 2, pp. 206–229.

Torres Santomé, J. (1998). *Globalización e interdisciplinariedad: El curriculum integrado.* Madrid: Morata.

Torres Santomé, J. (2001). *Educación en tiempos de neoliberalismo.* Madrid: Morata.

Torrione, M. (1994). El gitano-español: De la etiqueta germanesca a la catalogación lingüística (siglos XV–XVIII). In L. Martín Rojo, C. Gómez Esteban, F. Arranz Lozano, and Á. Gabilondo Pujol (Eds.), *Hablar y dejar hablar (Sobre racismo y xenofobia)* (pp. 95–112). Madrid: Universidad Autónoma de Madrid.

Troyna, B. (1995). The local management of schools and racial equality. In S. Tomlinson and M. Craft (Eds.), *Ethnic relations and Schooling: Policy and practice in the 1990s* (pp. 140–154). London: The Athlone Press.

Varela, J. and Álvarez-Uría, F. (1991). *Arqueología de la escuela.* Madrid: La Piqueta.

Vargas Clavería, J. and Gómez Alonso, J. (2003). Why Romà do not like mainstream schools: Voices of a people without territory. *Harvard Educational Review,* Vol. 73, No. 4, pp. 559–590.

Weis, L. (Ed.) (1988). *Class, race, and gender in American education.* Albany, NY: SUNY.

Whitty, G., Power, S., and Halpin, D. (1998). *Devolution and choice in education: The school, the state and the market.* Buckingham: Open University Press.

Willis, P. (1981). *Learning to labor: How working class kids get working class jobs.* New York: Teachers College Press.

Young, I. M. (2002). *Inclusion and democracy.* Oxford: Oxford University Press.

Zeichner, K. M. (1995). Beyond the divide of teacher research and academic research. *Teachers and Teaching: Theory and Practice,* Vol. 1, No. 2, pp. 153–171.

CHAPTER FIFTEEN

Understanding THE neoliberal context OF race AND schooling IN THE age OF globalization

CAMERON MCCARTHY

University of Illinois at Urbana-Champaign

This chapter is written against the backdrop of important changes in social dynamics taking place on a global scale—dynamics which have profound implications for racial affiliation and "its" cultural and social uses in the new century. In the early 1990s scholars such as Michael Omi and Howard Winant (1994), Cornel West (1993) and Jurjo Torres Santomé (2001) began to call attention to the increasing pattern of instability and uncertainty in the processes of racial affiliation and communal identification that had become apparent at beginning of that decade. The postwar political terrain, defined since the 1960s by civil rights struggles, the feminist movement, and the antiwar movement, the mobilization of "solid identities" (Asante, 1993) and clear lines of collective struggle now seemed to be warping into something else. The ideological, social, and economic cement that had held together industrial societies such as the United States had begun to crack and fall part. Much of this uncertainty was informed by the material reality of economic down turns in industrial economies and the continued influx of immigrants from the former colonies of imperial powers right into the heart of the major institutions, cities, and new industries of the metropolitan center. By these new demographic movements, new racial logics were being set in motion that made it difficult for the cultural purists in given racial groups to hold onto "their" putative constituencies or to offer racial manifestos for the future in which constituents could have guarantees of safe harbor or certain fulfillment of desires, needs, and interests. This all had a particularly poignant inflection in education as various custodians of culture stood ready to carve up the school curriculum like a carbuncle, assigning its different culturally determined/determinate sections to different types of group adherents.

This intensification of multiplicity in demography, culture, and economy posed serious philosophical and practical challenges to schooling. These multiplicities cut at right angles to and against the grain of enforced boundaries of culture and the disciplinary insulation and confinement that had marked, and continue to mark, the production of knowledge within schooling. In the process, the power and reach of scholarship on racial antagonism was particularly undermined. Paradoxically, the confinement and parochialism within the disciplines were not just features of the old established knowledges but characterized new discourses such as multiculturalism which rigorously avoided an engagement with critical knowledges, privileging instead a managerial discourse of cultural sampling in which all contending ethnic groups would be given their preserve in the curriculum (Appadurai, 1996). This full-scale retreat from critical discourses was also associated with an even more vigorous retreat from popular culture and what was deemed to be its corrosive hold on the young (McCarthy et al., 1999). A great battle over the representation of the present and future, and the ethnicization of culture, was taking place as modern life was being reordered by globalization,[1] mass migration, and the amplification and rapidity of movement of images around the world. Ironically, educators seemed to be out to lunch, overtaken by events, insisting on old ways of negotiating difference and school knowledge, and clinging on to a transcendent, idealized sense of the past as the fruition of Western civilization and Western culture (Ravitch, 1990).

This reactionary framework still mars schooling today. But what then had appeared in the beginning of the 1990s as emergent cracks in the racial order and the scholarly paradigms that had been advanced to understand these developments had, by the end of the past century, grown into a full-blown metamorphosis in the terms and conditions in which race could and would be articulated and struggled over. No longer could the old defenders of the status quo school curriculum comfortably hold Western Culture before the onslaught of racial and ethnic multiplicity like a vast antiballistic shield of protection. No longer could liberal and progressive scholars comfortably "place" culture with race into predictable multicultural slots. For as Ernest Hemingway's narrator had noted in a moment of premature exultation in *For whom the bell tolls* (1940/1996): "the ground had moved from beneath [our] feet." Culture and identity had been dirempted from place. And, the cultural porosity precipitated by the movement of people, economic and symbolic capital, and the proliferation, amplification, and circulation of images across the globe now deeply unsettled ethnic enclaves, even the dominant Eurocentric preserves. This is the moment in which we live—an historical moment of radical reconfiguration and renarration of the relations between centers of power and their peripheries.

Nothing has more powerfully illustrated and underscored this for us in the United States than the radical historical and earth shattering events of 9/11. For if there is anyone who still resists the ideas of globalization, transnationalism, post-colonialism, and their implications for how we live with each other in the modern world, their implications for the taken-for-granted organizing categories such as "race," "nation," "state," "culture," "identity," and "Empire"—the idea that we live in a deeply interconnected world in which centers and margins are unstable and are constantly being redefined, rearticulated, and reordered—then, such a person must have been awaken from their methodological slumber by the events of 9/11 and all that has followed afterwards. The critical events of that day—the attacks on the World Trade Center and the Pentagon, and the crescendo of the fallout attendant to these extraordinary acts—threaten to consume us all. It is striking, in the language of Michael Hardt and Antonio Negri's *Empire* (2000), how fragile modern forms of center-periphery arrangements of imperial rule are. It is striking—with the intensification of representational technologies, mass migration, the movement of economic and cultural capital across national borders, and the work of the imagination of the great masses of the people (the sorts of things that Arjun Appadurai talks about in *Modernity at large* [1996])—how it is now possible to send shock waves from the margins to the epicenters of modern life in the world in which we live. These after shocks and multiplier effects now sustain themselves indefinitely. Indeed, in addition to all the destabilizing effects and modulations taking place within the US metropolis itself—the declaration and prosecution of the war on terrorism; the war on Iraq, and the attendant pacification at home; the extension of the policing powers of the state; economic tremors of recession; deflation and downsizing across corporate enterprises; the daily hemorrhaging of the US labor force as lay-offs continue unabated—there are extraordinary ripple effects around the world. All of these developments have complicated the matters of race, identity, and representation considerably. And we see, for example, new and very tenuous alliances built under the symbolic umbrella of the flag and patriotism sucking in otherwise excluded racial minorities such as African-Americans and Latinos, along with traditionally hegemonic Anglos, into a newly expanded cultural dominant built around jingoistic symbolism and service to country. This process of new temporal and spatial configuration in certain contexts (contexts such as rising concerns about national security) is effectively displacing "others," namely, Arab Americans,[2] for instance, who are now being declared in a wholesale manner as the newly conspicuous enemy within and abroad (see Bueno Aguilar, this volume). We have seen, too, with the war on terrorism, the war with the Taliban in Afghanistan, and with Iraq, greater extension of regulation and surveillance at home in the United States as concerns and alarms are raised about the security of our borders, particularly the one to the South shared with Mexico. New biometric technologies of information gathering associated with face scanning, finger printing, and DNA sampling are being integrated into techniques of immigration control, surveillance, and policing as the United States attempts to widen the net of national security to the entire globe (Gates, 2004).

The central purpose of this chapter, then, is to bring concentrated theoretical, methodological, and policy reflection on this present historical conjuncture, characterized by new dynamics associated with racial formation and structuration, and their broader connections to the crises in the accumulation, legitimation, boundary maintenance functions of modern states, as they are impacted by logics associated with globalizing capital, information and surveillance and technologies, and network systems, and the movement of people and cultural and economic capital across borders. For sometime now, scholarship on racial antagonism in education and society has not quite kept pace with these extraordinary developments in the contemporary historical moment in which we live. Indeed, it might be argued that there is a growing atrophy of critical theoretical and empirical work on race within the educational field and the social sciences generally. This has prompted bellwether ringing in the popular press of the following kind:

> The era of big theory is over," declared one *New York Times* columnist in a recent article. "The grand paradigms that swept through humanities departments in the 20th century—psychoanalysis, structuralism, Marxism, deconstruction, postcolonialism—have lost favor or have been abandoned. Money is tight. And, leftist politics with which literary theorists have traditionally been associated have taken a beating. (Eakin, 2003, p. 9)

One is reminded here of a similar hand-wringing denunciation of the amorphous Left in the *New York Times* in the late 70s by the senior anthropologist, Marvin Harris. It was the occasion of the American Anthropological Association's Annual Meeting. On that occasion, Harris suggested that

> anthropology was being overtaken by mystics, religious fanatics, and California cultists; that the meetings were dominated by panels on shamanism, witchcraft, and 'abnormal phenomena;' and that 'scientific papers based on empirical studies' had been willfully excluded from the program. (Ortner, 1994, p. 372)

The *New York Times*, the newspaper that the late Edward Said liked to call the "newspaper of record" has made it its business to periodically prognosticate about the ridiculousness of the Left and its last days. In this chapter, I direct us to completely different territory, inviting readers to consider the seriousness of the malaise of mainstream life and mainstream schooling, underwritten as they are by state and corporate-driven imperatives of neoliberalism. The undersides of these neoliberal developments are marked by the intensification and multiplication of racial differences and inequalities in society. There is a great need for us to move beyond conventionalism and the institutional practices of confinement to embrace more critical understandings and interventions in the field of education and in social life. But this idea of movement, of change, must also be connected to stasis and the confining circumstances that underwrite the lives of modern racialized subjects. This suggestion of movement and change is the kind highlighted by Herman Melville in his magnificent novel, *Moby Dick* (1851). It is the suggestion of movement in the context of stasis, where for too many inner-city minority kids and their schools, as George Lipsitz argues, "we are locked on this earth" (Lipsitz, 2004)—locked in the bureaucratic deployment of characterization that Melville lays out on the deck of the Pequod in *Moby Dick* (arrayed around Ahab is the projection of contemporary 19th century social classification still relevant today: first mate, second mate, third mate; then, first harpooner, second harpooner, and third harpooner, Queequeg, Tashtego, and Dagoo of the Third World of Native American, Asian American and African backgrounds).

Movement and stasis are the powerful overarching tropes in our time. We must try to understand the context of this movement in stasis, this dizziness, this uncertainty that W. B. Yeats defines in "The Second Coming" as "the best lacked all conviction" (1994, p. 154). Of course, the worst now continue to seek to deepen and extend their hold on power in education and society. In what follows, I interpret and confront this context—this network of new relations that define race relations and schooling in our times. This is a context shaped by neoliberalism as a specific political-economic interpretation and articulation of globalization and multiplicity in the modern world—the world we live in. It is a context that has generated a set of dynamics that has effected the transformation of modern subject relations to the state and society at the dawning of the 21st century. Indeed, it might be argued that, instead of the end to the game of totalization announced in the declarations of the *New York Times* article I quoted earlier, we modern citizens, more than ever, are being seduced, inducted, incorporated into ever-larger discursive systems and materialisms, led forward as much by the state as by multinational capital. We are being seduced by large-scale programs of renarration of affiliation and exclusion holding out the possibility of identity makeovers, place swapping, material exchange, and immaterial rewards. Our daily lives are being colonized by massive systems of textual production that transgress the boundary lines between private and public life, and that seem to have, at the same time, the ambition to conquer all of global and planetary space. Here I am talking about the war on terrorism; new interoperable information technologies aimed at gaining fuller access to human characteristics for the purpose of sorting human bodies in a vast domestic and international project of surveillance and human capital extraction; the rise of state-driven post-Fordist authoritarianism in the name of national security; the human genome project and the dream of human perfectibility; the aspirations of corporate American sports, like basketball and football, to conquer the globe; one brand name after another; and one world series at a time.

How might we understand these developments? How might we theorize their conjunctural relationship to schools? What general organizing principles or terms might we deploy to both sum up these developments and identify their dominant vectors? It is not enough, as Dennis Carlson maintains in *Leaving safe harbors* (2002), to offer vain formulations at the level of abstraction of the mode of production. Neither is it enough to seek to isolate the variable of race from the other complicating factors of modern life in the pursuit of some vain form of methodological individualism and identity politics of clarity and authenticity. We need to pay proper attention to patterns of historical incorporation, and the work of culture and identification practices, in specific institutional contexts and programmatic applications.

UNDERSTANDING THE NEOLIBERAL CONTEXT
OF RACE, SCHOOLING, AND SOCIETY

One dominant but under-diagnosed complex or network of relations affecting schools can be conceptualized and identified as neoliberal rearticulations and transformations. It is this context of neoliberal hegemony itself and its relationship to what Michele Foucault (1991) has called *government* (i.e., the regulation of conduct of populations through systems of administration, the generation of media-driven discourses of truth, and the promotion of the self-management of everyday life) that we must examine in order to better understand the specific impact of current political, cultural, and economic forces on education, understood here as a public good. We must try to understand, particularly, neoliberal governance, its particular interpretation of globalization and multiplicity, and its transforming impact on schools. One way of talking about neoliberalism as it has arisen in the social science and political science literature of the last two decades has been to define neoliberalism in terms of the universalization of the enterprise ethic (Miyoshi, 1998). This is to see its logics in the context of the strategic translation of globalization by multinational capital and the usurpation of the role of the state in a broad range of economic and political affairs. Within this framework, neoliberalism is simply a new form of liberalism that marks the emergence of the new Right and its distinctive fusion of the political and economic that integrates 18th-and 19th-century notions of free market and laissez-faire into potentially all aspects of contemporary life. This is marked by policies since the Anglo-American pact of Ronald Reagan and Margaret Thatcher of extensive deregulation of the economy and markets, the overturning of Keynesianism and the disinvestment of the state in projects of welfare for the minority and working-class poor. It is defined further by the systematic reordering of state priorities in which the state's accumulation function is predominant in the modern systems of rule, and subordinates the processes of legitimation and the democratic involvement of citizens. Of course, many corporations like Nike, Starbucks, and Disney have appropriated Keynesianism, rearticulating "it" as an ironic substance or residue in the form of philanthropy and thereby morphing themselves into the role of state-like promoters of ecumenical feel-good affiliation, self-help forms of involvement in community, and so forth. Disney, in fact, provides a super-model of community ("of the way we are supposed to be") in the form of the fabricated town, Celebration—the new urbanist heaven in Central Florida, that Andrew Ross (1999) insightfully calls "Privatopia." For as the state disinvests in the public sphere, corporations move in to redefine community in neoliberal terms, absorbing and folding philanthropy into cause-related marketing, the building of new synergies and brand-share, and the wholesale appropriation of ethnicities in the cultivation of new products, new consumers, and new niche markets (King, 2003). If we were to follow the ideological direction of Teach for America and the No Child Left Behind Education Act, for example, by this logic, then, IBM and Xerox and, earlier, Ross Perot can do more for schools than the government or the state, or we the intellectuals in the university—"the bright but useless ones."

The second logic of neoliberalism, I want to argue, operates decisively through culture, at the point of integration of modern subjects into social institutions and the architecture of domestic and institutional space. Here, neoliberalism strategically addresses the new post-Fordist subject, the new cultural citizen of mobile privatization who exists within the self-contained unit of the home, the school, and so forth, and who mediates his or her environment through the new smart technologies driven by computer hardware and software—the smart Zenith TV and VCR that we can program; the remote control; the cell phone; video/digital games (hand-held or console based); and the ultimate phenomenon since 9/11 of the flag-car as the symbol of the nation riding on the back of the mobile patriotic citizen; the moving ground, so to speak, of a popular post-Fordist authoritarianism (Roman, 2005). These new technologies have helped to elaborate a discursive order and rearticulate time, duration, and the rhythm of production, consumption, and leisure in the constitution of our everyday lives, mobile and sedentary. We now have the ability to look out from within, to be vicariously active, to move while staying completely in place, to intercourse with the world while hiding from the light in a state of retreat. The surveillance camera, the scanning machine, the cable network uplinks in the school now allow us the illusion of control over environment while we monitor, often ourselves, from the safety inside. It is through these new social densities associated with electronic mediation, computerization, and the new digitally and genetically driven biometric technologies of surveillance, identification, and verification that neoliberalism operates as a supported master code translating the new terminologies of the Age associated with globalization, movement in stasis, place-swapping, and identity make-overs.

The university and schooling are not inured from these dynamic material practices associated with neoliberalism. There are three dimensions of neoliberalism, or the universalization of the enterprise ethic, that I argue are transforming the racialized context and life-world of schools and universities—understood as institutions for the optimization of the public good—molding culture, economy and politics, and ideology into a template of the new educational order. These three neoliberal tendencies can be identified as follows. First, there is *virtualization,* or the process of managing the university as an online community and a paperless world. Second, there is *vocationalization,* or the insistence on consistently derived and derivable returns on education. The third tendency in the process of educational neoliberalization is the practice of *fiscalization,* or bottom-line budgeting as the ruling measure of viability of all departments and units of educational institutions. Nancy Cantor and Paul Courant (2003) understand these trends as fiscal and budgetary dilemmas; I see them here as deeply cultural in the sense that they set off particular configurations of interests, needs, desires, beliefs, and system-wide behavioral practices in the life-world of universities and schools, with respect to ethos and milieu, and the organization of knowledge, the regulation of individual and group relations in these institutions, and the sorting and sifting of social and cultural capital. I will discuss very briefly below some of the main features of these neoliberal trends in schooling, highlighting their impact on racial relations in education. First let us talk briefly about virtualization.

Virtualization

The first trend that I want to discuss is the rise and intensification of virtual interactions in our educational activities, our online proclivity toward information craving, speed, efficiency, and maximization that now, as a set of dispositions, is rapidly displacing face-to-face interaction and embodied decision making and community feeling in our institutions. Education in its virtualizing tendency is susceptible to the "Internet paradox"—the other side of deregulation as the centrifugal logic of neoliberalism and *laissez-faire;* that is, "dependence on a social technology that often breeds social isolation" and insulation of knowledges and disciplines as much as it facilitates interaction" (Cantor and Courant, 2003, p. 5). This is not a Luddite argument; it is, as Cantor and Courant suggest, the proper concern that "the delivery of education solely on the Internet may rob students of the experience of the clash of ideas out of which emerges empathy with others and a desire for compromise" (p. 5). The arrival of the Internet for some heralded yet another clean technological break with the past. But unlike car manufacturers and fashion designers, we in the humanities need the past for more than nostalgia and the ephemeral. We cannot jettison it, ruthlessly bringing on stream the latest gizmo. We need the past to study it to better understand the present and the future. This raises questions of the public sphere and the fact that we have a multiplicity of publics in educational institutions in the Nancy Fraser sense—publics where conversations are shorn off by essentialism and tribalism (Fraser, 1997). Virtualization has not lived up to the promise of universalizing and transforming our particularisms. Indeed these ethnic particularisms, it might be argued, have intensified the generation of a great digital divide between ethnic groups and especially between racial minorities and Anglos. The coming of the virtual world may have heightened these latter tendencies—each man turning his key of endless data, in his own door, to use the imagery of T.S. Eliot ("And each man fixes his eyes before his feet" [Eliot, 1954, p. 53]). Second, let us discuss the matter of vocationalization.

Vocationalization

As Masao Miyoshi (1998) warned us a few years ago, in his essay, "Globalization, Culture and the University," transnational capital has overridden the line between the university and its outside, enveloping its sinews, reorganizing its infrastructures, and closing the distance between education and economy in the privatization of the organization of knowledge. As Miyoshi argued, then, students and administration seek to empty the rigorous content out of curricular knowledge, relabeling it "for sale." The goal is to maximize returns on investment as in the market: "our students' course-takings preferences often focus on areas likely to maximize future returns (preprofessional, technology-intensive-globalization)" (Cantor and Courant, 2003, p. 5). This investment in the enterprise ethic within the university has meant that on many campuses there has been an eroding of support for humanities and humanistic social sciences. For example, as Cantor and Courant have pointed out, "representation in superior humanities programs at public universities has dramatically declined between 1982 [and the present]" (p. 5). Indeed, it precisely these courses that provide the best preparation for democratic citizenship and critical thinking. Here, we have sacrificed this critical investment in knowledge for taking the pig to the market. Vocationalization of school knowledge also has the effect of marginalizing emergent knowledges such as African American Studies, Asian American Studies or Latino/a Studies as too ideological, too nonpractical, etc.

Third, there is the matter of fiscalization of the university and schooling, or the application of "bottom-line" budgeting.

Fiscalization

We live in a context of budgetary crisis within the economy generally, and within education. There are increasing demands for accountability and fiscalization—the application of bottom-line rationality to all education decision-making. These pervasive measuring, accountability, and feasibility pressures have placed the humanistic disciplines and alternative postcolonial and indigenous minority knowledges on the defensive. Neoliberals have proven themselves masters at blurring and bending political, ideological and cultural faiths to achieve viability. We live in such a time on campuses across the United States where the pressure of rationalization has placed humanistic programs in doubt, forcing them to establish new codes and rules of the game. Even programs such as literature, art history, philosophy, and so forth, which are unlikely to ever be profit-making enterprises, are feeling the pressure of the bottom line. We are trapped in the marketplace logic of student credit hours and sponsored research objectives. More teaching, less pay! Our relevant models are now the business school, the law school, and the natural sciences. Wherever and however money is to be made there lies justification and validation. The immediate casualties are ethnic and area studies programs, interdisciplinary research, collaborative research, and writing projects. The broader casualties are both our minority and majority students who now see their teachers and academic mentors less as models of thoughtfulness than as purveyors of knowledge fast-food. Ultimately, education as a public good is being compromised to privatization. Our greatest challenge, then, is to preserve the autonomy of the teaching-learning process, the autonomy of intellectual production, and the reproduction of critical minority and majority scholars. All of this has hit minority education quite hard making it difficult for subjugated knowledges in the field of African-American Studies and other ethnic studies programs to gain sure footing, except at the most elite universities.

RESEARCHING RACE IN TRANSFORMING CONTEXTS: MATTERS OF CULTURE, MATTERS OF IDENTITY, MATTERS STATE/PUBLIC POLICY

An understanding of the neoliberal contexts of education and society leads us to a third way, or course of analysis—away from the traditional opposition of theory versus practice, abstraction versus concrete studies, and so forth, that now dominate both mainstream and radical approaches to race. My aim here is to eschew the customary tendency to separate out these different strategies of race analysis. Instead, I want to consolidate efforts of fellow contributors to this volume aiming at models of research that cut across and integrate the theoretical, the empirical, and the practical. Moreover, to adequately address the complexities of race in this contemporary historical moment, students of race can not study race alone (Hall, 1980, p. 339), but must pay greater attention to contextualization, relationality, and conjunctural analysis. For, as Stuart Hall maintains:

> One needs to know how different groups were inserted historically, and the relations which have tended to erode and transform, or to preserve these distinctions through time—not simply as residues and traces of previous modes, but as active, structuring principles of the present society. Racial categories *alone* will *not* provide or explain these. (1980, p. 339)

Rather than offering vain formulations at the abstract level of the mode of production, I call attention to patterns of historical incorporation and the work of culture and identification practices in specific institutional contexts, as well as the spreading effects across and beyond local settings, linking the urban/local to the cosmopolitan/global. Specifically, I want to focus on three critical organizing categories through which I maintain neoliberalism has precipitated transformed circumstances for the practical and theoretical appropriation of racial logics in the new century. These central organizing categories are: *popular culture, identity,* and *state/public policy.* I foreground these categories here because I believe they materially and discursively embody some of the principal contradictions and tensions through which 21st century race relations in education are expressed. And, they ultimately force us to think about the operation of racial logics beyond the school, into society and the globalizing world context where the intersection of popular culture, identity, and state/public policy constitute critical fault lines through which the transformations and reconfigurations concerning race relations in the new century are being expressed.

Why then study culture? Why study identity? Why study state/public policy? What are the new developments affecting these categories of social, political, ideological, and economic organization through which contemporary race relations are being reconstituted and renarrated? Let's consider the matter of "culture."

Culture

First, with respect to the organizing category of popular "culture," I believe that scholars must consistently work toward the reformulation of this concept. We must offer retheorizations and reformulations in ways that are often not pursued in race-related debates in education and the associated identity politics in which the field is now conflagrated. One such area of debate, for example, would be the canon versus multiculturalism. The fact is that although pivotal to such discourses, "culture" is significantly undertheorized. "It" is often treated as a pre-existent, unchanging deposit, consisting of a rigidly bounded set of elite or folk-loric knowledges, values, experiences, and linguistic practices specific to particular groups. Moreover, I argue that even the critical perspective of the cultural studies paradigm which we invoked in this volume, and in which culture is defined as the production and circulation of meaning in stratified contexts, is also inadequate to a discussion of the new work of culture in a globalizing and information age, espe-cially as it bears upon race. Instead, I maintain that it might now be more useful to think about "culture" along the lines suggested by Tony Bennett in "Putting Policy into Cultural Studies" (1996) and *The birth of the museum* (1995), as well as the work of Toby Miller (see his *Technologies of truth* [1998] and his discussion of gov-ernmentality with Lawrence Grossberg in Bratich et al., 2003). These approaches combine the neo-Gramscian understandings, that underpin the cultural studies paradigm, with Foucauldian insight on the role of the discursive and the cultural in the differential production of citizenship and power discriminations in modern society. Here, too, theorization of culture moves beyond the "whole way of life" formulation in the Raymond Williams sense (although his linking of culture to moral sensibility and feeling, and his discussion of hegemony as a form of cultural saturation in *The long revolution* [1961] clearly apply). Rather, I conceptualize cul-ture as a set of dynamic, productive, and generative material (and immaterial) practices in the regulation of social conduct and social behavior that emphasize personal self-management (i.e., the modification of habits, tastes, style, and phys-ical appearance) and the expanded role of civil society in the state and vice versa in the rule of populations—"rule at a distance." This new emphasis forces us to link the cultural and economic work of difference in education to broader dynamics operating in society at large, to the politics of popular culture and public policy, and to the imbedded discriminations operating in the instrumental and expres-sive orders of the racialized state. Racial logics are articulated to the new cultural mobilizations precipitated by globalization that work paradoxically to emphasize locality, regionalism, subnationalisms, and the steady marketization of difference into commodified culture (Engel, 2007). Thus, local "taste" is also accessible as ecumenical form and address, as groups in one location of the world try on the garments of those dwelling in a completely different location.

As with culture, the category of "identity" is critical to the performance and impact of racial affiliation and antagonism in education and society. And like cul-ture, identity is also a material and imaginary terrain of struggle. How then should we begin to talk about identity in the changing circumstances affecting race in the new millennium?

Identity

With respect to the second organizing category to be foregrounded here—the category of *identity*—I want to announce the end of its auratic status. I argue, instead, that the notion of racial identity as residing in "origins," "ancestry," "linguistic" or "cultural unity" has been shattered, overwhelmed by the immense processes of hybridity, disjuncture, and renarration taking place in what Arjun Appadurai (1996) calls the new techno, media, and ideo scapes now disseminated in ever-widening areas and spheres of contemporary life. Migration, electronic mediation, and biometric and information technologies have separated culture from place. And, difference has become an abstract value that can be dirempted from specific groups and settings, and combined and recombined in ways that allow, for example, clothing designer magnates like Tommy Hilfiger, to appropriate elements of hip hop culture, to recombine semiotically these elements into new forms of clothing fashion, and then sell these new designs back into the inner-city itself. These stylized elements of black culture are further marketed, with overwhelming success, to an ecumenical community of ethnic cross-dressers. I want to conceptualize racial identity, then, as a contextual performance "produced within specific historical and institutional sites, within specific discursive formations and practices, and by specific enunciative strategies" (Hall, 1996, p. 4). Researchers must pay attention, among other things, to the ways in which minority urban cultural forms, linked especially to music and sports such as basketball and football (cultural forms that are a deeply important allure to school youth), are the vital carriers of the new messages of neoliberal imperatives now operating in US education and society, and elaborated on an expanded global scale (King, 2003). In looking at the field of sport for guidance on the matter of racial identity, I am also pointing to expanded terms of reference for understanding educational dynamics, pointing beyond the walls of the institution of schooling itself to the wider culture and society, where I believe the practices of the entertainment media, cultural practices of fashion and style, and the general circulation of popular images, serve to instruct and educate the young in patterns of identity formation and forms of affiliation, forms of inclusion and exclusion, and so forth. But it is not enough to address the matter of race through the prism of culture and identity; we also must look at the issue of *state* and *public policy*, and the regulatory landscape in which racial antagonism and forms of affiliation are administered and modulated.

State/public policy

What is the specific character of the modern racialized state? Is it, for example, merely a "traffic warden" equidistant from the ruler and the ruled while regulating competing interests, as that venerable group of mainstream social and political scientists such as Gabriel Almond, Lucien Pye, Dennis Jupp, and W. W. Rustow suggest? Or is it "instrumentalist," in the language of Ralph Miliband (1973), the blunt object of the bourgeoisie? Or, just a little more mildly in Leninist terminology, is it the "executive arm" (Lenin, 1917/1965) of the ruling class? Is the state, yet, corporatist, as Jurgen Habermas's student Claus Offe (1984) suggests—coordinating the interests of the bourgeoisie, and systematically disorganizing the interests, needs, and desires of the working class and racial minorities? Is the state a network of organizations deeply invaded by civil society and combative agents in the Gramscian model, and thus culturally surrounded as Rush Limbaugh argues in *I told you so* (1993)? Is the state, yet again, interred in the Foucauldian headless body politic, spreading its tentacles throughout the social order by means of technologies of truth, verification and identification, self-regulation, and discrimination, as the sources of a diffused program of government and rule at a distance? There is no simple answer to these questions about state governance. It may be that the state articulates policy along all these lines of regulatory practice suggested above. Nevertheless, these are all vital questions bearing upon the modern expression of racial antagonism in relation to which the state clearly plays a role of coordinating dominant identities while disorganizing subaltern ones. But contemporary research seems to be pointing us in contradictory directions about the nature of the state in light of the radical global transformations which I argue are powerfully reconfiguring modern race relations.

On the one hand, scholars such as Henry Giroux (1996), Naomi Klein (2002), and Anthony Giddens (1991, 2000) seem to be saying that, with respect to the racially and socially disadvantaged, the state is decomposing, disinvesting in programs of social welfare, giving way to the greater centrality of ironic programs of altruism, volunteerism, and philanthropy mounted by multinational corporations like Nike, NGOs like Teach for America, AmeriCorps, and so forth. These multinational projects of volunteerism and strategic deployment of welfarism are occurring in tandem with the altruistic practices of segments of the highly commercialized US sports industry such as NFL and NBA which, in turn, target high school and college-age youth as part of a project of image makeovers. These sports institutions have, as a critical goal, image making in the form of refashioning media-criminalized urban sports stars, reportraying them as big brothers to inner-city children, thoughtful and magnanimous gift givers to good causes like breast cancer research, and positive role models for avid book readers and the like (King, 2003). On the other hand, Michael Apple (2005), Kelly Gates (2004), Andy Green (1997), Saskia Sassen (2002, 2003) seem to be suggesting that the state is consolidating, digging itself back into modernist borders that are paradoxically reinforced by the new postindustrial biometric information technologies of surveillance and regulation, the extension of surveillance cameras and metal scanning technologies in schooling, and the like. They point, too, to the expanded and critical role of the state in brokering the interests of global capital as it seeks out new areas of value in the process of opening up new markets and colonizing new labor forces in the Third World and in the periphery of the First.

But it may be the case, that both sides of this story of the recomposing state are valid. The US state, for example, is at one and the same time what Hardt and Negri (2000) call a supranational state, putting out fires in the racialized Empire at great distances overseas (in places such as Iraq and Afghanistan). Yet, at the same time, attempts at pacification abroad involve a rigorous regime of controls and intrusions at home in the name of domestic security, revealing a state that is vulnerable, porous, and deeply invaded. Indeed, when President George W. Bush talks about interdicting international terrorists, he talks about this project in a policing, deer hunting, and "Wild West" language of the lone star state of Texas. These matters of legitimation in which the problem of international terrorism is made familiar and ordinary are spoken of in a desperately nativist vernacular— maybe, even, nationally and regionally specific to the South. Terrorists are pests, and the vigilant citizens at home are pesticide salesmen, like the former Republican congressman, Tom Delay, whose view of the world is informed by the partisan deployment of affect. But the logic of the US racial state, biometric and biotechnological, decisively expands abroad, interdicting, policing, and assisting (through treaties like NAFTA, for example) in the reorganization of the economic formulas and Keynesian arrangements of Third World national economies in the Southern hemisphere in a broad range of areas—from telecommunications and the clothing industry to vital areas important to the poor, such as health care. The other side of biometric paradigms of surveillance to protect US borders is the loosening of national control in Third World countries, over significant sectors of their economies and political and social life. A good example is the transformation that has taken place in the area of health care in periphery states at the behest of liberalization and deregulation. This has meant the deepening integration of the heath care of the poor and the middle-classes in the Caribbean and Latin America into the health care industry and privatizing formulas of the United States—a development in which the pursuit of new areas of value by the capitalist health care industry in the United States is wreaking havoc on what were formerly self-sufficient nationalized health care systems in these Third World countries, creating distortions, and deepening inequality of access for the periphery poor.

Understanding these matters of context on a broad scale is important for understanding the role of the state in race relations in education. For example, the state's commitment to neoliberal governance is now quite thorough-going. As documents such as the 2002 *No Child Left Behind* Education Act indicate, there is a broad project afoot to deepen the privatization of education in the United States. And with the proposition of vouchers to instigate school choice and charter schools in the air, the rightward swing of education policy threatens to aggravate racial inequality in education by siphoning off money from the hard-pressed public education system for the racially disadvantaged and the poor for the purpose of bolstering the privatization of schooling *tout court*. These developments underscore the point made earlier—that is, that the racialized US state is both intensely global, acting through multilateral policies like NAFTA to spread neoliberal principles and US interests in an imperialistic manner to periphery countries around the world. But the US racialized state acts narrow-mindedly at home as well, organizing the elite interests of the wealthy and disorganizing the identities and the interests of the white working-class and minority poor. All of this must be put in the context of developments associated with globalization, 9/11, the war on terrorism, and the war on Iraq—developments that reveal in the most fundamental sense both the strength and the vulnerability of the US racial state, the nativistic sense of boundedness and prerogative articulated by the US state agents, as well as the cultural multiplicity that continues to empty itself out into the heart of the metropolitan center. I call attention to these features of the racialized state and public policy, recognizing that developments in the United States are deeply connected to a wider world reality, linking up the particularity of the local/urban realities to the global and the planetary.

CONCLUSION: RACE, CULTURE, IDENTITY, PUBLIC POLICY, AND EDUCATION

What I have tried to underscore in this chapter, then, are all the ways these tensions around culture, racial identity, and public policy now play out *vis-à-vis* education. As I argued earlier, we live in an age of fundamental insecurity and vulnerability. All this has profound implications for education. More and more, young people must be prepared to live in a world that offers little recourse to personal, social, or economic stability. Smaller and smaller groups of elites are competing and thriving in the emerging information and knowledge economy, leaving the vast majority of youth and young adults with few prospects outside of poorly paying service sector jobs with limited benefits. Moreover, these young people cannot fall back on ready-made and stable notions of self and community, as did previous generations (Willis, 2003; Grossberg, 2005). As noted above, these, too, have been destabilized by global forces and trajectories.

Of course, the role and function of schools have been profoundly complicated in this context. The traditional twin roles of schooling—preparing youth for work and citizenship—no longer provide clear mooring. Increasingly, it must be said, our so-called new economy demands creative and flexible thinking, while our contemporary global terrain demands more cosmopolitan notions of citizenship. If nothing else, our moment is marked by difference and multiplicity. However, public policy initiatives around schools and schooling have tended to elide this complexity, opting instead to claim a kind of fullness of knowledge and control over the curricula. One sees "resentment" logics informing a range of school activities today, from the cognitive and intellectual to the political and social (McCarthy, 1998; Dimitriadis and McCarthy, 2007).

First, public policy has placed schools under enormous federal pressure to respond to standards, particularly around Language Arts and Math. The most notable of these movements, of course, has been driven forward by the *No Child Left Behind* legislation. The effects of this legislation have been broad and deep, although they have been particularly profound on the most vulnerable of public schools. At the most basic level, a corporate language has overtaken school discourse, a language that implies clear inputs and outputs, assessments, and measurements that can be correlated and compared across disparate sites. Knowledge itself has come to be treated like a perfectly transparent commodity, one that can be treated and dispensed independently of particular actors in context. A kind of technocratic approach to schooling and curricula has thus come to the forefront of public education today. While these impulses have of course been embedded in school life for nearly 100 years (Dimitriadis and Carlson, 2003), never before have they been so clearly pedagogically out of step with, and inappropriate for, the emerging social and cultural landscape young people face. According to Hargreaves, students in our so-called knowledge-society must learn to "create knowledge, apply it to unfamiliar problems, and communicate it effectively to others" (2003, p. 24). These require new modes and approaches to teaching and learning—constructivist and cooperative approaches that imply a range of learning outcomes and goals. New testing regimes, in stark counterdistinction, encourage just the opposite. They encourage a kind of rote drill-and-skill approach to teaching, one which helps encourage "teachers to focus on low-level knowledge and skills, resulting in less in-depth understanding and less focus on higher-order thinking skills" (Jones et al., 2003, p. 40).

Second, contemporary approaches to difference seem wholly informed by similar technocratic pressures. Narrow notions of "multiculturalism" have taken over discussion of multiplicity and complexity in our schools. Notions of "cultural competence" have provided school administrators with a managerial language which looks to contain difference, rather than engage it in productive ways.

Working against the tide of difference, many such educators have tended to draw a bright line of distinction between the established school curriculum and the teeming world of multiplicity that flourishes in the everyday lives of youth beyond the school. These educators still insist on a project of homogeneity, normalization, and the production of the socially functional citizen. Such technocratic approaches to difference insist on bringing the problems of multiplicity and difference into a framework of institutional intelligibility and manageability. Such approaches, however, are not well suited to help young people navigate the complex realities of our contemporary global terrain. More and more, young people will have to negotiate a world that is truly cosmopolitan—a world where one must coexist with difference—not simply control it. Recent world events have, at a minimum, complicated clear demarcations between "here" and "there," "self" and "other," "first" and "Third World." Our evolved reality is quite different—that of eternal and complex encounters between disparate ideas, ideologies, and peoples. Our schools must therefore prepare students to be "world citizens" in the most humble, partial, and reflexive sense of the term.

In sum, contemporary movements over racial antagonism in education can be regarded as attempts to control a reality that far outstrips popular imaginative capacities. If nothing else, these efforts to contain global complexity and difference both mask and highlight widespread uncertainty about the role and function of formal schooling institutions today. It should not be surprising, then, that many minority youth (but majority youth as well) are turning away from school when they look to the adult world to help them engage with the issues and concerns most relevant in their lives. Indeed, as I have argued elsewhere (McCarthy, 1998), young people are turning to popular culture and alternative schooling institutions in the face of these realities. First, young people are using a wide span of cultural forms to navigate their everyday lives today, including popular music, fashion, dance, and art. As several recent critical commentaries and ethnographies have demonstrated, we can not understand popular culture and young people's identities in predictable ways (Dimitriadis, 2001; Dolby, 2001). Ultimately, as this work makes clear, we must ask ourselves what kinds of curricula—broadly defined— young people draw on to understand, explain, and live through the world around them. This is messy terrain, one that exceeds a priori notions about identity often privileged by educators. As I have tried to make clear, the multiple uses to which popular culture is put challenge and belie easy notions of "cultural identification." Young people in the United States and around the world are elaborating complex kinds of social and cultural identifications through music like hip hop and techno in ways that challenge predictive notions about texts, practices, and identities.

Ultimately, the enormous social, cultural, and material dislocations of the last decade have destabilized any certainty around the traditional twin roles of schools—preparing young people for work and for citizenship. This new landscape, I argue, demands a different set of understandings as to what constitutes what some call "the research imaginary" in education today (Dimitriadis and Weis, 2007). How we contextualize and understand what we envision as education and how we think about students, particularly, minority students, has implications for who gets what type of educational experience and who gets what type of access to schooling. This seems to be at the heart of any discussion of youth culture today—the idea that we no longer can claim fullness of knowledge over young people's lives, and that we need to renegotiate, in a very fundamental way, what counts as "meaningful" education for youth.

In this chapter, I have sought to expand these terms, showing the ways in which the logics of neoliberalism and globalization (particularly after 9/11) are defining the new terms and new relations between education and society. In many ways, society has imploded into schooling, and education has expanded deep into society, where arguably, film, television, the Internet, popular culture, and popular music may be the ascendant centers for educating the young about each other and the foreigner in their midst and in the world. It is a context in which old ways of thinking about race are untenable and new methodologies and theories are in short supply.

NOTES

1. Globalization is understood here as the intensification and rapidity of movement of economic and cultural capital, migration, electronic mediation, and the amplification of mass-produced images across national borders (see McGrew, 1996).
2. Actually, the "other," the "enemy," "the terrorist" is not so easily defined in practice. As a consequence, national security policies that attempt to "identify" the enemy at various ports of entry, immigration and visa policies, the patrolling of the physical borders and ports of the United States, and so on, invariably end up netting innocent Asians (sometimes Asian Americans) or Latinos and Latin Americans who "look" like "Arabs" or even African people who are of the Muslim faith. What 9/11 demonstrated is that the inside/outside logic about the "enemy" could not hold up. And indeed, the very effort of the Bush administration to cleave the Other from the West has proven to be wholly inefficient, perhaps, unwise.

REFERENCES

Appadurai, A. (1996). *Modernity at large*. Minneapolis, MN: Minnesota Press.

Apple, M. (2003). (Ed.). *The state and the politics of knowledge*. New York: Routledge-Falmer.

Apple, M. (2005). Patriotism, democracy and the hidden effects of race. In C. McCarthy, W. Crichlow, G. Dimitriadis, and N. Dolby (Eds.), *Race, identity and representation in education* (2nd Edition) (pp. 337–348). New York: Routledge.

Asante, M. (1993). *Malcom X as cultural hero and other Afrocentric essays*. Trenton, NJ: Afro World Press.

Bennett, T. (1995). *The birth of the museum*. New York: Routledge.

Bennett, T. (1996). Putting policy back into cultural studies. In J. Storey (Ed.), *What is cultural studies?* (pp. 307–321). London: Arnold.

Cantor, N. and Courant, P. (2003). Scrounging for resources: Reflections on the whys and wherefores of higher education finance. *New Directions for Institutional Research*, Vol. 119 (Fall), pp. 3–12.

Carlson, D. (2002). *Leaving safe harbors*. New York: Routledge.

Dimitriadis, G. (2001). *Performing culture, performing identity*. New York: Peter Lang.

Dimitriadis, G. and Dennis, C. (2003). *Promises to keep: Cultural studies, democratic education, and public life*. New York: Routledge.

Dimitriadis, G. and Weis, L. (2007). Globalization and multisited ethnographic approaches. In C. McCarthy, A. S. Durham, L. C. Engel, A. A. Filmer, M. D. Giardina, and M. A. Malagreca (Eds.) *Globalizing cultural studies: Ethnographic interventions in theory, method, and policy* (pp. 323–342). New York: Peter Lang.

Eakin, E. (2003). The latest theory is that theory doesn't matter. *New York Times*, April 19, p. 9.

Eliot, T. S. (1954). The wasteland I.: The burial of the dead. In T.S. Eliot (Ed.), *Selected poems* (pp. 51–53). London: Faber and Faber.

Engel, L. C. (2007). Policy as journey: Tracing the steps of a reinvented Spanish State. In C. McCarthy, A. Durham, L. C. Engel, A. Filmer, M. Giardina, and M. Malagreca (Eds.), *Globalizing cultural studies: Ethnographic interventions in theory, method, and policy* (pp. 385–406). New York: Peter Lang.

Foucault, M. (1991). Governmentality. In G. Burchell, C. Gordon, and P. Miller (Eds.), *The Foucault effect* (pp. 87–104). Chicago, IL: University of Chicago Press.

Fraser, N. (1997). Justice interruptus: Critical reflections on the "postsocialist" condition. New York: Routledge.

Gates, K. (2004). *Biometrics at the border: Automated identification and race*. University of Illinois at Urbana, Institute of Communications Research: Unpublished paper.

Giddens, A. (1991). *The consequences of modernity*. Stanford, CA: Stanford University Press.

Giddens, A. (2000). *Runaway world: How globalization is refashioning our lives*. London: Routledge.

Giroux, H. (1996). *Fugitive cultures: Race, violence, and youth*. London: Routledge.

Green, A. (1997). *Education, globalization and nation state*. London: MacMillan.

Grossberg, L. (2005). Cultural studies, the war against kids, and the becoming of U.S. modernity. In C. McCarthy, W. Crichlow, G. Dimitriadis, and N. Dolby (Eds), *Race, identity and representation in education* (pp. 349–368). New York: Routledge.

Hall, S. (1980). Race, articulation and societies structured in dominance. In UNESCO (Ed.), *Sociological theories: Race and colonialism* (pp. 305–345). Paris: UNESCO.

Hall, S. (1996). Introduction: Who needs identity? In S. Hall and P. DuGay (Eds.), *Questions of cultural identity* (pp. 1–17). London: Sage.

Hardt, M. and Negri, A. (2000). *Empire*. Cambridge, MA: Harvard University Press.

Hargreaves, A. (2003). *Teaching in the knowledge society*. New York: Teachers Record Press.

Hay, J. (2003). Unaided virtues: The (neo)liberalization of the domestic sphere and the new architecture of community. In J. Z. Bratich, J. Packer, and C. McCarthy (Eds.), *Foucault, cultural studies, and governmentality* (pp. 165–206). Albany, NY: SUNY Press.

Hemingway, E. (1940/1996). *For whom the bell tolls*. New York: Simon and Schuster.

Jones, G., Jones, B., and Hargrove, T. (2003). *The unintended consequences of high-stakes testing*. Lanham, MD: Rowman and Littlefield.

Kellner, D. (1993). *Media culture*. New York: Routledge.

King, S. (2003). *How to be good: The NFL's rookie symposium, racialized sexuality, and the politics of philanthropy*. University of Arizona, Department of Physical Education: Unpublished paper.

Klein, N. (2002). *No logo* (2nd Edition). New York: Picador.

Lenin, V. I. (1917/1965). *The state and revolution*. Peking, China: Foreign Language Press.

Limbaugh, R. (1993). *I told you so*. New York: Pocket Books.

Lipsitz, G. (2004). *Locked here on this earth: Spatial politics and black expressive culture*. University of California at Santa Cruz: Unpublished paper.

McCarthy, C. (1998). *The uses of culture*. New York: Routledge.

McCarthy, C. and Crichlow, W. (Eds.) (1993). *Race, identity and representation in education* (1st Edition). New York: Routledge.

McCarthy, C. and Dimitriadis, G. (2007). Governmentality and the sociology of education: Media, educational policy and the politics of resentment. In H. Lauder, P. Brown, J. Dillabough, and A. H. Halsey (Eds.), *Education, globalization and change* (pp. 198–212). Oxford: Oxford University Press.

McCarthy, A. Durham, L. C. Engel, A. Filmer, M. Giardina, and M. Malagreca (Eds.) (2007). *Globalizing cultural studies: Ethnographic interventions in theory, method, and policy*. New York: Peter Lang.

McCarthy, C., Hudak, G., Miklaucic, S. and Saukko, P. (Eds.) (1999). *Sound identities*. New York: Peter Lang.

McGrew, A. (1996). A global society? In S. Hall, D. Held, D. Hubert, and K. Thompson (Eds.), *Modernity: An introduction to modern societies* (pp. 466–503). Oxford: Blackwell.

Melville, H. (1851). *Moby Dick*. New York: Harper & Brothers.

Miliband, R. (1973). *The State in capitalist society: An analysis of the Western system of power*. London: Quartet Books.

Miller, T. (1998). *Technologies of truth: Cultural citizenship and the popular media*. Minneapolis, MN: Minnesota Press.

Miyoshi, M. (1998). "Globalization," culture and the university. In F. Jameson and M. Miyoshi (Eds.), *The cultures of globalization* (pp. 247–270). Durham, NC: Duke University Press.

Offe, C. (1984). *Contradictions of the welfare state*. London: Hutchinson.

Omi, M. and Winant, H. (1994). *Racial formation in the United States* (2nd Edition). New York: Routledge.

Ortner, S. (1994). Theory in anthropology since the sixties. In N.B. Dirks, G. Eley, and S. Ortner (Eds.), *Culture/power/history: A reader in contemporary social theory* (pp. 372–411). Princeton, NJ: Princeton University.

Packer, J. (2003). Mapping the intersections of Foucault and cultural studies: An interview with Lawrence Grossberg and Toby Miller. In J. Bratich, J. Packer, and C. McCarthy (Eds.), *Foucault, cultural studies*. New York: SUNY Press.

Ravitch, D. (1990). Diversity and democracy: Multicultural education in America. *American Educator*, Vol. 14, No. 1, pp. 16–48.

Roman, L. (2005). States of insecurity: Cold war memory, "global citizenship" and its discontents. In C. McCarthy, W. Crichlow, G. Dimitriadis, and N. Dolby (Eds.), *Race, identity and representation in education* (pp. 73–94). New York: Routledge.

Ross, A. (1999). *The celebration chronicles: Life, liberty and the pursuit of property values in Disney's new town*. New York: Ballantine Books.

Sassen, S. (2002). *Global network/linked cities*. New York: Routledge-Falmer.

Sassen, S. (2003). *Denationalization: Economy and polity in a global digital age.* Princeton, NJ: Princeton University Press.

Torres Santomé, J. (2001). *Educación en tiempos de neoliberalismo.* Madrid: Morata.

West, C. (1993). *Race matters.* Boston, MA: Beacon Press.

Williams, R. (1961). *The long revolution.* London: Chatto and Windus.

Willis, P. (2003). Foot soldiers of modernity: The dialectics of cultural consumption and the twenty-first century school. *Harvard Educational Review,* Vol. 73, No. 3, pp. 390–415.

Yeats, W. B. (1921/1994). The second coming. In W. B. Yeats, *Michael Robartes and the dancer: Manuscript materials* (p. 147). Ithaca, NY: Cornel University.

Coda: Terrorism, globalization, schooling, AND humanity

JAMES G. LADWIG

The University of Newcastle

The soldier at My Lai reports his inability to feel in these words: "You feel it's not real. It couldn't possibly be …"

This man is six months out of public school. He is six months distant from the Glee Club, Flag Pledge, textbook, grammar-exercises, Problems of Democracy. It is essential that we be precise. It is not the U.S. Army that transforms an innocent boy into a non-comprehending automaton in six months. It is not the U.S. Army that permits a man to murder first the sense of ethics, human recognitions, in his own soul: then to be free to turn the power of his devastation outward to the eyes and forehead of another human being. Basic training does not begin in boot camp. It begins in kindergarten. It continues with a vengeance for the subsequent twelve years.

—JONATHAN KOZOL, *THE NIGHT IS DARK AND I AM FAR FROM HOME*
(KOZOL, 1975, P. 54)

In his lectures to the College de France in early 1976, Michel Foucault articulated many of the ideas and thoughts that developed into what many refer to as his theory of governmentality. In these lectures we see many of the concepts and ideas that have been brought from Foucault into our analyses and understanding of the institutions of "modern society." Here, the conceptual seeds of contemporary Anglo-applications of Foucault are sown: multiple relations of domination, the production of subject, technique. The sites to which he later focused his attention are all introduced as well. Here we see Foucault turn to the institutions of the margins, the sites of the pathological: prisons, hospitals, insane asylums.

In addition to these concepts, however, Foucault encases his discussion of the development of "society" without a theory of sovereignty (which he rejects) within an overarching diagnosis of Western institutions that is suggestive and potentially profound for our current times.

At the frontispiece of Foucault's lectures is the proposition that the historical construction of society has rested fundamentally on the discourses of war and racism, and that modern institutions need to be understood as sites of the application of heterogeneous techniques of power and discipline implicated in the production of subjects that lived by, and live, that war and that racism. In this light, striking a somber resonance with current events, the fulcrum of Kozol's point about schools being the source of the soldier's basic training in inhumanity (literally learning to consider some humans as not human) is located in Foucault's larger history of modern institutions. Of course, the recent English translation of Foucault's 1976 lectures is not the first glimpse we have of these ideas in the English speaking academy. Anne Stoler's provocation and compelling reinterpretation of these same lectures has been available for some time now, in her *Foucault and the Education of Desire* (Stoler, 1995). And of course, English-only Foucaultophiles will undoubtedly have been pouring over the newly available texts and discussing amongst themselves just what they imply. But these are grave historical times that warrant any and all attempts to bring reason to an understanding of just what is confronting our planet, our singular race, however feeble those attempts may be.

As a coda to this collection of important and insightful essays, I would like to offer just one more vision of how the world we inhabit has come to be the way it is. The point of this analysis will be to ask readers to consider just how it is that the dilemmas of injustice, inequality, and terror have come to be so clearly similar around the planet. For all the difference of which analysts are rightfully keen to remind us, from my readings of social theory, analyses of schooling and school reform, theoretical views from sociology, postcolonial analyses, and first-hand experience of working with students and teachers on the margins of state power, I would suggest we not forget to recognize schooling as a major and as yet remarkably stable foundation on which our societies build and manage us, our cultures, and our race. For all the specificity the essays in this volume rightfully declare, from amidst the detailed interactions which create the racisms, the awful inhumanity that all too many experience, the global structures of power constructed by schooling itself are the foundations of our current struggles. As Foucault reminds us:

> To put it in more concrete terms, we can obviously describe a given society's school apparatus or its set of educational apparatuses, but I think that we can analyze them effectively only if we do not see them as an overall unity, only if we do not try to

derive them from something like the Statist unity of sovereignty. We can analyze them only if we try to see how they interact, how they support one another, and how this apparatus defines a certain number of global strategies on the basis of multiple subjugations (of child to adult, progeny to parents, ignorance to knowledge, apprentice to master, family to administration, and so on). All these mechanisms and operators of domination are the actual plinth of the global apparatus that is the school apparatus. So, if you like, we have to see the structures of power as global strategies that traverse and use local tactics of domination. (Foucault, 2003, pp. 45–46)

The view I present below implies that most commentators misrecognize how this now global structure of schooling relates to the larger social struggles. Where many ask what implication globalization has for schooling, for example, I argue that globalization was sown into the seeds of schooling from its inception, and globalization as we know it could only ever have been plausible with the technologies of power embedded in schools as they currently function. Further, the techniques of power embedded in schooling, already well known and identified in radical analyses of schooling, are fundamentally linked to issues of race and racism.

This last claim is both more and less than how many would interpret it. The notion of radical analysis is not a statement about political extremism,[1] but a recognition that some analyses cut to the core, the fundamental roots of the object of their analyses. Etymologically, radical carries this sense, being about fundamental roots. The notion of schooling being radically linked to race and racism globally is not a statement about skin color, although the color of one's skin is the most obvious historical signifier of race. Race in this analysis is about the culturally created social groups stratified by some bizarre moral universes that have littered the pathways of human history. The notion of schooling being globally about constructing races is *less* than what many may think because it is not an exhaustive list of what schooling does—as a corollary to its main game, or in tandem with it—it is simply a declaration of the need to recognize the obvious central structure of our modern institutions. The notion of schooling being about globally constructing races is much *more* than a Zola impersonation, another *j'accuse*, making public the role schooling plays in maintaining and generating race itself. This notion raises the challenge posed by recognizing that modern schooling, world institutions, world culture have always and already been about race.

In this light, the struggle to reform schooling, curriculum, and pedagogy is about much, much more than reaching higher and higher levels of educational achievement, and more and more access to schooling in its modernist form. The struggle to reform schooling, to me, is about finding new forms of schooling that are more truly dedicated to the creation of humanity: humanity as singular collectivity and as a moral character. To that end, below, I explore the links between our understanding of schooling as an institution of world culture, pedagogical reforms as a key instrument of that institution's power, and I question the subject of our schools' creations. To begin, allow me to explain the context in which these theoretical speculations are at the fore in my mind.

AND STILL THEY SCHOOL

I've been working with Barrinji Central School in Barrinji, New South Wales,[2] for a couple of years now, on two separate projects. In one project, I am playing the role of a "critical friend," working with the teachers of the school on questions of improving pedagogy and curriculum. In the other, I am in continuous conversation with the Aboriginal parents and students of the school about what Aboriginal cultural knowledge teachers in the school need to be better able to teach the Aboriginal students of Barrinji Central. ("Central" schools in New South Wales are so named because they are located in remote areas with population centers, and they provide schooling from kindergarten to the completion of secondary schools: Grade 12 in New South Wales.)

It takes a long time to drive from Newcastle, Australia (on the east coast just north of Sydney) to Barrinji in the far west of New South Wales. One way is to go West on pavement out to the farthest small town on the main northwest road (the only pavement) and then turn back to the southeast on the only paved road to Barrinji for about an hour. The other way is more direct, but takes you along several hundred kilometers of dirt road. Either way takes about 12 hours if you are flexible with your adherence to speed limits, and you are willing to risk high speed collision with any number of animals, native and introduced. For international viewers, to understand this land, imagine the broad plains shown in the Mad Max movies and you have the picture. (The movies were shot not far from there, north of a mining town with wonderful labor heritage.) According to the local street sign, the population of Barrinji is around 980, but the census figures place the population below 400.

Barrinji is a small town on the banks of a river in the middle of a series of very large natural lakes. The lakes fill in flood periods but remain dry through drought and most other times. The area features in the diaries of the original white explorer Thomas Mitchell, where it is clear that the location was already a site of regular settlement for the Aboriginal mobs that lived up and down the river at the time of the first white explorations of the river in the 1830s. Today, the river provides irrigated water for local fruit and cotton industries (which are outside of the town) and for the mining town (via a water pipeline). The railway has played a significant role in Barrinji's history as this is where the main rail line across western NSW crosses the river.

The land around Barrinji is largely dry, desert scrub land, with the river being a line of life cutting through some of the oldest geological terrain on the continent (and therefore the world). Because of the old gums that line the banks of the river, the river land is visible from kilometers around. As some of the only large bodies of naturally formed standing water in the middle of Australia, the lakes have attracted human settlement as long as our memory lasts.

The Aboriginal community in Barrinji has strong ties to the Aboriginal river people Mitchell first encountered, but it is also strongly influenced by the white establishment and disestablishment of the local Mission, which operated from 1933–1949. Current Aboriginal residents in town recognize two main lines of traditional family lines: those who have traditionally spoken a well documented Aboriginal language up and down the river, and those who descend from the more overland mob. There are several transliterated spellings and pronunciations for each tribal name, but naming them here would reveal the town name. Aboriginal ties to the land and clear heritage in the area is evident in most parts of life in Barrinji, from local businesses, government agencies and with the nearby National Park. The National Park includes the river and lake lands and is the site of one of the largest inland sheep operations at the turn of the 20th century. Introduction to Aboriginal ties to the local area are readily available from the local council information centers and National Parks.

The importance of the Mission experience for the current Aboriginal Community can not be overstated, as it is associated with several forced movements in which families were forcibly transferred and physically separated. When first established, Aboriginal people were brought together in Barrinji from other, quite distant area missions, and when closed, then residents of the Mission were dispersed to several locations. In each move, some families were separated. As the local Council historical plaque puts it so ever mildly (the plaque can be found along one of the main central streets in town, next to the Civic Hall):

> When the [...] Mission opened in 1933, Aboriginal people were moved from towns on the river and [...] a mission site between (hundreds of kilometers away via dirt road). When the move was made, everyone was loaded onto several trucks, but unbeknown to the passengers the trucks had separate destinations. While one went to a rail siding to take people to Barrinji, the other vehicles went to (yet another remote site), hundreds of miles away. This caused families to be separated with some never to be reunited.

To this day, the daily life of families spread around the state has an impact on what young Aboriginal children experience in Barrinji, as parents and grandparents of the students in Barrinji, and the students themselves, are living with the consequences of this forced separation. In a place such as Barrinji, far from any large city anywhere on the planet, working with teachers whose students are largely from Aboriginal families that have been ripped apart from what was historically an overtly racist state, it is difficult not to ask just what schooling offers the students in Barrinji. Just as this question is rightfully raised by the international contributors to this volume, in many other sites of schooling around the world, where similar technologies of subjugation continue to be practiced on peoples such as indigenous Americans, African Americans, the Roma/Gypsies, and too many other groups. Parents, white and black, mostly see schooling as essential, needed for the social and economic advancement of their children. But the students in Barrinji rightly question the value of schooling themselves. And the Aboriginal students have exhibited behaviors all too well documented in the history of educational struggles to provide high quality educational outcomes for Aboriginal students: they often do not attend ("they don't rock up") either individual classes or school in general; they have been known to openly declare their lack of trust in the school and its teachers; they do not hide their boredom; and they have been known to not "participate" (do nothing but idly sit through classes).

This picture is not the whole story, of course—and the school is making great strides at the moment. However, the struggle of the school is not simply about better techniques of teaching or more meaningful and more just curriculum. The struggle is often over the core, basic cultural values embedded in school: people, space, time, bodies. Who the teachers are contradicts traditional Aboriginal culture: they are individuals who are not from the local community and are not likely to stay, who are not known personally and who are really too young to know much anyway (in the eyes of many Elders and children).

Where the learning takes place is also not particularly "natural." A small set of enclosed buildings, one of which was a site of historical angst for parents, in the middle of a dry heat, is not particularly where most students want to learn. After an excursion to the site of the old Mission, students repeatedly talked about how much they enjoyed the day, out amongst the trees along the river. Even on a typical day, given a choice, despite the persistent flies and the offer of air-conditioning, students do not hang about inside unless they are downloading music or otherwise using the web.

And time. From the minutes of daily start- and end-points for lessons, to curricular schedules for units over several days and weeks, time is always flexible, timetables rarely followed strictly, and the idea of the deadline is palpably one historically imposed by the bureaucratic structures of the school or its centralized authorities.

None of these is particularly new, and at this point in history it would be difficult to identify these as unique to Aboriginal culture, since these are the downbeats of the tempo to which life in the Barrinji flows. For Aboriginal students, however, the difference between these basic structures of school culture, world culture, and their own lives, is often experienced as a chasm: the faceless bureaucrat, space cut into right angles in rank and file, time carved into regular minutia.

AND BODIES

The mechanisms of schooling which identify specific characteristics, almost always with a less than subtle moralized value, with specific children's bodies are those which set one group of students apart from others: ability, learning difficulties, intelligence, talents. The grouping of students based on behaviors, read to be manifestations of internal capacities, sets up the playground divisions, the classroom groupings, the determinations of destinies.

None of these mechanisms are unknown to scholars of education. From Jules Henry's (Henry, 1963) incisive analysis of the psychic effect of schooling's ranking and instillation of compliance to Michael Apple's (Apple, 1979) cutting analysis of the politics of labeling, and the literally thousands of other radical analyses of the mechanisms of domination in schooling, a move to see how these specific techniques of power are the local specifications of the school apparatus Foucault identifies as global strategies, is not a great leap. And still, as Grumet (1988) reminded us two decades ago, even those of us who write such analyses school our children.

FINDING A NONRACIST WORLD CULTURE

For Howard Winant, the global order and world culture have a distinctively important history. His words on this matter are unambiguous:

> [...] But neither can there be any doubt that the complex of racial signifiers attained unprecedented comprehensiveness and ubiquity as the imperial order, the world capitalist system, the modern pattern of nation-states, first hove into historical view and then, as it were, dropped anchor. Cultural factors—understood here as ways of representing and assigning meanings to the varieties of human identity—must be seen as causative in this developmental process in two ways. First, they allowed and indeed necessitated the emerging global social structure to ascribe identities to all actors, individual and collective, consistent with the emerging new world social order aka "modernity". Second, only by ordering the social world along racial lines, only by assigning racial identities to all beings, only by generalizing a racial culture globally, was the new world order able to constitute itself as a social structure at all. It was a

> system of accumulation and unequal exchange, a set of world-embracing institutions
> of domination, rule, and authority, only to the extent that it was racialized. (Winant,
> 2001, pp. 29–30)

And so it is that we can see how the world culture, the social structures created by schooling, are part of this larger construction of who we all are—humans. The questions I would ask readers to consider are how the specific actions of schooling work to contribute to, to have made, this world order possible in the first place.

Is the fear of being caught out by the teacher all that different to the fear of being shamed in the eyes of the community? Is the terror of unknown others felt on the playground all that different to the terror against which the world shadow-boxes today? The techniques of surveillance and exposure deployed in Foucault's modern institutions have ascribed individual fears and collective terror in all of us who have been schooled. As the adolescent Aboriginal girls in Barrinji Central survive each day, not game enough to get up and leave a lesson they know to be worthless to them, but who remain silent, face down out of shame. As much anticipated potential as it is real, the causes of our fears and our own acts of terror lie historically in the institutions that have created the world culture against which many, if not most, struggle but without which none of us could survive for long.

On the backdrop of these institutional mechanisms of terror, schools build the meanings which make unequal distribution of rewards legitimate: meanings that individualize wealth, income, and success; meanings that collectivize security and safety. The attribution of relational social qualities to individual and collective bodies, the bio-mechanics of modern world culture is the core of schooling, and schooling the core of our own creation of terror. Until we find ways to reconfigure how schools construct subjects, Others, our struggles against wars on terror will be in vain. Before we manage to either use up the finite resources of our planet or commit ourselves to yet more waves of self-destruction, one first part of that struggle is simply to recognize the import of finding new forms of schooling. To that end, the essays in this volume carry the work of building that recognition globally and back home again.

NOTES

1. This said, being "extreme" in many nations doesn't take much, especially considering that in countries such as the United States the analyses offered by Marxist, feminist, or postcolonial scholars based there are often labeled as extreme, even when they prove relatively tame or straightforward by international standards.
2. The name and details of the location of the school and town are pseudonyms.

REFERENCES

Apple, M. W. (1979). *Ideology and curriculum*. London and New York: Routledge and Kegan Paul.

Foucault, M. (2003). *Society must be defended: Lectures at Collège de France, 1975–1976* (D. Macey, Trans.). New York: Picador.

Grumet, M. (1988). *Bitter milk: Women and teaching*. Amherst, MA: University of Massachusetts.

Henry, J. (1963). *Culture against man*. New York: Random House, Inc.

Kozol, J. (1975). *The Night is dark and I am far from home*. Boston, MA: Houghton Mifflin Company.

Stoler, A. L. (1995). *Race and the education of desire: Foucault's history of sexuality and the colonial order of things*. Durham and London: Duke University Press.

Winant, H. (2001). *The World is a ghetto: Race and democracy since World War II*. New York: Basic Books.

Contributors

Juan José Bueno Aguilar (1960, Zamora, Spain) holds a Ph.D. in Pedagogy from the University of Salamanca. He is currently Associate Professor (*Professor Titular*) of Multicultural Education at the University of A Coruña. He is author of *El lenguaje de los niños gitanos*, among other books and publications. His related research interests extend into the role of the mass media in the construction of new and multiple identities in today's multicultural world.

Mariano Fernández-Enguita studied Economics, obtained a Ph.D. in Political Sciences and Sociology, and graduated in Law. He is Professor (*Catedrático*) of Sociology and Chairman of the Department of Sociology and Communications at the University of Salamanca. He heads the Centro de Análisis Sociales and the Observatorio Social de Castilla y León. He has researched and published widely on social inequalitity, organizations and education. More information at http://www.usal.es/mfe/enguita and http://sociologia.usal.es.

Michael D. Giardina is Visiting Assistant Professor of Advertising & Consumer Studies at the University of Illinois, Urbana-Champaign. He is the author or editor of numerous books, including most recently *From soccer moms to NASCAR dads: Sport, culture, & politics in a nation divided* (Paradigm, forthcoming) and *Contesting empire, globalizing dissent: Cultural studies after 9/11* (with Norman K. Denzin, Paradigm, 2006).

Susan Harewood is Lecturer in Cultural Studies at the University of the West Indies. Her articles and chapters on communication, popular culture, performance and gender have appeared in a variety of journals and edited collections, including *Cultural Studies ↔ Critical Methodologies*, *Popular Music*, and *Social and Economic Studies*.

Emily Noelle Ignacio is Associate Professor of Sociology and is primarily affiliated with the Ethnic, Gender, and Labor Studies Concentration within the Interdisciplinary Arts and Sciences program at the University of Washington Tacoma and the Harry Bridges Labor Center at the University of Washington, Seattle. She is the Chair of the Race and Ethnic Minorities section of the American Sociological Association and an Executive Board member of the Asian American Studies Association. Her book, *Building diaspora: Filipino cultural formation on the Internet* (Rutgers University Press, 2005) examines how Filipinos around the world negotiate identities and form community in relation to Eurocentrism, Orientalism, globalization, and nationalism. Currently, she is researching the simultaneous (re)construction of Filipinos, Americans, the Philippines, and the United States of America via a close analysis of cultural tourism and the Filipino-Bolanon diaspora's responses to the effects of neoliberal economic policies on the small island of Bohol in the Philippines.

Dolores Juliano Corregido studied anthropology in Argentina and obtained her Ph.D. at the University of Barcelona where she has been a Professor (*Catedrática*) until her recent retirement. She has invested many years of scholarly activity in gender and the anthropology of education. Some of her most noteworthy publications include: *Cultura popular* (1986); *El juego de las astucias. Mujer y construcción de mensajes sociales alternativos* (1992); *Educación intercultural. Escuela y minorías étnicas* (1993); *Las que saben ... subculturas de mujeres* (1998); *Las prostitución: El espejo oscuro* (2002); *Excluidas y marginales. Una aproximación antropológica* (2004); and *Les altres dones. La construcció de la exclusió social* (2006).

James G. Ladwig is Associate Professor in the School of Education and the Research Institute of the Advanced Study for Humanity at the University of Newcastle, Newcastle Australia.

Cameron McCarthy is Professor and University Scholar in the Department of Education Policy Studies at the University of Illinois at Urbana. He has authored and coauthored numerous books, including *Race identity and representation in education* (2nd edition, Routledge, 2005), *Foucault, cultural studies and governmentality* (SUNY, 2003), *Reading and teaching the postcolonial* (Teachers College Press, 2001), *Racismo y curriculum* (Morata, 2001), *The uses of culture: Education and the limits of ethnic affiliation* (Routledge, 1997), and others.

Jin-kyung Park is a doctoral candidate in the Institute of Communications Research at the University of Illinois at Urbana-Champaign. Her research interests include cultural studies, postcolonial studies, and science/technology studies with a specific focus on East Asia. She is currently completing her dissertation on Japanese colonialism, women's health, and reproduction in colonial Korea.

Álvaro Pina is Professor (*Catedrático*) of English Studies, Faculty of Letters at the University of Lisbon. He is Head of the Department of English Studies. He teaches and researches in Cultural Studies and Cultural Theory. He is also Director of the Culture and Society Postgraduate Program, and Scientific Coordinator of the Communication and Culture degree course. He has published thirteen books and numerous articles.

Mar Rodríguez Romero is Associate Professor (*Profesora Titular*) and researcher of educational change and curriculum studies at the University of A Coruña. She is author of the books *El asesoramiento en educación* (Consultation in education) and *Las metamorfosis del cambio educativo* (Metamorphoses of educational change).

Teresa San Román has taught Anthropology at the School of Political Sciences at the Complutense University of Madrid and at the University de Barcelona, where she obtained her first *Cátedra* (full professorship). She obtained a second *Cátedra* in 1989 at the Autonomous University of Barcelona, where she continues to teach and head the research group GRAFO (*Grup de Recerca en Antropología Fonamental i Orientada*). She has conducted extensive fieldwork in Spanish Roma communities, shanty towns, marginalized elderly communities, and with Senegalese and Gambian immigrants, and is focused on developing a theory of social marginalization. She is author of numerous publications including *Vecinos gitanos* (Akal Eds. Madrid, 1976); *Vejez y cultura, hacia los límites del sistema* (Fund. La Caixa, Premio Investigación CC. Sociales, 1990); *Los Muros de la Separación: ensayo sobre alterofobia y filantropía* (Tecnos, Madrid, 1996); *La diferencia inquietante, nuevas y viejas estrategias de los gitanos* (Siglo XXI Eds. Madrid 1996); *Sueños africanos para una escuela catalana* (Pubs. de la Universitat Autónoma de Barcelona, 2002).

Jurjo Torres Santomé is Professor (*Catedrático*) of Curriculum, Instruction and School Organization, and Chairman of the Department of Pedagogy and Curriculum Studies at the University of A Coruña, Spain. He is author of *El curriculum oculto* (1991); *A Educação Infantil* (1991); *Globalización e interdisciplinariedad: el curriculum integrado* (1994); *Un currículo optimista fronte á desmemoria e o fatalismo* (2001); and *Educación en tiempos de Neoliberalismo* (2001). His latest book is *La desmotivación del profesorado* (Morata, 2006).

Cathryn Teasley is Adjunct Professor (*Profesora Asociada*) of Curriculum, Instruction and School Organization at the University of A Coruña. Her research is focused on the pursuit of cross-cultural justice through pedagogy, and she is contributing author to the two-volume work *Volver a pensar la educación* (Morata, 1995), on critical issues in education across the globe, and to *Globalizing cultural studies: Ethnographic interventions in theory, method, and policy* (Peter Lang, 2007).

Eduardo Terrén holds a Ph.D. in Sociology and is Associate Professor (*Profesor Titular*) at the University of Salamanca. He is author of books such as *El contacto intercultural en la escuela* (University of A Coruña, 2001), *Razas en conflicto* (Barcelona, Anthropos, 2002) and *Incorporación o asimilación: la escuela como espacio de inclusión* (Madrid, Catarata, 2004), and has published more than twenty chapters in volumes on racism and cross-culturalism. He has held research fellowships in London and Berlin and sits on various editorial boards for academic publications. He has participated in research projects on the education of Gypsies and immigrants, and on youth mobility. He currently heads a research group on second generation immigrants in Spain.

Teun A. van Dijk was Professor of Discourse Studies at the University of Amsterdam until 2004, and presently holds an appointment at Pompeu Fabra University in Barcelona. He has published several books on text grammar, psychology of text comprehension, racism, and the media, and has edited *The handbook of discourse analysis* (4 vols. 1985) and the two-volume introductory book *Discourse studies* (1997). He founded six international journals (*Poetics, Text, Discourse & Society, Discourse Studies, Discourse & Communication* and *Discurso & Sociedad*). His last monographs in English are *Ideology* (1998) and *Racism and discourse in Spain and Latin America* (2005), and his last edited book (with Ruth Wodak) is *Racism at the top* (2000). He is currently working on a new book on the theory of context.

Index

9/11, 75, 113-115, 321, 325, 334, 337
Action research, 12, 296, 312
Affirmative action, 164-166, 229, 232-233, 284
Afghanistan, 332-333
Afrocentrism, 133
Agency
    Anti-Doping Agency, 143, 147, 153
    Teacher agency, 294, 300, 310-312
Aggression, 45, 57
A-historicism, 9, 196
Allah, 88 n.11, 281
Alterity, 75, 277-278, 284
Alterophobia, 63
American
    African-American, 120, 125-129,
       131-134
    Arab-American, 321
    Asian-American, 323, 327
    Corporate American, 324
    Latin American, 161, 260
    Native American, 323
    North American, 4, 126, 247
Androcentrism, 203
Anglo-centrism, 1, 6
Anomie, 56, 58
    Anomization, 56
Anthropology, 10, 242, 246-252
Anti-racist education, 283
Appadurai, Arjun, 58, 69n4, 70n5, 80, 89,
    320, 321, 331, 337
Arab, 85-86, 98-99, 257, 267
Argentina, 3, 199, 352
Asian, 98, 106, 264

Assimilation, 35, 55, 159-161, 123-124, 241,
    252, 279, 283, 288, 302
    Assimilationist, 115, 120, 246, 258
Athlete Passport, 149-156
Audiovisual literacy, 287
Australia, 3, 95, 98, 105, 115, 153, 230, 344-345
Authenticity, 175
Authoritarianism, 127, 323, 325
Autonomous Communities, 295
Autonomy, 33, 228, 268, 328

Babelization, 186
Bacon, Francis, 187-188
Banking, 26
Barbados, 3, 44-48
Barrinji, 344-346, 348
Basque, 57, 253n6
Bauman, Zygmunt, 6-7, 19-23, 29-33, 35-36,
    56, 71, 74, 79, 88n6, 89, 198, 216, 244, 253
Beck, Ulrich, 20-23, 25, 36, 87n4, 88n6, 89
Behavior problems, 301, 307-308
Bhabha, Homi, 2, 3, 13, 14, 56, 58, 71,
    314n10, 315
Binarism, 76, 191
Biological determinism, 281, 284-285
Biometric, 322, 326, 331-333
Birmingham School of Cultural Studies, 2
Blackness, 6, 40-42, 50-51, 119
Borders
    Border-crossing, 3, 78
    National borders, 321, 337n1
Bourdieu, Pierre, 2, 194, 216, 247, 253, 308,
    309, 315

Bourgeoisie, 188, 221, 260-264, 269, 332
Brand
    Branding, 168
Brazil, 199
Britain, 6, 41, 115
Bush, George W., 12, 84, 102, 114, 121, 122, 126, 134, 333, 337n2

CAFTA, 8, 162, 169
Calypso, 6, 40, 42-44, 46-51
Canon, 76, 330
Caribbean, 1, 40-44, 46-51
Catalonia, 57, 253
Chilaba, 61
Christianity, 69n3, 75, 84-85, 161
Citizen
    Citizenship, 7, 20, 29-30, 42, 46, 61, 74, 78-80, 117, 121, 135, 145, 161, 327, 330, 335, 337
Civil rights, 9, 61, 96, 98-99, 127, 162-169, 175, 223, 262, 282, 319
Clash of civilizations, 75
Classism, 196, 207, 289, 299
Classroom, 97, 105
Clinton, Bill, 114, 118, 119, 120-122, 123, 125-127, 134, 136n5-7, 137n8, 138, 139, 140
Coeducation, 263
Coexistence, 73-87
Collaboration, 153, 155, 268, 307-309
Colonialism, 78, 93, 98, 102, 104-105, 135
Color blindness, 163, 284
Common humanity, 6, 30-32, 35
Common sense, 43, 46, 213, 235, 280
Commonsensical, 196
Communications, 173, 195, 288, 290
Community, 5, 17, 19, 24, 27-28, 30-33, 35
Compensatory, 295, 297
Compulsory education, see education
Conflictive, 196, 201, 233, 298-300
Conscientização, 26
Corporate culture, 310
Corporatism, 3, 224, 233, 307, 309
Cosmopolitanism, 12, 81, 87, 135, 235
Creativity, 35

Critical
    Critical knowledge, 320
    Critical pedagogy, 237n13, 289
    Critical theory, 220, 229, 236n5
Cross-cultural, 1, 3, 5, 9-10, 13, 96, 279, 288
Cross-dresser, 331
Cultural
    Cultural exclusion, 9
    Cultural studies, 1-6, 13, 17-24, 32-35, 143-145; American cultural studies, 40-41; British cultural studies, 4, 50, 115; Foucauldian cultural studies, 145
    Cultural stuff, 56
Cyberspace, 195

Decentralization, 12, 295, 309
Decontextualization, 196, 198
Deconstruction, 232-233, 322
Deficit, 126, 136
Deliberation, 10, 96, 213, 312
Democracy
    American democracy, 114,
    Participatory democracy, 229, 237n8
    Progressive democracy, 117
    Truncated democracy, 20, 23, 25
Deregulation, 325-327
Difference
    Cultural difference, 5, 19, 66, 81, 98, 105, 122, 133, 284, 309
    Racial difference, 122, 224, 284, 322
    Social difference, 224, 228, 231, 249
Differentialist racism, 282-284
Disciplines, 46, 185-186, 189, 309, 320, 326, 328
Discrimination
    Anti-discrimination, 211, 213
    Racial discrimination, 63, 85, 98
Disability, 203, 260
Disenfranchisement, 302
Disney
    Disneyfication, 9, 197
Distributive justice, 19
Diversity
    Cultural diversity, 7, 10, 64, 73-75, 77-78, 80-86, 313
    Ethnic diversity, 7, 105-106

Doping, 8, 143, 146, 156
Drug Free Sport Consortium (DFSC), 149, 152-154
Drug-testing technologies, 151-152, 155
Durkheim, Emile, 73, 76-77, 87n2, 89, 247, 253

Education
    Adult education, 33
    Compulsory education, 290, 293
    Higher education, 10, 272, 267, 269, 273, 293, 301
    Multicultural education, 288, 290
    Public education, 114, 176n2, 206, 265, 294, 334-335
    Teacher education, 195-196, 200, 301, 307
Educational
    Educational policy, 11, 258, 280, 289, 293-294, 308
    Educational reform, 9, 233, 265, 293-294
Eagleton, Terry, 2, 19, 23, 30-31, 36, 304, 315
El Salvador, 3, 8-9, 159-162, 169-174
Elite discourse, 8, 12, 76-77, 87n1, 96, 100, 106-108
Emancipation, 192, 220-222, 224, 227
Emigration, 58, 160
Empathy, 72, 163, 327
Empire, 321, 333
End of history, 209
Enlightenment, 22, 30, 46, 191, 249, 261
Enterprise ethic, 324, 326-327
Epistemology, 13, 191, 194, 220
Equality
    Economic equality, 232-233
    Educational equality, 259
    Racial equality, 120
    Social equality, 234
    Also see Inequality
Essentialism, 125, 284, 288, 327
Ethics, 155-156, 191, 312
Ethnic
    Ethnic identity, 55-59, 61, 241, 252, 314
    Ethnic militancy, 57
    Ethnic minority, 328
    Ethnic studies, 143-145

Ethnicity, 57, 59, 115, 176-177, 226, 228, 230, 244, 257, 265, 278, 282, 284, 297, 304
Ethnocentrism, 281, 299, 309
Ethnography, 296-297, 302
Eurocentrism, 285
Europe
    Contemporary Europe, 7, 78-79, 97-98, 110
    Eastern Europe, 98-99
    Modern Europe, 34
    Western Europe, 288
Exile, 25, 58, 243, 296

Fanon, Frantz, 69n4, 71
Feminist, 2, 39, 124, 220, 229, 319
First World, 4, 152-155, 200
Fiscalization, 326, 328
Flows
    Diasporic flows, 116
    Immigration flows, 259
Foucault, Michel, 2, 22, 143-144, 156, 193, 302, 341-342
Framing, 9, 76, 137n13, 162-163, 166-167, 170, 347-348
Frankfurt School, 232
Free market, 9, 162, 324
Freedom
    Freedom as concepts and practices, 5, 16, 19, 27
Freire, Paulo, 26, 314n11
Fundamentalism, 74-75, 84, 99-100, 196, 223

Galicia, 295
Galician, 57, 310n6, 314n7
Galiza, 295, 314n6
Galizan, 3, 295, 297, 300, 306, 308
Gender, 11, 51, 135, 167, 214, 222, 224, 230, 233, 260, 264, 269, 271, 274, 282, 284, 303-304, 310
Giddens, Anthony, 106, 135, 136n5, 332
Globalization
    Alternative globalization, 237n7
    Neoliberal globalization, 5, 251
Governmentality, 8, 143-146, 148, 154-155, 330, 341

Gramsci, Antonio, 9, 18, 22, 71, 77, 81, 86, 89, 114, 144, 162, 167, 178, 303, 316, 330, 332
Grand narratives, 192
Grassroots, 198
Gypsy, 12, 57, 59, 61-62, 70n5, 262, 280, 283, 284, 286, 287, 289, 293, 294, 296-299, 308-311, 314n3/n11, 315

Habermas, Jürgen, 22-23, 36, 61, 71, 332
Hall, Stuart, 2, 9, 36, 40, 41, 45, 52, 56, 71, 77, 78, 80, 86, 88n6, 89, 117-188, 122, 124, 133, 134, 135, 139, 162, 163, 178, 220, 238, 294, 303, 314n10, 316, 329, 331, 338, 339
Hegemony
    Counter-hegemony, 81
    Gramsci's hegemony, 77, 81, 330
    Neoliberal hegemony, 324
Heterogeneity, 12, 228, 311
Heterophilia, 62
Heterophobia, 62
Higher education, see Education
Hijab, 83
Homogenization, 6, 12, 58, 87n3, 248
Human achievement, 9, 202
Human genome project, 185, 279, 291n3, 324
Human rights, 2, 65, 68, 173-175, 192, 198, 214
Hybridity, 119, 122-123, 135, 318n10, 331

Iberian Peninsula, 1, 6, 57, 289, 296-297
Identity
    Cultural identity, 5, 80, 82, 120, 281, 294
    Ethnic identity, 55-59, 61, 70n5
    National identity, 6, 47, 62, 80, 114, 245, 263
    Racial identity, 331, 334
Immigrants, 4, 76, 78, 87, 93, 95, 98-100, 102, 104-108, 162, 241-242, 248, 257, 259, 288, 319
Imperialism, 44-45, 79, 135
Indigenous, 98, 229-230, 257, 328, 346
Individualism, 35, 166-167, 206, 324

Inequality
    Economic Inequality, 225, 229
    Ethnic Inequality, 108
    Racial Inequality, 97, 169, 334
    Social Inequality, 61, 95, 205, 219
Informational capitalism, 183-184, 197, 205
Injustice, 9-10, 173, 197, 200, 221, 223, 225, 232-233, 296, 305, 308, 340
Institutional racism, 94, 106, 165-168
Institutionalization of knowledge, 184-186
Interdisciplinarity, 3, 186
Indian, 62, 264
Iraq, 102, 113, 321-324
Islam, 60-61, 83-86, 102, 281
    Islamophobia, 98-99
    Islamism, 99

Kant, Immanuel, 190-191
Keynesianism, 126, 325
King, Jr., Martin Luther, 9, 161-163, 168, 176
Kulturkritik, 18-19, 23

Labor market, 11, 21, 84, 108, 203, 263-264, 266
Lifestyle racism, 282
Liminal servant, 301, 306, 313

Maghreb, 257
    Maghrebi 286
Malcolm X, 168
Managerial discourse, 10, 320
Marginalization, 95, 126, 134, 203, 241, 279, 282, 284, 296, 312
Marxism, 217, 316, 322
Marxist theory, 62, 118, 221, 224, 236,n3, 237n13, 348n1
Mass media, 11, 94, 100, 286-288
Mediterranean, 7, 66, 79, 248
Melville, Herman, 323
Mexico, 199, 322
Middle-class, 12, 43-44, 49, 115, 121, 123, 125, 202, 302, 333
Migration, 116, 135, 201, 243, 320-321, 331
Minority group, 126, 264, 283
Mixophobia, 6, 55

Modernity
    Alternative modernity, 34
    Liquid modernity, 20, 22, 31, 33
Mono-societies, 215
Moroccan
    Moroccan immigrants, 263, 265, 267,
        269, 271, 287
    Moroccan students, 266-267, 270, 272
Multiculturalism, 7, 9, 28-29, 79-80, 99, 105,
    116, 119, 168-169, 232, 248, 251, 283,
    289, 320, 330, 335
Muslim, 76, 83-84, 88n11,n14, 257, 287,
    341n2

NAFTA, 127, 333, 334
Nazi, 192, 280
    Neo-Nazi, 284
Negation, 221, 285, 301
Neoconservative, 84, 114, 121, 311
Neoliberalism, 3, 121-122, 160, 175, 322-326,
    328, 337
Neo-Marxist thought, 2, 225
New capitalism, 22
New racisms, 11-12, 286, 290
NGOs, 95, 99, 288, 332
Nietzschean resentment, 302
No Child Left Behind, 12, 114, 325, 334-335
Nonsynchrony, 289
Normalcy, 13
    Normality, 88n15, 280
    Normalization, 336
North African, 11, 61, 85, 88n15, 286

Occidental, 290n5
Olympic Movement, 147
Oppression, 10, 117, 164, 167, 173, 175-176,
    191, 196, 201-202, 208, 221-225, 283,
    289, 296, 311
Optimistic curriculum, 9, 183, 204
Orientalism, 26, 77-78, 86
Otherness, 74-77, 86-87

Participation
    Democratic participation, 33, 35, 312
Participatory action research, 312

Particularism, 41, 327
Philanthropy, 6, 59, 68-69, 325, 332
Polysemic, 234, 290
Popular culture,
    American popular culture, 117
    Black popular culture, 117
    Caribbean popular culture, 41
    Urban popular culture, 8, 117-118
Popular Party, 287-294
Portugal, 3-4, 103
    Portuguese, 3, 302
Positive discrimination, 284
Postcolonial, 2, 4, 289, 328, 342
Post-Fordist, 323, 325
Postmodernism, 10, 191, 220, 222, 236n5, 252
Poststructuralism, 222
Praxis, 21-22, 33-35, 224, 233, 313
Privatization, 233, 237n8, 294, 325, 327-328,
    334
Privatopia, 325
Professionalization, 184
Proletariat, 224, 261, 266-267
Public sphere, 3, 12, 97, 233, 325, 327
Puerile, 197

Racial simulation, 289
Racial stereotypes, 62, 77, 116
Racialization, 74, 282, 284
Racism
    Racism in the media, 286
    Racism through deception, 286
    Racism without race, 284
    Racist lexicon, 286
Relationality, 3-4, 313, 329
Religion, 73-87, 88n11-n14, 188, 203, 214, 226
Re-narration, 119, 321, 323, 331
Representation,
    Cultural representation, 86, 115, 227
    Ideological representation, 78
    Media representation, 80
    Racial representation, 8, 76, 121
    Social representation, 98, 101, 104, 290
Reproduction
    Reproduction of ethnic and racial
        inequality, 97, 310

Reproduction of racism, 7, 87n1, 94, 96, 103, 106
Republican, 136, 333
Resentment, 289, 306, 335
Retorsion, 64
Roma, 11-12, 98, 257-259, 261-264, 266-269, 272-274, 297
    Romani, 262
    Romanes, 57
Romero, Monseñor Oscar Arnulfo, 9, 159-160, 162-163, 168, 170

Said, Edward, 2, 26, 37, 69, 70, 71, 77, 78, 86, 90, 322
Salvadoran, 160-161, 171-174
Saussure, Ferdinand de, 57, 71
Schooling
    Egalitarian schooling, 258
    Mainstream schooling, 295, 297, 322
    Universal schooling, 11, 266
    Schooling as an institution of world culture, 343-348
    Schooling rate, 265, 269, 271
    Schooling and society, 10, 12, 342-343
Segregation, 67, 89n15
Separatist racism, 282
Sexuality, 51, 124, 233
Situated change, 230-231
Social
    Social justice, 2-3, 5, 50, 175, 200, 215, 220, 224-225, 229, 233-234, 289, 294
    Social welfare, 48
Socialist Party, 293, 316
South Africa, 95, 246, 280
Spain, 3-4, 6, 11-12, 57, 59, 83-86, 88n14, 98, 102, 199, 201, 203, 241, 244, 246-249, 257-260, 262, 265, 271, 273-274, 277, 279-280, 282-288, 293, 299, 304, 311-312
Spike Lee, 8, 117, 125-126, 168
Sports, 114, 120, 125, 128, 120, 150, 154, 324, 331
Stasis, 12, 323, 326
State
    Nation-state, 21, 25, 29, 42-43, 46, 61, 82, 116, 146, 155, 245, 294, 347

Racialized State, 330-331, 334
    Welfare State, 29, 101, 107
Stereotypes
    Cultural stereotypes, 87, 221
    Racial stereotypes, 62, 77, 116
Structural racism, 9, 162, 166-169
Subaltern, 4, 11, 13, 29, 34, 55, 313, 332
Subjectivity, 8, 115, 117, 124, 222-223, 278, 281
Subjugation, 343, 346
Surveillance, 114, 123, 148, 150-151, 322-323, 325-326, 333, 348

Taguieff, Pierre-André, 63-65, 68, 70n7/n8/n10, 71, 72, 285, 292
Teacher
    Teacher agency, see Agency
    Teacher education, 195-196, 200, 301, 307-308, 312
Technocratic, 214, 335-336
Territorialism, 281
Terrorism, 83, 85, 102, 321, 323, 333-334
Textbooks, 9, 93-97, 100-101, 104-107, 163, 189, 197-198, 202, 211, 286
Third World, 4, 8, 44, 143, 152-155, 192, 199, 248
Todorov, Tzvetan, 7, 55, 58, 72, 76, 90
Togetherness, 7, 74-75, 79, 204
Tolerance, 83
Totalization, 323
Transgression, 1, 3-5
Translation, 3-5, 11, 232, 324
Transnationalism, 321

Ulysses syndrome, 282, 290n7
United Kingdom, 3, 83, 99, 102-104, 106
United Nations, 147-148, 198
Universalism, 259, 269
Urban popular culture, see Popular Culture

Virtualization, 326-327
Vocationalization, 326

WADA (World Anti-Doping Agency), 143-156

Welfare
   Social Welfare, 48, 61, 198, 311, 332
   Welfare state, see State
Western Europe, see Europe
Williams, Raymond, v, 2, 5, 6, 17, 19, 23-27,
   29-33, 36, 37, 117, 141, 210, 217, 330,
   340
Willis, Paul, 275n6, 276, 302, 314n11, 317,
   334, 340

Working-class, 18, 25, 26, 34, 37, 191, 203,
   207, 210, 275n6, 276, 299, 302, 317, 325,
   332, 334
World Health Organization, 147,
World Social Forum, 226
World Trade Organization, 127, 198

Xenophobia, 63, 80, 99-100, 241, 279,
   281, 299

Intersections in Communications and Culture

Global Approaches and Transdisciplinary Perspectives

General Editors: Cameron McCarthy & Angharad N. Valdivia

An Institute of Communications Research, University of Illinois Commemorative Series

This series aims to publish a range of new critical scholarship that seeks to engage and transcend the disciplinary isolationism and genre confinement that now characterizes so much of contemporary research in communication studies and related fields. The editors are particularly interested in manuscripts that address the broad intersections, movement, and hybrid trajectories that currently define the encounters between human groups in modern institutions and societies and the way these dynamic intersections are coded and represented in contemporary popular cultural forms and in the organization of knowledge. Works that emphasize methodological nuance, texture and dialogue across traditions and disciplines (communications, feminist studies, area and ethnic studies, arts, humanities, sciences, education, philosophy, etc.) and that engage the dynamics of variation, diversity and discontinuity in the local and international settings are strongly encouraged.

LIST   OF   TOPICS

- Multidisciplinary Media Studies
- Cultural Studies
- Gender, Race, & Class
- Postcolonialism
- Globalization
- Diaspora Studies
- Border Studies
- Popular Culture
- Art & Representation
- Body Politics
- Governing Practices

- Histories of the Present
- Health (Policy) Studies
- Space and Identity
- (Im)migration
- Global Ethnographies
- Public Intellectuals
- World Music
- Virtual Identity Studies
- Queer Theory
- Critical Multiculturalism

Manuscripts should be sent to:

Cameron McCarthy OR Angharad N. Valdivia
Institute of Communications Research
University of Illinois at Urbana-Champaign
222B Armory Bldg., 555 E. Armory Avenue
Champaign, IL 61820

To order other books in this series, please contact our Customer Service Department:
(800) 770-LANG (within the U.S.)
(212) 647-7706 (outside the U.S.)
(212) 647-7707 FAX

Or browse online by series:
www.peterlang.com